Chop Suey, USA

ARTS AND TRADITIONS OF THE TABLE: PERSPECTIVES ON CULINARY HISTORY
Albert Sonnenfeld, Series Editor

Salt: Grain of Life, Pierre Laszlo, translated by Mary Beth Mader

Culture of the Fork, Giovanni Rebora, translated by Albert Sonnenfeld

French Gastronomy: The History and Geography of a Passion, Jean-Robert Pitte, translated by
Jody Gladding

Pasta: The Story of a Universal Food, Silvano Serventi and Françoise Sabban, translated by
Antony Shugar

Slow Food: The Case for Taste, Carlo Petrini, translated by William McCuaig

Italian Cuisine: A Cultural History, Alberto Capatti and Massimo Montanari, translated by
Áine O'Healy

British Food: An Extraordinary Thousand Years of History, Colin Spencer

A Revolution in Eating: How the Quest for Food Shaped America, James E. McWilliams

Sacred Cow, Mad Cow: A History of Food Fears, Madeleine Ferrières, translated by Jody Gladding

Molecular Gastronomy: Exploring the Science of Flavor, Hervé This, translated by M. B. DeBevoise

Food Is Culture, Massimo Montanari, translated by Albert Sonnenfeld

Kitchen Mysteries: Revealing the Science of Cooking, Hervé This, translated by Jody Gladding

Hog and Hominy: Soul Food from Africa to America, Frederick Douglass Opie

Gastropolis: Food and New York City, edited by Annie Hauck-Lawson and Jonathan Deutsch

Building a Meal: From Molecular Gastronomy to Culinary Constructivism, Hervé This, translated by
M. B. DeBevoise

Eating History: Thirty Turning Points in the Making of American Cuisine, Andrew F. Smith

The Science of the Oven, Hervé This, translated by Jody Gladding

Pomodoro! A History of the Tomato in Italy, David Gentilcore

Cheese, Pears, and History in a Proverb, Massimo Montanari, translated by Beth Archer Brombert

Food and Faith in Christian Culture, edited by Ken Albala and Trudy Eden

The Kitchen as Laboratory: Reflections on the Science of Food and Cooking, edited by César Vega,
Job Ubbink, and Erik van der Linden

The Secret Financial Life of Food: From Commodities Markets to Supermarkets, Kara Newman

Creamy and Crunchy: An Informal History of Peanut Butter, the All-American Food, Jon Krampner

Let the Meatballs Rest: And Other Stories About Food and Culture, Massimo Montanari, translated by
Beth Brombert

Drinking History: Fifteen Turning Points in the Making of American Beverages, Andrew F. Smith

Italian Identity in the Kitchen, or Food and the Nation, Massimo Montanari, translated by
Beth Archer Brombert

Fashioning Appetite: Restaurants and the Making of Modern Identity, Joanne Finkelstein

The Land of the Five Flavors: A Cultural History of Chinese Cuisine, Thomas O. Höllmann, translated
by Karen Margolis

The Insect Cookbook: Food for a Sustainable Planet, Arnold van Huis, Henk van Gurp, and Marcel
Dicke, translated by Françoise Takken-Kaminker and Diane Blumenfeld-Schaap

Religion, Food, and Eating in North America, edited by Benjamin E. Zeller, Marie W. Dallam,
Reid L. Neilson, and Nora L. Rubel

Umami: Unlocking the Secrets of the Fifth Taste, Ole G. Mouritsen and Klavs Styrbæk, translated by
Mariela Johansen and designed by Jonas Drotner Mouritsen

Chop Suey, USA

THE STORY OF CHINESE FOOD IN AMERICA

YONG CHEN

COLUMBIA UNIVERSITY PRESS New York

COLUMBIA UNIVERSITY PRESS

PUBLISHERS SINCE 1893

NEW YORK   CHICHESTER, WEST SUSSEX

cup.columbia.edu

Copyright © 2014 Columbia University Press

Library of Congress Cataloging-in-Publication Data

Chen, Yong.

  Chop suey, USA : the story of Chinese food in America / Yong Chen.

    pages cm

  Includes bibliographical references and index.

  ISBN 978-0-231-16892-2 (cloth : alk. paper)

  ISBN 978-0-231-53816-9 (e-book)

 1. Cooking, Chinese.   2. Chinese—United States—Social life and customs.

3. Food habits—United States—History.   I. Title.

  TX724.5.C5C54417 2014

  641.5951—dc23

2014012764

c 10 9 8 7 6 5 4 3 2 1

p 10 9 8 7 6 5 4 3 2 1

COVER PHOTO: GEOFF SPEAR

BOOK & COVER DESIGN: CHANG JAE LEE

To my parents, Rosalind, and Cynthia and Robert Chou

Contents

Preface
THE GENESIS OF THE BOOK

This book goes back to a kitchen encounter on August 23, 1985, when I first set foot in the New World. The sixteen-hour flight that took me from Beijing to New York was a great leap over an economic gap that had separated China and the West for more than a century. The eminent French historian Fernand Braudel called it "the essential problem of the history of the modern world."[1] Still looming large in the 1980s, it was the primary motivation for me and for millions of people from the third world to come to America.

The plane landed late at night. In the darkness that engulfed the city, I felt like a pioneer entering an unfamiliar wilderness. Yet I was not a total stranger in this new land. Like Alexis de Tocqueville's American pioneer of the early nineteenth century, I was "acquainted with the past, curious of the future."[2] I had heard much about America and looked forward to a new phase in my life. My path had been paved by a long chain of historical events, ranging from the arrival of American merchants in China shortly after 1776 in pursuit of such goods as tea and porcelain, which had become symbols of luxury in the colonies, to the coming of Chinese forty-niners who accompanied the emergence of the United States as "the newest empire."[3]

For me, the notion of the United States as an empire was a familiar one. During my childhood, I learned that it was an imperial power of aggression and capitalism from history textbooks and films about the Korean War and the Vietnam War. But the American empire remained a distant and abstract concept until the late 1970s and early 1980s, when Chinese citizens started to visit the United States in increasingly large numbers for the first time since 1949. American politicians love to talk about American political democracy to foreign audiences; yet upon their return from the United States, Chinese visitors like Professor Qi Wenying, my adviser at Beijing University, could not stop telling stories about the spacious American kitchen and the gigantic supermarket. With no equivalent in the Chinese lexicon then, a "supermarket" with open shelves of unimaginable amounts and varieties of foods affordable and accessible for everyone was an entirely foreign and enviably "enchanting" concept for many Chinese.[4] For someone like me, who had grown up under strict food rationing, such stories made tangible the idea that the United States was indeed an imperial superpower, an empire of mass consumption.

These tales rekindled China's American dream, harbored once by the Cantonese seeking their fortunes in the "Gold Mountain," and awakened consumer desires long suppressed under Communism. It also made America the most desirable place for the young and ambitious. The Chinese who traveled across the ocean during the early years of the reform era were among the nation's best educated and most fortunate, rather than its tired, its poor, and its huddled masses. But their motivation was the same as that of millions of immigrants from other parts of the world: the pursuit of the American dream, a dream signified first and foremost by America's material abundance.

Arriving in New York, I felt more like a migrant chasing this dream and a better future than a student en route to a doctorate at Cornell University. Growing up in China, we learned from Marxism that class struggle or revolution was the only way to change people's social status or material conditions. But for my generation, the United States offered an alternative: by crossing the Pacific Ocean, we could fundamentally elevate our situation overnight. This was why I did not hesitate to give up other enviable options I fortunately had at the time: to teach at China's best university, work for the central government, or study at Oxford University.

I did not enter the New World a lone wanderer. Howard and Renee met me at JFK Airport with Sondra and took me to their home on Long Island. I had become friends with Sondra and her husband, Bruce, when they taught in China in 1984. On the day of my arrival, she drove all the way from Connecticut to make sure that Howard and Renee would not miss the Chinese newcomer whom she had asked them to pick up.

As I stepped inside their house, Howard said in a warm and humorous voice that would become so familiar to me in the coming decades, "Welcome to

America; welcome home." Indeed, what I was entering was not just a house but American culture, and America was to become my home for the next quarter century.

In the kitchen, I had my first conversation with Americans on American soil. It also felt like a dialogue with American culture. Everything about my hosts was just so *American*: from the way they looked—I came with the typical Chinese presumption that American simply meant white—to the size of their kitchen, which was even more spacious than I had imagined. As Renee took a sandwich and a cup of milk from a giant double-sided refrigerator, Howard spoke to me in a consciously American way: "You are a Yankee now; please eat some American food."

It was not entirely a mere coincidence that my first intimate encounter with America took place in an American kitchen. Long considered a space for "transnational encounter," it had been a centerpiece of American culture and abundance.[5] During the famous "kitchen debate" that Richard Nixon and Nikita Khrushchev had in Moscow in 1959 in the model kitchen at the opening of the American National Exhibition, the Cold Warrior American vice president used the kitchen to showcase the superiority of capitalism and the American way of life.

As I chowed down on the American food in front of me, my hosts talked about their plans for the next few days to show me around New York, in Howard's words, to "Americanize" me. But I did not have a clear idea about what being American entailed. It would take years for me to appreciate its richness and complexity in meaning. I did not realize, for example, that my American hosts were Jewish. They told me they loved Chinese food, but I was unaware of the decades-old Jewish connection to Chinese food, which had become a part of the Jewish American identity and thus led many Jewish Americans to China in search of authentic Chinese food.

As much as I was excited about coming to America, my first close contact with the country generated a surging consciousness of my Chineseness. It did not amount to an intellectual articulation of cultural identity. Through invasions, intermarriages, and internal and overseas migrations over the centuries, the long stream of history has added layers upon layers of complexity to the meaning of Chineseness, making it extremely difficult to verbalize. Those Chinese like me, who grew up during the radicalism of the Cultural Revolution, had become a people with neither religion nor tradition—the kind of religion and traditions that defined peoples like the Jews. In a foreign country like the United States, food thus became our most important commonality, giving us a sense of affinity, a shared topic, and something to look forward to. Indeed, love of food has a long association with being Chinese. One of those who understood this association was Lin Yutang, a famous author and philosopher in China before World War II. He wrote of the Chinese in 1939: "If there is anything we are serious about, it is neither religion nor learning, but food."[6]

The unfamiliarity of the New World was accented by the new foods that my hosts introduced to me during my stay in New York: cereal, blueberries, spaghetti, pizza, and bagels. They fed me generously, but somehow I still felt quite hungry—not a physical hunger but a cultural one prompted by an increasingly unquenchable longing for Chinese food and home. It was the first time that my Chineseness became tangible—a Chineseness embedded in what many travelers from China have characterized as a "Chinese stomach."[7]

This led me on a continual search for Chinese food—first in Ithaca and later in cities across the country like Detroit, Honolulu, New Orleans, New York, Providence, San Francisco, and St. Louis. Before long, I started to wonder why there are so many Chinese restaurants in the United States. Such questioning about the popularity of American Chinese food turned my personal craving into an intellectual quest—which now includes a blog (www.chopsueyusa.com), where readers can also find various resources for exploring food—to comprehend the journey of Chinese food to America. This culinary journey, as I would realize over time, was also an integral part of the historical development of the United States, especially its emergence as an empire.

Acknowledgments

My father would have been thrilled to see the publication of this book. He had been nagging me for years before he passed away: "When are you going to finish your food book?" This was not because he was a foodie—to the contrary, consistent with his peasant roots and his puritanical revolutionary ideals, his food taste remained extremely spartan. He was concerned about my extracurricular activities, ranging from taking on administrative responsibilities at the university to visiting villages and corporations in China. Having gone through much turmoil in his life, he wanted me to be a pure scholar with a secure job and stable life, and cared less about my belief that to understand the world we must be in the world. When I saw him the last time, there was no more nagging. Lying in bed in the intensive-care unit at the Number Three Hospital in Wuhan, he could no longer talk or even eat. A stroke had partially paralyzed him. Feeling totally helpless as I watched my father in his last moments, I whispered gently and repeatedly to his ear: "I will finish the book."

My mother still finds it rather amusing that her scholar son writes a book on such a mundane topic. But having raised me to appreciate food, she is more responsible for my writing this book than anyone else. She has remained a true foodie all her life in spite of the varied obstacles she faced. The China of my childhood was a land of scarcity where food was strictly rationed. The monthly meat allotment was about one pound a month per person, enough just to make a few Big Macs today. The black market and a deficit family economy were what she relied on to put some meat on the table everyday. As an official in the government of the eight-county prefecture, she had a demanding job. In what the sociologist Arlie Hochschild dubs "the second shift," she went to the local market almost every morning at 5:30 and cooked two elaborate meals a day.[1] She received pungent condemnation for her gastronomical proclivities during the radical Cultural Revolution because they ran contrary to the puritanical vision that Chairman Mao had for Chinese society. In one of his most frequently quoted lines, Mao noted: "[To conduct] the revolution is not inviting guests to dinner parties."[2] After all, the Chinese Communist Revolution led by Mao was a "hungry revolution."[3] Like foodie characters that we encounter in films, such as Chef Chu in *Eat Drink Man Woman* and Tita in *Like Water for Chocolate*, my mother also expresses feelings through cooking. Like other Chinese mothers, mine never verbalized the three common English words "I love you" together. She just kept cooking. She sometimes stated, half jokingly, to live is to serve our mouth. Not until I started researching this book did I start to appreciate the insights of her statement into our existence and human history.

I owe the completion of this book to too many people to continue my procrastination. My wife, Rosalind, who stopped nagging me about it a long time ago, is another true foodie in my life; her love of food and her encyclopedic culinary knowledge have been a tremendous source of information and inspiration. Cookbooks, an increasingly favorite bedtime reading for many people, are her primary readings. She has been a partner in life and in food since the late 1980s, when she was a graduate student in food science at Cornell University. Our typical date then consisted of a trip to a local supermarket, such as Tops on Route 13, followed by cooking in our apartment kitchen.

Our cousins Cindy and Bob have been like a dear and supportive brother and sister but have never nagged me about anything. Their generosity and knowledge have helped me understand and experience the gastronomical landscape of America, Taiwan, and mainland China to the extent that would not have been possible otherwise. They turned every excursion we took together over the years, local and international, into enjoyable and intellectually stimulating culinary adventures.

Given all the transformation of my cultural identity, no one would see me as a Jewish person—except for Howard and Renee Stave, Bruce and Sondra Stave, my dearest Jewish friends, who warmly and kindly welcomed me to America and to their family since the very moment of my landing in New York. Occasionally and gently nudging me about the book, they played an indispensible role in shaping it and my American journey. They embody the thoughtfulness, generosity, tolerance, and hospitality of Americans. Sondra also read the manuscript and offered extremely valuable comments.

I am fortunate to have gotten an inside peak into the world of food in America thanks to the generous support of many food entrepreneurs and experts, such as Sunny and Jaime Lu, Mr. J. Chao, Mr. G. Wang, Richard Wing, Chen Benchang (Ben John Chen), Will Allen, Max Jacobson, William Grimes, Gabriella Gershenson, Pascal Olhats, and July Ding. Others, especially Frank Low, Sandy Yee Man Leung, Thomas Kong, Bill Hing, and Brian Tom, shared with me valuable stories and documents about their Chinese-immigrant ancestors' experiences in Chinese food.

I do not have sufficient space here to express my deep gratitude to the many friends, including Hao Ping, X. Y. Guo, Y. L. Du, Y. S. Ren, Long Yawei, Y. S. Li, Y. Jun, S. M. Zhou, and Sue Wang, in China for their support and for giving me opportunities to taste and appreciate the country's diverse and fast-evolving cuisines since 1997. Mr. and Mrs. S. Y. Wang helped me visit cities and towns throughout Anhui and Fujian, affording me precious insights into these two provinces' distinctively culinary traditions. L. Chen, a dear friend since 1979, helped to introduce to me the foodways of numerous ethnic minorities,

I cannot properly thank the individuals whom I have interviewed in America and elsewhere for this book in the past fifteen years in part because I want to keep their identities anonymous. Moreover, I do not even the know the names of many of them, including the street-food vendors in the Mexican American communities in Highland Park, California; the fishermen and -women on the Penghu Islands in the Taiwan Strait; and the countless restaurant workers in various cities, ranging from New York and San Francisco to Amsterdam, Beijing, Sydney, and Budapest.

Among those who have helped me to locate important sources in the United States, I owe special thanks to Gordon Chang, Sharon Block, Him Mark Lai, Vicki and Milt Feldon, Jacqueline Newman, and Harley Spiller. Hasia Diner's extraordinary work has been a model and an inspiration. The gastronomical giant Julia Child took time from her busy schedule to answer my questions and pointed me to important cookbook collections. I am deeply grateful to Cynthia Lee, my co-curator of the Have You Eaten Yet? exhibit on the history of American Chinese restaurants.

Over the years, I have greatly benefited from the professional expertise and selfless support from archivists at the Schlesinger Library at Radcliff Institute/ Harvard, the UCLA East Asian Library, the Special Collections at UC Irvine and UC San Diego, the National Archives in Washington, D.C., and College

Park, Maryland, and the Bancroft Library at UC Berkeley. I received generous help from the staff at local historical societies in numerous places, including Marysville and Watsonville, California; Providence, Rhode Island; Virginia City, Nevada; and the Chinese Historical Society of Southern California. Through their diligence and ingenuity, the staff at UC Irvine's interlibrary loan department helped me to get hold of countless difficult-to-access sources. Many other colleagues and friends, such as Chen Jianlong and Thomas G. Andrews, extended to me valuable support and opportunities. Jeffrey Pilcher, author of four important books on food and the editor of *The Oxford Handbook of Food History*, significantly helped me to comprehend the importance of food in history and the role of race.

I did not apply for extramural funding for this project but received support for my research trips from several units at UC Irvine: the Academic Senate, the Center for Asian Studies, and the School of Humanities. More important, UC Irvine, one of the fastest-growing institutions of higher education in postwar America, has been a productive intellectual home, where I have had the good fortune to work in sundry ways with visionary colleagues, such as Fred Wan, William J. Lillyman, and Bill Parker in various disciplines. I have learned much about food from the stories that Carol Sokolov, Tonya Becerra, and Brent Yunek shared with me. As a historian, I cannot ask for better colleagues than those at the History Department, whose collegiality and support have nourished me. Emily Rosenberg read the entire manuscript and offered extremely perceptive feedback. Steve Topik, a renowned coffee expert, constantly shared his insights on food. Anne Walthall encouraged me to write a book on food in the 1990s and continually urged me to finish it. I benefited immensely from Vicki Ruiz's knowledge and passion about food and support, and I am grateful to her and to Ana Rosa for the opportunities they offered me. Tim Tackett helped me better understand the development of restaurants in France. Ken Pomeranz has offered many constructive suggestions about my work over the years.

I also benefited tremendously from my students. A number of them have become close friends. Among them, Allen Lin, a history and engineering double major, went on to become an executive in the IT industry and has created a successful food blog; he also offered valuable comments on the book and helped me set up a blog for it. Megan Wycoff, another former student and passionate foodie with extensive experience in the food industry before coming to UC Irvine, provided critical assistance on several food research projects after her graduation.

I am fortunate to have had ample opportunities to work and interact with reporters of U.S. national media organizations like the *New York Times*, the *Los Angeles Times*, the *Chronicle of Higher Education*, and National Public Radio; local media like the *Orange County Register*, 89.3 KPCC, and the *Waterfront Times* of St. Louis; and Chinese American newspapers like the *World Journal*, *Sing Tao Daily*, *Taiwan Daily*, and *China Daily*. I extend my special thanks to Jeffrey Selingo, Valerie Takahama, Marla Jo Fisher, Charles Perry, Emma Wang, Esther Hsiao, Michael Luo, Lonny Shavelson, Charles Proctor, Malcolm Gay, Amy Lieu, Wendy Lee, and Wang Jun.

I am grateful for the support and encouragement I received from editors at numerous presses, such as Susan Ferber at Oxford University Press, Elaine Maisner at the University of North Carolina Press, Melanie Halkias and Kendra Boileau at Rutgers University Press, Sheila Levine at the University of California Press, Traci Mueller at Bedford/St. Martin's Press, and Ranjit D. Arab at the University of Washington Press. Mary Sutherland, my copy editor, has done an extraordinary job and turned the copy-editing process into an intellectually engaging and fruitful dialogue about history and food. The many constructive suggestions made by Irene Pavitt, my editor at Columbia University Press, significantly helped to improve the manuscript. Jennifer Crewe at Columbia University Press, in particular, patiently encouraged me for many years to finish the book. She read the entire manuscript and offered many extremely detailed and perceptive comments and suggestions. This book would not have been possible without her support and input.

Chop Suey, USA

Introduction

CHOP SUEY, THE BIG MAC OF THE PRE-MCDONALD'S ERA

The rise of Chinese food in America's gastronomical landscape in the late nineteenth and early twentieth centuries is one of the greatest epic stories of cultural exchange in world history. The arrival of Chinese food on American shores injected a refreshing air of diversity to a country long dominated by Anglo culinary monotony that many have lamented since the nineteenth century.[1] By 1980, Chinese food had become the country's most popular ethnic cuisine. The spread of Chinese restaurants facilitated a quiet but revolutionary change that enriched America's palate. More important, it marked the country's socioeconomic transformation, turning dining out into a democratic experience.

Making the epic story even more extraordinary, this colossal transpacific migration of cuisine did not involve the political power of government or the financial muscle of big corporations. Rather, it was engendered by a politically disfranchised, culturally despised, economically marginalized, and numerically insignificant group of people: individual Chinese immigrants. In their adopted country, these immigrants combated not only Anglo culinary conservatism but also unrelenting animosity toward Chinese food, pushing it into non-Chinese neighborhoods in cities across the nation. They did so with the only tool at their disposal in the early years: their labor. In the process, they created some of the most recognized dishes—such as chow mein—in the national food-consumer market without training or a marketing budget. Chop suey, in particular, came to epitomize the Chinese food that prevailed in the American restaurant market.

These circumstances raise an inevitable question: Why did Chinese food become so popular in America? It is also a central question of this book. The answer lies in changing socioeconomic conditions more than in the realm of gastronomy. First of all, the rise of Chinese food signified not simply a change in taste but a profound transformation in the economy. As a result, more and more people aspired to a more leisurely lifestyle, which included freedom from home cooking, as the country itself embarked on its transformation into a consumer society. Meeting such aspirations, the spread of Chinese restaurants was a logical extension of the role of Chinese Americans as service workers—a role that mirrored both the racialized domestic labor market and the geo-economic order in the transpacific world during this period.

As one of the most important chapters in Chinese American history, the development of Chinese food was also the result of the tremendous efforts of Chinese Americans in transplanting, preserving, and promoting their cuisine. Such efforts underscored the extraordinary socioeconomic and cultural importance of Chinese food for Chinese Americans as a marker of identity and a vital economic institution.

Since the early twentieth century, there have been many attempts to answer the question about the popularity of American Chinese food. Most important of all is the notion that Chinese food spread because it is the best cuisine in the world. This explanation has been a conviction of many Chinese, including Sun Yat-sen, the founding father of the Republic of China.

It would be easier to believe that American consumers fell in love with Chinese food merely or mainly because of its gastronomical superiority if they had accorded it more esteem—the kind of admiration they accorded French and now Italian food—or if they had accepted it from the very beginning. Contrary to a romantic notion that Americans have been eating Chinese food "since the days of the California gold rush," white America harbored a strong aversion toward Chinese food; they developed derogatory notions and stereotypes about its content and, in the words of many Anglo commentators, "odor."[2]

The long and winding journey of Chinese food to Main Street America is not simply a culinary story. It was intrinsically connected to larger historical developments that shaped America and the transpacific world. Indeed, human food preference—one of the most resilient human habits—is seldom just a matter of taste (sugar is one of the very few foods that people seem to like naturally) but is wrought by factors beyond gastronomy: our backgrounds and the larger natural and socioeconomic environment. Otherwise, we cannot explain why McDonald's—the maker of an insipid but very inexpensive burger—has penetrated

119 countries (as of August 2012), including those like China with a long-standing reputation for tasteful cuisines, making the Golden Arches more recognizable around the world than the Christian cross.

The ascent of Chinese food stands as a milestone in the development of the United States as an empire of consumption. Using the term "empire" here is unlikely to win any popularity contest among Americans because of its negative connotations, but the word underlines the essence of the country as a land of abundance, which laid the foundation for American freedom and democracy, as many Americans since Jefferson have keenly recognized. It also helps to explain the country's tremendous global appeal and dominance.

Aboard the *Arabella* en route to America in 1630, John Winthrop encouraged his fellow Puritans to build a "City upon a Hill" as an example for the world. More than two centuries later, the United States became a model that much of the world looked up to—not for its Puritan ideals but for its enviable mass consumption, which signifies the meaning of American liberty and freedom in the minds of millions of people around the globe. Many of them, including Chinese, have come to the United States in search of a better and more abundant life.

The immigrant Chinese labored as stewards of the emerging empire of consumption. Their service helped satisfy the growing appetite of American consumers for a better lifestyle by providing personal service as laundrymen, domestic cooks, and servants, and later as restaurant workers. Representing America's first truly national network of public dining, Chinese restaurants played a vital role in expanding the meaning of abundance and democracy by extending an experience that had been a privilege only of the wealthy to the masses: enjoying meals prepared by others on a regular basis. This helps to explain why underprivileged groups, such as marginalized Anglos, African Americans, and Jews, formed the primary customer base for American Chinese food in the initial years. The Chinese restaurant, in turn, offered an economically and socially accessible public space that was denied to them elsewhere.

To comprehend the development of America's Chinese food, therefore, is to understand the division of labor along the lines of culture and race within American society. Chinese Americans, in particular, were pushed out of occupations like mining and manufacturing into the service sector, and by the early twentieth century, restaurant work became one of the two primary lines of jobs open for them. Such a division of labor also prevailed in the global political economy, especially in the Pacific Rim. The lowly position of Chinese food in mainstream America's restaurant-market hierarchy has mirrored the inferior status of China both as a culture and as a supplier of cheap labor in the economy.

Therefore, the food that Chinese restaurant workers served to non-Chinese customers was in essence an "empire food." Its rise to popularity embodied the budding mass-consumer empire's desire for the convenience and service that Chinese laborers provided in restaurants, more than for the long and rich tradition of Chinese cuisine. This explains why the American dining public embraced the Chinese food characterized by simple and inexpensive foods like chop suey but largely rejected China's haute cuisine represented by exquisite dishes such as shark's fins. To those marginalized Americans, Chinese food has largely remained an inexpensive dining-out opportunity. Simply put, chop suey was the Big Mac of the pre-McDonald's era.

The rise of Chinese food is a story not just of marginalization and exploitation but also of the resistance and perseverance of Chinese Americans in the face of enormous hostilities. In order to fully comprehend the development of American Chinese food, we must also appreciate its importance for the Chinese community and the tireless efforts of Chinese Americans. Chinatown played an indispensible role as the cradle of America's Chinese food. It was Chinese food's landing field, where that cuisine first reached American shores. Chinatown also existed as a safe haven, preserving and shielding Chinese food in the years when it faced strong hostility. Moreover, Chinatown was the launching ground from which Chinese food spread to non-Chinese markets: it was here that many Americans had their first Chinese meal, and it was from Chinatown that Chinese restaurants ventured to non-Chinese neighborhoods, whose restaurants continued to rely on China-town as a source of labor, expertise, and ingredients.

The Chinese-food industry, in turn, remained a vital lifeline for Chinese America for a long time, generating revenue for the community and employment for individual Chinese Americans. Over the years, Chinese-food businesses have constituted prominent markers of the community through their distinctive physical presence and aroma. For individual Chinese Americans, Chinese restaurants provided not only familiar things to eat but also an important social space.

To understand the penetration of Chinese food into non-Chinese markets, we must appreciate the efforts and ingenuity of Chinese American restaurant workers. In promoting their food, they toiled for long hours, conducted effective public-relations campaigns, adopted various business practices such as the open kitchen and home delivery, and packaged Chinese dishes into easy-to-recognize product lines, such as chop suey, chow mein, and egg foo young.

They also made conscious attempts to accommodate the tastes of non-Chinese patronage and, over time, invented new dishes like the St. Paul sandwich

Steamed Savory Pork Belly with Preserved Vegetables

Serves 4

It is from my mother that I first learned about food and its significance in life. In the summer after my father passed away, I stayed with my mother in Wuhan for some time. She was in low spirits, and her memory was fading. When I realized that the topic of food magically rekindled her memories, I asked her to show me how to cook some of my favorite childhood dishes. While cooking together, we also talked nonstop. If the kitchen conversation with Howard, Renee, and Sondra back in 1985 introduced me to the New World, the time I spent with my mother in her kitchen reconnected me to a familiar past that we shared. The following is one of the dishes she taught me how to prepare.

   4 oz preserved vegetables*
   2 lbs pork belly
   2 tbsp cooking wine
   6 thin slices of ginger
   3 garlic cloves, mashed
   1 star anise
   1 tbsp honey
   ⅓ cup salad oil
   ⅓ cup (or less) dark soy sauce

Wash and finely chop the preserved vegetables. Boil the pork belly with the cooking wine, ginger, garlic, and star anise for 35 minutes or until you can poke a chopstick through the skin. Place it on a plate, and brush a thin layer of honey on the skin of the meat when it is still hot. Heat the oil in a wok or frying pan. Use chopsticks to poke a few holes on the skin. Turn heat to low to brown the skin side of the meat.

Cool the meat in ice water. Then cut it into slices (no thicker than ⅓ inch). Place the slices next to each other neatly in a deep and wide porcelain bowl with the skin side down. Cover the meat with a layer of the preserved vegetables. Pour the soy sauce over them. Steam for 1½ hours or until the meat is soft. Take the cooking bowl from the steamer, and place a serving plate on its top. Quickly turn the bowl over to transfer the food onto the plate, and then remove the cooking bowl. Serve it with steamed rice on the side.

Mei cai, which can be found in a Chinese supermarket.

(egg foo young patty / lettuce / tomato / pickle / mayo) and General Tso's chicken. As a result, many have wondered about the authenticity or Chineseness of the food catered to non-Chinese diners since the early twentieth century. The authenticity of Chinese food per se is a complex epistemological and historical one that food connoisseurs, restaurant operators, and cookbook writers have continued to tackle for decades. What constitutes *real* Chinese food has shifted a great deal over time. The Chinese food served in restaurants in non-Chinese neighborhoods has also experienced significant changes. In the post-1965 era, old foods under names like chop suey have gradually lost their predominance to new categories of dishes like "Kung Pao" and "Mongolian" in such restaurants.

On the one hand, the American Chinese food that started to rise in popularity around the turn of the twentieth century and its signature dishes, such as chop suey, were unequivocally Chinese in terms of cooking methods, principal ingredients, and origin as one of the most recognizable brand names in America's emerging mass-consumption market. On the other hand, American Chinese food was a commodity "made in the U.S.A." Its appeal stemmed from desires and demands generated by emerging mass-consumer markets. The prevalent food in Chinese restaurants serving non-Chinese patrons was shaped by negotiations between Chinese food operators and the taste preferences of their customers. And Chinese restaurants' multiplication followed the historical trajectory of the United States and is indeed a quintessential American story.

The active role of Chinese Americans in popularizing Chinese food is also evidenced in the multitude of Chinese-food cookbooks. More than 280 such cookbooks were published in the United States from the 1910s to the mid-1980s, the majority of which were written by Chinese Americans. In composing these cookbooks, Chinese American authors articulated and introduced Chinese cooking to non-Chinese audiences. While Chinese restaurants were located mostly in urban areas, the cookbooks brought Chinese food into American kitchens and raised public knowledge of it in areas without such restaurants.

A close examination of Chinese-food cookbooks by Chinese Americans, moreover, further reveals the significance of Chinese food for Chinese Americans as a marker and an expression of their identity. Cookbook writing created a visible and constant platform for Chinese Americans to speak to mainstream audiences. They spoke—with pride and authority—not only about China's cooking but also about its culture and history as well as their own experiences.

Discussing Chinese-food cookbooks gives me an opportunity to briefly look at the changes that have taken place in more recent years. The explosive increase in both the number of cookbook titles and the variety of Chinese food they cover bespeak the expansion of Chinese food the in the 1970s. This increase corresponded to the continued growth of Chinese restaurants and the introduction of cooking from regions other than South China. Writing this new chapter in the saga of American Chinese food were mostly new Chinese immigrants, who arrived in growing numbers following the passage in 1965 of the Immigration and Nationality Act.

In this book, my own voice is heard and my own experience supports the story: food connects the personal and the historical, as we can clearly see in cookbook writing. Equally important, the historical currents that engendered the rise of American Chinese food have also predicated my American journey in the past quarter century. Moreover, the epic of Chinese food is not merely a historical event that belongs entirely to the past but one that has continued to unfold in my lifetime and often in front of my eyes.

When I went back to China in 1997—for the first time since my initial departure in 1985—I found myself standing at a critical juncture of history. An unprecedented economic transformation was under way, which began to reduce the gap between China and the United States, a gap that Fernand Braudel and many others observed. This gap had also been an important condition for Chinese emigration to the United States and for the development of American Chinese food. China's tremendous socioeconomic and gastronomical metamorphosis made the country look and smell stunningly different from the homeland I had known as a child. Americans tend to regard China as the place for authentic Chinese food, but many of the foods and food places once familiar to me are gone. Evidently, the critical issues that I explore in this book—such as the geo-economic U.S.–China equation, the nature and meaning of Chinese food, cultural identity, and culinary authenticity—continue to unfold.

1
WHY IS CHINESE FOOD SO POPULAR?

This is the question that unavoidably arises from the ubiquity of Chinese food in the United States, but it is not a question that can be answered purely in gastronomical terms. Rather, the reasons for the migration of Chinese food from China to Chinatown to non-Chinese neighborhoods and eventually to the suburbs are found not in the merits of Chinese food as a cuisine but in the conditions of global labor and capital markets, changes in the American economy and consumption patterns, and demographic and occupational transformation of Chinese America.

THE GROWTH OF CHINESE FOOD'S POPULARITY

The pervasiveness of Chinese food in American public consumption has been conspicuously evident since the early twentieth century, when "there is hardly an American city that had not its Chinese restaurants, to which persons of every class like to go."[1] This phenomenon was also noticeable to visitors.

One such visitor was Sun Yat-sen. During his fourth visit to the continental United States in 1911, he traveled to numerous cities—including San Francisco, Stockton, Isleton, Courtland, Sacramento, Portland, Seattle, Spokane, Walla Walla, Austin, Carson City, Boston, and Denver—on a fund-raising tour for his fellow revolutionaries back in China[2] He noticed that "there is no American town without a Chinese restaurant."[3] Chinese food's extraordinary prevalence has since then become more and more apparent. But the precise extent of that prevalence remains somewhat murky, first of all because Chinese restaurants tend to be independent, small-size family operations, scattered all over the nation without significant horizontal connections. Second, many of the restaurants change hands or simply close doors quietly and often quickly in an industry characterized by a high rate of turnover. Finally, only a few people have attempted to systematically collect data on Chinese restaurants.

In 1946, a Chinese-language newspaper, *Hua Qiao Nian Bao* (*Annals of the Overseas Chinese*), estimated that there were 1,101 Chinese restaurants in eleven cities: New York (315), San Francisco (147), Chicago (142), Los Angeles (117), Washington, D.C. (82), Seattle (62), Boston (61), Philadelphia (51), Portland (42), Oakland (41), and Detroit (41).[4] Chen Benchang (Ben John Chen) was one of the first individuals to collect systematic data on Chinese restaurants. When I met him in his office in New York on October 24, 2000, the eighty-seven-year-old man did not look his age at all as he remained an active community leader and a busy businessman. He served as an officer in the expedition army during the war against the Japanese invasion in China. After coming to the United States in 1958, he established himself as a successful businessman in the food industry and an eminent figure in politics, whom President Ronald Reagan called "a special friend."[5] In 1971, he published a lengthy study of the Chinese restaurant industry in the United States. He was an ideal person to undertake such a study. A diligent writer and researcher, Chen also had extensive experiences in the food industry and created a successful food wholesale business (Benjohn Trading Company). According to his detailed survey, there were 9,355 Chinese restaurants across the country.[6] This number is consistent with that of Paul Chan and Kenneth Baker, who noted the 1970s that there were at least 10,000 such establishments.[7]

The popularity of Chinese food continued to grow. By 1980, Chinese food had clearly become the most popular ethnic cuisine in the restaurant industry, possibly constituting about 30 percent of America's major ethnic cuisines according to the geographer Wilbur Zelinsky, who found 7,796 Chinese restaurants in 270 U.S. and Canadian metropolitan areas; and Chinese restaurants maintained their dominant presence in the ethnic dining market throughout the decade.[8] The popularity of Chinese food continued to grow. A Chinese American named Tang Fuxiang, vice president of the committee to promote Chinese food, reported in 1988 that there were more than 21,000 Chinese restaurants in the United States and Canada, employing 240,000 people, or one-tenth of the Chinese population in these two countries.[9] In 2008, according to Jennifer 8 Lee, "there [were] some forty thousand Chinese restaurants in the United

States—more than the number of McDonald's, Burger Kings, and KFCs combined."[10] My own survey of Chinese restaurants in 62 cities across the nation in the summer of 2007 indicates that their number exceeded 30,000.[11]

AN UNLIKELY CUISINE TO RISE IN POPULARITY

Those who are used to its ubiquitous presence may find it hard to believe that few nineteenth-century commentators expected Chinese food to rise to popularity. Alexander Young concluded in 1872: "It is not likely that Chinese delicacies of the table will ever become popular in this country. On the contrary, John Chinaman, appreciating the dietetic conditions of our civilization, will probably conform to our customs in this as in other respects."[12] Thirteen years later, another observer drew the same conclusion that Chinese food was not expected "to be popular in this country."[13] Even in the early twentieth century, when the popularity of Chinese food became quite noticeable, some remained cautious about its future, believing that "a prejudice against Chinese foods must be overcome before their delicacy and economy can be enjoyed."[14]

There were ample reasons for such not-so-optimistic sentiments about Chinese food's prospects at the time, when mainstream American society exerted enormous enmity, even contempt, for Chinese food and the immigrants who brought it to American shores. Anti-Chinese forces persistently targeted the immigrants' food habits and invoked their eating of such items as rice as evidence of their un-Americanness.[15] In addition, the Chinese also faced other unfavorable conditions. First, the Chinese population remained small and was further reduced in size by different forms of racism, ranging from street violence to anti-Chinese legislation. It stayed under 110,000 throughout the second half of the nineteenth century and then declined from 107,488 in 1890 to 89, 863 in 1900, and 61,639 in 1920.[16] It would not return to the 1890 level until after World War II. Second, the small, shrinking community remained a predominantly immigrant population and was politically disfranchised.[17] Almost 90 percent of the Chinese in 1900 were immigrants and could not become citizens until 1943.[18] Third, facing discrimination in America, they received little help or protection from the Chinese government, which was initially hostile to overseas Chinese emigration. When the Qing court (1644–1911) adjusted its attitude and policies toward overseas Chinese immigrants around the turn of the twentieth century, it was too weak to offer meaningful assistance. And fourth, largely a laborer population, the Chinese had very limited economic resources.

"THE BEST IN THE WORLD": THE GASTRONOMICAL INTERPRETATION

Under such circumstances, the rise of Chinese restaurants in cities across the nation at the turn of the twentieth century was unexpected and "surprising" in the eyes of many people.[19] Why all the Chinese restaurants? they wondered. Some even surmised that they were backed by millionaires.[20] A more widespread and seemingly more conceivable interpretation emphasized the gastronomical excellence of Chinese food: Chinese food prevailed in the United States because it was the best cuisine in the world, and this has remained a conviction among many Chinese.

Hailed as the founding father of the Republic of China, Sun Yat-sen articulated this belief in *The Treatises of Sun Yat-sen* (*Sun Wen Xueshuo*, 1918). It is interesting that his purpose was not to make a purely gastronomical argument but to develop his thoughts on how to build a modern nation, which the republican revolution had failed to bring about. He began not with an action plan but with an epistemological deliberation, attributing the failure of the revolution to the influence of the ancient Chinese maxim that "knowledge is easy, but action is difficult." He employed several examples to prove its fallacy, and the first came from food, which the Chinese consumed daily but did not understand well. His deliberations conveyed a profound sense of the superiority of Chinese cooking:

> In the modern evolution of civilization, our China has lagged behind others in every aspect except the development of food and drinks, where it remains ahead of the civilized countries. Not only is the cuisine invented by China far more extensive and grand than that in Europe and America, but the exquisite quality of Chinese cooking has no equal in Europe and America. . . . Before commerce opened up between China and the West, Westerners only knew French food as the best in the world. After tasting Chinese food, however, everyone considers China as the best in the world [in cooking].

He also urged the Chinese to maintain their preeminence in cooking so that they could be a "mentor to the world" in this regard.[21]

China's culinary supremacy was a belief shared by many other Chinese. At a time when Western powers repeatedly defeated and humiliated China and looked down on Chinese culture, gastronomy was one of the few areas where the Chinese could find some solace and a source of pride. For Chinese Americans, defending their foodways was to defend their community and culture. Highlighting the use of chopsticks as a sign of backwardness and weakness, the New York–based weekly newspaper *Spirit of the Times* wrote: "The celestials, though claiming such a high descent, are not renowned for their chivalric spirit, or their skill in using a more warlike weapon than a chop stick."[22] The Chinese countered by mocking the Westerners' use of knife and fork at mealtime, saying that "the Englishman does the chief work of the slaughter house on his dinner table, and remits the principal work of the kitchen to his stomach."[23]

In 1910, Cui Tongyue compiled Chinese America's first known cookbook; it contained a collection of Western-food recipes intended for Chinese cooks and servants working for Anglo employers. In the preface, Cui expressed similar pride about Chinese food: "The finest food is found in China. Among all nations under the heaven, only France is nearly as good as China in terms of culinary development and cooking skills. The other countries lag far behind."[24] Early Chinese American cookbook writers harbored similar sentiments. Shiu Wong Chan wrote of Chinese cooking in 1919: "When you have eaten the food you will soon be convinced not only of its merits but, in fact, of its superiority over other kinds of food and ways of cooking."[25]

Such sentiments have persisted among the Chinese for decades. In explaining the attraction of Chinese food, Chen Benchang remarked in 1971 that the major reason for this is that Chinese cuisine possesses "better cooking skills and tastes better than foreign cuisines."[26] Gregory C. Chow, a noted economist and expert on China, offered a similar gastronomical interpretation of the rise of Chinese food by arguing that the Chinese "became cooks in the United States simply because they had the basic culinary skills that the Chinese had. Their home cooking skills were good enough to make their way to a Chinese restaurant to make money."[27]

The merit of Chinese food as a centuries-old tradition was certainly a factor in its appeal to non-Chinese consumers, and the culinary excellence of the Chinese also received praise from Western commentators. "Few people understand the popularity of Chinese cooking," wrote the *Chicago Daily Tribune* in 1906. This was because, the newspaper continued, "they do not know that the Chinese as a race are the greatest epicures since the famous feasters of ancient Rome."[28] Kenneth W. Andrew, who served as chief inspector of police in Hong Kong from 1912 to 1938, emphasized the gastronomical distinction of Chinese food as the reason for its popularity in Britain and elsewhere: "There is no need to stress that Chinese food is now accepted as being the best food in the world. It is eaten in every country, and is so popular that 'taking away' Chinese food has now become the most popular way to buy it; there are at present well over three thousand Chinese restaurants in the United Kingdom."[29]

Not ready to go as far as to say that Chinese food is the best in the world, the French historian Fernand Braudel nonetheless found it comparable to French food and believed that the reason for its prevalence is gastronomical. He placed his assessment in a historical perspective: "Chinese cookery, which has taken over so many restaurants in the West today, belongs to a very ancient tradition, over a thousand years old, with unchanged rituals, elaborate recipes: one that is extremely attentive both in a sensual and literary sense to the range of tastes and their combinations, displaying a respect for the art of eating which is shared perhaps only by the French."[30] Late-nineteenth- and early-twentieth-century Western epicureans adored French food, and comparing another cuisine to French food was a great tribute. And that was what some Americans did in praising Chinese food. Juliet Corson, a noted American food expert, observed in 1879 that Chinese food "greatly resembles" French food.[31] Without invoking the French-food comparison, the *Chicago Tribune* simply observed that the Chinese "as a race" were "the greatest epicures the world ever has known."[32]

Conscious of the respect that French food commanded among Americans, the early Chinese American food promoter Wong Chin Foo used it as a point of reference. "The epicure flourishes in the Orient as well as the Occident," Wong wrote. "In Europe he bows down before the genius of France; in Asia, before that of the flowery kingdom," he concluded.[33] Others, such as the writer Emily Hahn, held that Chinese food was better than French food: "I believe Chinese cuisine is better than any other in the world, and this is a view shared by many, including some who have long been devotees of French cooking."[34]

The problem with the gastronomical interpretation lies not merely in the highly subjective notion of Chinese food's culinary superiority. More problematic is the implied inevitability of its success. Chinese food remained looked down on in American culture for some fifty years after its initial arrival. Moreover, what eventually prevailed in public dining were not the exquisite dishes that Chinese epicures had cultivated over the centuries, dishes that Western food connoisseurs had widely regarded as best representing Chinese cuisine. Instead, it was the simplest and least trumpeted dishes that won over the American palate. In fact, recognized gastronomical preeminence alone has seldom been the deciding factor in the popularity contest among cuisines. French food, for example, whose grandeur culinary-minded Americans have always revered, has never attained the level of popularity of Chinese, Mexican, or even fast food.

Conversely, foodways with little gastronomical merit or sophistication in cooking or taste can become wildly trendy, as in the case of American fast food, which since the early 1990s has swiftly infiltrated all major restaurant markets in China, a country known for its long tradition in the culinary arts. Its stunning success in the marketplace was attributable to the hegemony of American capital and culture rather than its culinary virtue.

"DO THE CHINESE EAT RATS?": THE CULTURAL TRANSNATIONALIZATION INTERPRETATION RECONSIDERED

In order to trace the genesis of the rise of Chinese food, we must go beyond the realm of gastronomy. A more plausible interpretation is to see it as a result of cultural globalization or, in the words of Wilbur Zelinsky, transnationalization. This perceptive geographer and pioneer in the study of America's ethnic food argues that the ethnic restaurant "is a major component in the transnationalization of culture in North America and elsewhere. . . . [L]ike the other components of this rapid phenomenon, it offers its participants the opportunity for vicarious joys, for exotic vacations without airports or baggage."[35]

An important part of cultural globalization, curiosity about exotic cultures for vicarious pleasure was certainly a crucial factor. Symptomatic of this curiosity, the emergence of tourism created an important condition for the development of Chinese food, but cultural curiosity alone does not explain the spread of Chinese food.

America's curiosity about Chinese culture began with American merchants and missionaries in China. The missionaries, in particular, were important agents of transpacific cultural exchange because their writings significantly shaped American perceptions of Chinese culture, including Chinese food.[36] Warren I. Cohen pointed out in *Pacific Passage* that missionaries were also instrumental in opening "a window through which the Chinese could access the outside world."[37] However, missionaries and their compatriots in China hardly deserve much credit for the spread of Chinese food in the United States because the image projected by them was not only exotic but also largely repulsive.

S. Wells Williams, who went to China in 1833 as a missionary printer and eventually became a prominent Sinologist, was keenly aware of this imagery. He also understood that it helped to shape prevailing unfavorable perceptions of China as a whole. In *The Middle Kingdom* (1848), which saw several editions

WHY IS CHINESE FOOD SO POPULAR? 15

and reprintings, and was translated into numerous languages after its initial publication , Williams wrote: "The articles of food which the Chinese eat, and the mode and ceremonies attending their feasts have aided much in giving them the odd character they bear abroad, though uncouth or unsavory viands form an infinitesimal portion of their food, and ceremonious feasts not one in a thousand of their repasts." He listed foods that featured prominently and frequently in sensationalized misperceptions about the Chinese diet: "Travelers have so often spoken of birdsnest soup, canine hams, and grimalkin fricassees, rats, snakes, worms, and other culinary novelties, served up in equally strange ways, that their readers get the idea that these articles form as large a proportion of the food as their description does of the narrative."[38]

Williams's writing not only failed completely to dispel such misperceptions but also often echoed them: "Rats and mice are, no doubt, eaten now and then, and so are many other undesirable things, by those whom want compels to take what they can get." Nor did he demonstrate any intention to bring Chinese food to the table of his readers. He made it clear that "the Chinese eat many things which are rejected by other peoples."[39] "The art of cooking," he concluded, "has not reached any high degree of perfection."[40] Evidently, nineteenth-century American readers were unlikely to find such descriptions appetizing. Indeed, it is obvious that in the early years, cultural curiosity did not increase Americans' appetite for Chinese food.

Another important component of cultural globalization is international immigration, which constituted an extremely viable vehicle in the transplantation of Chinese food as well as several cuisines, such as Italian food, in the United States.[41] But there is no absolute correlation between immigration and the transplantation of cuisines, which is why the foodways of numerous large immigrant groups, such as the Filipinos, have stayed largely invisible. Some ethnic cuisines, though, like Thai food have become quite popular in spite of the small size of the ethnic community they represent. Brian Greenberg and Linda S. Watts report that "the popularity of Thai restaurants with American yuppies was one of the most striking features of the 1980s cuisine."[42] Yet, there were only 45,279 Thais in America in 1980,[43] and that number grew to merely 110,851 two decades later.[44]

The presence of Chinese immigrants in the United States alone does not necessarily guarantee the success of Chinese food in the marketplace. One of the seemingly insurmountable obstacles lying in its way to the mainstream palate was the image of the Chinese as eaters of repulsive foods, including rats—an important but unfortunate legacy that the American public inherited from Americans who had ventured to China.

Unappetizing depictions of Chinese eating strange items gained currency in the United States after the arrival of Cantonese immigrants. The Boston-based *Gleason's Pictorial Drawing-Room Companion* published the following joke in 1854: "A California paper gives the following as a bill of fare at a Chinese restaurant in that city: 'Cat Cutlet, 25 cents; Griddled Rats, 6 cents; Dog Soup, 12 cents; Roast Dog, 18 cents; Dog Pie, 6 cents.'"[45] But the allegation that the Chinese ate such things was no joking matter. Claiming to rely on sources in French "scientific journals," the *Saturday Evening Post* reported in 1860 the Chinese habit of eating such animals. After a long passage on eating dog and cat, the *Post* stated: "The rat is also an animal which occupies a large place in the food of the Chinese."[46]

By the 1860s and 1870s, negative attitudes toward Chinese food became intensely hostile. Most revealing of this attitude is the increasingly frequent use of the word "rat" in descriptions of Chinese food. Closely associated with filthiness, disease, and barbarianism, "rat" portrayed a pungent image, painting the diet of the Chinese as being not only undesirable but also despicable. More important, it was also seen as an integral part of Chinese restaurants. The message is clear: the Chinese were not just eating such disgusting stuff themselves but serving it to the public as well.

In an article in *Frank Leslie's Illustrated Newspaper* in 1870, Thomas W. Cox relayed a popular (but not authentic) story that in the early days of Chinese San Francisco, "a Chinese restaurant announced 'rat pies' on the bill of fare. The delicacy was not popular with the Americans, and after a week or so, it was stricken from the list. Next day, the restaurant advertised 'squirrel pies,' and found them in good demand."[47] In 1880, a defender of Chinese food used the cleanliness of a Chinese restaurant in San Francisco in an effort to debunk the popular fiction. After describing how "shining" and "clean" the table, kitchen, and cookware were, this author concluded: "It is a revelation to those who have been educated in the delusion that rats and garbage form the staple of the Chinese cuisine."[48] But such efforts apparently had little effect in stopping the denigration of Chinese food. By then, prevalent notions that rats were among "the staples of a Chinaman's diet" had helped to create the legend that the Chinese restaurant served such dreadful creatures.[49]

Fried Rice

Serves 3 or 4

If Chinese food is America's number-one ethnic cuisine, rice is the most recognizable staple food that American diners have associated with the Chinese diet since the nineteenth century. In the daily language in many parts of China, to eat is to consume rice. It is fitting, therefore, to cook a rice dish when contemplating the question about the popularity of Chinese food.

4 cups cooked rice
2 eggs
dash of black pepper
5 tbsp vegetable oil
dash of salt
1 tsp grated ginger
1 tsp minced garlic
2 Chinese sausages, chopped into small pieces
⅓ cup green bell pepper, cut into small pieces
⅓ cup yellow bell pepper, cut into small pieces
⅓ cup red bell pepper, cut into small pieces
⅓ cup Chinese cucumber, cut into small pieces
⅓ cup peas
1 tsp salt
¼ cup chopped green onion

Rice is a central ingredient and must be prepared properly. To cook Calrose (medium grain) rice in a rice cooker, my preferred water-to-rice ratio is 3 to 4. Do not use freshly steamed rice. Wait for at least a few hours.

Beat the eggs in a bowl with the black pepper. Heat 1 tbsp vegetable oil in a frying pan or wok with a dash of salt; add and stir in the eggs. Transfer the scrambled eggs to a plate. Clean and heat the wok until it is dry. Add 1 tbsp vegetable oil, and when it is hot, add the ginger and garlic and stir for 10 seconds; add the sausage and stir for 40 seconds. Then add the bell peppers and cucumber and stir for about 1 minute. Add the peas and stir for 1 minute. Set the vegetables aside. Heat the remaining vegetable oil in the pan. Add the salt and green onion, and stir until the onion is lightly browned. Turn the heat to medium. Add the rice, and stir continuously until any clumps are broken up. Add the eggs, sausage, and vegetables. Stir to thoroughly mix for 3 minutes.

The mass media continued to entertain this type of made-up story. In 1906, the *Monroe City Democrat* in Missouri published the following passage: "In Minneapolis they are investigating the chop suey restaurants. There is a suspicion that they do not use fresh rats."[50] Reports of Chinese as habitual rat eaters appeared not just in newspapers but also in writings by visitors to Chinese communities. After touring Chinatown in San Francisco, Joseph Carey reported in 1901 that the Chinese ate things "most repulsive to the epicurean taste of an Anglo-Saxon. . . . Even lizards and rats and young dogs they will not refuse."[51]

The notion of Chinese eating rats became so imbedded in American culture that in the early twentieth century, when Chinese food began to gain increasing appeal, prospective consumers still harbored anxiety about rats on their plate. Lucien Adkins observed: "Take a friend to Chinatown for the first time and watch his face when the savory chop-suey arrives. He looks suspiciously at the mixture. He is certain it has rats in it, for the popular superstition that the Chinese eat rats is in-bred." Adkins continued: "He remembers his schoolboy history, with the picture of a Chinaman carrying around a cage of rats for sale."[52]

Indeed, many nineteenth-century Americans acquired the image of the Chinese as a rat-consuming race in their school days. "Do the Chinese eat rats?" the *New York Times* asked rhetorically in 1888." It went on: "This has always been a mooted question. Geographers contain the assertion that they do, and an old wood-cut of a Chinaman peddling rodents, strung by the tails to a rack which he carried over his shoulders, is a standard illustration of the common school atlases of 10 years ago."[53] A reporter for the *New York Tribune* recalled similar geography lessons: "People of the older generation can recall in their geographies a picture of a Chinese coolie trotting along barefooted, with a string of rats suspended on his shoulders."[54]

In a book that he researched in the 1930s, Paul Siu recounted a children's chant:

Chink, Chink, Chinaman
Eat dead rats;
Eats them up
Like gingersnaps.[55]

Even in the twenty-first century, the idea of the Chinese eating and selling rats has not entirely vanished. On January 29, 2007, New York City's WPIX-TV reported the claim of a customer who had found a piece of meat that looked like a rodent in her take-out food from the New Food King restaurant in Brooklyn. Following the

report, that restaurant's business plunged: customers called in and asked its workers why it would sell rat meat; a few even told the owners to go back to China.[56]

Do the Chinese eat rats?—the very question that the *New York Times* posed back
in 1888—popped up unexpectedly in my e-mail inbox from a scholar and animal-
rights activist a few years ago. I found the question perplexing because it did not
come from an uninformed or a sinophobic source. Moreover, an adequate and
comprehensive answer lies beneath the intertwined complexities of political
and gastronomical developments. A simple factual answer would be yes. We can
find numerous records of the Chinese, especially the Cantonese, eating what
Americans commonly called rats in historical sources. But the Cantonese did not
eat indiscriminately every kind of the 66 recognized species within the genus
Rattus, and "rodent," another word that was sometimes used in association with
Chinese food, represents more than half of all the more than 4,600 mammalian
species, scientifically speaking. In the comprehensive book about Chinese life
during the Qing dynasty that he compiled in 1917, Xu Ke mentioned the unique
foodstuffs of people in East Guangdong Province, including rice-field mice.[57] But
this does not mean that the Chinese have been particularly fond of rats as food.
On the contrary, they have been aware of the threat posed by rats to human
health. Jia Ming, a Yuan dynasty (1271–1368) food writer, issued stern warnings
about rats when accidentally used as food in *Yingshi Xu Zhi* (*All You Must Know
About Food*), one of the earlier manuals on the health values and hazards of various
food stuffs. "If eaten by mistake, the bones of rats can cause people to lose weight,"
he wrote. It was a serious warning at a time when gaining weight was a sign of
good health and good fortunes. "Rat saliva is poisonous," and "if it is dropped
into human food and consumed by people, it can cause *shu lou* (scrofula)."[58] When
I was growing up in China, rats were officially labeled as one of the four pests
(*sihai*) that the central government mobilized the entire nation to eliminate.

But in post–Gold Rush American political and popular culture, whether the
Chinese ate rats—a word always used vaguely—was never a purely gastronomical question about the diet of the Chinese or the specific kinds of things deemed
edible. Rather, the association of their food with rats stemmed from prevalent
ideas about Chinese as a culture and a race, projecting them not only as a despicable and barbaric people but also dangerous propagators of epidemics. For
Americans, then, especially American public-health authorities, rats represented
dirtiness, diseases, and death, rather than the kind of cute little creatures that
we see today in animated films such as *Ratatouille*.

A revealing example is Frank Todd's *Eradicating Plague from San Francisco*, a
report issued by San Francisco's Citizens' Health Committee at the end of the

city's second bubonic plague of 1907/1908. The chapter "The Role of the Rat" linked the epidemic to rats: "From the earliest times . . . people have noticed that plague was apt to accompany sickness among rats." It concluded that "the plague is a disease of rats." The report then dissociated the rat from the Europeans: "People that suppose rats in some way necessary to humanity are mistaken. There was not aboriginal or autochthonous European rat." The report suggested that Asians were responsible for spreading rats to white people and launching the epidemic by reminding readers that "starting from China in 1334, the 'Black Death' killed 25,000,000 of these people, or nearly twentieth-four per cent [of the European population]."

Adding a racial twist to its historical analysis, the report noted that the plague had long been considered a "typically Oriental disease." The purpose was to connect the dangerous disease to the Chinese community and its restaurants, and rats embodied that connection: "In the Chinatown epidemic eighty-seven dead rats, eleven dead of plague, were found in the walls of a Chinese restaurant. Several cases of human plague had been traced to this place, but they immediately ceased when the rats were cleaned out."[59]

Acutely aware of the racial and political dimensions of the Chinese rat-eating question, Lee Chew, a Chinese living in New York, responded to the question defiantly around the turn of the century: "The rat which is eaten by the Chinese is a field animal which lives on rice, grain and sugar cane. Its flesh is delicious. Many Americans who have tasted shark's fin and bird's nest soup and tiger lily flowers and bulbs are firm friends of Chinese cookery. If they could enjoy one of our fine rats they would go to China to live, so as to get some more." He went on, "American people eat ground hogs, which are very like these Chinese rats, and they also eat many sorts of food that our people would not touch."[60] He understood clearly that ideas about edibility are often culturally constructed and serve as markers of social boundaries. Claims that the Chinese were rat eaters were not statements about their food preferences but were aimed at magnifying their undesirability and inferiority.

Such perceptions erected a great wall, separating American consumers from Chinese food for about half a century after it voyaged to the New World. If the culinary interpretation is flawed and the cultural transnationalization theory has apparent holes, then what can account for the rise of the Chinese food's popularity? A larger historical context sheds light on the ascent of such a highly undesirable diet: the evolution of the United States as an empire.

2
THE EMPIRE AND EMPIRE FOOD

"The Chinese are here by the order of Providence, the principles of the Declaration, and the provisions of treaty," proclaimed the Reverend M. C. Briggs in 1876.[1] So was Chinese food—it was carried to the American shores and palate by the same forces that generated Chinese immigration and transformed the United States into an empire.

The spread of Chinese food was inseparably connected to the geographic and socioeconomic expansion of the United States. This connection is best captured by the notion of "empire food," which was created in the process of empire building for the pleasures of its citizens. Consumption was indeed a significant goal and consequence of empire building, and recognizing Chinese food as empire food helps us appreciate its basic characteristics: ubiquitous but cheap.

Many Americans have been unwilling or unable to see their country as an empire. Different from many other traditional empires, the United States is, nonetheless, an empire of consumption characterized by extraordinary material abundance. It is the kind of empire that an American founding father like Thomas Jefferson aspired to build in order to ensure freedom and liberty, and it also explains the enormous appeal of the United States to prominent foreign visitors ranging from Alexis de Tocqueville to Boris Yeltsin as well as millions of immigrants. Standing as an important event in the expansion of the American empire, the multiplication of Chinese restaurants expanded the meaning of American freedom and abundance by extending the dining-out experience to the masses.

EMPIRE FOOD

The concept of empire food underscores that consumption, including food consumption, has been an extremely important goal and benefit of the process of empire building. It also recognizes that process as one of the vehicles for the global movements of food.

The transfer of food through imperial expansion is not entirely separated from culinary crossings beyond cultural and national boarders engendered by other historical forces, such as human migration, trade, and government or corporate interventions. But empire food has distinctive characteristics, evident in the individual foodstuffs that modern Western empires have produced—such as chocolate, sugar, coffee, pineapple, and tea—about which scholars have written in other contexts.[2]

These foods were "discovered" and spread in close association with the overseas conquest by modern European empires. They originated in non-Western societies and evolved into extremely important and popular commodities in mass consumption. They were often produced by those who were not citizens of the empire, especially non-white laborers. The introduction of such foods accompanied the transformation of the diet and lifestyle of western European countries. Sidney Mintz has argued that the introduction of sugar profoundly altered the starch-centered diet of what would become the United Kingdom within a century after 1650.[3] Such foods were also integrated into the social and cultural fabric of the empire. Tea, for example, evolved as a symbol of the British Empire and culture. Empire foods also marked the division of the globe into two—the world of production and that of consumption—a division often drawn along racial lines.

Chinese food is another significant empire food. But it also bears important differences from the individual foods mentioned earlier. First, the Chinese food we discuss in this book is a food *system*, rather than a singular food item. Second, tea has become part of the British identity, and coffee has been gentrified by corporations like Starbucks in the United States; yet the intimate relationship that Chinese food developed with mainstream America since the turn of the twentieth century has not evolved into a marriage of equal partners. Instead, its status reminds us of a humble maid or a Chinese servant in a nineteenth-century white household, who was sometimes regarded "as family," but whose real purpose of existence was there merely to serve.[4]

As the first class of food made for public consumption, Chinese food was a forerunner of McDonald's, another food system that appealed to the desires of the growing mass consumers for convenience and service in the postwar years. The expanding Chinese restaurants played an important role in the development of the American empire and its way of life, a role that McDonald's also assumed with low-paid workers. But when traveling to China, McDonald's resemblance to American Chinese food dissipates. Armed with American corporate muscle and cultural hegemony, McDonald's penetrated Chinese markets with stunning swiftness and became a favorite destination of well-educated and successful Chinese. By comparison, American Chinese food encountered much prejudice and resistance after its arrival on American shores, and it has not achieved much social respectability.

Chinese food, I must add, is also quite different from what Cecilia Leong-Salobir calls "colonial food," which Britain's colonizers embraced in its Asian colonies.[5] First, American Chinese food was initially patronized largely by those on the margins of society rather the social and political elites. Second, while British colonial food incorporated native and British dietary components, Chinese food retained its distinctive identity. Many Chinese restaurants served "American food," but it was invariably kept separate from things Chinese.

The development of American Chinese food followed the trajectory of America's evolution as an empire. The origin of its transpacific journey goes back to the transpacific commercial and religious expansion of the United States during the post-Revolutionary period. It led to the initial Chinese presence in the New World, consisting of a limited number of sailors, students, merchants, cooks, and servants in the Northeast. These pioneers were followed by the Chinese forty-niners, who arrived in California during the Gold Rush years and first transplanted Chinese food to American soil.

Moreover, extending its global presence, the United States also experienced a tremendous growth in its economy and consumption at home, and the rise of Chinese food constituted a significant landmark in this domestic expansion. Scholars have written about the Chinese contributions to freedom and democracy in the legal and political systems;[6] equally important, the Chinese have played a vital role in democratizing consumption. Readily available in different parts of the country from the turn of the twentieth century, Chinese food helped to turn the luxury of enjoying meals prepared by others into a universally affordable experience, engendering an indispensable component of the modern world's most powerful empire of mass consumption. Ching Chao Wu, a doctoral student in the Sociology Department of the University of Chicago, put it in plain language in 1928: "If the poor and out of luck wanted cheap and substantial meals, they patronized the Chinese restaurants."[7]

At the beginning of the twentieth century, a well-traveled white epicure characterized chop suey as "the great contribution of the orient to the occident."[8] Reminiscent of the famous travel writer Norman Douglas's notion that curry is "India's gift to mankind," this seemingly complimentary characterization undoubtedly reflects an Orientalist and condescending view of China.[9] At the same time, chop suey's enormous popularity does symbolize the contribution of Chinese restaurant workers to the expansion of the American empire's lifestyle.

EMPIRE IN DENIAL

The use of the appellation "empire" to characterize the United States will certainly raise eyebrows among many Americans. As citizens of a nation liberated from an oppressive empire, they have tended to view that term as a dirty word, associating it with evil, as Ronald Reagan did in reference to the Soviet Union in a speech he gave in 1983.[10] Walter Lippmann perceptively pointed out in 1927 that "all the world thinks of the United States today as an empire, except the people of the United States."[11] Echoing Lippman, William Appleman Williams wrote in 1980: "The words *empire* and *imperialism* enjoy no easy hospitality in the minds and hearts of most contemporary Americans."[12] In the twentieth-first century, the United States largely remains "an empire in denial"—in the words of Niall Ferguson, the conservative British historian and advocate of the American empire.[13] In the commencement speech he delivered at West Point in June 2002, President George W. Bush repeated the long-standing idea that "America has no empire to extend." Knowing that Americans resent the appellation, the scholar Charles S. Maier avoided "claiming the United States is or is not an empire," even though it "reveals many . . . of the traits that have distinguished empires."[14]

Throughout the world, the notion of empire since the late nineteenth century acquired negative connotations due to of its connection to European imperialism and colonialism: the exploitation of distant peoples and natural resources, dominance, subjugation, and conquest. Of all the 193 member countries of the United Nations as of 2011, not one calls itself an empire.

DEFINITION OF EMPIRE

Since the nineteenth-century debates on empire and imperialism, there have been various theories on the topic. In this book, I use the word "empire" as a his-

torical concept. Empire is a centuries-old form of human government and organization, marked by the domination of one nation over other peoples. It has the
following four features.

First and most basically, it is the expansion of one nation's sovereignty and
territory at the expense of others. Second, as John Gallagher and Ronald E. Robinson pointed out in the context of the British Empire, such domination had also
existed informally.[15] Third, informal and formal empires share the same goal of
economically benefiting the mother nation. Consumption is the end of empires,
simply put. Needless to say, the privileged got fed extremely well in private homes
and public events, sometimes with exotic foods from faraway areas that only an
extraordinary empire could reach. The following quotation is perhaps the only
menu from such an event at that time, showing the food served at a dinner party
that Julius Caesar presented to the college of high priests in honor of the ap-
pointment of Lentulus Flamen Martialis around 70 B.C.E.:

> For hors-d'oeuvres sea urchins, as many raw oysters as they wanted, palourdes,
> mussels, thrushes under a thatch of asparagus, a fattened chicken, a *patina* of
> oysters and palourdes, black piddocks, white piddocks; then more mussels,
> clams, sea anemones, blackcaps, loin of roe deer and wild boar, fowls force-
> fed on wheatmeal, *Murex trunculus* and *Murex brandaris*. The dinner was ud-
> der, the split head of wild boar, *patina* of fish, *patina* of udder, ducks, roast
> teal, hares, roast fowl, frumenty and Picentine loaves.[16]

Rome also strove to feed the rest of its population. As Caesar admitted in 71
B.C.E., Rome provided free food to as many as 150,000 residents (Rome's total
population was about 463,000 in 86 B.C.E.).[17] Giving food to their citizens was
a predominant concern shared by other empires, such as imperial China, where
population was counted in terms of the number of "mouths" that had to be fed.
The lifeline of the British Empire was, essentially, a food line. The imperial
poet Joseph Rudyard Kipling understood this well, as he wrote in "Big Steamers," a poem published in 1911 in *A School History of England*:

> "Oh, where are you going to, all you Big Steamers,
> With England's own coal, up and down the salt sea?"
> "We are going to fetch you your bread and your butter,
> Your beef, pork and mutton, eggs, apples and cheese."
> "And where will you tech it from, all you Big Steamers,
> And where shall I write you when you are away?"

"We fetch it from Melbourne, Quebec, and Vancouver,
Address us at Hobart, Hong Kong, and Bombay."
"But if anything happened to all you Big Steamers,
And suppose you were wrecked up and won the salt sea?"
"Why you'd have no coffee or bacon for breakfast,
And you'd have no muffins or toast for your tea."

. . .

"Then what can I do for you, all you Big Steamers,
Oh, what can I do for your comfort and good?"
"Send out your big warships to watch your big waters,
That no one may stop us from bringing you food.
For the bread that you eat and the biscuits you nibble,
The Sweets that you suck and the joints that you carve,
They are brought to you daily by all us Big Steamers
And if anyone hinders our coming you'll starve!"[18]

This also reminds us that that empire building is the extension of individual consumption desires, spilled over the national boundaries. Gary Okihiro writes, "Desires have fueled travel to near and distant seas and lands in the form of exploration, trade, and conquest."[19]

Fourth, in spite of the tendency to distinguish empires from nation-states, the two have coexisted for centuries.[20] The distinction between empires and states—especially those multiethnic states that have formed and developed through physical expansion and exercised hegemony beyond their borders—is not as clear-cut as some have assumed. In fact, we may legitimately use the term "empire-states" to characterize such multiethnic entities, which came into existence as a result of territorial expansion. At the same time, however, they possess important characteristics of nation-states, including a shared language and a strong sense of common national identity. China clearly fits the characterization, as does the United States.

RESEMBLANCE TO OLD EMPIRES

By Niall Ferguson's tally, the United States is the sixty-eighth empire of the world—and he counts Communist China as the sixty-ninth.[21] In many ways, indeed, America looks much like empires of the past, such as those of Rome and Britain. After independence, the United States legally diminished and overtly denied the property rights of Native Americans in order to conquer their land.[22]

It has also taken land—by force or money—from other native peoples in the Pacific, from European powers, and from Mexico. Its physical size has grown fourfold from about 820,000 square miles in 1783 to 3.79 million square miles today.[23] Ellen C. Collier, a specialist in U.S. foreign policy, identifies 234 instances of American military interventions abroad from 1798 to 1993.[24] In the first decade of the twenty-first century, as Herfried Münkler notes, the country had 250,000 troops stationed on more than 700 military bases in more than 150 countries.[25] Acting like a traditional empire, the U.S. government also thinks like one. Before its integration into the State Department in 1999, the U.S. Information Agency (USIA) developed individual country-based communication (propaganda) plans. In 1952, one such plan under the agency's auspices directed its overseas posts to collect information on the Chinese communities in Southeast Asia and the attitude of the host country toward them.

The Pentagon divides the globe into five regional commands: Latin America, Europe, the Middle East, the Pacific, and North America. Although Americans love to call their country a republic, the United States—with its daunting global presence and dominance—reminds us more of Imperial Rome than of Athens. Also similar to what Rome did in its heyday, the American empire devotes increasing resources to entertain its populace and feed some of its poor, beginning after World War II, when it became the most powerful and richest country on earth.

The American empire bears particular resemblance to its British predecessor. Like Britain, it has exerted its global influence "informally," using its soft power in popular culture. Besides its global military installations, it has seven hundred Graduate Record Examinations (GRE) test centers in more than 160 countries, as just one example of its cultural domination. On the front of food consumption, McDonald's serves 68 million people in 119 countries each day. Economically, the United States has succeeded Britain as the world's most vocal and most aggressive player in international trade. At the first World's Salesmanship Congress in Detroit in 1916, President Woodrow Wilson told the more than three thousand salesmen, executives, and managers in various industries: "You are Americans and are meant to carry liberty and justice and the principles of humanity wherever you go, go out and sell goods that will make the world more comfortable and more happy, and convert them to the principles of America."[26] Promoting American goods and businesses has since been an unofficial but important job description of every president. The position of the U.S. dollar as the unrivaled world currency—established first at Bretton Woods after World War II and then reinvented when it was coupled with petroleum in global transactions after its delinking from gold in 1971—has marked America's dominance in world trade and turned the U.S. Treasury into a magic cash cow.

Nonetheless, I use the word "empire" not simply to condemn or criticize America. It undoubtedly deserves to be rebuked for its horrendous atrocities, immoral activities, and high cost, as numerous Americans on both the Left and the Right have noted.[27] At the same time, however, the country has stood from its beginning as a symbol of freedom and liberty. Its association with freedom is not merely rhetorical or self-proclaimed but also one of its most remarkable features in the minds of many people around the world. In Communist China, both political dissidents and high-ranking Communist officials have sought U.S. protection when their liberty and safety were in jeopardy.

Ronald Steel wrote in 1996 of America's difference from traditional empires: "[W]e are not content to subdue others: We insist that they be like us."[28] But not so infrequently did the United States have to do much insisting because many have aspired to be like Americans or to live like Americans. Millions of people have turned to the United States for the freedom from want. The number of annual immigration went over the 200,000 mark for the first time in 1847 and rose to almost 500,000 in 1900, when the country's total national population was under 76 million.[29] For more than a century, the U.S. government has actively trumpeted its political values—freedom and democracy—around the world, but it is America's unsurpassed capacity to satisfy people's consumer desires that has had a lasting and profound impact on the rest of the world.

THE UNITED STATES AS AN EMPIRE OF CONSUMPTION

The enormous international and domestic appeal and influence of the United States as the home of a "people of plenty" sets it apart from other large empires of the past. Powerful empires left their own distinctive footprints in history: the Chinese emperors put up great walls; Rome built roads; the British Empire turned the tongue of an island nation into a dominant global lingua franca. Beginning in the late nineteenth century, the United States pushed consumer aspirations to levels the world had never before thought possible. Noting America's "unprecedented affluence" in the 1950s, the economist John Kenneth Galbraith reminded us that nearly all nations "throughout all history, have been very poor."[30] This does not mean that the United States has always had a better standard of living than all other countries. Australians, for example, were economically better off than Americans around the turn of the twentieth century.[31]

But what makes America different is its promise of a better life for an ever-growing number of people.

The American empire of consumption—called "a way of life" by William Appleman Williams—is not only enjoyed by its citizens but also desired and seen as a trademark of the country by millions of people around the globe. Alan Thein Durning points out the American origin of inflating consumption aspirations: "In the perception of most of the world's people, the consumer life-style is made in America."[32] Lawrence B. Glickman writes in like fashion: "Consumption has long been central to American identity, culture, economic development, and politics."[33]

Consumer desire is not uniquely American. The anthropological economist Marshall Sahlins reminds us that "it is not that hunters and gatherers have curbed their materialistic 'impulses'; they simply never made an institution of them."[34] In spite of their mutual enmity during the Cold War, the capitalist West and the Communist countries shared the same objective: building a superior consumer society. Although the soldiers of the United States and the Soviet Union never faced each other in combat, President Richard Nixon and Premier Nikita Khrushchev had a personal face-off in 1959 at the American National Exhibition in Moscow, turning the American model kitchen into a Cold War battleground of ideology. During the famous "kitchen debate," the two men pledged that their countries would enter into a contest "in the production of consumer goods." Khrushchev declared: "The system that will give the people more goods will be the better system and victorious."[35] In the late 1950s, the Chinese leaders also made it a goal for the young Communist country to "surpass Britain and catch up with America" (chao ying gan mei); this led to the Great Leap Forward, which resulted in the starvation of as many as 38 million people, according to the controversial book Mao: The Unknown Story.[36]

Nor was opulent living an American invention. Old World empires like China had boasted luxurious styles of consumption long before the United States came along, but lavish life remained for centuries a privilege of the rich and powerful. What is distinctive about the United States is that it developed the world's first extensive system of mass consumption. This new model democraticized for increasing numbers of common people once exclusive luxuries like meat consumption or meals prepared and served by others, and it has affected the lives and aspirations of millions of people around the globe. At a level of influence that few other empires had seen, America became a model for the world—not as a puritanical "city upon a hill" envisioned by John Winthrop but as a consumer's paradise.

The democratization of consumption marks the internal expansion of the empire of consumption, extending its appeal and benefits to its critics. Among them, racial minorities have criticized Jefferson's empire of liberty as a racially exclusive one of and for white men. Besides upholding slavery, the critics point out, the nation deliberately prohibited non-white immigrants from naturalization from the very beginning. Such a racial definition of America laid a crucial legal foundation for subsequent exclusive measures like the Chinese Exclusion Act of 1882. In many cases, however, such criticism largely represented a desire to be accepted by and included in the kingdom of consumption. Some even fought battles on behalf of America in imperialist wars. While such minorities and immigrants desired to join the empire, others were born into it. William Appleman Williams, a most vocal critic of the empire, acknowledged that "I was born and reared in our American womb of empire."[37]

Noting the intrinsic democratic nature of mass consumption, the American economist George H. Hildebrand asserted in 1951 that "consumer sovereignty and the liberal system . . . stand or fall together."[38] Over time, the democratic characteristic of mass consumption grew more obvious, as working-class people in England in the 1960s and elsewhere could live like the middle class, and consumers would find a sense of freedom through consumption choices.[39] In 1992, the conservative commentator Ben J. Wattenberg declared that the remote-control television zapper, as a symbol of the consumer culture, was "one of the great democratic instruments in history."[40] About the political meaning of such choices, Gary Cross writes: "In the context of consumerism, liberty is not an abstract right to participate in public discourse or free speech. It means expressing oneself and realizing personal pleasure in and through goods."[41]

THE BEGINNING: A COUNTRY OF ABUNDANCE AND AN EMPIRE OF LIBERTY

In a letter to Judge Spencer Roane written on September 2, 1819, in which he insisted on the authority of the federal government over state courts, James Madison explicated that "in the great system of Political Economy having for its general object the national welfare, everything is related immediately or remotely to every other thing."[42] To understand the United States as an empire of consumption, we must recognize the connections and interdependence among four of its fundamental components: abundance, expansion, consumption, and liberty and freedom.

Essential to America's evolving consumer society is its extraordinary material abundance. Sustained and increased by the continued territorial expansion of the United States, it has provided not only an enviably high standard of living but also a critical foundation for American freedom and liberty. The interdependence of such key aspects of American life was keenly appreciated by the nation's founders like Thomas Jefferson and James Madison.

In creating a country of liberty, they also wanted to build an empire. Madison advocated empire building, arguing that the "Republican Government . . . in order to effect its purpose, must operate not within small but an extensive sphere."[43] In his mind, a nation with an extended territory would help to preserve liberty and freedom by preventing the majority political faction from having absolute power over minorities.[44]

Jefferson was the primary architect of the Louisiana Purchase in 1803, which nearly doubled the land size of the United States. The purchase contradicted Jefferson's anti-federalist ideals, such as states' rights and strict constructionism. Acquiring such a large piece of land would change the terms of contract between the states and the federal government, significantly amplifying its power.[45]

In Jefferson's mind, only an expanding empire could continuously provide the material abundance so essential for the principles of liberty and freedom. He wrote in defense of the Louisiana Purchase, "The nation's best interests demanded the extension of the empire for liberty."[46] In a message to the legislature of the Indiana Territory in 1805, Jefferson argued that "by enlarging the empire of liberty, we multiply its auxiliaries, and provide new sources of renovation, should its principles, at any time, degenerate, in those portions of our country which gave them birth."[47] Jefferson was influenced by Thomas Malthus's theory that all societies were bound to become overpopulated, corrupt, and senile because of the limitations of resources.[48] But the United States was to be different.

The difference was in its economic abundance, which was on the minds of colonial Americans from the early years. In *New-England's Plantation* (1630), Francis Higginson drew food pictures of such abundance, an idea that appears repeatedly in the following passage:

> This country aboundeth naturally with store of Roots of great variety and good to eat. Our Turnips, Parsnips and Carrots are here both bigger and sweeter than is ordinarily to be found in England. Here are also store of Pumpions, Cowcumbers, and other things of that nature which I know not.

Also, divers excellent Pot-herbs grow abundantly among the Grass, as Straw-
berry leaves in all places of the Countrey, and plentie of Strawberries in
their time, and Penyroyall, Wintersaverie, Sorrell, Brookelime, Liverwort,
Carvell, and Watercresses; also Leeks and Onions are ordinary, and divers
Physicall Herbes. Here are also abundance of other sweet Herbs, delightful
to the smell, whose names we know not.[49]

Economic plenty became amply evident in the years leading to independence.[50]
American colonists acquired a taste for imperial commodities, especially tea,
which they enjoyed extensively. A historian of colonial America writes: "Americans looked at eighteenth-century England with new eyes, admiring its cosmopolitan culture."[51]

Territorial acquisitions added to the resourcefulness of the young nation.
The material plenty of the United States became one of its most striking features in the eyes of foreign visitors in the early nineteenth century. One of the
numerous well-educated and perceptive visitors was Alexis de Tocqueville, who
toured the country in 1831 and 1832. In *Democracy in America*, he wrote: "[T]he
country is boundless, and its resources inexhaustible."[52] People from the outside world continued to be awed by America's material plenty. Michael Schudson remarked that "it takes an immigrant or outsider to speak of American
abundance in beatific terms."[53] This has proved especially true when the foreign visitors were from places of food scarcity. More than a century and a half
after Tocqueville's visit, Boris Yeltsin was astonished by the quantity of goods
he saw in American supermarkets during his tour of the United States in 1989,
noting: "You can't imagine it. It makes the people secure." He wanted at least
100 million Russians, especially their leaders, to come to "the American school
of supermarket."[54]

MEAT AS A SYMBOL OF ABUNDANCE

The plentitude of food, particularly meat, became an unmistakable symbol of
America's abundance. In fact, meat eating was a sign of status and power in
many cultures. In ancient China, for example, the phrase "meat eater" specifically referred to rulers of the country. During the Spring and Autumn period
(770–476 B.C.E.), when a farmer named Cao Gui was recommended to serve as
the military adviser to the king of the Lu Kingdom, one of his fellow villagers
thought that he should not go because of his low social status: "The meat-eaters
are making the strategies. Why do you want to intermeddle?"[55] At that time, as

a physical manifestation of the effect of meat eating, social elites were said to have a face without darkness, which was regarded as a sign of malnourishment and poor health.[56]

Meat remained a precious commodity in China for a long time. In 1873, the *New York Times* reported that a Chinese commoner "rarely indulges" in meat at all.[57] A late-nineteenth-century missionary handbook informed prospective China-bound missionaries that "meat is a luxury" in that country.[58] During the Cultural Revolution years, the monthly meat ration per person in Hubei Province was less than a pound—even poor nineteenth-century Englishmen had twice as much as we did. One of the things that struck my mother the most during her visit to the United States in 1992 was steak, which she considers as something extremely American and extravagant—in Chinese cooking, expensive cuts of meat usually have to be finely sliced or chopped to be served in small quantities. The scarcity of meat was also a prominent feature of the diet of common people in nineteenth-century Italy. In the weekly journal *All the Year Round*, Charles Dickens reported in 1870 that "the peasantry of the Tuscan Alps rarely, if ever, eat meat, except on Sundays and the holidays of the Church."[59]

Meat was a luxury for most people in western Europe throughout the nineteenth century. As Vaclav Smil notes, in the 1860s the bottom half of English society had barely more than twenty pounds of meat a year per person. And it not until after World War II that the wealthiest European countries attained the meat-consumption levels that the United States had reached more than century earlier.[60]

During the nineteenth century, the United States developed a reputation not only as an abundant and free nation but also as the home of a carnivorous people. In the Civil War, a time of food shortages in both the North and the South, an English visitor was impressed by the availability of meat, noting that Americans "usually have meat three times a day, and not a small quantity at each meal either."[61] Americans themselves knew that they were devouring a lot of meat. A southern planter stated in 1841: "There are few things in the habits of Americans, which strike the foreign observer with more force, than the extravagant consumption of food—and more especially of meat. Truly we may be called a carnivorous people."[62]

Representing America's material abundance, meat was also associated with the Anglo male identity. It was commonly believed that meat was a symbol of macho manhood. In fact, meat consumption "is seen, in a sense, as the ingesting of the very nature of the animal itself, its strength and aggression."[63] Jeremy Rifkin reminds us that "the identification of raw meat with power,

"Fish" Eggplant

Serves 2

In the nineteenth century, the United States became not only a global power but also a carnivorous country that privileged meat over vegetables. As a balancing act, I selected an eggplant recipe. The eggplant in the Chinese diet and in the American supermarket is a product of global cultural crossings. Domesticated in South or Southeast Asia, it is believed to have been introduced to Africa by the Persians and to Europe by the Arabs and reached China by way of Southeast Asia.*

- 2 Chinese eggplants or one large eggplant
- 6 tbsp vegetable oil
- 2 tbsp minced garlic
- 2 tbsp minced fresh ginger root
- 2 tbsp chopped green onion
- 3 tbsp soy sauce

Cut the eggplants into ½-inch slices. Deep-score on one side to form a diamond or rectangular pattern (do not cut through). Heat 5 tbsp vegetable oil in a sauté pan, turn the heat to medium. Brown the scored side of the eggplant slices. Transfer the eggplant to a plate and keep warm.

Heat 1 tbsp vegetable oil in the pan; sauté the garlic, ginger, and green onion for 1 to 2 minutes; then add the soy sauce. Gently put the eggplant slices back into the pan until heated through. Pour the soy sauce mixture evenly over the top of the eggplant. Serve with the scored side up.

*Frederick J. Simoons, *Food in China: A Cultural and Historical Inquiry* (Boca Raton, Fla.: CRC Press, 1991), 169.

male dominance, and privilege is among the oldest and most archaic cultural symbols still visible in contemporary civilization,"[64] which helps explain why the anti-Chinese forces characterized its campaign to exclude the Chinese as a struggle of "Meat vs. Rice" and of "American Manhood Against Asiatic Coolieism."[65]

As an emblem of abundance, America's carnivorous habits have also left irreversible marks on its natural environment. The country developed a love affair with beef, which intensified after 1870 as a result of railroad development, improved food refrigeration, and the demographic changes of immigration and urbanization.[66] The *Daily Picayune* declared in 1898 that beef was Americans' "most important food."[67] This was also an expensive love affair (the amount of feed for producing one pound of beef can produce more than four pounds of poultry and about two pounds of pork), which engendered an important impetus for continued land expansion.[68]

Visitors to central and northern Illinois and Iowa may find it hard to imagine that the vast cornfields there were once part of the "prairie triangle," which during the nineteenth century was completely and swiftly turned into farmland. Allan G. Bogue writes about this region: "In 1830 the farm-makers had hardly begun their task; by the 1890's the land was tamed, the corn belt a fact."[69] Much of the corn was grown to feed cattle in order to satisfy the increasing demand for beef. The physical transformation from prairie to farmland also took place elsewhere in the Midwest. A lengthy survey of American meat production in the 1880s reported that "Eastern Kansas is now mainly a great corn region, and feeds grass-grown stock from Western Kansas for beef."[70]

OVERSEAS EXPANSION AND POLITICAL RAMIFICATIONS OF MATERIAL ABUNDANCE

Thomas Jefferson's legacy lived on. After the end of the frontier, the United States increasingly relied on overseas expansion to enlarge its material wealth. As Alexis de Tocqueville had already noted in *Democracy in America,,* "Reason shows and experience proves that no commercial prosperity can be durable if it cannot be united, in case of need, to naval force."[71] In 1894, in the midst of rapid U.S. global expansion, John G. Carlisle, secretary of the treasury in Grover Cleveland's cabinet, explained to Congress how it benefited the domestic conditions: "The prosperity of our people . . . depends largely upon their ability to sell their surplus products in foreign markets at remunerative prices in order to secure money or establish credit abroad with which to pay interest and dividends upon loans and other investments which our customers there have made here."[72]

In the twentieth century, the conviction persisted that "America's domestic well-being depends upon such ever-increasing overseas economic expansion."[73] And this is exactly how the American global dominance has worked, according to the William Appleman Williams–inspired scholar Andrew Bacevich: "Expansion made the United States the 'land of opportunity.'"[74] The German scholar Herfried Münkler concurs: "From World War II into the 1960s, more power abroad meant greater abundance at home, which in turn, paved the way for greater freedom."[75]

Sustained by a growing empire, the material abundance of the United States predicated the nation's liberal, democratic political system. Tocqueville realized the political ramifications of American abundance when he wrote: "It is in America that one learns to understand the influence which physical prosperity exercises over political actions, and even over opinions."[76]

Despite its narrow perceptive on the frontier as a one-directional process and its other deficiencies, Frederick Jackson Turner's frontier thesis echoes Tocqueville, recognizing the profound political effects of America's burgeoning material plenty as a result of its westward expansion.[77] Turner wrote: "Not the Constitution, but free land and an abundance of natural resources open to a fit people, made the democratic type of society in America for three centuries while it occupied its empire."[78] Others also regarded material abundance as a foundation of America's political freedom. In 1954 ,the historian David Potter argued that "economic abundance is conducive to political democracy."[79]

American Cold Warriors often interpreted the meaning of freedom in terms of consumer goods available to American consumers. The short cartoon *Destination Earth* (1956) describes the benefits of a petroleum-based free market economy and shows the connection between freedom and consumption abundance and how it could undermine Communism.[80] In "What Freedom Means to Us," a speech delivered at the American National Exhibition on July 24, 1959, Richard Nixon emphasized to his Russian audience that "the great majority of American wage earners" owned nice consumer goods, such as houses, television sets, and cars.

America has also used its material plenty as a tool to deal with domestic social problems. Reinhold Niebuhr pointed out in a reflective examination of the nation's past that "through a strategy of commercial and territorial expansion, the United States accrued power and fostered material abundance at home. Expectations of ever increasing affluence in turn ameliorated social tensions and kept internal dissent within bounds, thereby permitting individual Americans to pursue their disparate notions of life, liberty and happiness."[81] Social tensions were particularly high in industrializing and urbanizing European countries during the late nineteenth and early twentieth centuries, leading to tremendous labor unrest and the rise of radical political ideologies (such as socialism in European countries). Europeans wondered why American society, including its working class, seemed relatively immune to socialism and Marxism. In an essay "Why There Is No Socialism in the United States," the controversial German sociologist Werner Sombart provided his answer: "All socialist utopias come to nothing on roast beef and apple pie."[82]

To the list of roast beef and apple pie as social and racial painkillers, Thomas Nast added turkey. A popular and influential nineteenth-century illustrator, Nash created such American cultural icons as the Republican elephant and Democratic donkey. He painted a famous Thanksgiving dinner scene in 1869, a time when rapid socioeconomic changes intensified social conflict. Two short phrases at the lower corners of the painting read: "Come one; come all," and "free and equal."[83] The painting projects an image of men and women of different races—besides whites and African Americans, there was a Chinese man with the pigtail hanging down his back—coming together to share and celebrate American abundance.

Reminiscent of Rome's pledge to provide food for its populace, American presidential candidates have often promised to bring abundance to the dinner table of the American people. "A full dinner pail," William McKinley's presidential campaign slogan from 1900, featured prominently in the Republican presidential campaign of 1928 as a potent metaphor for American prosperity. In his presidential nomination speech, Herbert Hoover vowed to top it: "Our workers with their average weekly wages can today buy two and often three times more bread and butter than any wage earners of Europe. At one time we demanded for our workers a 'full dinner pail.' We have now gone far beyond that conception. Today we demand comfort and greater participation in life and leisure."[84] In a campaign speech in October 1928 in New York, Hoover articulated clearly and loudly his belief in the interdependence between economic prosperity and political liberty: "Liberalism is a force truly of the spirit, a force proceeding from the deep realization that economic freedom cannot be sacrificed if political freedom is to be preserved."[85] Franklin Roosevelt understood this interdependence between economic and political freedom as well. In a speech delivered in Pittsburgh in October 1932, the presidential candidate accused the Republicans of "shifting the boast of the full dinner pail, made in 1928, to the threat of the continued empty dinner pail in 1932."[86] The "four freedoms" that FDR proposed in 1941 as his vision of the new world order includes "the freedom from want." For him, evidently, a hungry world could not be completely free.

In the minds of so many American policy makers, it would be impossible to uphold the United States as a country of freedom and democracy without economic abundance—a point that they emphasized during the Great Depression, when such abundance was gravely threatened. Gardiner C. Means, who served on the Consumer Advisory Board under the National Recovery Administration, suggested that safeguarding the interest of the consumer "may well be the key that will open the way to a truly American solution of the problem which is leading other countries in the direction of either fascism or communism."[87] As FDR's principal architect of the New Deal, Harry Hopkins was more blunt: "This country cannot continue as a democracy with 10 or 12 million people unemployed. It just can't be done."[88] Jefferson would have agreed.

TO COOK OR NOT TO COOK: THE CHANGING MEANING OF ABUNDANCE

To understand the importance of Chinese food as a critical part of the emerging empire of consumption, we have to recognize that for those in pursuit of American abundance, it entailed not simply the multitude of goods but also the quality of life. In the realm of food, it involved not only its quantity. Beginning in the late nineteenth century, it increasingly meant how food was prepared and consumed.

The growing empire of consumption extended its socioeconomic boundaries to include a growing number of non-elite white Americans, which is clearly seen in the emergence and growth of the middle class. Historians do not have a consensus on precisely when and how the American middle class emerged. But a sure sign of its appearance is the effort by more and more American households to enjoy and emulate the consumer goods and the lifestyle of the upper class. Besides carpeted floors, comfortable sofas, and a piano, the rising middle class in the nineteenth century also had better food and more refined table manners than before. Men learned, in Stuart Blumin's words, "to eat more slowly, and with a fork rather a knife."[89] Men's unhurried eating meant that the meals of middle-class families became more elaborate, as did their dining rooms.[90] More elaborate meals also meant more work for the women, who were urged to follow the Victorian "cult of domesticity" by staying home to take care of their children and husbands. Increasingly, middle-class families hired domestic servants.[91] As the middle class continued to expand during industrialization and urbanization, personal service became an important occupation. There were 22,243 servants in 1850, which grew to about 730,000 in 1870 and had passed the 1 million mark by 1880.[92] The number of people engaged in domestic and other personal service jobs more than doubled from about 1.4 million in 1880 to over 3 million in 1890, and grew to more than 4.7 million in 1900.[93] I must add that cooking became a top responsibility of servants.

Having the service of other people for basic personal needs like cooking constituted a vital marker of social distinction. This was manifested most clearly in food consumption, where the society was conspicuously divided into those who cooked and those who did not. Keenly aware of this division, many early cookbook writers consciously wrote for the former. For instance, Amelia Simmons, once a servant herself, wrote *American Cookery* (1786) for domestic servants.

In the nineteenth century, having their meals cooked by others was a particularly important threshold in the middle class's aspirations to emulate the lifestyle of the top strata of society. Having a cook was not as prohibitively expensive as certain other aspects of being upper class, such as owning large real-estate properties; the presence of plenty of racial minorities and immigrants as low-paid servants increased its affordability.

Moreover, because of America's material wealth, the gap between the top strata of society and all the rest seemed quite bridgeable in the area of consumer goods. The historian Daniel Boorstin notes that by the mid-nineteenth century "in America, it was far more difficult than in England to tell man's social class by what he wore."[94] Similarly, luxury-food consumption was not entirely off-limits to the non-wealthy. One example is the drinking of imported tea in colonial America. In 1744, Dr. Alexander Hamilton, a physician who immigrated to America from Scotland and became known for his acute social observations, traveled along the Hudson River. In the cabin of a poor family, he and his companion spotted superfluous consumer goods: "Half a dozen pewter spoons and as many plates, old and wore out but bright and clean, a set of stone [stoneware] tea dishes, and a tea pot."[95]

Technological improvements in the kitchen, such as the woodstoves that replaced open hearths after the Civil War, did not necessarily ease the burden of labor, especially for women.[96] Nineteenth-century Americans knew very well how arduous housework was at the time. In Edward Bellamy's science fiction novel, *Looking Backward*, the young protagonist, Julian West, wrote about his world: "In my day, even wealth and unlimited servants did not enfranchise their possessor from household cares, while the women of the merely well-to-do and poorer classes lived and died martyrs to them."[97] Having others do the chores, such as cooking, was a widespread ambition of the middle class. As Alice A. Deck illustrates, food advertisements that adopted the image of African American women as domestic cooks in the first half of the twentieth century reveal "white middle-class America's deep-laying desires [for] black domestic servants."[98] When these servants were not around, white middle-class Americans turned to young Irish women, and they also found Chinese immigrant men to be desirable servants.

No One Likes to Cook: Marx's Deficiencies

The desire to avoid home cooking is a universal human tendency and an especially important part of being middle class in America.

Undoubtedly, many individuals have enjoyed cooking throughout the centuries. But no one likes to cook when it is not a choice but represents compulsory, strenuous, routine, and tedious work. Extraordinarily diligent and idealistic people who take pleasure in work for the sake of work itself might strongly disagree with my proposition.[99] Karl Marx would be one of them. An idiom that I became familiar with as a child in China captures the essence of the Marxist vision of the ideal society, where work becomes an end itself: "From each according to his ability, to each according to his needs."[100] Yet this idiom contains two deficiencies in Marx's understanding of human nature.[101]

The first stems from a mistaken premise that human beings would be intrinsically willing to work on their own and based on their abilities. Like Marx, Thorstein Veblen regarded work, or what he termed "workmanship," to be a human instinct. But he nonetheless acknowledged that leisure became "honorable" and "imperative" when work was divided into "noble and ignoble employments."[102] Even the Bible, which often expresses a positive view of work, promises leisure (rest) from labor as part of eternal life: "Blessed are the dead which die in the Lord from henceforth: Yea, saith the Spirit, that they may rest from their labours" (Revelation 14:13 [KJV]). A fundamental demand of workers in industrializing societies is therefore shorter hours of work and more leisure time.

Nineteenth-century white, middle-class American women exhibited a similar attitude toward kitchen work, which Catherine Selden loathed as "the tyranny of the kitchen."[103] Writing in a women's magazine in 1870, Minna Wright explained middle-class women's resentment of confining kitchen chores: "With weak nerves, precocious children, and the great social problem of the age to solve in societies and meetings innumerable, we have neither time nor strength left to be queens of the kitchen." Without servants, they just could not sustain a "New England Kitchen," she concludes.[104] In the minds of people like Wright, evidently, home cooking was the antithesis of being middle class.

This attitude about home cooking continued to manifest in the twentieth century. In the 1940s, *The Good Housekeeping Cook Book* simply referred to home cooking as "the meal problem."[105] In 1960, in her enormously popular *I Hate to Cook Book*, Peg Bracken openly admitted her resentment toward cooking, calling it one of three activities that "become no less painful through repetition" (the other two being childbearing and paying taxes).[106] Resonating with American audiences, the book sold more than 3 million copies and made Bracken a household name.[107]

This loathing for household chores like cooking was not confined to white middle-class women. Many years later, the African American author Toni Morrison spoke of housework as "drudgery."[108] Cooking was an activity largely shunned by men, particularly men of high social status. A member of the social elite of his time, Confucius cherished meat and stated that he would offer instruction to anyone who brought him a bundle of dried meat.[109] But he exhorted that a gentleman should stay away from the kitchen and the slaughterhouse.[110]

Compared with traditional Chinese society, cooking as an occupation garnered even less respect in late-nineteenth- and early-twentieth-century America, where cooks—especially women—were usually regarded as synonymous with servants. Even the Bureau of the Census did not make a clear distinction between these two kinds of work in collecting occupational data.[111] In 1894, Ah Yow, a Chinese proprietor of a restaurant in Seattle, was barred by the collector of customs from reentering the United States upon his return from a visit to China. A district judge by the name of Hanford denied his petition because, in the judge's view, "a restaurant keeper, [who] is a caterer, who keeps a place for serving meals, and provides, prepares, and cooks raw materials to suit the tastes of his patrons . . . is not a merchant."[112]

Edward Bellamy's Julian West, the narrator of *Looking Backward*, woke up from his hypnotized state to find himself in a utopian society in the year 2000 where people no longer had housework, including cooking, to do at home. West exclaimed, "What a paradise for womankind the world must be now!"[113]

The other deficiency in Marx's comprehension of human nature was his focus on need or necessity as a timeless, natural constant. When talking about human nature and human needs, however, Confucius spoke about desire as that which encompasses both the physical necessity of humans and the social needs that are continually refined by changing social conditions. The energy that the adult human body needs to keep it going is about two thousand calories a day, which can be generated by about twelve medium-size (6 ounce) baked potatoes.[114] Thus once people sustain the most rudimentary bodily calorie and nutrition needs with regularity, they then desire to consume better foods such as meat and wine in greater variety. In addition, they want to have such foods prepared by others. Such desires help us understand the historical conditions and forces that brought Chinese immigrants and their restaurants to a prominently dominant position in food consumption.

THE CHINESE CONTRIBUTION TO THE DEMOCRATIZATION OF DINING OUT

With the growth of the emerging middle class in both size and appetite came the increasingly difficult question of who would do the work in the kitchen. Immigrants and racial minorities were the answer. In the South after the Civil War, freed slaves assumed the duties of slaves as domestic servants, "adding a despised race to a despised calling."[115] In other regions, immigrants became an increasingly important force in domestic service.[116] From 1880 to 1890, the number of immigrants engaged in domestic and personal service increased from 967,094 to 1,438.080.[117] By 1910, immigrants, their children, and racial minorities outnumbered native whites by nearly 2.5 times in such jobs.

Outside private homes, the public-service sector also grew in the late nineteenth and early twentieth centuries to meet the needs of those who could not afford domestic help. Here again, immigrants and minorities filled service jobs. The historian William Leach reports that "the number of service workers, including those entrusted with the care of customers, rose fivefold between 1870 and 1910, at two and half times the rate of increase of industrial workers."[118] Many service workers were immigrants and racial minorities. Like middle America, the U.S. Navy also used minorities, notably African Americans and Filipinos, as domestics with the official designation "stewards."

In the American West, the despised race was Chinese, and they increasingly became domestic servants in both private homes and the public-service sector. Other immigrants took similar service jobs. For Europeans like the Germans, Irish, and Italians, however, domestic service was more of a temporary position, and it involved only certain segments of their communities. For the Chinese, however, it was a predominant and lasting occupation.

The rise of Chinese restaurants is a logical extension of the Chinese presence in domestic service. The shortage of servants helped to spur the growth of the restaurant industry. "As it became increasingly rare for middle-class families to have full-time, live-in servants," Andrew P. Haley writes, "restaurants offered an alternative to eating and entertaining at home."[119] In spreading to cities across the nation, Chinese restaurants not only created its first lines of standardized restaurant foods but also turned dining into a form of mass consumption. In these establishments, Chinese Americans continued their designated role as personal-service providers in the emerging consumer economy. In this role, they helped to extend the material abundance (in the form of lifestyle) of the empire not merely to the middle class but also to marginalized groups.

Gary Okihiro acknowledges the contributions of marginalized minorities like the Chinese in preserving and advancing "the principles and ideals of democracy" and in making America a freer place for all through their political struggle for equality.[120] In addition, the Chinese have also played an indispensable role in extending American democracy to the market of consumption. As providers of cooked meals and other personal services, they helped the United States to fulfill its promise of an abundant life to more and more people, and this of course included the less privileged groups. In a word, they were empire stewards. Fulfilling an important social need, the food they served in Chinese restaurants was indeed an empire food.

3
CHINESE COOKS AS STEWARDS OF EMPIRE

Got up half past 4 this mor[ning] and made the graham biscuits for breakfast. and wash the dishes done clean the stove dust or ashes and made 170 cookies this afternoon . . . and have the apple pie for the dinner. and translate the second hymn of sweet hours of prayer. read the 4th chap[ter] of Romans.

These lines are from the diary of Ah Quin on March 12, 1878, when he worked as a cook for a mining company on a small island in Alaska. For Ah Quin, thirty years old, nearly six feet tall and skinny, weighing no more than 130 pounds, this was a fairly typical day during his time in Alaska from 1877 to 1878. The hard-working man got up very early in the morning, and no matter how tired he was, he would always find time to read the Bible and write a diary entry every day—a habit he kept for many years. And the food he cooked at the company was invariably Western. Besides biscuits, apple pies, and cookies, he also had a rather extensive repertoire of things to make: cornmeal pudding, muffins, mutton pot pies, pancakes, sponge cakes, donuts, clam chowder, roast turkey, and cod—a repertoire built from his previous experiences as a cook in California following his arrival in the United States in 1868.

The conspicuous absence of Chinese food from Ah Quin's menu was a common experience of the majority of Chinese domestic servant cooks, a reminder that Chinese entered the food sector not to proselytize the art of Chinese cooking but to provide the service needed by their Anglo employers. Cooking was an integral part of domestic service, and it quickly became one of the most prominent occupations of Chinese Americans in the post–Gold Rush years. The magazine *Youth's Companion* characterized this development as "The Chinaman's Conquest."[1] The entry of the Chinese en masse into servitude as cooks and servants paralleled and was intrinsically connected to their growing predominance in the laundry business. Such service jobs illustrate their historical role as stewards of the emerging empire of consumption and represent a precursor to their future conspicuous position in the restaurant business.

The Chinese presence in the service sector is marked by three features. First, their preponderance in certain geographic areas such as California. Second, long before being officially christened as a model minority in the late twentieth century, the Chinese were praised as exemplary cooks and servants, used by white employers as the ideal for personal- and domestic-service work. Third, in time Chinese America would become virtually a population of service workers, cooking food and washing clothes for Americans.

They were also pioneers in cultural change. They navigated the new and often hostile world with much curiosity and courage; they exhibited their autonomy in close interactions with their employers and customers.

THE NEEDS OF THE EMPIRE

Rome conquered its world with Roman legions, the British Empire with the Royal Navy, and the United States with its mass consumer culture. In modern history, China has been an empire of cheap labor. Still a pillar of the accelerating Chinese economy, Chinese labor in the nineteenth century started to significantly extend China's global presence to new markets created by expanding Western capitalism.

As ever, powerful Western empires needed not only soldiers to fight battles but also laborers to perform services. In Rome, slaves accounted for a great proportion of the population, and their cheap labor constituted a vital foundation for its glory and the prosperity enjoyed by its citizens.[2] As an important part of Roman life, slaves worked on farms and large estates, cleaned roads and streets, and cooked for well-to-do families. In antebellum America, indentured servants and African American slaves carried out such duties. Then came the Chinese. During the late nineteenth and early twentieth centuries, large numbers of Chinese laborers worked as domestic servants, cooking in private homes, in company kitchens, and on oceangoing ships. They and their compatriots in the laundry business joined other racial minorities and immigrants in providing services that satisfied the growing appetite among more and more Americans for a more convenient and leisurely lifestyle.

The presence of Chinese service workers first became noticeable in the American West, where anti-Chinese sentiments began to surge in the early 1850s. The *Sacramento Union* remarked in 1852, "What at first appeared rather novel and interesting in respect to Chinese immigrants, is becoming an alarming evil."[3] In an 1853 report, *Alta California* called them "innumerable hordes of semi-human Asiatics."[4] Rodman W. Paul summarized the quickly deteriorating situation: "In the half dozen years since their arrival in California, they had drawn upon themselves political debates and attacks, and had been the cause of a state-wide popular agitation among the mining class."[5]

The Reverend William Speer was one of the few whites openly sympathetic to the Chinese. Speer had been a medical missionary in the Pearl River Delta, home to native communities of Chinese immigrants. Because Speer knew their "language and the needs," he opened the first Chinese Christian mission in San Francisco in 1853.[6]

While the anti-Chinese antagonism from the working class had an apparent economic motivation, others, who regarded Chinese immigration as another racial element in the political economy, wondered about how to "receive this new element in our republicanism."[7] Keenly aware of this question and understanding the socioeconomic status of the Chinese, Speer offered several reasons for their presence in California. One was the need for "the Chinese as servants." "For patience, docility, willingness to receive instruction, and economy, we have not seen the equals of the Chinese," he explicated.[8] In a lengthy plea to the California legislature, he reiterated the same reasoning:

> Our wives and families have a very deep interest in the presence and labors of the Chinese. In a country where females are yet few, and the cares of large households exhausting to their feeble strength, the aid of these patient, busy, economical people, many of whom have had a previous training in various departments of domestic drudgery in the houses of American, English, and other foreign residents along the Chinese coast, has been felt to be a boon.[9]

Other advocates of the Chinese continued this line of defense. In defending the Chinese, they were also protecting the right of American consumers to cheap but outstanding Chinese service. As many of them knew well, it was "a blessing" and "a convenience" that "has contributed largely to our prosperity, our comfort and our wealth."[10]

George F. Seward, America's top diplomat—his exact title was "envoy extraordinary and minister plenipotentiary"—to China between 1876 and 1880, accorded Chinese domestics "a high degree of commendation" and cited extensive evidence from testimonies collected during the 1876 congressional investigation of Chinese immigration to show that "the Chinese do very well as servants."[11] During the debate about the desirability of the Chinese in 1902, Clara E. Hamilton made the same argument by demonstrating what "Pacific Coast life would be like without the Chinese." Furthermore, she understood that household chores in the private sphere were part of the political economy. The Chinese question, she wrote, "touches the horizon of our own households. This may be 'personal and circumscribed,' doubtless, but the domestic affairs of a people figure too largely in the prosperity of the commonwealth to be ignored with safety."[12] Her remarks reveal why topics like the virtue of Chinese domestic servants and the value of Chinese cooks loomed large in political debates of Chinese immigration.

In the lexicon of political economy in late-nineteenth- and early-twentieth-century America, the words "servant" and "cook" were often synonymous; most servants also performed cooking duties, except in those families that hired more than one servant. A contemporary American numerated the responsibilities of Chinese servants in small families: "They cook and serve meals . . . make beds, sweep, and dust."[13] Many people commented on the qualities of the Chinese both as servants and as cooks. Even before the arrival of large numbers of Chinese servants in the East, for example, the *New York Tribune* expressed an appreciation of the "domestic aptitude of the Chinese," which the newspaper noted "fits them especially for cook, stewards, and table waiters."[14]

A RACE OF COOKS

Chinese food remained a target of ridicule and attack in American society, and this makes the widespread admiration of the Chinese as good cooks ironically worth noting. Anglo commentators frequently identified excellence in the kitchen as a natural trait of Chinese. Indeed, the kitchen became an inevitable destination for many of these immigrants. However, it was a position predestined not by nature but by geo-economic conditions. In a world where the Chinese were looked on as undesirables excluded from most occupations, they began to be seen as valuable only when performing duties shunned by whites. This also explains why idealizing the Chinese as good cooks and servants almost invariably focused on Chinese men, who became a major force of cheap labor in the global economy.

The praise of the Chinese for their merits as a cooks became increasingly pronounced in the late nineteenth century. Robert Henry Cobbold, an English missionary of the Church Missionary Society, spent about eight years in the coastal Chinese city of Ningpo. In 1860, he published *Pictures of the Chinese*, which quickly reached American readers. In it, he noted the quality of Chinese men in kitchen work: "Almost every Chinaman is, by a kind of natural instinct, good both at cooking and at bargaining."[15] "The Chinese are a nation of cooks," proclaimed *Lippincott's Monthly Magazine* in 1892. "There is scarcely no individual in their vast community who is not more or less competent to cook himself a respectable dinner. Chinese tradition points to a date, some thousands of years before the Christian era, at which an inspired ruler of old first taught mankind the application of fire to food."[16]

Such accolades continued well into the twentieth century. One article noted at the beginning of the twentieth century: "If there is one sphere of European domestic life in which, more than another, the Chinaman finds scope for the exercise of his own peculiar ingenuity, without doubt it is in the regions dedicated to the pursuit of the culinary art."[17] Alice A. Harrison put it more bluntly in 1917: "A Chinaman is naturally endowed with Epicurean tendencies."[18]

Yet many white employers exhibited a fondness for Chinese cooks because of the fine service provided by the Chinese, rather than because of their culinary expertise. The outstanding qualities of the Chinese as cooks listed in 1879 in a missionary tract have little to do with cooking per se: "They are good cooks, the best in the world, the French excepted. They will obey orders to the letter and spirit. They work all day, and are satisfied with moderate wages—who says all this? The Pacific Mail Company from San Francisco employs only Chinese—Chinese sailors, cooks, waiters. They speak in the highest terms of their honesty, sobriety, faithfulness." It concluded that Chinese possessed "all the qualities of good servants."[19] According to residents of a "fashionable suburb of Los Angeles" at the turn of the twentieth century, Chinese cooks were "Yellow Angels," and, again, this was largely because of their patience and loyalty in performing their domestic duties.[20] After all, servitude was what white Americans saw and wanted in Chinese cooks. Will Irwin, a well-known San Francisco reporter, summarized a widespread sentiment: "The Chinaman was an ideal servant."[21]

Good Housekeeping, a source of authority on domestic matters, offered an idealized depiction of the servant, who by

> temperament and training . . . fitted for the task beyond the dreams of the eastern house-wife of moderate means. He likes, or at least expects, to work hard . . . likes the family he works for and has no wish to emulate the lady of the house, to rise above the caste into which his parents and grandparents were born. Furthermore, he is clean, honest, thrifty and methodical. Like a well-regulated clock he ticks off his duties. By certain hours each, if you let him alone, your house will be in order; your meals served; the table cleared and each dish returned to its place.

On the whole, he "will do more work and make less trouble than any other class of servant."[22]

The Chinese were thought to fit this profile almost perfectly and thus were bound to become servants. This reflected a deeply embedded mentality among many Westerners. While in political exile in California in the early 1850s, the Chilean journalist Benjamin Vicuña McKenna got the impression that "the Chinese seem unfitted for any but domestic service." The otherwise largely unsympathetic report of Canada's Royal Commission on Chinese Immigration noted in 1885: "The universal testimony is that they make good domestic servants." It mentioned specifically that "[o]f all the gifts . . . which the Chinese have given the State of California that, for which many seemed most grateful and about the character of which, with hardly a qualification, all are agreed, is the domestic servant."[23] Some Americans, who had had Chinese servants while living in China, wanted to bring them home to the United States because of their excellence.[24]

The idea of service jobs naturally befitting the Chinese also illustrates a reality in the global division of labor between whites and non-whites, and between rich and poor nations. This labor division was transplanted by international migration to U.S. soil, where the Chinese performed jobs avoided by white Americans. In 1880, after lamenting that "our boys and girls" became "idle, incompetent 'hoodlums' . . . ashamed of honest toil," a middle-class "California housekeeper" praised the Chinese, who "occupy the places which in healthier state of society would be filled by men and women, boys and girls, of our own race; but these latter refuse to do the work required."[25] Ho Yow, the Chinese consul-general in San Francisco, exhibited an awareness of this global division of labor when he stated that "Chinese fit into the world's industry in ways which do not conflict with white labor."[26] But the statement underestimated the extent to which this racialized division of labor was imposed on the Chinese by whites, especially white workers, who viewed the Chinese with intense hostility. The whites drove the Chinese out of mining, manufacturing, and agriculture; some corporations also made a deliberate policy not to hire Chinese men for more profitable jobs. One such corporation was Miller and Lux, a company formed by two German immigrants and a holder of vast lands and water rights. This company decided to use Chinese only as cooks in the late nineteenth century. The logic of its management was, as David Igler reports, "the Chinese as a race were cooks."[27] But those Chinese working as cooks still did not escape white labor's wrath. After the Chinese cook was fired at Gale's Mining Company in 1909, for example, one of its white workers hoped that the new one would "be white and give us white men's grub."[28]

In such an extremely anti-Chinese political climate, hiring a domestic Chinese cook could be politically dangerous. Governor Henry Gage of California, who had watched his popularity plunge during the bubonic plague outbreak in 1901, was attacked for employing a Chinese cook for his family in 1902. The *San Francisco Chronicle* remarked that it "does not indicate friendship or respect for free white labor on the part of the Governor."[29] And indeed, Gage failed to win his party's nomination as a candidate for governor. In places like Tacoma, Washington, some people feared that using Chinese domestic help could jeopardize the safety of their families.[30] Such fear perhaps also explains why sometimes even dining establishments like the well-attended Anderson's in San Diego found it necessary to publicly announce that they employed "No Chinese."[31] The Park Boarding House in Riverside, California, similarly emphasized in an advertisement that that it had no Chinese cooks in its dining room.[32]

A target of white labor's animosity, Chinese domestic workers were at the same time constantly compared by their middle-class employers with white service workers and were used to judge them. White employers generally preferred Chinese servants not just because of their diligence but also because political marginalization made them less likely to be troublemakers. In reference to Chinese servants, Alfred Wheeler testified at the 1876 congressional hearing: "I have always found them extremely subordinate and respectful, quiet, attentive, and rather avoiding difficulties."[33]

The *Oregonian* proclaimed in the 1880s that "one of the principal reasons that hotel keepers, restaurant men, and others have always given for employing

Chinese labor instead of that of white men has been that the Chinese could be depended upon, while the white help, after working a week or so, would get drunk and leave their employers in the lurch."[34]

Clearly, Chinese laborers were "model" servants. Clara E. Hamilton, in a 1902 article, bluntly explained the reason why she preferred them: "We need the Chinese here as a check upon our other working people, if for no other reason, but we have also a strong partiality for the quality of work of which they are capable. They are entirely reliable. If you have a well-trained Chinese cook you have a treasure. . . . He is quiet, usually respectful, and always orderly, deft and capable."[35] These qualities were mentioned by many others. In 1936, the San Francisco native and writer Charles Dobie concluded that Chinese servants and cooks were "more efficient, less complaining, always on the job . . . [and] worked on Sundays, holidays, rain or shine."[36]

"The Chinaman was an ideal servant," another San Franciscan declared in a letter to the *New York Times* in 1880—long before Will Irwin in 1909 reached the same conclusion. The letter recounted his family's experience with servants. The family was middle class or lower middle class and on a limited budget, and the two daughters were expected to help with house chores. Nonetheless, the family had managed to have servants. After the two Irish maids left, the family hired a Chinese, who also assumed cooking responsibilities after the cook left. The family then saw its daily food expenses reduced from $5 to $2 and still lived better than before. The two daughters, now freed from house chores, lived like privileged princesses.[37] Service from the Chinese enabled this and other middle-class households to elevate their lifestyle beyond their means. Charles Crocker testified before the congressional joint investigation committee on Chinese immigration in 1876: "Mechanics who have a family and must have a servant to do a little work, when they could not afford to pay thirty and forty dollars for a female servant. They are willing to take a Chinaman at twenty dollars. They can afford that, but they could not afford forty dollars for white servants."[38] James Beard, the legendary figure in American gastronomy, grew up in the early twentieth century in Portland, Oregon, where his mother owned a small residential hotel. Beard recalled in 1983 that his own middle-class family was "spoiled" by Let, their Chinese chef.[39] From various accounts, we can picture the life of middle-class and sometimes lower-middle-class families with Chinese cooks and servants: the mister rang for water from the comfort of his sofa, the mistress waited in bed for her breakfast, and the whole family enjoyed a quality time over Western meals prepared and brought to the table.

A POPULATION OF SERVICE WORKERS

Concentration in service jobs was a striking characteristic of the Chinese population, which joined other minorities and immigrants in satisfying the growing consumption desires of the United States in the years after the Gold Rush. The Irish, the largest immigrant group in this occupation, did so largely in the East, and African Americans did the same in the South.[40] By the 1870s, Chinese service laborers were predominant in the West, especially in California, where the number African Americans and the Irish was limited.[41]

More than 77 percent of the Chinese population was located in California. By 1870, domestic service/cooking had become the third largest occupation of the Chinese in the United States:

Miners	17,069
Laborers	9,436
Domestic servants	5,420
Launderers	3,653
Agricultural laborers	1,766
Cigar makers	1,727
Gardeners and nurserymen	676
Traders and dealers	604
Railroad workers	568
Boot and shoemakers	489[42]

While indicating the distribution of Chinese in diverse occupations at the time, the list also shows a clear pattern of the Chinese concentration in the service sector. These numbers most likely did not include those who were hired to perform service duties on a short-term basis; this concentration would become more significant as the number of Chinese in personal- and domestic-service jobs almost tripled in the years between 1870 and 1920. In 1920, those engaged in such jobs represented almost 60 percent of all gainfully employed Chinese.[43]

Most nineteenth-century Chinese servants were very young. Of the 159 male servants identified in the 1870 census manuscript schedule for San Francisco, 81 were under the age of twenty; 70 were in their twenties; and only 8 were in their thirties. The youngest was a ten-year-old boy named Ah Kee. There was only one female servant.[44] Domestic servitude was also often the first job that young immigrants took after their arrival in the United States. Lee

Chew, who worked for the first two years after his arrival in America in the early 1880s as a domestic servant, knew that "my start was the same as that of almost all the Chinese in this country."[45]

These Chinese servants became a major force in western states. In 1880, for example, California alone boasted about eight thousand Chinese servants, representing 34 percent of the state's total servants employed.[46] There were more than five thousand launderers, representing almost 80 percent of all laundry workers in the state. Ten percent of the state's hotel and restaurant owners and employees were Chinese. They also held similar jobs in other western states. A resident of Ellensburg, Washington, wrote to the *Oregonian* in 1886 after traveling along the railroad to the Cascade tunnel: "I find Chinese employed in the kitchens of every hotel and in a large number of private residences. They have almost a monopoly of the laundry business."[47] By then, a labor market of Chinese servants was fairly well established; their service could be secured through the numerous Chinese employment agencies in San Francisco. In 1885, four such agencies ran advertisements in the *San Francisco Bulletin*, along with the ad of the employment office of a famous anti-Chinese agitator, Denis Kearney. One of these agencies promised to supply "first-class Chinese cooks and waiters, for city and country."[48]

Indeed, the presence of Chinese cooks was found not only in urban white families but also on ranches and farms throughout the West. In *Cattle on the Conejo*, J. H. Russell recalled that "up to forty or fifty years ago Chinese were almost always the ranch cooks."[49] Richard Street writes that working as farm and camp cooks, "the Chinese did exert an early, overwhelming influence," which lasted for half a century.[50]

The Chinese presence could be seen and heard in the western mountains as well. A Chinese cook reportedly gave name to the Tunemah Trail, which stands at 11,894 feet in the High Sierras.[51] We can only guess what thoughts occupied his mind when he uttered the exclamation (supposedly a Chinese curse word), "Tu-ne-mah!" but the echo undoubtedly reached far. So did the socioeconomic impact of his labor and that of his fellow cooks.

This does not suggest that the Chinese story is only a regional one. In 1870, the Chinese were found in thirty-two of the thirty-seven states and in eight of the ten territories. While opportunities in mining triggered the earliest large waves of Chinese immigration to the American West, the need for personal service— generated by accelerated industrialization and concurrent urbanization— provided the initial impetus for the Chinese presence in eastern cities. Chinese workers arrived in increasing numbers to meet such a need in urban America, and their arrival also spearheaded Chinese communities in the East. Of particular importance were the laundrymen.

Chinese laundry workers formed another regiment of a large and growing army of Chinese service workers in the evolving consumption empire. While the Chinese cooks liberated many middle-class families from the tyranny of the kitchen, the laundrymen helped to add convenience and luxury to the life of working-class people. The laundrymen's experiences are pertinent not only to Chinese domestics but also to Chinese restaurants. The title of a cartoon published in the *New York Tribune* captured that connection between the two industries: "Exit Washee. Enter Chop Suey." The text underneath it reads, "Driven out of business by the Steam Laundry, they changed the lettering of their signs. Instead of 'laundry,' they made their signs read 'restaurant.'"[52] One common thread that linked the laundry shop, the restaurant, and the middle-class family kitchen: Chinese labor serving non-Chinese clientele.

By the early 1850s, the Chinese presence in the laundry business was already visible in San Francisco, pointing up the importance of the service sector for Chinese America from the very beginning. John David Borthwick, a Scottish journalist, who traveled to the city in 1851, gave a detailed description its Chinese laundry shops:

> Owing to the great scarcity of washerwomen, Chinese energy had ample room to display itself in the washing and ironing business. Throughout the town might be seen occasionally over some small house a large American sign, intimating that Ching Sing, Wong Choo, or Ki-chong did washing and ironing at five dollars a dozen. Inside these places one found two or three Chinamen ironing shirts with large flat-bottomed copper pots full of burning charcoal, and, buried in heaps of dirty clothes, half-a-dozen more, smoking, and drinking tea.[53]

The significance of laundry work became even more pronounced as the Chinese moved eastward to swiftly expanding cities. Pittsburgh, the birthplace of America's steel industry, stood as a leader in the creation of a new "manufacturing belt," which started in the 1870s.[54] Spurred by rapid economic development, Pittsburgh's population swelled from 77,923 in 1860 to 139,256 in 1870, before rising to more than 450,000 in 1900.[55] As early as 1874, four of the laundries listed in the city directory were unmistakably Chinese, located in different parts of the city. The number increased to eight a year later.[56] Detroit was another city that experienced rapid growth in this manufacturing expansion. In 1875, that city had at least four Chinese laundries.[57]

Chinese laundries appeared in many cities outside the American West with an amazing level of simultaneity, showing the pivotal role of the Chinese in the emerging service sector within a fast-growing economy. The first Chinese laundry showed up in Chicago in 1872, and by 1874 there were four.[58] In St. Louis, there were six Chinese laundries in 1873.[59] Boston had four such laundries in 1875.[60] This seemingly synchronized entry of Chinese laundries into multiple cities in the East is certainly attributable to the rapid improvement in transportation, which facilitated the Chinese dispersal from the western states, particularly California. The origins of these laundrymen were common knowledge; for example, in a directory of Boston in 1875, Lee Sing was identified as "Chinese Californian Laundry."

Before the arrival of their compatriots from California, the Chinese in the East were already entrenched in the service sector. The Chinese in antebellum New York, for instance, included sailors, servants, and cooks, who had been brought to the busy port city by international trade.[61] The *New York Tribune* estimated in 1870 that there were about two hundred Chinese in the city, and many of them were servants.[62] Before an employment agency was established, uptown white middle-class women would travel downtown to the budding Chinese quarter around Mott Street to look for domestic help.[63]

As in other East Coast cities, laundry work quickly became the dominant occupation among working Chinese in New York and the surrounding areas, providing an important personal service outside white American homes. In the early 1880s, more than one hundred Chinese worked in a laundry company in Belleville, New Jersey.[64] By the late 1880s, the Chinese population in New York was no longer confined to Chinatown around Mott and Canal Streets, as Chinese laundries sprouted up "all over the city."[65] The growth met an increasing need of the swelling urban population.

The cost threshold for opening a laundry business was a relatively low, sometimes requiring just a modest amount of about $100 in the 1880s.[66] And in some cities, Chinese laundrymen achieved local dominance. In Providence, Rhode Island, which experienced rapid economic and population growth in the second half of the nineteenth century, two of the nine laundries in 1878 there were Chinese.[67] Two years later, Chinese owned seven of the city's fourteen laundries. In 1883, they became the major force in that business, owning perhaps twenty-three of the thirty-three laundries, and in 1900, 99 of the city's

136 laundries were Chinese.[68] A similar predominance was found in Chicago, where the most popular names in laundries were Chinese—there were, for example, twenty-one Sam Sing's and eleven Sing Lee's.[69] The pattern simultaneously repeated itself in Philadelphia, where 511 of the city's 767 laundries were Chinese. These laundries were so numerous that they commanded their own subheading, "laundries, Chinese," in the city's business directory.[70] And in New York, *Harper's Weekly* reported in 1890 that "it is hard to find any neighborhood where there are no Chinese laundries."[71]

Chinese San Francisco in the late nineteenth century had a more diverse economy than many other Chinese settlements, but laundry work constituted an important source of employment. By 1870, the Chinese had become the most numerous group among San Francisco's more than two thousand launderers. In 1880, the 5,435 Chinese workers represented about 80 percent of California's labor force in the laundry industry.[72]

Chinese laundrymen's work brought convenience and style to the life of white workers. William F. Babcock testified before the 1876 congressional investigation commission that "the very employment of the Chinese in laundry work causes mechanics to change their clothes much oftener than they did when they paid a high price for their washing. Take the tops of these houses where the Chinese laundries are, and look at the lines of ragged clothes, old red shirts, pantaloons, and every common thing, garments that I do believe were washed half as much before, and that were not even fit for a woman to wash."[73] By 1910, Chinese service labor had established its presence in most states. The only state that might not have had at least a Chinese servant or laundryman was West Virginia.[74]

The labor force in the nation's service sectors never became entirely Chinese, but the Chinese themselves became largely a service-worker population, setting them apart from European groups such as the Irish, Germans, and Italians. For these, domestic service was mainly for certain segments of their communities, especially young women. In 1910, for example, the female:male ratio was almost 18:1 among native white servants; it was nearly 24:1 among children of immigrants and more than 14:1 among white immigrants. Among African Americans, domestic servants also tended to be women, for whom the ratio was 5:1.[75] For the Chinese, Japanese, and Indian immigrants, the situation was reversed: the ratio was more than six men for every female servant. Among the Chinese alone, the ratio was undoubtedly even higher. The same pattern was also apparent in another type of personal service: laundry work—a predominantly female occupation among whites and African Americans but that became almost entirely a male line of work for the Chinese.

Moreover, for white immigrants, including young Irish women, servitude was often a temporary position. An Anglo employer remarked: "It is true that our piquant damsels from the Emerald Isle are very ambitious, but it is in the style of our chignon, and the liberties of the free and equal American citizen, that they would emulate. That these peculiar aspirations do not add to the harmony of our home is a notable fact. . . . Our German girls, after becoming intelligible, are recaptured by young Hans to care for his cabbages."[76] By comparison, the possibilities of career upward mobility available to Chinese servants were much more limited, which is one reason that they tended to stay on their servitude jobs. In other words, the Chinese were designated as servants of the empire.

By 1940, almost the entire Chinese population had been relegated to the service sector. The laundry business and restaurant work had become the two principal occupations of the Chinese, a fact that contemporary Chinese were keenly aware of. In a 1930 investigative report series "The Present and Past of Chinese Restaurants in New York," published in a New York–based Chinese-language newspaper, an author by the name of Tiexin noted that job opportunities of the Chinese lay mainly in these two areas.[77] Well-educated Chinese were no exceptions. A Chinese man, who received his doctorate in history in 1950, could not find a job in his profession because "Americans thought every Chinese was either a laundryman or a cook."[78]

Chinese servitude was an integral part of America's capitalist economy and budding consumer culture. Lewis Coser once suggested that domestic service is a premodern condition that tends to become obsolete in a modern society.[79] This does not hold entirely true for nineteenth-century America as a whole, as we can see from an analysis of figure 1. On the one hand, less "modern" southern states—such as Alabama, North Carolina, and Tennessee—did have large numbers of domestic servants and corresponding low numbers of modern facilities like restaurants and saloons. On the other hand, in more capitalistic and industrialized states—like New York, California, and Massachusetts—the stronger presence of restaurants and saloons coexisted with a multitude of domestic servants. The enterprising western states, in particular, experienced a rapid increase in the number of domestic servants during the late nineteenth and early twentieth centuries.[80] Clearly, the desire for a life of leisure free from household chores knows no geographical or temporal boundaries.

Figure 2 compares the number of Chinese, Japanese, and Indian servants with that of African Americans in 1910 in selected states. It shows the "modern" nature of Chinese domestic service, which was found in capitalist and industrializing

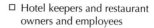

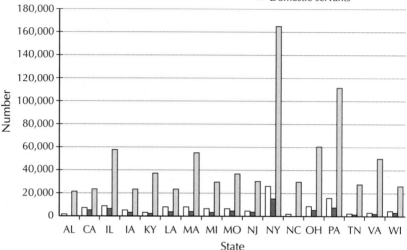

FIGURE 1 The number of food- and domestic-service workers in selected states, 1880. (U.S. Census Office, *Compendium of the Tenth Census* [Washington, D.C.: Government Printing Office, 1883])

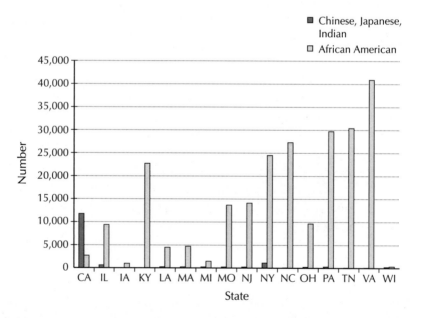

FIGURE 2 The number of Chinese, Japanese, and Indian compared with African American servants in selected states, 1910. (U.S. Bureau of the Census, *Thirteenth Census of the United States*, vol. 4, *Population 1910: Occupational Statistics* [Washington, D.C.: Government Printing Office, 1914])

states, rather than the less developed South. Furthermore, Chinese servants and cooks tended to work in large metropolitan areas. Because of their close association with industrialization, international migration, and urbanization, they were harbingers of modernity.

LIFE IN THE KITCHEN WORLD

Empire building is also a key element in globalization.[81] The evolution of the United States into an empire encompassed a process of cultural encounters. As empire "stewards," the Chinese laborers in personal service were also active agents of cultural exchange. Working and often living away from their own communities, their job was quite personal in nature, putting them in close and constant contact with their white employers. The historian Sucheng Chan notes that "other than miners, the only Chinese who interacted with whites were cooks, servants, and laundrymen" in nineteenth-century California.[82] Roi Ottley noted in an article about Harlem in 1936 that "the Chinese are daily in our midst, with their restaurants and laundries."[83]

Of particular importance were those who took on cooking responsibilities. They were directly involved in an essential aspect of the private lives of their employers and, in many cases, lived with them under the same roof. Even those who lodged in Chinatown still spent a significant amount of time interacting with whites on a personal level.

Needless to say, the relationship that Chinese cooks formed with their patrons was anything but equal. "Despite its complexity and importance, cooking in the home traditionally has been an occupation of low status," as Rebecca Sharpless notes in her study of African American women domestic cooks in the South.[84] For Chinese cooks, the kitchen could also be a precarious space because of racial prejudice that permeated every corner of society throughout the late nineteenth century. For example, Prentice Mulford recalled in 1869 an incident at the Polyglot House restaurant in what is now Placerville, California, where a Texas man beat the Chinese assistant in the kitchen and demanded better coffee.[85] A year earlier, the *Daily Morning Chronicle* reported another incident of bloody violence that took place in the Wilkin's Hotel at Beckwourth Pass, Nevada: when a white man named Pierce missed breakfast and the Chinese cooks would not send him food, he went to the kitchen and shot them, wounding one and seriously injuring the other.[86] The *Independent* mentioned that in 1878 a white man killed his Chinese cook but received no punishment.[87]

Overall, the relationship between Chinese kitchen workers and the recipients of their service was characterized more by immediate personal exchanges than by bloody violence or extremely harsh hostility. Ah Quin left extensive records of his interactions with the whites in the Alaska mining camp. At 10:00 A.M. on June 1, 1878, after he had made breakfast, he called E. T. Gourley to cut his long queue so that he could look more "like the white people." Gourley and another white workman named A. K. Thompson cheerfully laughed at him, as Ah Quin gave each of them a "few hairs."[88]

Not uncommonly, a personal bond developed between the Chinese cooks and their white employers. Chinese domestic-service laborers, a Chinese reported in 1902, "frequently become much attached to the families they serve, and keep their positions for years."[89] Richard Street concurs: "Many Chinese cooks became best friends with their employers and children."[90] The words "best friends" are clearly an exaggeration, but many Chinese developed long associations with white families.

One such family, the Roths, employed Kee Low as their cook for more than two generations. The family moved to Filoli, a 654-acre estate located in Redwood City, California, after it was purchased in 1937 by William P. Roth and Lurline Matson Roth, heir of the Matson Navigation Company. Kee Low continued his job until his retirement in 1961.

In May 2012, I gave a public lecture at the estate, which had been donated by Lurline Roth to the National Trust for Historic Preservation in 1975. Lynn Norris, its education program director, invited the grandson of Kee Low to join us for the day. Norris explained, "We consider the Lows part of the Filoli family." That was a sentiment shared by the Roths, who supported in various ways members of the Low family over the years, paying for the college education of one of Kee Low's two sons. The Roth children loved Kee's international cooking, which included such things as tamales, curry chicken with garlic and spices purchased in India, and oyster chowder (both Boston and Manhattan) made with broiled California baby oysters, as well as reproductions of dishes that Lurline Roth liked in restaurants. But just as in the case of Ah Quin's cooking, Kee cooked little Chinese food. The Lows also identified closely with Filoli and the Roths, and Kee's son assisted in the kitchen and often invited his friends to visit.[91]

J. H. Russell, a well-to-do cattle rancher, was born in 1883 and grew up on the Russell Triunfo Ranch in California's Ventura County. In his memoir about life on the ranch, he wrote about some of the family's Chinese cooks, who "still stand out in my memory."[92]

These stories indicate that Chinese cooks' presence extended beyond urban middle-class homes. There were also Chinese cooks in the U.S. military, serving officers, as Ah Quin did on Angel Island and at the Presidio in California from 1879 to 1880.[93]

Another Chinese, who worked as a cook in the U.S. military was Richard Wing, one of the four Chinese from Hanford, California, to enlist during World War II.[94] His cooking skills became noticeable while working in the mess hall, and he soon got the assignment as General George Marshall's personal cook, a position he held for about three years. During Marshall's trips to China and Moscow, Wing also served as his food taster. The two men developed an amicable relationship, which Gerald M. Pops attributes to Marshall's "egalitarian instincts."[95] In 1948, when Marshall visited California as President Truman's secretary of state, he invited Wing, who was no longer his cook, to be his guest.[96]

Some white employers developed a dependency on their long-standing cooks, and this became a recurring theme in stories they told. In one such story published in 1907 in the *Overland Monthly*, Mrs. Caxton became so dependent on her cook, Ah Gin, that she refused to live with any of her grown-up daughters. The two formed this relationship in part because of the loyalty of Ah Gin, who once risked his own life to protect her house during a terrifying earthquake.[97]

But Chinese cooks did not achieve their autonomy and influence only through loyalty. In America as well as in China, they did so through their assertiveness and skills. "A widely traveled American said not long ago," the popular magazine *Outlook* relayed in 1915, "'You tell your Chinese cook to put salt into the soup and he obeys because he is an admirable servant; but every time he makes the soup he reflects on your ignorance and lack of cultivated taste in soups.'"[98]

In 1895, *Manford's New Monthly Magazine* carried a dialogue between a white woman in San Francisco and her new Chinese cook. After the Chinese man told her that his name was Wang Hang Ho, she said, "Oh, I can't remember all that. . . . I will call you John." Upon learning that her name was Mrs. Melville Langdon, the Chinese responded: "Me no memble all that. . . . Chinaman he no savey Mrs. Membul Landon—I call you Tommy."[99] It was one of the popular jokes intended to mock the Chinese for their pigeon English. But its repeated appearance in various publications over the years suggests a widely recognized pattern of Chinese cooks' autonomy and defiance of racial and class prejudice.[100]

A few Chinese even broke a gigantic social taboo by entering the emotional world of their white employers. Their stories were invariably and predictably represented in the media as being disastrous and even fatal. The *Riverside*

Independent Enterprise, for example, published an article in 1894 about a Chinese cook named Sing Ngui, whose marriage to a "pretty German girl" became like a prison, from which she had to be rescued.[101] The *National Police Gazette* ran a story, in a harshly disapproving tone, about a beautiful white woman's love affair with her Chinese cook. What made the situation even more alarming for the tabloid is that it took place in San Francisco's Nob Hill, a "citadel of Wealth, social position and respectability."[102] She was portrayed as a victim of the "slant-eyed, sleek" Chinese man's "specious arts and Oriental vices."

The autonomy of Chinese cooks reminds us that we must not see them merely as victims. In general, they received a share, albeit a small one, of America's economic prosperity. Contemporary estimates show that their income was relatively high in comparison with the earnings of their compatriots in China and America. In 1870, Chinese cooks could earn at least $15 a month and board, and that was considered a low wage for them.[103] In the early 1880s, a servant with some experience like Lee Chew could earn $35 a month with board.[104] A competent cook earned about $35 or $45 a month in the early 1890s.[105] According to some contemporaries, the monthly wages for Chinese cooks ranged from $25 and $40 to $70 a month at the turn of the century.[106] Based on Russell Conwell's 1870 estimate that rural laborers in the immigrants' native communities in the Pearl River Delta earned the equivalent of $8 to $10 a year, a Chinese cook's income was at least twenty times higher.[107] Wages in Canton were among the highest in China, where a cook could make as much as $6 a month in the late 1890s, still considerably lower than wages of his countrymen in America.[108] Moreover, the cooks' income also put them at a higher bracket than that of many of their compatriot, such as those working in agriculture in the South, who made about $22 a month at the time.[109] The cooks' pay-plus-board was also better than the $31 monthly wage of the Chinese railroad workers,[110] who often had to pay for their food and board.

Service work also constituted an important lifeline for the entire Chinese community to sustain the horrendous assaults of anti-Chinese forces, whose goal was "not only to restrict Chinese immigration, but to expel the Chinese from the country."[111]

Finally, in spite of the enormous limitation the Chinese faced in upward social mobility, a number of individual service workers did move on to become small business owners. After he settled in San Diego, Ah Quin started his own retail business, as did Lee Chew, who opened a laundry shop in Chicago and increased his capital to $2,500 in three years before he went to Detroit. Compared with the previous two cases, John Nipson's experience is more unusual and colorful. Known among the Chinese as Ah Sing, he spent much of his time before the 1850s as a steward on oceangoing ships and mastered English. He was apparently fluent in French because he reportedly served as steward to the exiled French emperor, Napoleon Bonaparte, on St. Helena Island in 1815.[112] In 1856, the sixty-two-year-old Nipson had turned himself into a merchant in import and retail.

In 1960, a noted scholar of Chinese America appeared to suggest that America's negative image of China and the Chinese was related to the Chinese presence on the West Coast.[113] It is a sentiment that more than one well-educated Chinese immigrant expressed: those Chinese who held lowly jobs as cooks, servants, and laundrymen caused American society to look down on all Chinese, but I have found no evidence to support that claim. The immigrants' concentration in less desirable occupations reflected only the preexisting conditions: the huge economic gap between China and the United States, and the intense anti-Chinese prejudice in American society. Because of the personal nature of their work, cooks and other service workers actually gave many whites their first opportunity to interact with the Chinese and raise their awareness of Chinese culture. Contrary to the prevailing view in political and legal discourses that the Chinese were not trustworthy, most white employers came to the conclusion that the Chinese were honest and reliable. A number of them, including the Roths, became deeply interested in Chinese art and porcelains, directly and indirectly because of the influence of their Chinese domestic workers.

However, Chinese food was not among the things that Chinese domestic cooks introduced to their employers. "The Chinese adopted Western dishes much faster than whites accepted Chinese food," writes the historian Liping Zhu.[114] Chinese cooks' deft mastery of Western cooking explains their popularity with the white middle class. *Overland* magazine noted in 1869 that "our Chinese cooks imitate the American style with a painful accuracy." Chinese domestic workers continued non-Chinese cooking early in the twentieth century. In the hotel run by James Beard's mother in Portland, Oregon, its Chinese cooking staff mastered French cooking "technique and style."[115]

In the nineteenth century, those Chinese who could "do first-class French cooking" were deemed "high-tuned" servants.[116] Coming to the United States with limited experience in cooking, not to mention Western cooking, they quickly learned the trade by necessity. Many did so from their employers, who often talked about teaching their Chinese cooks how to make certain foods. Lee

Gumbo

Serves 6

Nineteenth- and early-twentieth-century Chinese domestic servants like Ah Quin cooked non-Chinese dishes for their Anglo employers. I have not found evidence that they cooked gumbo, but it is one of the non-Chinese dishes that I have come to love in America. The recipe is easy and convenient to cook at home, especially for those "servantless American" households.*

> 3 lb rotisserie chicken
> 1 tsp chopped fresh parsley
> 2 bay leaves
> 4 garlic cloves, chopped
> ½ cup vegetable oil
> ½ cup flour
> ½ lb andouille sausage, chopped
> 1 medium yellow onion, chopped
> 1 yellow bell pepper, chopped
> 1 cup chopped celery
> 1 tsp cayenne pepper
> ½ tsp salt
> dash of black pepper
> 8 oz okra

Before you leave for work, boil the chicken with the parsley, bay leaves, and 2 garlic cloves in 6 cups of water in a stainless-steel thermal vacuum cooking pot. Turn off the heat and immediately place the pot in the vacuum flask. Take the pot out when you return from work and remove the chicken from the pot. Discard the bones, but save the broth. Coarsely chop the breast and leg meat into 1-inch cubes.

Heat the oil in a large saucepan and add the flour to make a roux. Stir until the roux turns dark brown. In a stockpot, sauté the sausage, and add the onion, bell pepper, and celery and cook until soft. Add 2 garlic cloves and stir 2 for minutes. Sprinkle in the cayenne pepper. Add 4 cups (or as much as you prefer) chicken broth from the pot in the vacuum flask. Add the chicken cubes and the roux, simmer for 15 to 20 minutes, and season with salt and black pepper. Add the okra, turn to low heat after the soup boils, and simmer for about 10 minutes.

*Julia Child, *Mastering the Art of French Cooking* (New York: Knopf, 2004), 1:xxv.

Chew learned "how to cook" from the lady of the first household where he worked.[117] Another important but seldom discussed source is cookbooks, which some Chinese like Ah Quin used.

In his diary, Ah Quin inserted four pages of recipes, all for Western dishes, and the ingredients include beef, wheat flour, milk, butter, sugar, salmon, and potato, which "the American deemed . . . indispensable to a meal," as a nine-teenth-century commentator put it.[118] We can make an educated guess that these recipes came from cookbooks. Ah Quin did not mention their origins; and his Cantonese-based, idiosyncratic translation renders the meaning of some of the handwritten words illegible, making it difficult to pinpoint the sources that he consulted. But we know for sure that Ah Quin read English-language cookbooks because of his language ability.[119] Others unable to read English, however, could resort to translations of Western recipes and cookbooks. One of them was published in 1910 in Chinese San Francisco.

NAVIGATING THE NEW WORLD

Cui Tongyue's *Hua Ying Chu Shu Da Quan* (*Chinese-English Comprehensive Cookbook*) is not an ordinary cookbook but an extensive multifaceted volume that includes 344 pages of recipes, a bilingual multitopic English-language conversational handbook, and a glossary of food words. It is a vital source of knowledge on Western cooking as well as a cultural guide to help Chinese cooks navigate the New World. This encyclopedic publication is testimony to the continued importance of the cooking job for Chinese immigrants in the early twentieth century, and it also opens a window into the life of the Chinese cook.

The handbook contains a long list of English conversational sentences rendered into Chinese. Focused on simulated dialogues with white employers, the first section includes sentences like "Are you a cook?" " Yes," and "Where was your last situation? In a hotel or restaurant?" "No, it was in a private family." This guide taught the readers not only survival skills but also negotiation techniques: "What were you paid per month?" "Twenty-five dollars." "That is not enough for me." "How much do you want?" "Forty-five dollars."[120] Clearly, the autonomy and assertiveness of Chinese cooks that we noted earlier were not merely individual behaviors but reflected a collective strategy and mentality consciously cultivated in the community.

Besides food preparation, Chinese cooks performed other duties, as we can tell from sentences in the section on lunch:

Sweep the bedroom.
Change the bed linen.
Pull up the window blind.

We can also picture how a middle-class family got a taste of the lifestyle of the upper class by ordering its Chinese cook to

Bring me a box of cigars.
Take a piece of cloth to dust the piano.
Carry the rocking chair to the library.
Bring me a newspaper from the writing desk.
Take the order down to Mr. J's Grocery Store.
And one more cup of tea.

The "Travel on a Railroad" and "Travel on a Steamship" sections illustrate the itinerary nature of a cook's existence. The places that appeared in these two sections included big cities like San Francisco, Chicago, St. Louis, Boston, New York, and Hong Kong as well as smaller paces like Ogden, Utah, showing how widely dispersed Chinese cooks had become.[121]

It is also notable that while some of the English sentences were rendered into Chinese according to their meaning, all of them were transliterated based on how they sounded in Cantonese. In other words, the Cantonese-speaking cooks with little English skills could just mimic the sound. It was a practical solution to a daily challenge for both the itinerant immigrants and the English-speaking Americans who interacted with them. In response to such a challenge, several bilingual handbooks had already appeared in the late nineteenth century and were readily available. In fact, one could even find a Chinese-language newspaper advertisement for such a book.[122]

One of the earliest books was compiled by a teacher named Benoni Lanctot; his *Chinese and English Phrase Book* saw its second edition in 1867. Intended to help English speakers communicate with Cantonese-speaking immigrants, this 113-page book provides translations of basic English words and sentences as well as their translations based on Cantonese pronunciation.

Reminiscent of titles like *Gardening Spanish*, which today's suburban Americans can get in print and audio format for communicating with their Mexican gardeners, *Chinese and English Phrase Book* has a chapter titled "Dialogue on Getting a China Boy." [123] In it, readers without knowledge of the Chinese language could learn to ask questions in Cantonese like "Can you cook?" and "Can you wash?" Middle-class Americans with upper-class aspirations could learn to give such orders in Chinese: "Bring me some hot water," "Make some tea," "Brush my coat," "Make some soup," or "Buy a piece of good beef." The author considered all these "familiar sentences," suggesting that many Anglos must have used such commands frequently.[124] With other sections that cover topics clearly related to the work of servants and cooks, such as names of extensive household items and foods, this made a useful manual for those who had Chinese domestic help.

Compiled by "Wong Sam" in 1875, *An English–Chinese Phrase Book* was one of the earliest bilingual handbooks intended for the Chinese. It is not difficult to imagine the popularity of this book, which Wells Fargo printed and placed copies in its 130 offices throughout the American West.[125] It offered basic English sentences, each with Chinese translations, on miscellaneous topics ranging from American socioeconomic conditions and legal systems to travel and work. Although not a primary subject, kitchen work was covered in sentences like "Put the butter in the cupboard" and "Empty the sugar into the milk-pan."[126]

Chinese service workers, especially those on the East Coast, would find similar information in another publication, Thomas Lathrop Stedman and K. P. Lee's *Chinese and English Phrase Book in the Canton Dialect*, published in New York in 1888.[127] Compared with Wong Sam's book, it is more structured and contains more comprehensive subjects. Organized into individual lessons, the subjects include such common topics as "The Weather," "The Seasons," and "The Time." Most of the subjects are simulated situations that Chinese immigrants were likely to encounter, such as "A Social Visit," "At a Police Station," "At Court," "A General Clothing Store," "With a Lawyer," "With a Physician," and "At the Bank." The sentences in the two sections of "Travel on the Railroad" and "Travel on a Steamship" give us a clear idea about the physical mobility of the Chinese.

Three sequential situations concerning the Chinese laundry business are covered in three lessons. Lesson 17 is about renting store space for a laundry; Lesson 19 deals with "A Customer in a Laundry"; Lesson 20 contains sentences for dealing with the "Loss of a Laundry Ticket." In Chinese transliteration, the handbook taught Chinese laundrymen how to say no to non-Chinese customers who had lost the laundry ticket: "Then I can't let you have your clothes." This policy was so widely adopted that the phrase "no tickee no washee" (and its variations) became proverbial and eventually found its way into movie titles (Edmond F. Stratton's *No Tickee, No Washee*, 1915; and Henry D. Bailey's *No Tickee No Shirtee*, 1921) and Archer Taylor's book *The Proverb* (1931).[128] This kind of derogative slur many Chinese still find offensive, but it must have also reflected the frustration that many white customers felt at the firmness of the Chinese in upholding the rules of their shops.[129]

Five additional lessons deal with matters that would concern Chinese cooks. The beginning of Lesson 27, "Hiring Out as a Cook," gives us a sketch of young Chinese job hunters, knocking on doors in white neighborhoods following the tips from their countrymen: "Does Mrs. Brown live here?" "I hear she wants a Chinese cook."[130] The subsequent conversation reveals some of the expectations that the white employer had for the prospective cook: previous experience as a family cook, excellent references, the ability to make good pastry and dessert, being punctual in having the meals ready. Sentences in Lesson 28, "Duties of a Waiter," also spell out such expectations: "Your hours will be from seven in the morning to nine at night;" "Do you drink? for if you do, I don't want you."[131]

The remaining three food lessons contain sentences for shopping at grocery stores and meat and fish markets, and were clearly for Chinese cooks working for non-Chinese employers. The reason is clear: few Chinese men would find it necessary to memorize English phrases to do food shopping for their individual consumption. They certainly did not have to buy two bushels of sweet potatoes or five pounds of macaroni or four pounds of lamb chops at a time for their personal use.[132]

Such sources give us a glimpse into the life of Chinese cooks and servants, who themselves seldom had the time or education to document their experiences, but indirect sources like these still leave many questions unanswered. For example, they do not tell us how Chinese cooks felt about having to make Western foods for Anglo employers. Some Chinese American elites expressed such feelings, though. For Cui Tongyue, the editor of the *Chinese-English Comprehensive Cookbook* and a man deeply proud of China's culinary traditions, Chinese men cooking American food in order to make a living was a bitter fact that reflected the geopolitical reality of the time and America's racism. It was caused by, in his words, "the weakness of our motherland [that] forces us to migrate overseas."[133] It was also because in the United States, he wrote resentfully, the Chinese were excluded from the better opportunities and "only the occupation of Western cooking was available for the Chinese to make a living."

Cui Tongyue compiled the volume in order to make sure that the Chinese would keep their advantage in this trade as cooks of Western food in the future. But by the time he was writing, Chinese food had already quietly but surely made an indelible mark on the American palate.

The development of Chinese food in America's consumer market is a continuation and extension of the historical role of Chinese immigrants as service workers. The experience in private kitchens, furthermore, prepared many for entry into the restaurant business. For example, after leaving the Russell Triunfo Ranch, one of the family's Chinese cooks opened his own restaurant in Chicago.[134] After returning to the family restaurant business in Hanford, California, in January 1957, Richard Wing (George Marshall's former personal cook) expanded his family's Imperial Dynasty into a famous restaurant that served French-influenced food. Its French flavor remained distinctively clear on the menu that its staff graciously gave me in 2003 with such dishes as Escargots à la Bourguignonne. Most other Chinese who entered the restaurant business in the twentieth century, however, did so in more urban areas and cooked Chinese food.

The rise of Chinese restaurants was part of the story of immigrants and minorities laboring to serve the expanding appetite for a more leisurely life style in an emerging empire of consumption. But the socioeconomic interpretation of Chinese food's popularity still has another question to answer: Why have other marginalized immigrant groups, who also perform service jobs, not brought their food to national prominence? One such group are the Filipinos, whose profile bears striking similarities to that of the Chinese. By 1980, they and the Chinese had become the two largest Asian communities in the United States,[135] and the two groups' per capita income levels were also comparable ($14,876 for Chinese, and $13,616 for Filipinos), according to the 1990 census.[136] More important, Filipino immigration, which started in the early twentieth century, also represented a flow of labor. Like the Chinese, Filipino immigrant labor had long remained predominantly male. And a significant number of them worked as stewards in the U.S. Navy, performing cooking duties—a duty that some Filipinos still carry out.[137]

Nonetheless, Filipinos have not put their food on the American gastronomical map. Ronnie Alejandro, a well-known Filipino American chef who has written extensively on Filipino cooking, remarked, "The Philippine cuisine, actually, has never been formally introduced so to speak."[138] In an article published in New York–based *Filipino Reporter* in 1994, Edmund M. Silvestre noted, "The Philippine cuisine is still very much out of the ethnic food race and will probably remain so beyond the turn of the century." His pessimistic projection about Filipino food has remained true. One contributing factor, indentified by Silvestre, is "a lack of restaurant tradition among Filipinos."[139]

A comparison between the historical experiences of the Filipinos and the Chinese reveals another significant difference: the relative dearth of physical Filipino settlements. While the extent to which this led to the invisibility of Filipino food remains to be examined more precisely, Chinatowns have clearly played indispensable roles in the development of American Chinese food.

4
THE CRADLE OF CHINESE FOOD

In 1991, my wife and I moved to southern California. After living for six years in the small town of Ithaca in upstate New York, the first question I asked was how to get to Little Taipei, the nickname of Monterey Park among the Chinese: I had heard so much about the good Chinese food there. A friend offered me a simple instruction. Go north on Interstate 405 to I-710; take I-10 east; roll down your window, and then just follow the smell. We took the advice. As we exited I-10 at Atlantic Boulevard and headed south, a familiar aroma of food rushed into the car.

I had arrived.

Like conjoined twins, Chinese food and the Chinese community have been inseparable and interdependent. We have seen America's growing consumption desires and the marginalization of Chinese Americans as historical contexts in which to fully understand the spread of Chinese restaurants. Here, I examine the critical role that the American Chinatown played in the transplantation and spread of Chinese food.

As a cradle of America's Chinese food, Chinatown was where this food was first transplanted in the early 1850s. In the following decades, when anti-Chinese animosity was on the rise, Chinatown existed as its sanctuary; at the end of the nineteenth century, then, Chinatown became a launching pad for Chinese food to extend to non-Chinese neighborhoods.

Simply put, without Chinatown, there would be no American Chinese food as we know it. At the same time, Chinese food defined Chinatown. Various food places represented not only the biggest cluster among all businesses in the Chinese community but also its most conspicuous markers—visual and olfactory—for both Chinese and non-Chinese. Of particular importance were the restaurants that offered familiar food and a social respite for Chinese immigrant men in the early decades (Chinese women seldom came to the restaurants).[1] In the first half of the twentieth century, these dining establishments constituted a vital lifeline of the urban Chinatown economy.

The symbiotic relationship between Chinese food and the Chinese community reminds us of the extraordinary importance of food as a marker of cultural identity. Chinese immigrants continued to cherish their food, even though it was derided as evidence of their reclusiveness and un-Americanness. Likewise, Americans who traveled to China during this period clung to Western food in spite of the enormous logistical difficulty they faced in finding it. The culinary allegiance in both cases demonstrates that cultural identity is not an abstract academic concept but a lived experience, one that manifests itself in people's daily life.

The Chinese and Americans maintained allegiance to their respective culinary traditions for different reasons. In avoiding and ridiculing Chinese food, Americans articulated a sense of cultural superiority over the Chinese. Chinese immigrants maintained their own culinary tradition because it gave them a source of comfort and home in a foreign and hostile environment. And it also represented their defiance to the mounting anti-Chinese prejudice.

THE ARRIVAL

The Chinese American community emerged together with the arrival of Chinese food. In 1849 and early 1850, while some of the seven hundred or so Chinese in San Francisco still lived in tents, others began to construct permanent houses, using building materials and furniture imported from China, which were also utilized widely by non-Chinese San Franciscans. In early 1850, an eyewitness reported that "at least 76 houses have been imported from Canton, and are put up by Chinese carpenters." The report also mentioned two Chinese restaurants, "kept by Kong-sung and Whang-tong, where very palatable chow-chow, curry and tarts are served up by the celestials."[2]

For the Chinese, such restaurants were both eating establishments and social meeting places. On November 19, 1849, about three hundred Chinese went to a "Canton Restaurant" on Jackson Street to conduct important community affairs, forming a committee to hire an Anglo "arbitrator and adviser."[3]

The appearance of Chinese restaurants was noted by others. In 1849, Bayard Taylor traveled to California on assignment to report on the Gold Rush for the *New York Tribune*. In *Eldorado*, Taylor mentioned three Chinese restaurants: Kong-Sung's house near the water, Whang-Tong's on Sacramento Street, and Tong-Ling's on Jackson Street. Besides, he added, "in Pacific street another Celestial restaurant had been opened."[4] These early establishments did not merely cater to the Chinese but also were "much frequented by Americans," serving "their chow-chow and curry as well as excellent tea and coffee."[5]

San Francisco was a critical Gold Rush gateway, which swelled from a quiet small town of one thousand people in 1848 to a booming city of thirty-five thousand in 1850.[6] Public eating places popped up to feed this mobile and predominantly young and male population—in 1849, only 2 percent of the population in the city was female, and most of them were between the ages of twenty and forty.[7] These places expanded so fast that they immediately became an important revenue source for the city of San Francisco. For example, in the month of July 1851, the city collected almost $13,000 from drinking and eating houses, making them the single most significant tax base.[8]

William Shaw, an Englishman who visited San Francisco in 1849, believed that the Chinese restaurants were the finest in town: "The best eating houses in San Francisco are those kept by Celestials and conducted in Chinese fashion. The dishes are mostly curries, hashes and fricassee served up in small dishes and as they are exceedingly palatable."[9] Evidently, these restaurants had white customers and served Chinese food.

Writing about the Chinese in San Francisco at this time, James O'Meara noted that Chinese restaurant owners "accumulated rapid wealth."[10] By late 1850, some Chinese restaurants had become fairly large establishments in the city's budding restaurant industry, as is evidenced by estimates of property damage caused by fire, a threat that San Francisco faced repeatedly at the time. On October 1, *Alta California* reported that a Chinese restaurateur suffered a loss of $2,800.[11] The loss was considerably smaller than that of some non-Chinese establishments such as Keil McCarty's Universal Restaurant, which reported a loss of $4,000. But it was substantially more than the amount lost by some of the drinking places like the Mariposa saloon.

The assertion in *Alta California* in 1852 that "at one time nearly all the restaurants in the city were conducted by the Chinese" is undoubtedly an exaggeration.[12] But Chinese restaurants did become quite numerous in San Francisco.

As a result, the Chinese-language newspaper, *Golden Hill's News,* found it necessary to announce in detail to its Chinese audiences the license fees that restaurant owners must pay.[13]

In 1856, the Chinese business directory compiled by the bilingual newspaper *Oriental* listed five restaurants.[14] Chinese restaurants also found their way into the city's general directories. Charles P. Kimball's *San Francisco City Directory* of 1850, for instance, listed such establishments: "Canton Restaurant" and Norman Assing's Macoa and Woosung Restaurant at the corner of Kearny and Commercial Streets.[15]

Non-white patronage of Chinese restaurants at this time was more a matter of circumstance than an indication of racial tolerance in San Francisco's nascent years. The Western notion of "the restaurant" began in France first as a medical term and a therapeutic place before becoming defined as a public dining place in Paris in the early eighteenth century.[16] In antebellum America, meals outside one's own home constituted a foreign concept for most people; even many rich people still entertained extensively in their homes. Restaurant dining began to pick up in major cities in the post–Civil War decades, but the motivation varied. Unlike aristocratic New Yorkers who went to Delmonico's for social distinction, San Franciscans flocked to restaurants primarily to feed themselves. It is not surprising that Chinese restaurateurs rose to the occasion. Their experience was not simply a food story but a highly political one that intersected with the cultural and socioeconomic currents in the fast-changing city.

THE POLITICS OF GASTRONOMY

For many non-Chinese San Franciscans, Norman Assing was already a familiar name in the early 1850s.[17] Numerous records about him have survived, giving us a glimpse into the life of one of the first Chinese restaurateurs, who also was one of the Chinese community's high-profile leaders.

Before arriving in San Francisco in 1850, Assing had traveled to the West from Macao in 1820 on a ship that brought him to New York.[18] He later lived in Charleston, South Carolina, where he became a naturalized citizen and a Christian. The historian Him Mark Lai noted that his Chinese name was Yuan Sheng. Another Chinese source gave his Chinese name as Chen Yanqing.[19]

In the early 1850s, when Assing became a successful restaurateur, he was also involved in international trade and emerged as the community's most vocal leader. He led his fellow Chinese in frequently participating in public ceremonies.

On August 28, 1850, the Chinese marched to Portsmouth Square, near San Francisco's Chinatown, "and arranged themselves in a circle upon the platform" during the funeral ceremony for President Zachary Taylor. Afterward, he wrote a letter to the mayor to thank him on behalf of the Chinese for the invitation to be part of the event. During the first celebration of California's admission to the Union on October 29, 1850, Assing commanded a Chinese contingent of fifty with a banner of crimson satin and the English words "China Boys."[20] This group also took part in the public celebration of George Washington's birthday in 1852.

Assing strenuously fought the surging anti-Chinese racism in the state. In 1852, for example, he wrote a public letter to the governor protesting his proposal to restrict Chinese immigration.[21] He also played a visible and busy leadership role in various social affairs, ranging from posting a reward for finding a missing person to publicly expressing gratitude to a ship captain for bringing newcomers from China. In 1852, when the Tong Hook Tong theater group came from China to San Francisco, Assing was one of the men who managed its performance. In 1852, he served as the official interpreter for the Three-District Association, one of the immigrants' most important social organizations.[22] He was also a founder of the Yanghe Huiguan (Yeong Wo Native-Place Association) and often worked with other prominent Chinese. One was Tong Achick, one of the first six pupils at the Morrison School, founded in the 1830s in memory of an English missionary to China, Robert Morrison.

Assing was neither a stereotypically humble Chinese nor a modest Christian. On his forty-second birthday, he threw a party at his restaurant and, as *Alta California* reported, "all the China boys were present."[23] Under the section "Foreign Consuls in San Francisco" in the 1854 city directory, he was listed as a consul representing China: "CHINA–NORMAN ASSING, Sacramento street, between Kearny and Dupont."[24] In part because of the distinctive romanization of his name and because of Norman Assing's high visibility, it is safe to assume that the Assing in the directory is our restaurateur. But the first Chinese consul did not come to San Francisco until the 1870s. Gunther Barth suspected that Assing distributed missionary tracts in 1850 while wearing "'a singularly colored fur mantle . . . and a long sort of robe,' whom a reporter assumed to be 'a mandarin at least.'"[25] If Barth was right, we have further reason to believe that Assing may have given himself the consul title to boost his standing in public.

Assing, indeed, was a controversial figure. Some of his fellow Chinese viewed him as a tyrannical man hungry for power and control. Barth, one of the first scholars to look into Assing's life, apparently shares that view and reports his scheme to "tighten his control over his countrymen."[26] James O'Meara, a resident of the city at the time, called him a Chinese "boss."[27] But even within the Chinese community, Assing did not always have his way. Atoy, an adventurous and "very pretty" twenty-year-old Chinese woman, who became a visible figure shortly after coming to California, defeated his repeated attempts to have her deported and returned to her alleged husband in China.[28] She enlisted help from Chinese and non-Chinese allies, claiming that she was single and accusing Assing of attempting forceful abduction.[29]

Like his influence, his wealth was limited. Apparently, the restaurateur sometimes had to visit food retailers personally for food supplies. During one such trip, he got into a fight over the price of cauliflower with a white butcher.[30]

An imperfect person in a far less perfect world, Assing nevertheless should be remembered not as an evil man but as someone who helped put the Chinese presence on California's gastronomical and political map. At a time of mounting anti-Chinese hostility, such a vocal, assertive, and ambitious personality was what the emerging community needed.

But the political climate for the Chinese continued to deteriorate, as anti-Chinese forces started to exclude them from mainstream political and economic life. In the case of *People v. Hall* (1854), the California Supreme Court ruled that Chinese were ineligible to testify against whites. Such institutionalized racism was also shared and endorsed by individual legal authorities. During a trial in 1855, when someone proposed that Tong Achick defend his case, the judge "threatened to knock Tong Achick down in the presence of the Court, if he dared to say anything insulting."[31] Anti-Chinese hostility became widespread throughout the American West in the 1850s. Section 6 of Article II of the Constitution of Oregon (1857) stipulated clearly: "No negro, chinaman, or mulatto, shall have the right of suffrage." It also prohibited the Chinese from owning "real estate or mining claim."[32]

Such an increasingly hostile society had no place for a colorful and feisty Chinese personality like Norman Assing, whose life in the public eye was relatively short-lived. Nor did the society have any serious appetite for the food of a people that it hated and despised so much. As the *Evening Bulletin* noted, "In San Francisco, and in cities in the interior, the Chinese restaurants of '50 and '51 have been driven out of the business."[33] Here as well as other cities, it was Chinese customers, rather than white patrons, who created and supported Chinese-food places, which had sprung up in conjunction with Chinese communities.

FOOD TOWN: A TALE OF THREE CITIES

To a large degree, the urban Chinatown existed as a "food town" for Chinese immigrants in the late nineteenth century because food businesses, like restaurants and grocery stores, were among the first institutions to appear in it. Located almost exclusively within Chinatown, moreover, such businesses constituted not only its most noticeable physical characteristic but also its appeal to Chinese immigrants.

Three of the largest cities that emerged in the Gold Rush years were Marysville, Sacramento, and San Francisco, where the most significant Chinese communities had settled. During these years, Marysville stood out as the state's third largest city; it was also a supply hub for the northern mining areas and a conduit that connected the mining district and San Francisco. It was accordingly called Third City (*san bu*) by the Chinese (later, Stockton inherited the title). In the 1850s, a Marysville merchant wrote in a letter that "there are twelve or fifteen teams on an average week leaving this city with loads for Chinese merchants in the mines."[34] Equally important, a Chinatown also emerged to serve a growing number of Chinese laborers, who worked as launderers, cooks, and servants in the growing local economy, and, of course, food was a central part of the service that Chinatown offered. By 1853, there were already two Chinese restaurants and three Chinese stores. All were on or around First Street, where a Chinatown would evolve.[35]

The number of Chinese cooks and servants increased from 18 in 1860 to 211 in 1870, and laundry workers grew from 53 to 154.[36] Chinatown expanded accordingly, increasing its businesses to twenty-five in 1878 and forty-two in 1882.[37] Remaining in Chinatown and serving Chinese customers, the restaurants had not yet become a broad-based industry. At this time, Chinese restaurant workers were fewer than laundrymen and servants, and they remained under the radar screen of census takers. The manuscript census of 1860 recorded only one waiter/dishwasher, who subsequently disappeared from the 1870 and 1880 censuses.[38] This does not mean that the Chinese-food industry was less important than laundry and domestic service. Food places constituted an important economic pillar of Chinatown, while laundry shops and servants were more widespread, as we can see clearly in the case of Sacramento during the same period.

The next largest city created by the Gold Rush, Sacramento was known among the Chinese as Second City because of its significance in Chinese America. Its number of Chinese reached 980 in 1860 and grew to 1,331 in 1870 and

1,674 in 1880.[39] By that time, the city's sizable community boasted more than 100 businesses. Chinese providing personal services to white consumers represented the largest cohort of the Chinese labor force. Of the 104 Chinese businesses that found their way into the bilingual Wells Fargo directory in 1878, the 40 laundries were the largest category.[40] In 1880, the 638 Chinese who worked as laundrymen, cooks, and servants constituted the largest group among the city's Chinese population.[41] These individuals and laundries spread across the city. Twenty-four of the twenty-six food places were clustered on I Street between Second and Fifth Streets. Constituting the core of Chinatown's economy, they also made it an elaborate food marketplace. Besides the nine general grocers, there were also specialty food stores: four fish merchants, two vegetable stores, and six butchers and poultry retailers. Read-to-eat food was not only available in the three restaurants but also offered by two "merchant(s)" and seven grocery stores.

The Chinese gave the crown of First City or Big City to San Francisco. Its Chinatown, the largest Chinese settlement in the United States, was unequivocally a food town from its beginning. In 1856, for example, the thirty-three grocery stores outnumbered all other businesses in the community. Together, the food places—grocery stores, five restaurants, and five meat markets—accounted for nearly half of all businesses in Chinatown. Their proportion in Chinese businesses declined over time, though. Of the 423 Chinese firms listed in the Wells Fargo directory in 1878, about 23 percent were food places due to the diversification of the ethnic economy into areas like cigar- and shoemaking and laundry. But the absolute number of clearly identifiable food stores increased to ninety-seven, which turned Chinatown into an even more sophisticated food market than the community in Sacramento. For example, of the nine stores that sold rice, five were rice specialty stores, and there were two tofu places. Of the grocery shops, twenty-eight specialized in seafood, fifteen in pork, and six in poultry—all of which were frequently used in Cantonese cooking, in spite of the image of the Chinese as only rice-eating people. And when these articles were difficult to come by, the immigrants were willing to pay a high price. As early as the 1850s, a "butcher in the Southern mines" reportedly noted the immigrants' food habits: "They preferred pork, even at twenty-five-cents a pound. I have sold in one day as high as fourteen hogs, averaging seventy-five pounds each. They are very fond of fowls, and buy a great many. For a large one they pay two dollars, the general price now is about a dollar and a half. . . . They like fish too, whenever they can be got, and use dried or salt fish daily."[42]

Steamed Fish

Serves 1 or 2

*Most Chinatown residents discussed in this chapter were Cantonese, known for their love of seafood. For complicated fish dishes, one can just go to a Cantonese seafood restaurant, which was what nineteenth-century Chinese immigrants liked to do in Chinatowns. This recipe is simple and fast to prepare at home.**

    2 tbsp Chinese fermented black beans
    2 tbsp Chinese rice wine
    6 thin slices of fresh ginger root
    3 cloves garlic
    ½ lb ¾-inch-thick white fish filet (preferably sea bass)
    ¼ cup chopped green onion
    3 tbsp vegetable oil
    2 tbsp soy sauce

Soak and rinse the black beans. Coarsely chop them into smaller pieces and place them in a small bowl. Add the rice wine, ginger root, and garlic; allow the mixture to macerate for at least 30 minutes. Place the sea bass in a shallow plate and smear the wine mixture evenly over the top. Cover the plate and allow to marinate for 15 to 20 minutes. Boil water in a steamer and steam the fish for 8 to 10 minutes. Turn off the heat but do not open the steamer; let the fish rest inside for another 5 minutes. Then take the plate out and place the green onion evenly on top. Heat the vegetable oil until it is very hot and pour it onto the green onion. Drizzle with the soy sauce.

*For a slightly different version of this recipe, see Yong Chen, "Try It, You May Like It," *Irvine (Calif.) Spectrum News,* June 14–18, 1999, B2.

Much less numerous than food places in 1878, laundries became the largest business category in 1882 in San Francisco. But such numerical preponderance did not turn the city's Chinatown into a "laundry town." As in Sacramento and other cities, the 176 laundry shops were scattered, covering seventy-three streets across San Francisco and serving mostly a non-Chinese clientele.[43] Their Chinese names, as recorded in the bilingual Wells Fargo directory, often explicitly indicated that they "wash barbarian clothes." Meanwhile, Chinatown continued to be defined by food, as the number of food places increased to about 150, all located in Chinatown and serving a largely Chinese clientele. These included one hundred or so different grocery stores, six confectionary shops, and twelve butchers. A pattern of business cluster also emerged among food stores: eight of the ten poultry stores were on Washington Alley, while all four rice shops were on Dupont Street. For those who did not have the time or a place to cook, meals were available not only in the twelve so restaurants but also in the four boarding houses. Offering diverse foods and services, Chinatown stood as a convenient and exciting gastronomical mecca, where individual restaurant goers had ample choices and merchants fetched their supplies in the different food wholesale stores. As a clear indication of Chinese San Francisco as a food-supply center, the main Chinese-language newspaper frequently listed food wholesale prices on the front page in the 1870s. For example, on October 23, 1875, it displayed the per-hundred-pound price for more than twenty kinds of foods, including rice, dried fungus (*muer*), sugar, ham, eggs, and beans.[44]

The story of the three Gold Rush cities was repeated elsewhere. Chinese eating places followed the steps of Chinese immigrants to small towns and provided a magnet for the community. One such town, Hanford in central California, owes its existence to the arrival of Chinese who worked for the Southern Pacific Railway. To serve these workers and, later, Chinese laborers in the fields, a Chinatown emerged, known as China Alley. One of the early residents was Shu Wing Gong (Henry Wing, the grandfather of the famous restaurateur Richard Wing), who catered to Chinese railroad workers shortly after his arrival in the early 1880s. Then he opened a Chinese restaurant, selling noodles to Chinese customers for as little as 5 cents a bowl.[45]

Many Chinese workers—a significant number of them in the service sector—ventured beyond California. And in the Chinese communities that evolved to serve them, food businesses occupied a central place. By Marie Rose Wong's count, the twenty-two Chinese in Portland, Oregon, in 1860 included two merchants, three laborers, and twelve in the laundry business. The city's Chinese population increased to 1,612 in 1880, among whom the 1,024 laborers, 229 laundrymen, and 122 people in personal-service jobs represented the three largest groups.[46] By that time, the city already had a good-size Chinatown. The Wells Fargo directory of 1878 lists thirty Chinese businesses, including perhaps three restaurants.[47] We do not know precisely how many of them were restaurants because the names of most businesses in either Chinese or English do not indicate their exact nature. But one had an easily recognizable restaurant name, Hong Fer Low. Sometimes spelled Hong Far Low, its Chinese words are *xing hua lou*, meaning "apricot blossom building." It was also the name of a small restaurant that a Cantonese reportedly opened in Shanghai in the early 1850s, which later became famous and moved to a bigger location on Fuzhou Road in 1928.[48] There was a Hong Far Low in Boston's Chinatown as well. The Hong Fer Low in San Francisco's Chinatown opened in the 1850s and lasted until 1960, according to Andrew Coe, and remained a famous establishment for many years.[49] In the late nineteenth century, it was a favorite of tourists. The *Morning Call* described it thus: "The restaurant was most gorgeously fitted up, the walls being made of carved woods imported from China and inlaid in places with precious stones. . . . Some of the chandeliers in the place cost $1500 each."[50]

Portland's Hong Fer Low was on Second Street—the heart of Chinatown. In fact, the Chinese called Second Street *tang ren jie* (Street of the Chinese), which was the Chinese equivalent of the English "Chinatown." Located next to the Zhonghua Huiguan (Chinese Association), the Chinese community's leading social organization, this restaurant stood as a reminder of the importance of food in Chinatown life. The Hong Fer Low in San Francisco was also located in the heart of Chinatown, as were numerous other good restaurants.

In 1869, the first sizable group of Chinese—250 former railroad workers— arrived in St. Louis, then the fourth largest city in the United States.[51] That city's Chinese population remained small, and many worked in the laundry business for years. In 1888, the Chinese population numbered fewer than 170, employed mostly in the seventy-six Chinese laundries.[52] Around that time, groceries and restaurants appeared in the city's Hop Alley to serve the Chinese.

As Chinese immigrants moved out of the West, usually to work as laundry-men and servants, urban Chinatowns developed in many eastern cities, and again food businesses played a pivotal role in this development. The nineteenth-century ethnographer Stewart Culin, who studied Chinese settlements in the East, described the community-building process: "The store is the center which life in a Chinese colony revolves. As soon as several men have collected in a town or city, one of them will send to the nearest place of supply and purchase such Chinese groceries and other wares as may be needed by the colony. . . . If the colony increases in numbers he may rent a small store and with the assistance of some of his friends form a store company." The establishment of a Chinese restaurant was a signal that the community reached a significant level of stability and critical mass: "In time the shop-keeper, knowing the advantage of increasing the attraction of his place, may procure a tolerably skillful cook and open a restaurant in an upper story of his building."[53]

WHITE NOSE, CHINESE SMELL

Food businesses have also been the urban Chinatown's most sensible marker
for both Chinese and whites. "Fancifully decorated and illuminated on their
balconies and upper stories during the evening," Chinatown restaurants left a
deep visual impression on nineteenth-century non-Chinese visitors.[54] In day-
time, however, the architecture of the buildings housing the restaurants resem-
bled that of other structures.

Perhaps even more sensible than their physical appearance is the distinctive
aroma from Chinese-food places. Traditionally ranked at the lowest end among
human senses,[55] the sense of smell is now increasingly recognized as being "important to human beings and had always been so."[56] As neural- and marine-
science research in recent decades has discovered, in navigating the outside
world humans, other mammals, and sea creatures rely not only on visual and
hearing senses but also on olfactory cues. Salmon, for example, swim hundreds
or thousands of miles in the open water to return to their river home by following familiar smells.[57] Smell functions in humans as an emotionally charged
geographic and cultural compass. In a passage about the inventions of smoking,
drinking, and tea, Lin Yutang showed his appreciation of food smells: "They
are all to be enjoyed through the nostrils by acting on our sense of smell."[58]
Smell is important because this significant sensory property of food is also
closely connected to memory. The anthropologist David E. Sutton writes that
"smells evoke what surrounds them in memory."[59] Because of its social significance, therefore, the smell of food becomes a marker of cultural boundaries. As
Sutton puts it, "Good and bad smells also make claims for social distinction."[60]

Permeating the air, the scent of food announces the presence of Chinatown.
It was a smell of home that I always longed for when living in Chinatown-less
upstate New York. The smell of familiar food and culture was also an important appeal of Chinatown to early immigrants, such as Wah-chung Leung.
When he first arrived in San Francisco on February 3, 1922, the fragrant smells
in Chinatown triggered his homesickness.[61]

To Anglo noses, however, it signaled just the opposite: the "strange odors of
the East" is how the journalist and author Charles W. Stoddard described Chinatown in San Francisco, a city he began to know well from the 1850s. For
many white observers, the smell was not just unfamiliar but also repugnant.
John David Borthwick, a Scottish journalist who reached San Francisco in 1851,
reported his impression of the city's Chinese quarter: "A peculiarly nasty smell
pervaded this locality."[62]

The practice of using the sense of smell to distinguish the racial or socioeconomic "other" has occurred in various other contexts. Industrializing France, for example, developed notions of the smell of the poor.[63] The idea that African Americans had a distinctive odor prevailed in the minds of nineteenth- and twentieth-century white Americans, including those who had no direct contact with them.[64] Belonging to a culture so different, however, the Chinese smell seemed particularly detectable to white noses. Otis Gibson—who continued to work among the Chinese in California after spending ten years in China as a missionary—wrote of the food smells associated with various nations: "The French smells of garlic; the Irishman smells of whisky and tobacco; the German smells of sour krout [sic] and lager, and smells strong too; the Englishman smells of roast beef and 'arf and 'arf'; the American smells of corn-cake and pork and beans." Gibson then devoted the rest of the passage to the smell of the Chinese, which he found especially unforgettable:

> The Chinese smell is a mixture and a puzzle, a marvel and a wonder, a mystery and a disgust; but nevertheless, you shall find it a palpable fact. The smell of opium raw and cooked, and in the process of cooking, mixed with the smell of cigars, and tobacco leaves wet and dry, dried fish and dried vegetables, and a thousand other indescribable ingredients; all these toned to a certain degree by what may be called a shippy smell, produce a sensation upon the olfactory nerves of the average American, which once experienced will not soon be forgotten.[65]

Gibson's mixture of smells clearly had strong social dimensions, containing allusions to the exotic and mysterious nature of the Chinese and their association to vices.

Like Gibson, some other early writers mentioned diverse sources of the smell, such as the "burning opium."[66] But frequently, it was the smell of Chinese food that triggered white visitors' olfactory nerves. Many identified the particular Chinese "odor" or "the peculiar Chinese smell" as coming from food places, such as restaurants and butchers.[67] In 1865, Samuel Bowles, a newspaper editor from Massachusetts, attended a grand banquet in honor of the visiting Speaker of the House hosted by Chinese business and community leaders in San Francisco. He recalled his experience: "I went to the table weak and hungry; but I found the one universal odor and favor soon destroyed all appetite." Moments later, he was called out by another guest at the same table who had left earlier. Together they went to an American restaurant and "the lost appetite came back."[68]

Iza D. Hardy, a British novelist who visited Chinatown with police escort early in the 1880s, went to a Chinese restaurant first, but he left without eating because of "the rancid odour" of the food there.[69]

Many white visitors to Chinatowns in other cities also noted the smell of Chinese food. Entering a Chinese restaurant in New York in 1887, a reporter sensed "a pungent odor" from "something being cooked."[70] In Chicago's Chinatown, which had become fairly sizable by 1889, another white reporter found "odors from the style of cooking" "repulsive."[71] In 1890, a newspaper article relayed the experience of a white visitor to a restaurant in Philadelphia's Chinatown, whose nose "tells him that he is in peculiar quarters."[72]

For Anglos, that particular smell was an essential part of the Chinese and their community. In 1880, a reporter for the *New York Tribune* wrote about San Francisco's Chinatown: "The floors of these balconies, the sides of the houses, the windows, and doorways . . . all reek with the filth which never seems to disturb the Chinese eye, to be an offence in the Chinese nostril." To the reporter, "the air is heavy and offensive, laden with the powerful odors of native tobacco—the same smell which taints the atmosphere of all the shops, and which clings to the Chinese."[73] By the early twentieth century, white observers had developed a popular notion of a distinctive Chinese smell that "unlike almost any other odor that ever was," as visitors to St. Louis's Hop Alley put it in the early twentieth century.[74]

Human olfactory physiology is universal: the air we breathe into the nose brings in odorant molecules (called ligands) that then bind to our odorant receptors, causing a change in the membrane potential and sending a signal to the olfactory bulb of our brain, where the information is coded and remembered.[75] But the process by which white brains and minds registered the smells of Chinatown was more cultural and racial than physiological. White noses sensed and comprehended the Chinatown food scent differently from the way Chinese nostrils did because whites relied not only on their olfactory receptor cells but also on prevailing ideas about Chinese culture and the Chinese race. What was an inviting aroma to the Chinese became a repulsive odor to many whites.

Associating the Chinese with odor was also extremely political. Politically and racially motivated people often traced the smell to specific things, such as squid, rats, and offal, all of which were regarded as embodying the strange and repulsive lifestyle and diet of the Chinese. In Monterey, California, in the late nineteenth and early twentieth centuries, for example, Chinese fishermen were condemned for the offensive smells they generated.[76] Dr. Charles Kaemmerer, a French immigrant who had lived in New York for more than twenty years and had worked as the city's sanitary inspector, accused Chinese men of cooking and eating cats or rats, claiming that he sensed "a very peculiar odor."[77]

In cities like San Francisco, the depiction of Chinatown as a place of stink represented an attempt to "demonize and isolate the 'other.'"[78] In 1880, under the auspices of the infamously anti-Chinese Workingmen's Party of California, an investigating committee issued a pamphlet titled *Chinatown Declared a Nuisance*. It included a street-by-street report of itemized nuisances in San Francisco's Chinatown. In describing the conditions of Chinatown's streets and alleys, the report used words like "stink," "stinky," and "stench" on more than ten occasions to paint a graphically abhorrent image of Chinatown as a filthy and odorous place. It described 741 Pacific Avenue this way: "Upon entering through an adjoining wood-yard, we found a very paradise of Chinatown; piles of dirt, filth, stench, and slime, enough to sicken the stomach of any white person." Here is another description: "An Alley on Mr. Sheppard's property behind Stockton street, off Jackson is an indescribable hole of filth and stench. Piles of dirt, mixed with human excrement, garbage, etc., defies all civilization."[79]

In the minds of many whites, clearly, the odor of Chinatown and Chinese food signified an inferior race and an undesirable culture to be shunned and excluded from America.

FOOD AS IDENTITY

Less politically motivated commentators, however, usually found the smell from Chinatown food places "impossible to describe."[80] This was not just because of the absence of a sufficiently developed lexicon of smells in the English language; the indescribability of the Chinese smell was consistent with long-standing Western perceptions of the Chinese and their culture as exotic and mysterious. Westerners living in China also played an important role in developing such perceptions. Many of them found Chinese cooking odorous. During a journey to Chengdu in southwestern China in 1887, for example, the American Methodist Episcopal missionary Virgil C. Hart used words like "unpleasant odors" to describe the cooking of native Chinese.[81]

The extensive and persistent attention of Westerners to the smell of food in their observations of the Chinese reminds us that food preference constitutes a central and conspicuous element of cultural identity. Westerners had long viewed food habits as an important part of the national identity. The famous French gastronome Jean Anthelme Brillat-Savarin pronounced in 1825: "The destiny of nations depends on the manner in which they are fed."[82] Inheriting this view, Americans attached great national importance to individual dietary preferences. A 1910 advertisement for the *National Food Magazine*, for instance, linked "the health of the individual" to "the health of the nation."[83]

For Americans and other Westerners in the nineteenth and early twentieth centuries, food constituted a most sensible foundation on which to form their first impressions about China. "One of the first things which impress the traveler in China is the extremely simple diet of the people," noted Arthur Henderson Smith, an American missionary in China for more than half a century.[84] Such impressions derived from food were far from benign or positive, as was clearly noted by Samuel Wells Williams, one of nineteenth-century America's most influential China experts. In *The Middle Kingdom*, Williams wrote: "The articles of food which the Chinese eat, and the mode and ceremonies attending their feasts, have aided much in giving them the odd character they bear abroad."[85] Americans, it seemed, disliked Chinese food not just because of the food itself but because Americans identified themselves as the superior "other" of the Chinese. In a memoir of his experiences in China, an old-time British merchant compared Westerners and the Chinese: "We were different from them; we ate strong flesh of cows and sheep, which they avoid."[86] Such a food-based consciousness of racial and cultural difference also manifested itself in the daily life of Americans and other Westerners in China.

Westerners did not stay unchanged in China, though. Both the British and the Americans fell in love with tea, for example. As a measure of identity, however, more revealing than individual foodstuffs and incidental eating events are certain long-term food patterns: the staple ingredients and how to prepare them in daily meals.

Ample evidence shows that for their regular meals, many Americans tried to avoid Chinese food and clung to their own foodways, relishing Western foods shipped to China. The Massachusetts native Osmond Tiffany, who visited China in 1848, tasted Chinese food but concluded that "no enthusiast would care to go through two Chinese dinners." "The dishes," she continued, "have a very strong smack of castor oil, and you can scarcely find one that has not some repulsive taste." She also reported the importation of dairy products such as butter from outside China: "If a lot arrives . . . it is eagerly seized."[87] While traveling in China, some Americans brought not only food but also their own cooks.[88] Like their American counterparts, the British in early-twentieth-century China "ate their domestic cuisine, reproducing as far as possible the tastes of their home with Chinese or imported ingredients, and they mostly found Chinese food disgusting."[89]

Americans did not abstain entirely from Chinese food; some, especially children, become "fond of Chinese food."[90] Many adults occasionally tasted Chinese food as an adventure. Eating it on a more regular basis, however, became an ordeal that they had to endure when they did not have enough Western food or money.[91]

A few Americans made a deliberate effort to live on Chinese food. They included members of the China Inland Mission, one of the largest and most influential missionary organizations in modern Chinese history, known as the "pigtail mission" because of its unorthodox and deliberate efforts to localize culturally.[92] Localizing involved not only wearing native attire but also eating Chinese food. As one missionary instructed new members in a story published in the *Independent* in 1901, "Wearing Chinese clothes and eating Chinese food, you are to live and work and die among these people."[93]

Still, regular consumption of Chinese food required an effort because it was considered a hardship. At the end of the nineteenth century, the *New York Evangelist* published a letter remembering the late Presbyterian missionary Fannie Wright. It counted the difficulties that she had encountered while faithfully serving God in China: "She had often been without supplies from home and subsisted entirely on the Chinese food."[94]

Like their compatriots back home, many Americans in China employed Chinese servants to cook Western food. In 1866, the American Presbyterian Mission Press published a Chinese-language cookbook, *Zhao Yang Fan Shu (Foreign Cookery in Chinese)*, in order to teach such servants how to make Western food with non-Chinese ingredients like wine, butter, cream, and "foreign carrots." The preface notes: "Everyone knows how difficult it is to teach native cooks to prepare dishes suited to the taste and habits of foreigners."[95] The cookbook also includes a set of rules about keeping things clean and orderly: not only did the food have to taste Western but the kitchen had to look Western.

Because of their cultural propensities, Americans in China, especially the nineteenth-century missionaries and merchants, missed an opportunity to become culinary ambassadors; otherwise, Chinese food could have reached the mainstream American palate much sooner. More important, their avoidance of Chinese food and their aversion to its aroma reveal how strongly they associated their own American identity with food. Many years later, the anthropologist Margaret Mead wrote about this association: "Being American is a matter of abstention from foreign ways, foreign food, foreign idea, foreign accents, foreign vices. So whisky drinking becomes identified with the Irish and, by coincidence, with Catholics, beer drinking with Germans, and marijuana with black musicians and zoot suits with minority group adolescents."[96] Many immigrants and their children comprehended cultural and national identity in gastronomical terms. "Americans were people who ate peanut butter and jelly on mushy white bread that came out of a plastic package," wrote an American-born Italian, who never realized that he was an American citizen while growing up in the 1940s and 1950s.[97] Naturally, as Netta Davis notes, "the primary image of American immigrant adaptation is a culinary one."[98]

Similarly, different Chinese coming to the United States maintained their allegiance to their culinary traditions in both their consciousness and their daily lives. Many students from China longed for Chinese food after arriving in America, as I did. In the first decade of the twentieth century, when six Chinese students arrived in the United States to study in the New Bedford Textile School, they "sighed for dishes more familiar to a Chinese palate."[99] Blanche Ching-Yi Wu, who came to the United States as a graduate student in the early 1930s, recalls that she and her fellow Chinese students at the University of Michigan were "homesick for Chinese food," and relied on a Chinese-food peddler, who visited Detroit on weekends, for things like "salted duck eggs and the 'ancient eggs,' bean curd, mung beans, soybeans, soy sauce."[100]

Visiting government officials from China also demonstrated a strong attachment to Chinese food. Upon reaching San Francisco in 1885 as China's minister to the United States, Zhang Yinhuan complained about two things in his diary: the harassment from immigration officials, who initially refused to let him land, and the unpalatable Western food that he had to live with during the long journey. "Western food," he wrote, "was elegant but not to my liking." The day after his landing, local Chinese community leaders came to his rescue, inviting him to a Chinese dinner. He apparently enjoyed the familiar food prepared by his Cantonese compatriots as they chatted about hometown foods with "laughter."[101] Arriving in Washington as Zhang's successor in 1889, Cui Guoyin found himself "unable to eat the hotel's Western food." Fortunately, Zhang arranged to send him a pot of rice and three Chinese dishes.[102] After attending the coronation ceremony of Czar Nicholas II, Viceroy Li Hung Chang (Li Hongzhang in pinyin) visited the United States in 1896 with his own chefs, and his efforts to cling to Chinese food even during public functions generated much media fascination.[103]

Senior scholar-statesmen in this period often regarded eating Chinese food as a statement of patriotism. During the second Opium War (1856–1860), British solders took Canton and captured Ye Mingchen, the viceroy of Guangdong and Guangxi Provinces. Imprisoned in Calcutta, he refused to eat foreign food when his food ran out and starved himself to death in 1859.[104] It was not just because he found the Westerners' food unpalatable; it was an act to protect his honor as a Chinese and a loyal subject to the emperor.

Chinese food also accompanied the immigrants en route to the New World. For example, during his voyage to the United States in 1876 on the *City of Peking* of the Pacific Steamship Company, a Chinese intellectual named Li Gui noticed that there were 109 Chinese passengers' lower-class cabins as well as 38 Chinese on the kitchen staff.[105] The Chinese cooks undoubtedly prepared palatable food for their compatriots on board, and Chinese food remained available in transpacific voyages for years. For instance, the American Mail Line, which ran passenger service between China and the United States beginning in the late 1920s, offered Chinese meals on a daily basis for its third-class Chinese passengers on all its presidential liners.[106]

The immigrants who lived in the United States largely maintained their food habits, as demonstrated by ample historical records and archaeological evidence.[107] They did so in spite of daunting obstacles. First, there was much hostility toward Chinese food. Not intimidated by it, however, the Chinese defended their foodways publicly. In a widely publicized address to President Ulysses S. Grant, the Chinese argued: "It is charged against us that we eat rice, fish, and vegetables. It is true that our diet is different from the people of this honorable country; our tastes in these matters are not exactly alike and can not be forced. . . . But is that a sin on our part, of sufficient gravity to be brought before the President and Congress of the United States?"[108] Second, the ingredients for making Chinese food were not readily available in the New World. In the early years, the Chinese had to import from China many different foodstuffs, including rice, orange skins, tea, mushrooms, bamboo shoots, shark's fins, bird's nest, and sea cucumber.[109]

During the nineteenth century, immigrant Chinese working as miners, farmhands, railroad laborers, laundrymen, and cooks outside Chinatown could not easily avail themselves of Chinese food. Occasionally, there was a single store selling it, as was the case for the seven hundred or so Chinese building a railroad near the San Joaquin River. As Charles Nordhoff noted in 1873, "There was a store kept in several cars near the end of the track" that had a variety of Chinese foods like dried oysters, sweet rice crackers, dried bamboo sprouts, salted cabbage, Chinese sugar, and Chinese bacon. This demonstrates one reason why the Chinese stuck to their own food—it had far greater variety than "the beef, beans, bread-and-butter, and potatoes of the white laborers."[110]

Whenever possible, Chinese workers traveled to Chinatowns in cities like San Francisco and Marysville, and later in New York and Philadelphia, for food in restaurants, turning the Chinatowns into food towns. For them, doing so was an affirmation of their Chineseness—it met their practical needs for food, rest, and socializing. Their cultural identity was seldom an abstract concept but was always intertwined with practical issues in daily life.

Chinatowns in the American metropolis were invariably crowded. In 1885, the Board of Supervisors of San Francisco appointed a special committee to investigate Chinatown. Full of anti-Chinese animosity, its report nonetheless revealed the cramped living conditions in the Chinese community: "The Chinese herd together as compactly as possible, both as regards living and sleeping-rooms and sleeping-accommodations."[111]

Individual Chinese, especially laborers, had limited private spaces for cooking and relaxing. Just as Chinese boarding houses often provided food, many restaurants took in boarders. In San Francisco, many Chinese took advantage of such service provided by the restaurants for an average charge of $10 a month.[112] As the veteran Chinese missionary Otis Gibson reported in 1877, "Plain living in a common restaurant can be had by a Chinaman for eight dollars a month. Good living will cost from fifteen to twenty dollars a month, according to the ability of the boarder."[113]

Chinatown restaurants also provided inexpensive food for the immigrant laborers. In the late 1870s, immigrants like Ah Quin could grab a supper for as little as 10 cents in San Francisco's Chinatown; this was the same price as a theater ticket.[114]

Moreover, the restaurants gave the Chinese a place to socialize and recreate. In cities from New York and Washington, D.C., in the East to San Francisco in the West, white observers noted Chinese customers eating and relaxing in Chinese restaurants, and often characterized these restaurants as a "resort." The *Washington Post*, for example, wrote in reference to a good Chinese restaurant that opened in the city in 1899: "This restaurant is the resort and meeting place of East Asiatics, living in the Capital, who, when they are not at their stations, are pretty certain to be in this little corner of Asia."[115] Feeling at home, relaxed and cheerful Chinese diners were often seen "talking loudly in their native tongue" while eating or "playing cards and dominoes and dice."[116]

The restaurant was indeed a social resort for the Chinese. In an article about restaurants in San Francisco, Noah Brooks wrote in 1868: "The Chinese are social and cheerful in their habits. They seize every possible occasion for a feast, and the restaurants of the race in this city are almost constantly lighted up with the banquets of their numerous customers."[117] Gibson also noted that Chinese individuals enjoyed social dinners together in San Francisco's Chinese restaurants. In New York, as Wong Chin Foo reported in 1888, the Chinese restaurants "are most thronged on Sunday, when the Chinese laundrymen of New York and neighboring cities come in for a general good time."[118] And good times and homey Cantonese food were what such establishments continued to offer. In the Chinese restaurants in Chicago's Chinatown during the 1930s, as Paul Siu observed, "on every Sunday evening, the laundrymen dine together. These are the busiest hours of the week for the restaurant."[119]

For Chinese as well as non-Chinese, culinary traditions constituted a critical element in both their consciousness and their daily lives. Chinese food traveled to America together with immigrants from China and remained a prominent fixture in Chinese communities. It was in urban Chinatowns that Chinese food took root on American soil and thrived during the time when it was shunned by the larger society. Chinatown food places gave Chinese immigrants not only familiar things to eat but also precious space for relaxation and social life. Forming the primary clientele of these places, Chinese customers supported and preserved Chinese food before launching it to non-Chinese markets.

Over time, as antagonism toward Chinese food began to lose its intensity, Chinatowns inspired non-Chinese Americans' interest about Chinese food. One of the earliest comprehensive publications about Chinese food was a pamphlet issued by the U.S. Department of Agriculture about the vegetables in Chinatown.[120] And it is also in Chinatown where many American consumers had their first taste of Chinese food.

5

THE RISE OF CHINESE RESTAURANTS

"It has taken the American public a long time to swallow its chop suey," noted a reporter in 1908 on the mounting popularity of Chinese food in America.[1] Indeed, it had been largely shunned by American consumers for almost fifty years after its initial landing in California. This dramatic turn of events for Chinese cooking came as a result of two new developments: (1) a profound demographic and socioeconomic transformation of Chinese America, and (2) the extraordinary expansion of the American economy. At the conjunction of these developments is Chinatown's metamorphosis from a target of intense racial hatred to a popular tourist destination.

The growing appeal of Chinatown among non-Chinese leisure and pleasure seekers was not a development to rejoice over in Chinese American history. This phenomenon followed the destruction of most of the once-thriving rural Chinese communities, and the subsequent urbanization and occupational marginalization of the shrinking Chinese population.

At the same time, turning the United States into a global power, the fast-growing economy at home generated more wealth and leisure as well as a swelling army of tourists, hungry for new things to see and to savor. A steadily increasing number of these travelers, especially those in the lower-middle and working classes, went to Chinatown to sightsee. It is in Chinatown that many American mass consumers discovered Chinese food.

THE AMERICAN ECONOMIC EXPANSION

The quickly improving U.S. economy and standard of living in the late nineteenth century prepared a larger economic context for the spread of Chinese food. Analogous to the economic miracle taking place in China in the late twentieth century, in the last three decades of the nineteenth century, U.S. manufacturing increased at an annual rate of about 8.7 percent, and the economy at about 7.4 percent (figure 3).[2] Measured in 1985 USD, the American gross domestic product per capita increased from $2,254 in 1870 to $3,757 in 1900 and $4,559 in 1910.[3] During World War I, the United States became the world's largest creditor and leading export nation.[4]

Needless to say, the economic expansion did not equally benefit all social classes and racial groups. From 1923 to 1929, another period of economic prosperity, the share of total income received by the wealthiest 1 percent increased by 35 percent while the wages of unskilled workers actually declined. Still, many groups benefited from the economic growth. In the years after 1890, for example, the white elderly saw their incomes rise sharply.[5]

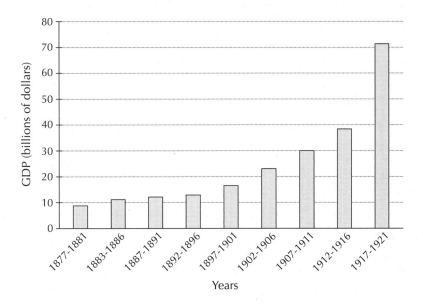

FIGURE 3 The growth of the GDP (gross domestic product) of the United States, 1877–1921. (U.S. Bureau of the Census, *Historical Statistics of the United States, Colonial Times to 1957* [Washington, D.C.: Government Printing Office, 1960], 143)

Charles S. Maier has correctly pointed out that America "began its ascent to global power in the late nineteenth century pursuing its industrial vocation."[6] That ascent was also accompanied by soaring consumer desires. With more money in their pockets, a great number of Americans developed a lust for leisure travel. The middle and upper-middle class joined the wealthy in trips to see the world. After the Civil War, a few visits to Europe within a lifetime became a sign of the American bourgeoisie, including an education tour for adolescents and a requisite wedding trip.[7] The lower echelons of society also sought to jump on the bandwagon of leisure travel. The sociologist Dean MacCannell sees the turn of the twentieth century as the beginning of mass tourism. His focus is on "the international middle class," but in the United States the leisure travel craze also reached less privileged groups like immigrants and minorities.[8]

Unable to afford the time or money for long-distance travel, less-fortunate segments of society took short and inexpensive excursions within American cities, and these trips became increasingly popular around the turn of the century. Although the "raw, young American cities were barren of classical history and art," they had certain attractions to offer.[9] Among them were the ethnic communities with exotic appearances and smells. The decades-long political and media focus on "the Chinese problem" had turned Chinatown into an exoticized urban ethnic community, one that emerged as a popular destination of urban excursions.[10] In an article about New York City's ethnic communities, Forest Morgan pointed out in 1910 that "in all New York the most bizarre and interesting colony is of course Chinatown. . . . This is a great locality for sightseers."[11]

THE EMERGENCE OF CHINATOWN AS A TOURIST ATTRACTION

The emergence of Chinatown as a tourist site embodied a profound transformation of the demographic and occupational character of America's Chinese population, altering the meaning of Chinatown for white Americans and the Chinese alike.

This transformation took place on three fronts. The first was the disappearance of Chinese communities in small-town America. For many people, the word "Chinatown" invariably invokes the Chinese settlement in large cities. But for years after the Gold Rush, the American Chinatown existed in both small towns and big cities. Things changed quickly after the early 1870s, when the anti-Chinese movement became more intense and violent, and garnered widespread support throughout society. Signaling the beginning of a long-lasting wave of anti-Chinese violence, an anti-Chinese riot broke out in Los Angeles in 1871, resulting in the deaths of nineteen Chinese.[12]

In what Jean Pfaelzer insightfully calls "the forgotten war against Chinese Americans," the anti-Chinese movement did not succeed in eradicating the entire Chinese presence, but it destroyed about two hundred Chinatowns in the Pacific Northwest and drove out their residents by the end of the 1880s.[13] The Rock Springs massacre in 1885 reveals the level of anti-Chinese brutality and the acquiescence it received. In one of the worst racial riots in American history, fifty-one Chinese laborers, who worked in the coal mines along the Union Pacific Railroad in Rock Springs, Wyoming, were killed.[14] While the perpetrators went unpunished, the survivors of the ruined Chinese community were forced to leave. In 1887, more than thirty Chinese miners perished in another massacre that took place in Oregon's Hell's Canyon Gorge on the Snake River. The criminals, who "robbed, murdered, and mutilated" the Chinese victims, remained free of convictions.[15]

As the survivors of such attacks in small towns moved to Chinese communities in cities in both the West and the East, Chinese America began to be urbanized. In 1880, those Chinese living in cities with a population of at least 100,000 represented only 21.6 percent of the Chinese population. That amount grew to 71 percent in 1940.[16] For the Chinese, then, the transformed Chinatown in the American metropolis was no longer merely a cultural, socioeconomic center within Chinese America. It had come to epitomize Chinese America.

The second significant change in Chinese America was its occupational concentration in the service sector of the economy. This was largely because the anti-Chinese forces that ravaged small-town Chinese communities also pushed the Chinese out of the more profitable occupations, such as mining and manufacturing. By 1940, restaurant jobs had become one of the two main lines of work for the Chinese.

The third transition occurred in the minds of Americans, for whom Chinatown shifted from primarily a target of hatred to an object of curiosity, and from a place of danger to a site of pleasure. For much of the second half of the nineteenth century, a host of white Americans—including labor union members, public health officials, politicians, and reporters—had concertedly created the image of the Chinese as a grave threat. In a widely distributed and cited pamphlet, the prominent physician Arthur B. Stout regarded the Chinese community as a potential cause of the physiological "decay of the nation";[17] others depicted Chinatowns in cities like San Francisco as dark places of immorality and sources of sexually transmitted diseases and epidemics.[18]

The nineteenth-century American city itself was not a very desirable place. "Walking into an American city in the mid-nineteenth century," the historian Catherine Cocks tells us, "was an act fraught with moral and political peril."[19] But in the minds of white Americans, walking into an urban Chinatown entailed unknowable physical hazards, even though it had never been a threat to their physical safety. Quite often, white visitors to Chinatown in San Francisco requested a police escort for protection "against the possible dangers."[20] Some depicted Chinatown as New York's "most forbidden quarters."[21]

Toward the end of the nineteenth century, the sense of danger and the intensity of enmity regarding Chinatown began to subside, replaced by growing curiosity because the perceived threat of the Chinese had been curbed and controlled. The various exclusion measures, starting with the Chinese Exclusion Act (1882), had virtually shut the door on Chinese immigration. Showing the effect of such measures, in 1890 the Chinese population in the United States started its long downturn. In 1904, when Congress made Chinese exclusion a permanent policy, even the notoriously anti-Chinese Democratic Party in California felt—for the first time in its history—no need to mention the Chinese issue in its platform.[22] The anti-Chinese forces simply cleansed Chinese settlements from the open space of small-town America. Now safely contained in the confines of a few urban blocks in major cities, the Chinese community became a pleasurable site and a tourist destination for those eager and curious to see and taste the Orient.

America's curiosity about China was not a new development and had often associated Chinatown with China and all things oriental since the early 1850s.[23] For Easterners, in particular, Chinatown represented a unique feature of the American West before its creation in East Coast cities. A. W. Loomis suggested in 1868 that people would learn about how the Chinese lived "without the trouble and expense of a voyage by sea" by visiting Chinese stores and restaurants in California.[24] During their visit to San Francisco in 1873, a group of Philadelphians took a tour of Chinatown, which "they regarded as good as a trip to China."[25]

Beginning in the 1880s, there was a new development: Chinatown as a *specimen* of China became its predominant image and social utility. Contemporaries noticed a "remarkable" change: the softening of the popular prejudice again the "once hated and despised" Chinese.[26] San Francisco's Chinatown was the first Chinese settlement to emerge as a significant urban travel destination. From time to time, Chinatown residents would spot VIP visitors. When Rutherford B. Hayes visited the city in 1880—the first U.S. president to do so—

he took a trip to Chinatown. In 1881, a group of "distinguished French visitors" paid a visit to the city's Chinese quarters "under the escort of the Chief of Police."[27] In September 1882, during his stay in San Francisco en route to British Columbia, the Marquis of Lorne, governor-general of Canada, and his wife made a trip to Chinatown, where they watched a performance in a theater for a half hour before heading to the Pen Sen Lan restaurant for Chinese food and tea.[28] Prominent domestic travelers also visited Chinatown. In June 1885, the editor of the *New York Tribune* toured Chinatown, accompanied by members of the city's board of supervisors and "the usual escort of detectives."[29] By the 1890s, as tourism traffic increased, visiting Chinatown was no longer primarily for special occasions (such as the Chinese New Year) but occurred more regularly, and tour guides had replaced police escorts.

In New York, Chinatown tours became a frequent occurrence around the turn of the century. Chinatowns in many other cities, such as Chicago and St. Louis, also witnessed an increase in tourist traffic.

Visitors and tourism promoters now characterized Chinatown as a place for "harmless" entertainment.[30] So harmless, indeed, that taking a Chinatown tour turned into a "constantly growing practice," and sometimes even a family event. A Chinatown sightseer by the name of M. H. Cross wrote to the *New York Times* that "the usual Chinatown tours are interesting and harmless." He noted, "I have taken my wife and daughters and young lady visitors; I have made at least one trip under the guidance of 'Chuck' Connors. I have never seen there anything which a young woman might not properly see."[31] Born George Washington Connors, "Chuck" made a career and became famous by conducting Chinatown "vice tours."[32] His staged scenes brought Chinese vices, which had become proverbial in the media, in front of the bare eyes of his visitors, free of risk.

A passage from a San Francisco city guide of 1897 reveals the stimulatingly paradoxical appeals of Chinatown to white tourists: "If the average citizen of San Francisco were asked to place his finger on that part of his city which is the most attractive to strangers and at the same time the most objectionable to himself, he should be sure to indicate Chinatown."[33]

Objectionable because it had long been regarded as a "vice district."[34] In San Francisco, it was part of the red-light district known as the Barbary Coast, and in San Diego, it was located in a similar neighborhood called the Stingaree.[35] Objectionable, yet "Chinese vice" constituted a major attraction of Chinatown. For many non-Chinese visitors, part of the pleasure and sensation of visiting Chinatown was to experience a sense of superiority, culturally and morally. In their eyes, Chinatown stood in sharp contrast with white society: progress

Pork Chop Suey

Serves 1 or 2

When Chinese restaurants started to venture outside Chinatowns, chop suey became the most famous line of dishes. It remained a synonym of America's Chinese food for decades. However, its origin has been shrouded in mystery. Cooking it can help us better understand this simple and versatile traditional Chinese dish, which has become a quintessential American story.

   2 tbsp cornstarch
   1 tsp sugar
   1 tbsp water
   1 tbsp rice wine
   1 tsp sesame oil
   3 tbsp light soy sauce
   dash of black pepper
   1 lb lean pork, sliced into thin strips
   4 tbsp olive oil
   1 tbsp chopped green onion
   1 clove garlic, minced
   ¼ tsp salt
   3 cups sliced napa cabbage
   4 cups (soy) bean sprouts
   ⅓ cup diced celery
   1 cup shredded carrot
   4 button mushrooms, cut into wedges
   ½ cup chicken broth

Mix the cornstarch, sugar, water, rice wine, sesame oil, soy sauce, and black pepper in a bowl. Add the pork and marinate for 1 hour. Heat 2 tbsp olive oil in a wok or nonstick frying pan, and add the green onion and garlic. Stir for about 10 seconds.

Add the marinated pork. Stir until cooked. Transfer it to a clean container and set aside. Heat the remaining 2 tbsp olive oil, and add the salt and then the cabbage, bean sprouts, celery, carrot, and mushrooms. Stir for 2 minutes or until almost cooked. Put the pork back in the wok and add the chicken stock. Stir thoroughly and bring to a boil.

versus stagnation, vice versus morality, dirtiness versus hygiene, and paganism versus Christianity. A French visitor to Chinatown put it bluntly in 1880: "We have seen to night what we have never seen before, and what we hope never to see again."[36] Clearly, touring Chinatown gave some visitors a feeling of superiority.[37] For this purpose, Chinese scenes or "mini -Chinatowns" were staged by the budding tourism industry not just in New York but also in other cities like San Francisco to magnify the moral inferiority of the Chinese. In 1910, New York City closed one such make-believe Chinatown that had long been on Doyers Street when it became too unsanitary.[38] Nonetheless, the fake opium den continued to exist there for many years.

We can easily envision the cultural and moral superiority that many white visitors to Chinatown felt when riding at night in hay wagons and listening to white tour guides like Chuck Connors, known then as the "mayor of Chinatown," who declared that "these poor people are slaves to the opium habit and whether you came here or not to see them they would have spent this night smoking opium just as you see them doing it now."[39] White middle-class tourists in St. Louis also took such tours to the Hop Alley Chinatown. One tour on the night of January 4, 1904, included three couples and two single women. Like Chinatown sightseers elsewhere, they visited an opium den. Then they went to a Chinese restaurant, "where tea and chop suey were served."[40]

In St. Louis and other major cities, evidently, vice was not the whole story behind the Chinatown tourism boom. Chinese food was one of the standard features of a "usual" Chinatown tour. Together with the temples, the theater, fake opium dens, and souvenir shops, Chinese restaurants played a critical role in supporting Chinatown's tourism-oriented economy during the first half of the twentieth century, a role that is yet to be fully researched.[41]

Chinese restaurants represented an important tourist attraction, as the *Washington Post* observed in 1902: "The person who sets out to see sights of the Capital and fails to visit the Chinese restaurants misses one of the features of the city."[42] "Of all the places in Chinatown," a newspaper report of New York's Chinese settlement noted as early as 1888, "the most interesting are the restaurants."[43] Dining establishments were important for four reasons. First, they were extremely noticeable, visually and olfactorily. Second, they were less controversial than some other attractions, such as opium dens, which met strong objections among both Chinese and whites. Third, among all Chinatown attractions, restaurants were the most important generators of revenue as well as jobs. Peter Kwong reported in 1987 that fifteen thousand people worked in the 450 restaurants in New York's Chinatown.[44] To this day, according to a study of Chinese restaurant workers, restaurants are the largest employer of Chinese immigrants across the nation.[45] And fourth, restaurants have been the most enduring features of Chinatown. Over the years, the opium dens have long faded away, and tourists' interest in the temples, the theater, and even the shops has ostensibly waned, but the appeal of Chinese food has remained high. Even in the early years, many equated Chinese food with Chinatown. Helen Worden remarked in 1933, "If you prefer to bring Chinatown to your door, call either Mr. Chin or Mr. Lee at Chelsea 3-6840. They will deliver to your apartment for $3.00 a gallon some of the best chow mein I have eaten. This will serve sixteen people."[46]

In cities without a substantial Chinese community, Chinese restaurants themselves functioned as a tourist attraction. Craig Claiborne, one of the most famous American culinary experts, grew up during the Great Depression in Mississippi, where "anyone's idea of excitement and genuine adventure was a trip to a big town like Birmingham or Memphis." In the 1970s, he recalled his first trip to Birmingham when he was seven or eight years old: "[T]he only thing I do remember about that trip" was "being taken to a Chinese restaurant. There were hanging Chinese lanterns and foreign waiters and real Chinese china and chopsticks and very hot and exotic tea."[47]

Nonetheless, the popular interest in Chinese food was not a mere by-product of tourist curiosity about the exotic Orient. Otherwise, most Chinese restaurants would have stayed inside Chinatown, where visitors could also experience other exotic elements of Chinese culture, such as groceries, fish markets, and storefront shops. Instead, Chinese restaurateurs marched en masse to non-Chinese neighborhoods and communities. More than just a change in taste, the spread of Chinese food also signaled a profound transformation in lifestyle and the beginning of mass consumption in the realm of food. Accompanying an increasing desire for travel, more and more people coveted the convenience and luxury of having their meals cooked and served by others. As a result, average Americans' expenditure on dining out also began to grow steadily and visibly around the turn of the century.[48]

Popularizing the dining-out experience, the ascent of Chinese food marked a significant domestic expansion of the empire of mass consumption. Richard Pillsbury regards fast food as the "first class of food" produced and consumed outside the home.[49] But Chinese food is actually more deserving of this dubious honor. It is also the longest-lasting type of food for mass consumption at a national level. Representing a comparable case are the American diners, which appeared in the late nineteenth century and were also independent operations.[50]

During their prime in the 1940s, there were as many as six thousand diners in the country. But diners were mainly regional phenomena, concentrated in the Northeast, while Chinese restaurants multiplied from coast to coast. The diners began their decline in the 1970s, while the number of Chinese restaurants has continued to grow, dueling with American fast-food outlets and eclipsing even McDonald's in number. Meals cooked and served by others had been an exclusive privilege enjoyed only by the social elites. Chinese food played a significant role in liberating this privilege from the monopoly of the wealth by turning dining-out into a universally accessible experience in cities across the nation.

6

THE MAKERS OF AMERICAN CHINESE FOOD

Panda Drive in Huntington Beach was one of the first independently owned drive-through Chinese restaurants in California. After its brief initial success, however, business slid sharply. In the summer of 2004, its owner invited me to work with her to revamp the establishment. But the efforts to bring customers back were too late, and the restaurant eventually folded along with an otherwise refreshing food-business concept. I learned an important lesson firsthand: the creation of a successful restaurant hinges on the negotiations between the restaurateur and the clientele, and small operation restaurants, in particular, must provide the kind of food and service that corresponds to the taste and lifestyle of the consumers. This lesson also helped me better understand the development of early Chinese restaurants, which were invariably small operations. In order to fully understand the making of Chinese food and its meaning, I investigate key players in the process: Chinese American food providers and their non-Chinese clientele.

The mushrooming of Chinese restaurants resulted from the strenuous efforts of Chinese Americans in promoting their food. At the same time, such restaurants would not have developed so extensively without the patronage of non-Chinese customers. While educating these new patrons about unfamiliar Chinese ingredients and utensils, Chinese restaurant workers also labored tirelessly and deliberately to accommodate and satisfy those patrons' needs and preferences. The American Chinese food that rose to prominence in turn-of-the-century mainstream markets was shaped by the interplay between Chinese restaurant owners and their non-Chinese consumers.

Before discussing Chinese American players, we must look at several groups—the so-called slummers, African Americans, and Jews—who provided an indispensible customer base for the expanding Chinese restaurants. The social status of those three groups helps to further illustrate the point I made in chapter 2: Chinese Americans played an important role in extending the reach and meaning of American abundance and safeguarding the principle of democracy in the realm of consumption.

A TRULY DEMOCRATIC DEVELOPMENT

The making of American Chinese food was indeed a democratic process in the marketplace, and its spread was one of the most successful grassroots marketing stories in American history. This is a story of the business ingenuity of enterprising individual Chinese restaurateurs and food workers. Without a well-organized trade association or sales force, they turned Chinese food from a disdained and unfamiliar object to one of the most recognizable commodities in the budding mass-consumption market.

Moreover, promoting Chinese food often entailed combating racial prejudice. In popularizing their cuisine, then, Chinese Americans also defended their culture and freedom, thus advancing American political democracy.

The rising Chinese restaurants themselves constituted a democratizing force in the realm of public food consumption. In bringing Chinese food to the non-Chinese palate, they also served to fulfill the empire's promises of a better lifestyle by providing meal services to the masses. If the Chinese domestic cooks helped to free white middle-class women from kitchen chores, now the expanding Chinese restaurants offered similar personal services to the less privileged, whose patronage, in turn, provided the critical support for their expansion.

Andrew P. Haley points out that it "was not until the end of the nineteenth century that the upper class's influence over dining for pleasure was challenged."[1] By making restaurants accessible, the multiplying Chinese establishments fundamentally shook the old regime in gastronomy. Haley focuses on the middle class. Yet those Chinatown-touring members of the white middle class, whom scholars like Dean MacCannell associate with the ascent of mass tourism in this period, deserve only partial credit for the rise of Chinese food. They were more likely to have visited Chinatown as tour-wagon sightseers than as regular patrons at its restaurants. Frequenting Chinese dining places with much greater regularity—especially the non-showcase establishments—were the socially and racially underprivileged groups, including marginalized whites, the working class, immigrants, and racial minorities. In New York, for example, the ordinary Chinese restaurants were "patronized by the laboring classes and outlaws, and quite largely by the lower classes of white people who visit Chinatown for vicious purposes or mere curiosity."[2] Noting the similar class backgrounds of Chinese restaurant-goers, the New York *Sun* reported that Chinatown "everywhere draws the very lowest of the white population towards the haunts of race considered inferior." It also pointed out that many such whites lived on the fringes of Chinatown; they went at night to shop in the stores, visit the gambling houses, and "feast at the restaurants."[3]

Such groups, who could not afford to join the more affluent crowd in globe-trotting or lavish dining activities, found Chinatown and Chinese restaurants a convenient and exotic enough site for a leisure outing. For the elite of the country, French food was the best and most desired.[4] The less fortunate, meanwhile, discovered Chinese food. As the *New York Tribune* explained in 1901, "So many, who, while possessed of a small share of this world's goods, still affect 'sportiness' frequent the restaurant for its cheapness and grow to enjoyed the highly flavored dishes."[5] Eating in a Chinese restaurant thus became a memorable adventure. Arthur Chapman wrote in 1921 that "a meal of chop suey in New York's Chinatown was an outstanding event. The thrill of forbidden surroundings and the taste of strange food combined to make an experience to be talked of as one of the real ventures to be found in New York."[6] In Chinatown and Chinese restaurants, non-middle-class groups found out that both travel to exotic cultural sites and the freedom from having to cook their own meals did not necessarily have to be the exclusive domains of the privileged. In Chinese restaurants, socially respectable guests sometimes found themselves among those "not far removed from the hobo class." For these reasons, consuming Chinese food was a "truly democratic" experience, as the *Washington Times* remarked in 1903.[7]

For those who faced strong racial and cultural prejudice in society, socially and economically accessible Chinese restaurants provided not only an opportunity to eat out but also a space in which to socialize. Here, rebellious youth rendezvoused in defiance of traditional values and authorities, and Jews found a place to hang out on Christmas and indulge in "their love of discussion and debate" over what to select from the long menu.[8]

Such non-Chinese customers, in turn, extended Chinese food's customer base far beyond the numerical constraints of the dwindling Chinese community, creating a vital condition for its explosive multiplication. Moreover, their preferences significantly predicated the nature of Chinese food that prevailed in non-Chinese neighborhoods.

THE SLUMMERS

Among the conspicuous Chinese-restaurant customers in the early years were the "slummers," adventurous and rebellious city youth. Hungry for amusement and for social space, they turned slumming into a noticeable "trade" in the nascent Chinatown in Manhattan beginning in the late 1880s.[9] For these young men and women, roaming Chinatown's streets "without proper escort" was part of the excitement that came from evading the police, who would drive them away or even arrest them.[10] Slummers frequented Chinese restaurants so often that some believed that "wickedness in New York thrives luxuriantly in an atmosphere of stewed chicken, bamboo sprouts and mushrooms."[11] On April 14, 1918, New York police conducted an early-morning massive raid of thirty chop suey places, rounding up some two thousand people and taking three hundred of them to the police station. At least fifty of these youths on average were in each restaurant, showing how popular Chinese restaurants were among such customers. The district attorney's office claimed that it had received one hundred letters from parents complaining that "their daughters have been lured to chop suey houses."[12] In 1918, news of such arrests of "girls from 14 to 20 years in the tenderloin cafes, chop suey joints, and back rooms of saloons" reached the town of St. Joseph, Missouri. Disapproving of the behavior of such young women, the *St. Joseph Observer* stated that "girls ought to be obliged to be at home at 10 P.M.," suggesting that it was "necessary to spank a girl for deliberate lies."[13]

These insubordinate youths went to Chinatown restaurants to eat and, more important, to cultivate a social space for themselves. In Chicago, for example, "young girls with braids down their backs daily are escorted into" many chop suey joints "by boys wearing their first long trousers," reported the *Chicago Tribune* in 1910.[14] And this, of course, made chop suey restaurants a target for the police chief and the health commissioner. Young white women also frequented Chinese restaurants in Philadelphia early in the twentieth century. In 1916, Philadelphia police arrested six girls in a Chinese restaurant, accusing them of using heroin.[15] The same year, a New York high-school teacher on a trip to Philadelphia went to a Chinese restaurant, where he saw about a dozen girls.[16] Such young females apparently had a regular presence in Chinese restaurants. By

1903, slumming had become a fad in Washington, D.C., as the *Washington Times* reported that "a visit to a Chinese restaurant is looked upon as an excursion into Bohemia, a taste of slumming."[17]

This trend also found its way into small cities, such as Portland, Maine, where in June 1908 the police searched a newly opened Chinese restaurant, the Canton Low, to look for a young and unescorted white girl. Instead of finding the girl, the police saw four Chinese laundrymen and arrested two on charges of opium smoking.[18] By the end of the nineteenth century, similar kinds of customers frequented Chinese restaurants in Boston, prompting attempts to close these dining businesses after midnight or even "for good."[19]

Part of the appeal of Chinese restaurants to the slummers and the like is that they stayed open late into the night. A newspaper report of Chinese restaurants in Philadelphia in 1890 stated that "they flourish in their chief glory after night falls, and from dark until two o'clock in the morning the flavor of Chinese hot soup fills the air."[20] In the many Chinese chop suey joints in Brooklyn at the beginning of the twentieth century, "there is nothing doing until after midnight."[21] The Chinese restaurants in Washington, D.C., also did most of their business in the evening and at night. A report by the police chief of Los Angeles in 1906 indicated that "theatrical and sporting people" and other "night owls" had developed a "remarkable hunger for chop suey."[22] In San Francisco, Chinese restaurants had long been known to stay open late. These restaurants were also filled with noise from customers chatting and sometimes from the loud music played.

The late-night hours and loud noise in Chinese restaurants helped to create an inviting "free and easy" setting not only for rebellious youngsters. In New York City, these establishments also attracted the so-called bohemians, "as well as a goodly share of class below the lowest grades of the city's many graded Bohemia," in the words of the *New York Tribune*.[23] Rerunning the same report, newspapers in California announced in headlines that "Chopstick Dinner" was a fad.[24] These bohemians constituted a loyal clientele who not only dined in Chinese restaurants but also ordered takeout. "Few Bohemian gatherings are complete without a pail of chop suey, brought, fresh and hot, from Chinatown," declared the *New York Tribune* in 1903.[25]

Such visitors did not always make good customers, though. In 1898, two boys tried to run away without paying after eating dinner at a Chinese restaurant in Sacramento.[26] Two years later at another Sacramento Chinese restaurant, one William Donnelly showed up looking penniless. When asked to pay in advance, he broke windows and beat the Chinese waiter. Finding him guilty, a white judge also declared that "any white man who would patronize a Chinese restaurant ought to be confined in jail on general principles."[27]

If the judge's principles were to be followed, American cities would soon have run out of jail space because the popularity of Chinese food continued to grow among whites. It also caught on among non-white groups, most notably African Americans, and Jews. Patronage of Chinese restaurants by rebellious youth and bohemians involved a relatively limited number of people and was confined largely to Chinatown in major cities. And this represented a trend with a limited life span. Slumming in New York, for example, tapered off by the late 1910s and early 1920s, as police crackdowns intensified. In 1918, the New York *Sun* already referred to its heyday as the "old slumming days."[28] African Americans and Jews, by comparison, created a much bigger and far more sustainable customer base for Chinese food.

THE AFRICAN AMERICAN CONNECTION

African Americans already had established a noticeable presence in Chinese restaurants by the beginning of the twentieth century. The *New York Tribune* reported in 1901 that they frequented the city's Chinese dining establishments "in disproportionately large numbers." It went on, "They seem to like the Chinese, and, indeed, the noise in the kitchen reminds one of the similar condition of southern kitchens under negro management."[29]

The ambience was not the only reason that attracted them to the Chinese restaurant; it was one of the few public places that welcomed them. Racial and ethnic discrimination at public institutions like restaurants was rampant throughout the United States at this time. In response to such prejudice, in 1895 New York became one of the first states to enact a civil rights law, which tried to protect equal access to such places as "inns, restaurants, hotels, eating-houses."[30] The law targeted, in particular, hotels and restaurants that usually closed their doors to Jews and African Americans. But that law had little substantive effect: until its amendment in 1913, victims of discrimination had to show proof of damage in court.[31]

White customers brought their prejudicial attitudes to Chinese restaurants. Quite often, such customers would walk away at the sight of African Americans dining in a Chinese restaurant. In order to keep their white patrons, sometimes snobbish Chinese restaurateurs put their African American customers in an "inconspicuous corner" with little or no service; a few even refused to welcome them altogether.[32] In 1918, a lawsuit was filed against the proprietor of a Chinese restaurant in Worcester, Massachusetts, for its refusal to serve African Americans in the main dining room.[33] Some Chinese discriminated against African Americans in other ways as well. For example, in 1904 Suey Pang, the owner of a chop suey restaurant on Sixth Avenue in New York, attempted to charge an African American real-estate agent named W. Nathaniel Walker $2.50 for a 25-cent chop suey. When Walker insisted on being served, Pang, who was waiting on two white messenger boys, called him a nigger and hit him with a club. The magistrate, who fined Pang $5, also reminded him of his racial position. "As a Chinaman," he scolded the Chinese man, "you are scarcely a fit person to set yourself up as a judge between respectable colored business men and white messenger boys."[34]

But overall, a close relationship evolved between Chinese food and African Americans. In St. Louis, African Americans were among the regular "devotees" of Hop Alley, where Chinese restaurants and other businesses clustered.[35] The African American–Chinese food connection persisted in subsequent decades in St. Louis as well as elsewhere.[36]

In some cities, Chinese restaurateurs took their restaurants to African American communities, such as Harlem, where the presence of Chinese food increased visibly in the early twentieth century. Wallace Thurman, a well-known Harlem Renaissance novelist, wrote in 1927 that "Negroes seem to have a penchant for Chinese food—there are innumerable Chinese restaurants all over Harlem."[37]

The long and sometimes ambivalent relationship between Chinese food and African American communities remains palpable in St. Louis. This was first brought to my attention by Malcolm Gay, an energetic and insightful reporter for the *River Front Times* of St. Louis. He called me in 2006 to discuss an article that he was researching on the chop suey houses in St. Louis. From my conversations with him and the article he published subsequently, I learned that there are still forty or fifty such restaurants in St. Louis, almost all exclusively in African American communities. Even though African Americans by and large support Chinese restaurants, they also harbor discernible resentment to the Chinese, seeing them as non-contributing outsiders. In the early twentieth-first century in St. Louis, a sign inside a now-closed African American–owned tavern, Gino's Lounge, reveals such resentments: "No Chinese food."

The chop suey joints that have persisted in St. Louis's African American neighborhoods not merely are a reminder of Chinese food's initial popularity among the underprivileged but also bear evidence of the transformation that Chinese food has gone through over time. Many now offer a locally famous new product: the St. Paul sandwich. "Comprising an egg foo young patty, slice of tomato, pickle and iceberg lettuce sandwiched between two slices of mayonnaise-laden white bread," it is hardly a direct gastronomical offspring of chop suey.[38] And the face of the city's Chinese community has also changed. When I visited St. Louis in 2003, the city's Hop Alley Chinatown was long gone. A local Chinese couple, Mr. and Mrs. Law, took me to Olive Street, where a cluster of food businesses, including several Chinese restaurants, had shown up. On Saturdays and Sundays, a large number of Chinese customers come for restaurant dining and grocery shopping, turning the usually quiet street into a busy weekend Chinatown.

The itinerary of first-time visitors to the United States usually includes New York, the heart of Western capitalism, whose skyscrapers have symbolized American material abundance for more than a century. But those who have already been to New York and would like to take an in-depth look at this country should also pay a visit to Detroit. Its development has been closely pegged with profound transformative moments in the evolution of the United States into an empire. Detroit's rapid growth beginning in the late nineteenth century coincided with America's expansion in manufacturing and global power. It then evolved into the heart and soul of the once-storied American automobile industry, which radically transformed American life and redefined the American dream in the twentieth century. A long and steady decline has now turned it into what *Harper's* characterized in 2009 as "the wreck of the America dream."[39] Besides its glorious history, there is still another good reason to go there: an abundance of Chinese restaurants in African American neighborhoods.

"If, like me, you're a Detroit native who recently went home to find out what went wrong, your first instinct is to weep," wrote Daniel Okrent in 2009.[40] I, too, found the sight of pervasive urban decay profoundly disheartening when I spent a few days in Detroit in 2011, driving through various neighborhoods and strolling through the streets. But if, like me, you are searching for evidence of African Americans' lasting connection with Chinese food, you will not be disappointed in Detroit.

Unlike San Francisco, New York, and Chicago, Detroit is not particularly known for its Chinese food, but Chinese food in that city has a long history. Before its demolition in the 1950s, Detroit's Chinatown boasted such famous restaurants as Henry Yee's Forbidden City.[41] The New Life Chop Suey restaurant at 13991 Gratiot Avenue made the list of the Chinese establishments that the cookbook writer Wallace Yee Hong recommended in the early 1950s.[42] By the 1920s, Chinese food had extended beyond Detroit's Chinatown. As evidence of the popularity of Chinese cooking in the city, a Korean American from Hawaii, Yang Yi Jhung, opened a chop suey and chow mein wholesale business in Detroit.[43]

Syd Pollock, the owner and promoter of the old Indianapolis-Cincinnati Clowns, took his son Alan to their "favorite Chinese restaurant" in downtown Detroit in the summer of 1953 when the African American touring baseball team played there.[44] Several of the African American customers I interviewed in Detroit also indicated that they had been regularly eating Chinese food for many years. Inside the Great Wall Chinese restaurant, a stand-alone structure on the edge of downtown, a cab driver in his late fifties told me while waiting for his food, "I cannot even remember when I first started going to Chinese restaurants. It was a long time ago." Another longtime regular consumer of Chinese food is a retired policeman, who has lived in Detroit for many years after emigrating from Jamaica.

In spite of their physical proximity, cultural and class differences have erected a palpable wall separating African American consumers from their Chinese-food providers. The Great Wall had a dining area, but it was very small, with only a couple of tables, and none of the African American customers sat down to eat or chatted with the chef and waitress during my stay there. Several other Chinese restaurants—such as Paradise Chop Suey on Grand River Avenue, a family business of more than thirty years—that served African American consumers had no chairs and no tables. Golden Bowl Chop Suey on McNichols Road West is an even more extreme example, where all the customers I observed were African American. Bearing little resemblance to our conventional concept of a restaurant, its storefront is fortified with heavy, black, iron bars. Inside, customers place their orders and take their food through a window. Such limited contact between operators of Chinese-food places and their patrons helps to explain why some African Americans feel that Chinese restaurants are in their community but are not part of it. Some Chinese restaurant workers do not identify with the community either. The chef in one restaurant, an illegal immigrant who had paid $50,000 for his voyage from Changle County in Fujian Province, referred to his African American customers derogatively as "black ghosts" (*heigui*).[45]

Standing in sharp contrast with chop suey places serving African Americans are Chinese restaurants in white communities in suburban cities. One such city is Taylor, about eighteen miles from Detroit, named after President Zachary

Taylor, whose 1850 funeral parade in San Francisco included Chinese participants. Eighty-seven percent of Taylor's population is white, according to 2010 federal census data; by comparison, Detroit's population is almost 83 percent African American.[46] In Taylor's Chinese restaurants like Panda Gardens on Telegraph Road, a large full-service establishment, most of the customers are white. During my lunch at this restaurant, some customers were engaged in conversations with the waitresses, and they appeared to know each other quite well. The restaurant also offers a long list of alcoholic beverages, including wines, beers, and cocktails. The differences in terms of the physical environment, service style, and range of foods between the Chinese restaurant in suburbia and its counterpart in African American communities reminds us that American Chinese food was shaped by negotiated interactions between restaurant operators and their varied consumers.

We have yet to fully explore the depth and extent of the African American–Chinese food connection. Evidence suggests that in cities across the country in the first half of the twentieth century, African Americans constituted a significant portion of Chinese restaurants' customer base. In 1930s Philadelphia, for example, it was estimated that African Americans accounted for 60 percent of the consumers at the Chinese restaurants.[47]

Eastern European Jews were another group that patronized Chinese restaurants in large numbers. Compared with the African American case, the Jewish connection to Chinese food is more clearly documented—and it has been a strong and persistent relationship.

A JEWISH LOVE AFFAIR

More than ten years ago, a close Jewish friend of mine went to Europe on a family vacation, and before long, one of his boys wanted to return home to southern California because he missed the Chinese food there. This story reveals changes in both American cultural identity and the meaning of American Chinese food; it also reminds us of the long association between Chinese food and American Jews. A saga in cultural crossing, the Jewish–Chinese food connection is an important chapter in the development of American Chinese food.

A large exodus of Jews from eastern Europe started in the late nineteenth century. From 1880 to 1920, 2.5 million eastern European Jews left Europe, and probably as many as 90 percent of them emigrated to the United States.[48] Many settled in New York, where the Jewish population increased from 80,000 in 1880 to 1.25 million—or more than 25 percent of the city's population—in 1910.[49] By the end of the nineteenth century, going to Chinese restaurants had become a routine for many Jewish families. In 1899, the New York–based magazine *American Hebrew* warned that the food served in Chinese restaurants and food places in basements and stores was perhaps not as kosher as it claimed to be.[50] But the trend of patronizing Chinese restaurants continued to grow. In 1928, an article in *Der Tog*, a Yiddish daily published in New York, characterized that trend as "the war between chop suey and gefillte fish."[51] The war was won by Chinese-food lovers, who sustained the practice over the decades, turning it into a great Jewish American tradition.

For example, in the 1920s Patricia Volk's grandmother took her mother to a Chinese restaurant on West 181st Street regularly on Thursdays when the family housekeeper had the day off.[52] Vicky, a second-generation Jewish American born to immigrant parents from Romania, grew up in the Bronx in the 1930s. She remembers going to Chinese restaurants as a special treat, an adventure, and a rebellion: "We would go to have Chinese food, and then go to the movies afterwards . . . on Saturdays, Saturday afternoon. And then, as we got a little older, in the late teens when there were periods of rebellion, to show that we were becoming sophisticated, we would eat shrimp in Chinese food."[53] Sandye is another Jewish woman from the Bronx, where she grew up in a Jewish neighborhood during the 1940s and 1950s. Her parents took her to a Chinese restaurant in her neighborhood once a month, usually on Sundays. For her and the Jews she knew as a child, Chinese cuisine was "the most popular, acceptable non-Jewish food."[54] She loved Chinese food so much that her mother said jokingly that she had a Chinese great-grandmother. When she was in college and started dating, she and her fiancé, Bruce, would go to Chinatown for more authentic Chinese food.[55]

The Jewish–Chinese food connection became a family tradition and was passed on through generations. During the long courtship of Patricia Volk's parents, they dined in Chinese restaurants many times. When Volk was seven, it became a regular three-generation family event to make Sunday dinner trips to the old Ruby Foo's on West Fifty-second Street, a restaurant that she still remembers in the early twenty-first century. When she was old enough, she went to Chinese restaurants with her kosher-keeping paternal grandmother, who "would put on sunglasses and hat and look both ways."

Gradually, more and more Jews took Chinese food home—not just takeouts from restaurants but also ingredients for making it in their own kitchens. Chinese cooking quietly found its way into cookbooks written by Jews. Perhaps the most famous Jewish cookbook author was Lizzie Black Kander, a native of Milwaukee. In 1896, she founded the Settlement House, where she offered popular cooking classes to Jewish immigrants. In 1901, she published *The "Settlement" Cook Book*, written as a textbook for her classes, and this extremely popular cookbook includes a chop suey recipe.[56] Betty Dean's *The New Jewish Cook Book* (1947) shows a noticeable Chinese flavor and offers chicken chop suey recipes and a whole section on soybean dishes.[57] The *Rochester Hadassah Cook Book* (1976), compiled by a group of Jewish women in Rochester, New York, to memorialize their community, contains recipes like "easy chop suey."[58] Many Jews cooked Chinese food at home, as Sandye did regularly—so regularly that, she said in an interview, her son must have believed that Chinese food was part of the Jewish tradition as a child. Indeed, eating Chinese has become an important tradition by Jewish Americans in many different cities.

Several Jewish informants and friends who grew up or lived in other cities—such as Chicago, Philadelphia, and Los Angeles—told me that they ate Chinese food on a regular basis. It is also a practice that Jews in small towns experienced. My good friend Richard, an Orange County Jewish American who does business with China, vividly remembers going to the Paradise Chinese restaurant while he was growing up in Asheville, North Carolina, in the 1960s and 1970s. In the summer of 2012, he recalled his past food experience over lunch: "The food there was not as good as here, but it was the only Chinese restaurant in town." Allon came from a lower-middle-class family, and his father never went beyond the seventh grade. Growing up in Cleveland Heights in the 1930s and early 1940s before he attended Yale, Allon regularly went to his favorite Chinese restaurant. He gave two reasons for his passion about Chinese food: it is cheap and delicious.

Long-standing interest and curiosity have led many Jews to travel to China in search of culinary authenticity in the years since Richard Nixon's visit to China in 1972. The decades-old family tradition of dining in Chinese restaurants made Patricia Volk wonder what food was like in China. On a trip there, she even brought a menu from a Sichuan restaurant in New York with her, only to discover that the food in China did not bear much resemblance to the fare in her local Chinese establishment.

Sandye and Bruce went to Hong Kong in the 1960s and to China in the 1980s, with curiosity about food in China. But when she first got to Beijing, she was somewhat disappointed because "it did not smell like wonton soup and laundry." In the Bronx neighborhood where she spent much of her childhood, there was a Chinese laundry on Tremont Avenue, not far from the Chinese restaurant she frequented. It was also the smell that she associates with China-town, which, she said, "still gives me a feeling of comfort and belonging."[59]

This close connection with Chinese food has certainly become part of the Jewish American folklore. Vicky has lived in southern California for many years with her husband, Milt, who served in the U.S. Army Air Forces in China during World War II. A warm and funny man, he was also an avid lover of Chinese food. In the early 1990s, Vicky and Milt invited me to give a talk in their community about Chinese food and helped me to get acquainted with the local gastronomical landscape. One day, when we were sitting in a Chinese restaurant in Westminster in southern California, he said to me: "The Jewish calendar goes back to about 5,700 years ago, and the Chinese calendar goes back to about 4,600 years ago. Do you know what that means?" Before I had time to respond, he went on with a big smile, "It means the Jews went without Chinese food for more than 1,000 years." In time, I realized that this is a popular Jewish tale told on various occasions—in newspaper stories, Talmud classes, scholarly publications, and dinner conversations.[60]

The wide circulation of similar stories and jokes about the Jewish–Chinese food connection reveals and reinforces its importance in Jewish American identity. People who have watched the film *My Favorite Year* (1982) might remember a line that the protagonist, a young Jewish writer, said to his non-Jewish date: "Katherine, Jews know two things: suffering, and where to find great Chinese food." As Matthew Goodman recalled in 1999, Billy Crystal, a Jewish native of Long Beach, New York, once said to the host of a late-night talk show: "I'll tell you, the other night I was feeling Jewish. I mean really Jewish. You know how Jewish I felt?" Crystal explained, "I ordered takeout Chinese food—that's how Jewish I felt."[61] The popular comedy-drama television series, *Gilmore Girls*, which debuted early in 2000, had an episode called "Jews and Chinese Food."

Around the end of 2011, two Jewish friends alerted me to a handwritten message on a photographed sign posted online. It reads: "The Chinese Rest. Assoc. of the United States would like to extend our thanks to The Jewish People. We do not completely understand your dietary customs. . . . But we are proud and grateful that your GOD insists you eat our food on Christmas." Through e-mail, the message reached Stuart Schoffman, a fellow of the Shalom Hartman Institute and the editor of *Havruta: A Journal of Jewish Conversation*, who realized that it was a cartoon by the writer David Mamet. Nevertheless, as Schoffman writes, "this one touches the soul, pierces to the heart of the matter, and also tickles the taste buds, at a critical moment in Jewish history."[62]

Kung Pao (Gongbao) Chicken

Serves 4

Turn-of-the-twentieth-century American Chinese food was shaped by the negotiation between Chinese restaurant owners and their customers. It has continued to evolve. Today, Kung Pao has replaced chop suey as the most popular line of dishes on restaurant menus. It is Sichuan in origin and is allegedly named after a Sichuan governor in late Qing: Ding Baozhen, whose title was Gongbao (Palace Guardian).* Kung Pao chicken is the most popular among all Kung Pao dishes.[†]

>   2 lbs boneless and skinless chicken breast, cut into ¼-inch cubes
>   2½ tbsp soy sauce
>   4 tbsp cornstarch
>   2 tbsp water
>   2 tbsp rice wine
>   2 tbsp salad oil
>   12 dried red chili peppers
>   several dashes ground Sichuan peppercorn
>   1 garlic clove, thinly sliced
>   1 tsp chopped green onion
>   3 slices of fresh ginger
>   ½ cup roasted unsalted peanuts
>   3 tbsp bean sauce (*doubanjiang*)[‡]
>   1 tsp sugar

Marinate the chicken in the mixed soy sauce, cornstarch, water, and rice wine for 1 hour. Heat the oil in a wok on high heat. Add the chili peppers, ground peppercorn, garlic, green onion, and ginger. Stir for 20 seconds without burning them. Add the marinated chicken and stir until the meat is almost cooked. Add the peanuts, bean sauce, and sugar. Stir to thoroughly mix for 2 to 3 minutes without overcooking the meat.

---

*Wu Zhenge "Gongbao Ji Ding Tan Yuan" (Exploring the Origins of Gongbao Chicken), *Zhongguo Shi Pin* (*China Food*) 6 (1986): 38–39.

[†]Buwei Yang Chao called this dish "chicken cubelets" in *How to Cook and Eat in Chinese* (New York: Day, 1945).

[‡]Use Pixian *doubanjiang* if possible.

Chinese food has become an important part of Jewish American consciousness, and it has grown to be an integral element of the Jewish American community, as Chinese restaurants followed the Jews to uptown neighborhoods, to the boroughs, and to the suburbs. Gaye Tuchman and Harry Gene Levine pointed out in a well-researched and thoughtful article, "In most Jewish neighborhoods, Chinese restaurants outnumber Jewish delis. In most non-Chinese ethnic neighborhoods, the Chinese restaurants tend to be small and modest or simply store fronts selling only take-out food. But neighborhoods with many Jews (or Chinese or Korean) possess more Chinese restaurants and more large fancy ones."[63] Many Jews know this from their own experiences. Eleanor, who went to Chinese restaurants once a week while growing up in the 1930s in New York, said to me in 2000, "You can tell whether it is a Jewish neighborhood or not by the number of Chinese restaurants."[64]

The deep and lasting relationship between Chinese food and Jews was forged by a multitude of factors. Various people point to similarities between Chinese and Jewish cooking. Mimi Sheraton, the former *New York Times* food critic, noted "a shared taste for chicken soup, tea and dishes seasoned with garlic, celery and onion."[65] Sandye remembers that her mother cooked a lot of chicken. And Chinese food, like kosher cooking, does not "mix meat with milk."[66] But it also features pork and shellfish—early operators of Chinese restaurants were seafood-loving Cantonese. These were unfamiliar, forbidden, and even repulsive foods to the Jewish palate, including that of many non-kosher Jews. Tuchman and Levine mention another factor: eastern European Jews had the motivation and skills to "explore and adapt to their new urban environment."[67] But, again, this alone does not sufficiently explain why Jews chose Chinese instead of other cuisines, such as French, which appeared excitingly exotic to several of my informants.

The most fundamental motivation for eastern European Jews to eat in Chinese restaurants stemmed from their desire to be American.[68] This is not simply because Chinese food appeared American or cosmopolitan, as Tuchman and Levine have emphasized; it was that Chinese food represented a divergence, often a deliberate one, from traditional Jewish ways. Sandye recalls that her family kept a kosher kitchen, "but somehow you were allowed to go Sunday to the Chinese restaurant and eat a lot of pork." Her father was more concerned about keeping kosher than was her mother. When he did not come home for dinner, her mother would buy non-kosher food, and they would eat out of the bag that contained the food so that the pots, pans, and plates in the house would not be polluted. At the age of twelve, when she realized the contradiction in this practice, she said to her parents: "It is interesting: our kitchen is kosher but our toilet is not."[69]

More important, going to Chinese restaurants meant a change and improvement in lifestyle, a milestone in the Jews' pursuit of the American dream. As people like Sandye and Vicky remember, going to a Chinese restaurant represented a special event for many Jews in the 1930s and 1940s. In the early twentieth century, dining out became an increasingly imperative part of the white middle-class lifestyle and a very American thing to do in the eyes of the Jews. Eastern European Jews harbored strong aspirations to move up the social ladder and, in fact, achieved the highest rate of upward occupational mobility among all new immigrant groups.[70] It is not surprising that more and more Jews also wanted to live like middle-class Americans and join the expanding American dining-out crowd.

Nonetheless, their options were limited. French food was too expensive, and some found it too rich. By the 1930s, Italian restaurants had entered some Jewish communities, such as Vicky's childhood neighborhood in the Bronx; in addition, Italian food was cheap, like Chinese food in the 1940s and into the 1950s as several informants remembered. But a number of factors caused Chinese food, rather than Italian, to become Jews' chosen ethnic cuisine.

First, with a much larger ethnic consumer base, Italian restaurateurs did not have the same need to branch out as the Chinese did. In 1910, for example, there were more than 340,000 natives of Italy but only 3,904 Chinese immigrants in New York City.[71] And for the small Chinese community, with virtually no other occupational options beyond the few service industries like the laundry business, the budding restaurant industry, which offered better pay than laundry work, looked like a golden opportunity.[72] The Chinese made strenuous and successful efforts to capitalize on the new trend, turning Chinese food into an extremely popular cuisine throughout the nation in spite of a continued decrease in their population. Arthur Chapman noted in 1921 that "in New York City Chinese cooking has made more rapid headway than any other kind—and that despite the lack of increase in the Chinese population here."[73] Chinese restaurants stood as a steady source of employment for Chinese Americans, including newcomers. Even Chinese students, who came to study in American universities from the 1950s to the early 1990s, often worked in Chinese restaurants to help fund their education.

The next three factors are simpler: Chinese restaurants carried much less dairy food; they stayed open on Sundays and Christmas Day; and they had no Christian iconography and no anti-Semitic antagonism.

Another factor is perhaps the most important and complex: Jews could feel "American" in Chinese restaurants more than they could in Italian establishments. The Irish, who faced strong ethnic prejudice on the East Coast, migrated to the West and "whitened" their ethnicity by positioning themselves as the opposing "other" of the racial minorities there, especially the Chinese.[74] The Jews *became* American in Chinese restaurants. They never harbored the same anti-Chinese hostility as did the Irish, and no evidence suggests that large numbers of Jews went to Chinese restaurants as a so-called whitening act. But for many, eating Chinese did indeed represent an acculturating and Americanizing experience. If Chinese food stood as "safe treyf" to Jewish eyes, then Chinese restaurants offered a safe social space.[75] Here Jews could feel secure and American in the presence of the Chinese, who seemed to speak less English and certainly did not resemble white Americans. Alexander Portnoy in Philip Roth's celebrated novel, for example, thought the Chinese in Chinese restaurants saw Jews as white or even "Anglo Saxon."[76]

Besides eating Chinese, Jews in New York wrought their new American identity by being Democrats and Brooklyn Dodgers fans. Compared with the latter two, eating Chinese was a much less pronounced act, especially in the beginning. People like Patricia Volk call the Jewish bond with Chinese food a love affair, but it was kept almost a secret for many years. "Memoirs and autobiographies of the immigrant era made few reference to eating Chinese food," Hasia Diner concludes, likely because it touched on an important Jewish taboo.[77] Equally important, association with the food of a perceived inassimilable people would not advance the image of the Americanness of those eager to settle and succeed in the New World. Thus many Jews kept a discernible mental detachment from the Chinese restaurants and food physically located so close to them. Some referred to eating Chinese as "eating chinks." The phrase did not necessarily constitute a consciously derogative term, as several of my informants recall. But it does reveal an awareness among some Jews of the socioeconomic and cultural distance between them and the Chinese. Moreover, there is little indication that many Jewish diners developed any close personal relationships with Chinese restaurant workers. Among the many Jewish people who have shared with me their Chinese-food experiences, few remember the names of their neighborhood Chinese restaurant or the people who worked there. While it is undoubtedly attributable to the passage of time, this memory lapse also suggests that like the laundry shop nearby, the Chinese restaurant signified little more than a place for affordable and convenient service. Going there represented a desire to become American and middle class rather than to associate with the Chinese.

When I met him in the summer of 2009, Max still remembered his experience working as a Chinese restaurant waiter in a New York Jewish neighborhood during the late 1960s. But it was not a fond memory because he felt as if he had been treated like a robot. The customers seldom had a real conversation with him. "When they needed something, they just waved their index finger at me and said 'give this or that,'" he recalled.

Nevertheless, persistent Jewish support was critical for the rise of Chinese food, especially in East Coast cities, where the number of Chinese restaurants quickly multiplied early in the twentieth century. In the early 1930s, some Chinese knowledgeable about the restaurant business in New York and Philadelphia estimated that Jews accounted for 60 percent of the white clientele at their establishments in the two cities.[78] But the Jewish connection to Chinese food is by no means merely a story of Jews wanting Chinese food. Chinese restaurateurs made extraordinary efforts to make their food available to Jews. They did so by keeping their restaurants open at Christmastime, giving Jews a place to go on the Christian holiday. And they also delivered their food to Jewish neighborhoods and to individual customers. In 1935, Eng Shee Chuck, a Chinese restaurant owner in Newark, New Jersey, did more than that. He and his relatives prepared eighty chow mein dinners and eighty toys with red ribbons. He took the food and toys to the Jewish Children's Hospital, where he told Jewish children ancient Chinese fairy tales.[79]

PROVIDERS OF AMERICAN CHINESE FOOD

Eng Shee Chuck's story reminds us of the creative and effective roles of Chinese Americans in the making of America's Chinese food. Like most successful creators of mass-consumer products, Chinese Americans—food entrepreneurs, workers, and promoters—swiftly responded to emerging consumer demands for a better life and more exotic things to eat, carving out a new niche within the confines of the service sector. In broadening the reach of Chinese food, they were not just passively reacting to changing market conditions but made conscious and strategic attempts to combat anti-Chinese perceptions and shape the taste of mainstream food consumers. Over the years, they adopted and developed different practices. Takeout became popular with the bohemians and others in turn-of-the-century New York; called "carryout" in cities like Detroit and

Chicago, it remains a common practice of Chinese restaurants. At the same time, many Chinese restaurants also featured a visible cooking area. Chinese restaurateurs in Oregon in the early twentieth century adopted open-air (outdoor) dining.[80] In addition, they often integrated dancing and performance with dining, a business model that became extremely popular during the 1930s and 1940s: one of the first restaurants to do so was the New Shanghai Café, a branch of San Francisco's Shanghai Low, which opened its doors in 1922. Another format was the all-you-can-eat buffet. It has been pushed—primarily by newcomers from Changle County in Fujian Province—to be the latest trend in the Chinese-food industry.

The making of American Chinese food entailed more than effective business strategies, though. The efforts to promote Chinese food closely intersected with the long-standing political campaign of the Chinese community to combat persistent racial prejudice. If that campaign had had a Medal of Honor to award, it would have undoubtedly gone to Wong Chin Foo. In many ways, he was the East Coast counterpart of Norman Assing. He moved to New York in 1874, about a quarter century after Assing's arrival in San Francisco.[81] Like Assing, Wong was an energetic and high-profile community leader, visible in various affairs, ranging from creating a Chinese theater to mediating financial disputes among fellow Chinese.[82] And he was also a complex person, constantly involved in disputes and sometimes even physical fights with fellow Chinese; the naturalized U.S. citizen once worked as a Chinatown tour guide and as an agent to help U.S. authorities to catch Chinese smugglers of immigrants and opium into the United States.[83]

Wong Chin Foo embodied the connection between efforts to promote Chinese food and the Chinese community's campaign to defend its rights and freedom. Like Assing, he was a fearless and tireless civil rights fighter, establishing the Chinese Equal Rights League in 1892 and representing his countrymen as a court interpreter and the like. While Assing's arena remained largely local, Wong brought the Chinese struggle for justice to a national level through his extensive writings in high-profile newspapers and magazines. He introduced Chinese culture to wide and diverse audiences in his public lectures across the country. Although a victim of racist violence on numerous occasions,[84] he was never intimidated but was always ready to confront it head-on. He once challenged Denis Kearney to a duel, eventually defeating the famous anti-Chinese agitator in a debate.[85] Many have called Wong a "true American hero."[86]

Although Wong never owned a restaurant, he was Chinese food's first ambassador. A media heavyweight, who commanded a rate of $500 per public lecture by the 1880s, he drew considerable public attention to Chinese food.[87] Respected as an "authority" on Chinese food, his comments and articles appeared, sometimes repeatedly, in numerous newspapers throughout the country.[88] Besides introducing the basic features, popular dishes, and utensils in Chinese cookery, he also defended it against prevailing negative perceptions, offering a $500 reward for hard evidence of Chinese eating rats and cats.[89] Sharing the fate of Assing, Wong faded away from the pubic eye, making the rest of the life of this versatile, colorful activist and food promoter a mystery forever.

In dealing with an unfriendly and often hostile environment, Chinese Americans organized various public-relations events, using food as an effective tool. Community leaders frequently invited prominent whites to lavish banquets. Samuel Bowles, a Massachusetts journalist, who traveled to the West with U.S. House Speaker Schuyler Colfax in 1865, noted that the "managers of the six Chinese companies and the leading Chinese merchants of San Francisco all hold friendly relations with the leading citizens and public men of California. Occasionally, when distinguished people are visiting here, they extend to them the courtesy of a grand Chinese dinner."[90] When Colfax arrived in San Francisco, Chinese leaders held in his honor a long and elaborate banquet, which consisted of three stages with multiple courses in each. In 1907, Boston's Chinese merchants hosted a banquet dinner in Chinatown for the governor, lieutenant governor, and governor's council.[91]

Ordinary Chinese also did the same. In 1877, three hundred Chinese employees at Lewis Brothers, a tobacco import company, hosted an annual banquet for their white employers and colleagues as well as twenty other white guests at the luxurious Hung Fer Low (also spelled Hong Fer Low) restaurant in San Francisco. Considering the food habits of their guests, the Chinese hosts ordered various Western dishes; but they did not miss the opportunity to introduce their own cuisine, providing chopsticks as well as "pyramids of indescribable Chinese entrees."[92] When reporters and other curious whites requested Chinese companionship for a dinner in a Chinese restaurant, the Chinese readily complied. On one such occasion in 1859, three white men asked Lee Kan to join them for a Chinese meal.[93] Lee was a famous interpreter in San Francisco's Chinatown, who had attended a missionary school in China and worked as the Chinese-language editor of the *Oriental*, a bilingual newspaper published by the Reverend William Speer. Lee also managed to bring to the dinner a successful Chinese merchant and the head of the Siyi Huigan, one of the so-called Chinese Six Companies (Chinese Consolidated Benevolent Association). Chinese restaurateurs also entertained white guests, joining the community's public-relations campaign while publicizing their businesses at the same time. In New York, for example, three Chinese businessmen invited Mayor William L. Strong to dedicate their new restaurants in 1895.[94]

The following example best indicates the extensive involvement of the community in promoting its culture and food. In January 1883, less than a year after the Chinese Exclusion Act was signed into law, the Chinese celebrated the lunar New Year loudly and proudly in Santa Barbara. They published a public notice in the local paper, inviting everyone to join the celebration, during which they offered Chinese food to the visitors.[95] This "Chinatown open house" type of public-relations strategy would be used more often and more widely in the 1930s and 1940s.

Occasionally, the Chinese went to mainstream venues to promote their community and food. From June 1 to June 12, 1899, for example, Chinese New Yorkers conducted a Chinese fair in the Grand Central Palace.[96] Intended as a public-relations stunt, its purpose was to demonstrate Chinese Americans' advancement in "Western education and customs."[97] And it also included an extensive food show with a hundred kinds of different Chinese foods.[98]

Furthermore, the Chinese promoted Chinatown and their food by appropriating attempts to exoticize their culture. Despite public negativity and animosity, the Chinese never lost their pride in their culture. Over time they trumpeted their cultural uniqueness in a deliberate effort to capitalize on the thickening tourist traffic. They turned the tourist favorites, such as the theaters, restaurants, and temples, into visually impressive cultural artifacts. These buildings, in the words of G. B. Densmore, "are fancifully decorated and illuminated on their balconies and upper stories during the evening, and Chinese lanterns of all sizes and shapes flutter and flicker in front of all public places."[99] Among them, the upscale restaurants were the most visible, leaving a deep impression on contemporary white observers. In New York at the end of the nineteenth century, for example, according to Louis Joseph Beck, "the most gorgeously decorated and illuminated buildings in Chinatown are those occupied by these restaurants."[100] These restaurants were usually on the upper floors in three- or four-story buildings that were "gaudily painted in deep green with red and gilt trimmings. Chinese lanterns are suspended in reckless profusion from every available point."[101] When Chinese restaurants spread to other parts of the city, they did so "without flourish of trumpets but with considerable gilding and decoration,"[102] carrying with them what Arthur Bonner characterizes as "pseudo-Oriental glitter."[103]

Decorating Chinese restaurants with the same glitter for the visual consumption of customers became a common practice among Chinese restaurateurs across the country. The New York Chinese restaurant view depicted by Beck bears striking similarities to Otis Gibson's description of a Chinese restaurant in San Francisco during the 1870s: "Here is a three-storied building, with balconies on the second and third stories, gaudily painted with deep green, and trimmed with red. A profusion of Chinese lanterns suspended in these balconies helps to give the place a peculiarly Oriental appearance."[104] Ira Miller Condit, a veteran missionary both in China and among the Chinese in California, never seemed to have developed a penchant for Chinese food or an appreciation of the Chinese passion for food, but he recalled in his memoir the physical appearance of Chinese restaurants as visually "notable institutions": "They are three-story buildings, having balconies gaily painted and gilded, with an array of great lanterns hanging in rows."[105] An article published in the *Cornhill Magazine* concluded that in San Francisco's Chinatown, "the restaurants are the largest and most attractively fitted [and] painted buildings."[106]

Chinese restaurateurs and workers also made the Chinese motif a conspicuous feature in the interior of upscale restaurants. In 1877, *Harper's Weekly* published a large drawing of the interior of a San Francisco Chinese restaurant, which "is richly decorated with carvings in wood, gorgeously painted and gilded; Chinese lamps depend from the ceiling; quaint paintings and inscriptions adorn the walls; and a stranger might almost fancy himself transported to the Celestial Empire."[107] The famous Hong Fer Low restaurant emerged as a favorite of tourists in the late nineteenth century. It "was most gorgeously fitted up, the walls being made of carved woods imported from China and inlaid in places with precious stones. . . . Some of the chandeliers in the place cost $1500 each."[108]

In Philadelphia's Chinese restaurants in 1890, many white patrons noticed distinctively Chinese features in the interior: "The walls are hung closely with strips of crimson paper, bearing characters in black and gold. Red curtains hang at the windows, and red draping depends from the mirror frames."[109] Red was a favorite color of the Chinese for "every joyful occasion."[110] Over time, the interior of many restaurants in Chinatown remained conspicuously red, giving an impression of "almost like a Buddhist Temple."[111]

Such a conspicuously Chinese motif had existed long before non-Chinese diners flocked to Chinese restaurants. As non-Chinese patronage grew, however, this motif became a deliberate attempt to satisfy non-Chinese customers' curiosity about the distant and exotic "Far East." In the five restaurants that catered to non-Chinese clientele in New York's Chinatown in 1919, for example, "the walls have tapestry and the lights are shrouded in fantastic shades."[112] And over the years, such ornamentation became more accentuated, acquiring new elements, such as colored pictures of "pretty Chinese girls."[113]

Chinese restaurateurs and workers also made every attempt to ensure that their customers could feel and see the cleanliness of their restaurants—not a trivial matter in those days. Long associated with religious and social notions of purity, cleanliness in food had always been important. In turn-of-the century America, it was critical for attracting non-Chinese visitors for two specific reasons. First, this could help to overcome a rampant perception that the Chinese were filthy, producing the particular Chinese "odor" and spreading contagious diseases. Second, it resonated with a growing sanitation consciousness in American society, which is evidenced by the highly publicized investigative reports by activists like Jacob Riis.[114]

To compete for the slumming business, the New York *Sun* reported in 1896 that Chinatown restaurant owners "have cleaned up their places and made attempts at decoration"[115] As early as 1903, the journalist Harriet Quimby noted their deliberate strategy to give "evidence that everything is done in a cleanly manner."[116] Indeed, cleanliness soon became a trademark in Chinese restaurants.

Inside the restaurants, the "eating rooms are kept with scrupulous cleanness, and no unusual dirt will be found in the kitchens."[117] Beginning in the late 1880s, some Chinese restaurants, such as Been Hong in New York,[118] had an open kitchen so that customers could see that "the food is prepared in an extremely cleanly manner."[119] In fact, the Chinese established a reputation that "Chinese kitchens are as clean as many a white tiled dairy," which the *New York Tribune* listed in 1903 as one of the reasons for the growing popularity of Chinese restaurants.[120] An article in the *San Diego Union* in 1887 noted that the Chinese restaurant environment was "clean, neat, and attractive."[121] In other cities, such as San Francisco, Chicago, and Washington, D.C., white seekers of Chinese food—including those who had reported odors in Chinese restaurants—generally agreed that these establishments were cleanly kept, and this remained a feature of Chinese restaurants.[122] In a book about New York's restaurants, George S. Chappell wrote that "Chinese restaurants are everywhere, most of them clean and attractive."[123] J. S. Tow, secretary of the Chinese Consulate General in New York, who had studied the condition of the Chinese, concluded that the success of Chinese restaurants was "due to the cleanliness with which they prepare their food and keep their kitchens and restaurants." "Their kitchens are often visited by American ladies, whose verdict is usually that that they are as clean as, if not cleaner than, American restaurants," he wrote.[124]

A number of factors combined to shape the Chinese food that prevailed in Main Street America until the second half of the twentieth century: the efforts of Chinese-food workers and promoters, the early non-Chinese customers' socio-economic and cultural backgrounds, and the tastes of these customers. Some Chinese in the restaurant industry used the term "Chinese-American cuisine" to characterize this kind of food, and that notion effectively captures a new cuisine that is both Chinese and American.

7
"CHINESE-AMERICAN CUISINE" AND THE AUTHENTICITY OF CHOP SUEY

For contemporary non-Chinese observers and diners, the appeal of Chinese food stemmed from its inexpensive prices and its convenience, due to Chinese restaurants' long hours of operation and speedy delivery. This type of food was also what non-Chinese consumers expected of Chinese restaurants. Such expectations reflected their clear choice between two kinds of Chinese food that were made available to them: the simple and inexpensive dishes like chop suey, and China's haute cuisine featuring delicacies like shark's fins. The prevalence of the former in the multiplying Chinese restaurants reminds us that the rise of Chinese food performed a social service rather than an admiration of Chinese cooking as a culinary art, and this explains its success.

The triumph of chop suey over shark's fins magnified the lowly position of Chinese food in the minds of Americans. It also fit the lifestyle and socioeconomic backgrounds of many non-Chinese customers. In addition, it was based on the prevailing puritan/utilitarian approach of mainstream society. By the early twentieth century, the chop suey type of Chinese food emerged as a distinctive cuisine, characterized by some Chinese Americans as "Chinese-American food." This characterization asks an important question: How Chinese is it really? An in-depth analysis of chop suey, the epitome of such "Chinese-American food," clearly indicates that it was indeed Chinese in origin. At the same time, however, as a highly commodified system of dishes that reached extraordinary levels of brand-name recognition in American food consumption, it was undoubtedly American.

It isn't feasible at this point to offer a definitive gastronomical definition of what constitutes "authentic" Chinese food. Simply put, it contains enormous regional variations, and it has changed a great deal over time. So has "Chinese-American food," as old dishes like chop suey gradually lost their prominence in the post-1965 era. In spite of such changes, Chinese food has largely remained at the lower end in the hierarchy of mainstream American consumption

THE MOST REMARKABLE FEATURE
OF CHINESE RESTAURANTS

In Manhattan's nascent Chinatown in 1887, a thriving restaurant on Mulberry Street near Canal Street drew the attention of a *New York Tribune* reporter. "The most attractive sign, however, reads as follows: 'A good dinner 8 cents,'" the reporter wrote. "This was sufficient to lure a reporter to the place," he continued.[1] The price was very good indeed in New York, where people had to pay more for a meal of bread, butter, potatoes, and pickles at the "15-cent eating houses" around that time.[2] Similar stories of non-Chinese customers lured to Chinese restaurants by advertised lower prices appeared in many newspapers.[3] The tendency of non-Chinese consumers seeking inexpensive foods in Chinese restaurants was a fact that Chinese restaurateurs knew but often lamented: "They study matters closely, and manage to get their meals for about ten cents."[4]

Affordability had been a trade mark of Chinese restaurants from the beginning. In the early years in San Francisco, Chinese restaurants briefly enjoyed noticeable non-Chinese patronage because of the low prices of their food. Bayard Taylor, who went to California in 1849, reported that in these restaurants "meals are $1 each, without regard to quantity," while at "another restaurant at the corner of Kearny and Jackson, "the dinner will cost us $5."[5] James O'Meara recalled a similar price difference between Chinese and non-Chinese establishments in the city at that time:

> Single meals at the ordinary restaurants, conducted by white men, Americans or foreigners, or those of Spanish blood, cost from one dollar to two dollars, for the simplest dishes, and a nice dinner could not be had for less than five dollars; but at these Chinese restaurants a "square meal" could be had for one dollar and to regular boarders the charge was sixteen dollars per week, while at the other restaurants the charge was from twenty to thirty dollars.[6]

When Chinese food began to spread to non-Chinese markets in the 1880s, low price was the most critical selling point. The Chinese-food promoter Wong Chin Foo wrote that one could get "ready-made dishes," consisting of fish, chicken, duck, pig's feet, rice, tea, and so forth, at prices cheaper than in any other restaurant. "The prices run from five to twenty-five cents," he noted.[7] Affordability remained a prominent characteristic of Chinese food as the Chinese restaurant business continued to grow. In 1901, a Chinese merchant named Lee Wing expressed confidence that Chinese restaurants would do well because their food was a bargain and there was a large variety of ingredients in one dish. He used as an example a noodle dish called "'yokaman,' which is served in a bowl and consists of a hard boiled egg, slices of chicken and pork, macaroni and a gravy for 10 cents. . . . Another one of our cheap and popular dishes is chop suey." [8]

Low price was also a main attraction of Chinese restaurants elsewhere. In Washington, D.C., low-paid customers like messenger boys ate in Chinese restaurants because "they have found out that Chinese rice and cabbage is cheaper and better than the American brand."[9] Yet competitive price alone would not be enough to lure patrons, since there were other inexpensive dining places in major cities. Non-Chinese customers also swarmed into Chinese restaurants because they found the food there appetizing. Indeed, the savoriness and the wide variety of Chinese dishes were among the most often cited merits of Chinese restaurants around the turn of the century.

But few seemed to find Chinese food attractive only because of its gastronomical merits. In commentary praising Chinese food, indeed, the mention of such merits was almost invariably coupled with an emphasis on its cheapness. An in-depth article about Chinese food in the *New York Tribune* in 1901 commented that in terms of cheapness and savoriness, Chinese food "can easily outclass similar places run by Americans cooks. . . . The Chinese is a master of the art of making palatable dishes out of next to nothing or rather a little of everything. Not even the French cook can rival him. The insipidity of cheap chophouses and the sameness of the dairy lunch counters are escaped by frequenters of these restaurants."[10] Noting the continued growth of Chinese food in New York City, the *Independent* explained in 1917 that this was because the public recognized its merits and value: "For 30 cents" a person can get a meal "of soup, a generous serving of chop suey (meat and secondary vegetables), rice and unlimited supply of tea with rice cakes."[11]

Besides low price, Chinese food was usually served in generous portions, "cheap and substantial" as one reporter put it.[12] In Philadelphia's Chinese restaurants in 1890, a bowl of noodle soup with tea cost only 10 cents, and "the bowl is liberal in size."[13] The *San Diego Union* noted in 1904 that Chinese chop suey restaurants were increasing in popularity in most American cities, where "very large portions are always served" and "most dishes are cheap."[14] The Old Dragon Chinese restaurant on Market Street in San Francisco noted on its menu that "all Chinese dishes are served in very generous portions, almost any order, except soups, being sufficient for two or three persons if supplemented by some other order."

In 1896, reporting Chinese food's growing acceptance, another newspaper article concluded, bluntly but perceptively, that "the most remarkable feature of the Chinese restaurants is their cheapness."[15] This assessment evidently resonated with non-Chinese consumers, who made the lowest-priced Chinese dishes the most popular.

Inexpensive food was such a common customer expectation that when rising food costs forced Chinese restaurateurs to increase prices, they sometimes felt obliged to issue a public explanation.[16] Nonetheless, Chinese restaurants emphatically highlighted low price in their advertisements. In a 1904 ad targeting railroad workers, the Chi Ock Chinese restaurant in Ardmore, Oklahoma, for example, noted both the cheap price and the large portions of its food, mentioning that its 25-cent meals contained "more to eat."[17] Like many elaborate Chinese restaurants with prominent Chinese décor, the Far East Restaurant in Washington, D.C., promised "modest price" to its prospective non-Chinese consumers in 1917.[18]

Besides affordability, Chinese restaurants also met the need of urban dwellers for convenience. They stayed open for long hours. Those in early-twentieth-century Philadelphia, for example, remained open from around 11:00 A.M. until 2:00 or even 4:00 P.M. the next day.[19] Important holidays such as Christmas were no exceptions. And, too, Chinese restaurants advertised their promptness in serving food. As early as 1894, the ad for the Sam Kee Chinese restaurant in Waco, Texas, announced that it had expert Chinese cooks and cheap meals. The restaurant also declared that short orders were its "specialty."[20]

SHARK'S FINS VERSUS CHOP SUEY

Such simple and cheap dishes served conveniently and promptly would not fit the notion of Chinese cuisine in the minds of either self-anointed white food connoisseurs or the epicures of China. These dishes did not represent Chinese food in its entirety.

Regarded by many as "the world's first great cuisine," Chinese cooking as a system of foodways can be traced at least back to the Song dynasty (960–1279).[21] In the subsequent centuries, Chinese food evolved into a rich and complex culinary tradition with a burgeoning variety of dishes that encompassed both simple everyday meals and sophisticated exotic foods.

By the early twentieth century, the food in Guangdong Province had become among the most developed in China. In his analysis of foodways during the Song dynasty, Michael Freeman points out three conditions for the formation of a cuisine. First, there must be a multitude of ingredients, made available through not only local production but also importation from other regions. He argues that "cuisine does not develop out of the cooking tradition of a single region."[22] Second, there must be a sufficient consumer base. Third, people have to develop the mentality to think of food as pleasure.

Guangdong Province, home to almost all Chinese immigrants in the early decades, had the ideal conditions for culinary development. It had been at the forefront of China's international trade, interacting with regions beyond the national boarders. By the mid-nineteenth century, the province, especially the Pearl River Delta (the native area of most early Chinese immigrants in America), had also developed one of China's most dynamic and prosperous regional economies. The Cantonese had a long-standing reputation for their epicurean passion and cooking skills, a reputation of which Chinese Americans like Wong Chin Foo were fully aware.[23]

Proud of their long and sophisticated culinary tradition, the Chinese tried to introduce an extensive repertoire of Chinese dishes to Americans in both China and the United States. But the dishes that the Chinese elites and restaurateurs proudly used to demonstrate their hospitality and to showcase the elegance of their cuisine were luxurious foods like shark's fins and bird's nest soup and other complex dishes. These foods also captured the Orientalist imagination of white American commentators and connoisseurs of Chinese food alike.

When writing about Chinese food as a cultural novelty, many Americans who traveled to China invariably focused on such fanciful foods as hallmarks of this cuisine. William Hunter, who spent a long time in China after his first arrival in 1825 and who studied Chinese, recalled a "'chopstick' dinner." The banquet, which he apparently regarded as embodying authentic Chinese food, featured "such delicacies as bird's nest soup, with plovers' eggs and Beche-de-Mer, curiously prepared shark's fins and roasted snails."[24] Such banquets also took place in Chinese restaurants in the United States. In the words of Juliet Corson, one of nineteenth-century America's foremost food experts, "Innumerable are the newspaper correspondents' accounts of state dinner given in China to honored 'foreign devils'; and the wealthy Chinese merchants of San Francisco and New York sometimes feast their American friends."[25] The lavish multiple-course feasts that white journalists, invited guests, and food connoisseurs encountered in Chinese restaurants in Chinatown seldom failed to highlight the likes of shark's fins, bird's nest, and sea cucumber.

In the early 1870s, a white journalist had a twenty-six-course feast in San Francisco's Hong Fer Low with Chinese merchants. On the menu were sea cucumber, "one of the most cherished delicacies of Chinese epicures," and bird's nest (or, more precisely, "swiftlet's nest," as it is known to the Chinese), "worth one dollar per pound."[26] Found mostly on the high cliffs of islands off the coast of Southeast Asia in countries like Vietnam, Indonesia, and the Philippines,[27] this foreign food was known to the Chinese as early as the Tang dynasty (618–907), and it had become a signature dish in China's haute cuisine by the late nineteenth century.[28] White culinary connoisseurs who were interested in tasting real Chinese food, including the three white men who dined with Lee Kan in San Francisco in 1859, usually ordered such delicacies..[29] When inviting their white VIP guests to "public-relations" banquets, the Chinese hosts clearly customarily offered similar delicacies. For example, the first phase of the lavish 1865 banquet in honor of House Speaker Schuyler Colfax included signature dishes of Chinese haute cuisine, including shark's fins and bird's nest.[30] These two dishes were also expectedly present at the 1907 banquet in Boston for the governor of Massachusetts. It is understandable that Chinese as well as Anglo-American elites regarded such exquisite delicacies as representative components of Chinese cuisine, since there has long been a tendency to define a nation's foodways through its haute cuisine. "Developmental models of the creation of high cuisine typically focus on the role of the elites," argues B. W. Higman.[31]

Except for a very limited number of Chinese-food buffs, American consumers in general never developed an appetite for China's haute cuisine represented by such lavish items. Jerome A. Hart wrote in 1909 that "Americans, as a rule, do not care for the Chinese delicacies such as shark's fins and bird's nest soup."[32] Surviving menus from the early twentieth century indicate clearly that other than a few Chinatown establishments, most Chinese restaurants did not offer these fancy foods because they had few buyers.

A great many American consumers rejected Chinese haute cuisine because it contradicted prevailing ideals about food. And, at the time, Americans had plenty of food but did not seem to care much about its preparation. The famous

Beecher sisters—Harriet Beecher Stowe, author of *Uncle Tom's Cabin*, and Catharine Beecher, founder of the American Woman's Educational Association— knew this well. In their influential cookbook, *The American Woman's Home*, which was regarded as Stowe's second most important book, they asserted that "the American table . . . presents a fine abundance of material, carelessly and poorly treated."[33] The French economist Michel Chevalier, who visited the United States in the 1830s, asserted that this tendency stemmed from Americans' preoccupation with work. For the American, he wrote, "meal-time . . . is only a disagreeable interruption of business, an interruption to which he yields because it cannot be avoided, but which he abridges as much as possible."[34]

Americans ate much but not well also because of another preoccupation: a scientific and home-economics approach to food that predominated during the late nineteenth century. Together with the mainstream society's strongly puritanical tradition, it significantly discouraged and disapproved of gastronomical passions. The wordy subtitle of the Beecher sisters' cookbook—*Being a Guide to the Formation and Maintenance of Economical, Healthful, Beautiful, and Christian Homes*—reveals both that puritanical aversion to fine dining and an emphasis on food as a matter of health to be managed economically and efficiently. While the former had long biblical roots, the latter was vigorously promoted by affluent middle-class and largely New England reformers like the Beecher sisters. The scientific approach to food was also discernible in Fannie Merritt Farmer's *The Boston Cooking-School Cook Book*. A phenomenal success, the book sold out immediately after its first publication in 1896 and had sold more than 2.5 million copies by the eighth edition in 1946. "Food is anything which nourishes the body," states the first sentence of the book. It then offers information of the body's physical components: oxygen, 62.5 percent; carbon, 21.5 percent; hydrogen, 10 percent; nitrogen, 3 percent; and calcium, phosphorus, potassium, sulfur, chlorine, sodium, magnesium, iron, and fluorine, the remaining 3 percent.[35]

The writings and career of Ellen Henrietta Richards, a pioneering leader in the field of home economics, best represent the confluence of the religious and secular currents:

> In America to-day, the situation which confronts us, whether working man, student, or millionaire, is not how to get food enough, but how to choose from the bewildering variety offered that which will best develop the powers of the human being and make him efficient, and, what is of greater importance, how to avoid that tempting variety, indulgence in which weakens the moral fibre and lessens mental as well as physical efficiency.[36]

This kind of utilitarian approach and China's haute cuisine were worlds apart.

It was a cuisine cultivated by China's leisure classes and was characterized most notably by the rare and expensive foods known as "treasures" (*zhen*) that were also extremely time-consuming to prepare. Shark's fins serve as a good example: a relatively latecomer to the recognized list of such treasures, this food took two days to cook, according to Yuan Mei, an eighteenth-century scholar-statesman, famous poet and essayist, traveler, and perhaps the best known ancient Chinese food writer among food lovers in pre–World War II America. Mann Fang Lowe, one of the Chinese restaurants that tried to serve haute cuisine dishes to non-Chinese customers at the beginning of the twentieth century, needed one full day to prepare it. This restaurant's all-English menu states that such "special orders . . . must be given the day before."[37] The famous late-twentieth-century chef Kenneth Lo remarked that it took three days to prepare.

I have never tried to make shark's fins in part because I do not find the food particularly appealing. Like bird's nest soup and similar treasures, it has no apparent or intrinsic health or culinary value; its desirability has been highly cultivated and stems mostly from its rarity. By itself, the soup has little flavor. Its gelatinous texture serves merely as a "carrier" for the highly savory taste from other ingredients in the soup. As I realized more consciously while participating in discussions over the 2011 controversy that arose from the proposal (Assembly Bill 376, introduced by Paul Fong and Jared Huffman) to ban its sales, the practice of finning sharks is extremely inhumane. Thrown back into the ocean with their fins taken away, the sharks almost immediately drown or become a feast for other sea creatures. But early American consumers' aversion to shark's fins hardly had anything to do with humanitarian considerations. For them, it was simply because foods like this were prohibitively expensive and much too exotic and complex.

In addition, Chinese fine dining also required meticulous and time-consuming preparation, which only China's aristocracy could afford. To further understand this, you need only look at Yuan Mei's famous recipe book. After serving as a county magistrate for a number of years, he retired to his residence in Nanjing and traveled extensively. Like other Chinese government officials, Yuan lived well; his residence consisted of twenty-four "pavilions, standing separately in the grounds, or built round small courtyards," as well as an artificial lake large enough to accommodate boats.[38] But he put his leisure to productive use; at the end of the eighteenth century, he became a famous and knowledgeable epicurean, compiling *Suiyuan Shidan* (*Food Menu of the Suiyuan Garden*, 1792), a cookbook that includes menus from different parts of the country.

Yuan's conception of food as a leisurely pleasure to be enjoyed and savored was the opposite of the Anglo-American austere and scientific approach. It is also different from those Chinese food manuals published before his time that placed a greater emphasis on the medicinal and health aspects of food, such as Jia Ming's *Yinshi Xu Zhi* of the Yuan dynasty (1271–1368) and the diet segments of Gao Lian's *Zun Sheng Ba Jian* (*Eight Treatises on the Principles of Life*, 1591). Yuan's book centers on issues directly related to food preparation, such as the quality of foods used for cooking, the choice of sauces, the fitting combination of ingredients, the precision in the timing of cooking, the selection of the appropriately elegant utensils, and the order in which dishes are served during a meal. A true gourmand, Yuan believed that good food depends on exquisite cooking rather than merely on expensive ingredients. Simple and affordable ingredients like tofu could be better than bird's nest, he said. But these must be meticulously prepared and unhurriedly enjoyed.[39]

Chinese fine dining was also available in large Chinese communities in cities other than San Francisco. In New York's Hong Ping Lo restaurant in the late 1880s, for example, one could order a feast by the table (called a "spread") for $50, and it would take two days to consume.[40] But Chinese food never took off in the United States as fine dining. This is not just because it ran contrary to mainstream America's ideals about food. Moreover, accepting Chinese food as high-class dining was the last thing we would have expected from the American leisure class and those with leisure-class aspirations and pretensions. For these American consumers, the value of the Chinese lay in their utility as lowly providers of cheap labor.

It is the less privileged, such as marginalized whites, northern urban African Americans, and eastern European Jews, who embraced Chinese food and formed a critical initial customer base. They chose the Chinese food represented by inexpensive dishes—a choice that shaped the nature of the American Chinese cuisine.

Therefore, cheap and convenient dishes like chop suey carried Chinese restaurants beyond Chinatown. In New York City, Chinese restaurants that had moved uptown by the beginning of the twentieth century offered more limited menus than their Chinatown counterparts, and according to the *New York Tribune* in 1901, "'Yockaman,' 'chop suey' and 'chowman' [chow mein] are the pièces de resistance."[41] Consumers in African American areas, as Roi Ottley noted of Harlem in the 1930s, "only order pork fry rice and chicken chop suey . . . and ignore the more delicate and native Chinese dishes."[42] In Jewish neighborhoods from the 1930s to the 1960s, as several of my informants recall, chop suey was one of the most popular Chinese dishes.

As chop suey quickly gained national brand-name recognition, many Chinese restaurants came to be known simply as chop suey joints. In responding to the new trend, some restaurants adjusted their menus. Richard Wing's family, for example, turned their restaurant into a chop suey place when the national trend reached the rural town of Hanford, California, as they began to cater increasingly to non-Chinese customers. "The Americans do not like authentic Chinese food," Wing remarked in 2001.[43]

"CHINESE-AMERICAN CUISINE"

While non-Chinese customers did not go to Chinese restaurants to explore China's haute cuisine, the majority of Chinese restaurateurs did not regard themselves as uncompromising culinary missionaries. In fact, few Chinese restaurant cooks and owners had any previous training or experience in kitchen work. Most of them learned to cook in America in order to make a living. This in part explains why even the "high-toned" Chinese restaurants in San Francisco in the 1870s were ready and eager to serve non-Chinese food. They "kept knives, forks, plates, table-clothes, and napkins, and can, on due notice, get up quite a respectable American dinner."[44] In the early twentieth century, many of the multiplying Chinese restaurants served "American" food on a regular basis. In 1903, a police captain in New York named Burfriend, who was quite familiar with Chinese restaurants in his jurisdiction, once asked a chop suey restaurant owner why his establishment had "a bill of fare mixed with such commonplace things as hams and eggs and mutton chops with fried French fried potatoes," rather than a strictly Chinese-food menu. The Chinese restaurateur replied that this was "necessary for him to do in order to satisfy his customers."[45]

The Nankin American and Chinese Restaurant in Philadelphia announced the availability of such mixed food by including the word "American" to its name in 1919.[46] Others did so in newspaper advertisements. The Orient (its Chinese name means "East Garden") in Washington, D.C., advertised such dishes as chow mein, chop suey, and egg foo young in 1942; and its ad also pointed out in capital letters: "Oh, YES, AND AMERICAN FOOD."[47] At Thanksgiving, some offered special American holiday meals. In 1914, white sailors violently wrecked the New Republic Chinese restaurant on Race Street in Philadelphia because they did not get the Thanksgiving dinner that they wanted.[48] We do not know their motivation precisely, but most likely it had something to do with the unsatisfied expectation that one could get such American food in a Chinese restaurant. Soon thereafter, the city's diners would see ads from several Chinese restaurants, such as Wong Kew, which called itself a "Chinese and American Restaurant" and offered a "Wonderful Thanksgiving Treat" at $1.75 per cover.[49]

Non-Chinese customers could also find a relatively long list of American dishes on the menus of many Chinese restaurants in different cities from the 1920s to the 1940s. For example, Yuen Faung Low, known to its non-Chinese patrons in Minneapolis simply as John's place, had a two-page menu, half of which was devoted to American dishes. Even Chinatown's Shanghai Low in San Francisco, a longtime establishment that opened in 1913, included a section called "American menu" on its bill of fare. Besides its Chinese dishes, similarly, the Old Dragon Chinese restaurant in San Francisco had an elaborate American menu, including salads, oysters, poultry and game dishes, steaks and chops, eggs, and sandwiches along with an extensive list of alcoholic beverages.[50]

Such a division of dishes into Chinese menu and American menu was a common practice found in many Chinese restaurants across the nation. They served inexpensive American food along with Chinese dishes at comparably low prices. The Lun Far (Chinese for "orchid") restaurant at 1409 Sixth Avenue in New York, for example, served typically affordable Chinese dishes, such as yat gaw mein at 45 cents, and a small plate of beef chop suey at $1.50 as well as American dishes in six categories from appetizers to desserts. The Shanghai Village in Denver also served conventional American-style Chinese food like chop suey dishes (including one named "Chinese or American chop suey" for 60 cents), chow meins, and various egg foo youngs. In addition, its American dishes, which take an entire page of the two-page menu, included a $2 T-bone steak and a 35-cent hamburger.

Not all Chinese restaurants offered American food. But in Chinese restaurants serving non-Chinese clientele, their all-English menus prominently featured popular dishes such as chop suey, as customers could see in San Francisco's Mandarin Café in 1925, Boston's Joy Yong Chinese and American Restaurant in 1943, and Minneapolis's Yuen Faung Low in the 1920s.

Restaurant menus are fascinating documents, not just gastronomically but also historically, as Lily Cho has shown in her nuanced analysis of Chinese restaurant menus in small-town Canada.[51] Reading American Chinese restaurant menus can tell us a great deal about the clientele, the Chinese restaurateurs' ideas about what Chinese food was, and their business practices.

The menu of the Joy Young restaurant, located on 65 Mott Street in New York City, was one example.[52] This six-page menu plus a page-long wine/liquor list was more elaborate than the menus mentioned earlier, offering three kinds of food, which reveals the way Chinese restaurateurs categorized the meals served in Chinese restaurants. The first kind was universally available in all Chinese dining establishments: the inexpensive simple dishes. This included seventeen different chow mein dishes, twelve chop sueys, and six egg foo youngs. The least expensive among them cost less than $1; the most expensive chop suey, made with fresh lobster, was under $2. The next group featured a few American dishes that were also reasonably priced: for 35 cents, one could get a fried egg sandwich; the most expensive dish in this section was half of a fried spring chicken at only $2.75. Although it was located in Chinatown, the restaurant made an apparent attempt to cater to non-Chinese customers. And demonstrating an understanding of what constituted "authentic" Chinese food, the third kind of food was characterized as "special Chinese dishes," listed in the last section of the menu. It included more expensive dishes than those in the previous two sections. For instance, a large shark's fins soup with minced chicken cost $12, and according to the menu, dishes like this one "must be ordered in advance." However, high price was not the primary characteristic of dishes in this section, which also included less expensive dishes, such as a bok choy soup at $1. The dishes in this section were "special" because they were intended for those who wanted authentic Chinese food. The menu presented these items as "real Chinese food" and as "identically the same kind of dishes you would be served if you were in China." And while the dishes in the first two sections were written only in English, the names of those in the third group were given in both Chinese and English.

Chinese restaurateurs, especially those working in non-Chinese neighborhoods, mainly offered cheap Chinese and sometimes simple American dishes to non-Chinese mass consumers. The growth of Chinese restaurants outside Chinatowns, therefore, signified a significant expansion of mass consumption more than the spread of the gastronomic art of Chinese cooking per se.

This does not mean that the Chinese involvement in the restaurant industry was accidental. It was instead an opportunity that the Chinese actively and consciously pursued. They were well prepared to do this by their extensive experiences in food-related service jobs: They cooked meals for middle-class families, supplied virtually all the vegetables for Los Angeles,[53] and operated grocery stores and, later, supermarkets in northern California and elsewhere.[54] Those working in the restaurant business continued the historical role of the Chinese as service workers, doing their best to satisfy and accommodate the tastes and needs of their clientele, rather than insisting on serving what they regarded as authentic Chinese food.

This explains why Chinese Americans operating as individual proprietors without professional association with one another created highly consistent and recognizable lines of dishes across the nation. Lee Gain You, a Chinese restaurant chef/owner, designated these dishes as "Chinese-American cuisine," and this term was taken up by others in the field. Paul Chan and Kenneth Baker wrote: "Even though Americans like the Chinese food they now are getting, it must be admitted that most Chinese restaurants are producing a type of food that is not really Chinese: It is more properly called 'Chinese-American,' that is, a type of food, based on Chinese cooking, that has been designed for Americans."[55] And in *Chinese Kosher Cooking*, Betty S. Goldberg categorized the recipe for beef chop suey as "Chinese-American."[56]

Lee Gain You arrived in the United States in 1922 at the age of twenty-four from the village of Mong Aye in the Pearl River Delta. In his restaurant in Baltimore, the Oriental Café, half of the bill of fare, written only in English, belongs to "Chinese-American cuisine." In a practice also seen in other Chinese dining establishments, it lists dishes for non-Chinese customers in four groups: chow mein, chow suey, egg foo young, and fried rice. And all are within a price range from 50 cents to 85 cents. The other half is the bilingual menu for "Chinese cuisine," which included more elaborate foods like bird's nest soup and Sai Wo Ap (Western Lake Duck) at reasonable prices. The city at that time simply did not have enough Chinese customers to support higher-priced Chinese foods.[57]

Throughout much of the twentieth century, Chinese customers often requested "more authentic" dishes in Chinese restaurants outside Chinese communities. The bifurcation of Chinese food evolved into another common practice among Chinese restaurateurs in the late twentieth century: to prepare two physically separate sets of menus, one in Chinese and the other in English. The Chinese-language menu and chopsticks were reserved for Chinese diners. I have seen this practice more than once when dining with white friends, and it also was noticed in the early 1980s by Fred Ferretti, a *New York Times* food writer, who was once denied chopsticks in a Chinese restaurant until he asked for them, with a smile, in Cantonese.[58] Speaking Chinese politely, Ferretti concluded later, would also get you "authentic" Chinese food.

CHOP SUEY: CHINESE FOOD, AMERICAN STORY

Such a practice brings up the question of the authenticity of the Chinese food served to non-Chinese customers. We care deeply about authenticity because it matters a great deal in many aspects of life, such as art, our beliefs, our identity, and the claims and promises that people make. Curiosity about the cultural authenticity of cuisines has generated similar questions in other contexts. Jeffrey Pilcher, for example, asks, "What is authentic Mexican food?" He notes that "just as chop suey and pepperoni pizza are not typical of the foods of China and Italy, few people in Mexico actually eat the burritos (made with wheat flour tortillas) and taco shells (pre-fried corn tortillas) that often pass for Mexican cooking the United States."[59]

Like many people, Pilcher does not regard chop suey as truly Chinese. An analysis of this food will help us understand the nature of American Chinese food. Chop suey was for many years the most famous and most popular of all Chinese dishes in the United States. In New York, "chop suey has specially captured the popular fancy, and few are the downtown business men who do not relish it," a reporter noted at the end of the nineteenth century.[60] It loomed large in the movement of Chinese restaurants uptown and all the way to Harlem at the very beginning of the twentieth century.[61] It also occupied a conspicuous place in advertisements for Chinese restaurants throughout the country. The ad posted by the Wuey Sen Low restaurant in Salem, Oregon, in 1905, began by announcing in large bold print: "Chop Suey at the Chinese Restaurant." Then it specified that the restaurant offered "the famous Li Hung Chung Chop Suey, and Yakama."[62] These restaurants, as J. S. Tow concluded in the early 1920s, "came into existence in America because of Chop Suey."[63] Jessie Louise Nolton, one of the earliest Chinese-food cookbook writers in America, estimated that chop suey was "the foundation of three fourths of all the dishes served in the Chinese restaurants."[64] This exaggerated estimation nonetheless conveys an understanding of the preponderance of chop suey in Chinese restaurants.

As another indication of chop suey's popularity at this time, Willie Woo, a local chop suey chef and aspiring student at the University of Chicago, offered to teach co-eds there how to make the dish in exchange for his tuition.[65] In an article about the difficult time that chop suey joints were facing in 1908, the *New York Tribune* mentioned that Chicago "was long the best chop suey town in America. The business amounted to about $2,000,000 a year."[66] Moy Jim, manager of the Wide East House, declared that "chop suey is a necessity in life."[67]

In St. Louis, also around this time, chop suey was the favorite item in Chinese restaurants.[68] The city's craving for the dish continued to grow. In the early 1920s, it even became a symbol of freedom for newly divorced women, who "eat chop suey to show their emancipation."[69] The extraordinary popularity of this food inspired theatrical shows, such as Wallace Irwin's *Chop Suey*—a story not of food but a mixture of tongs, white tourists, and romance in Chinatown—that opened during the last day of the Chinese New Year celebration in 1903 at the Theater Republic in San Francisco.[70]

The prevalence of chop suey also stirred up resentment among those who were unhappy to see Chinese immigrants thrive in the restaurant business. Inspector J. G. Fowler of Minnesota's dairy and food department proposed in 1906 to investigate chop suey to see if it contained only "wholesome and nutritious ingredients."[71] In Chicago the same year, a proposal floated for an ordinance that would allow only American citizens to own chop suey establishments.[72]

The fast-increasing consumer craving for chop suey promoted various non-Chinese imitators—men and women of diverse backgrounds, including white natives and immigrants from Europe and Asia. Some opened their own chop suey houses. A German immigrant played German music in his Chinese restaurant in New York in 1908—a "chop suey with Beethoven" experiment that never clicked with American consumers.[73] People also made chop suey at home. For example, Brent did not realize his dream of becoming a culinary professional but has remained passionate about food. A few years ago, he and his mother compiled a collection of family recipes, including his grandmother's chop suey casserole recipe. It was his mother's favorite while growing up in the 1940s in Cherry Valley, Illinois, a small farming community seventy-six miles northwest of Chicago.[74] By then, several food companies, such Beatrice Food's La Choy and Fuji brands, had developed successful prepackaged chop suey products. In Chicago, where ready-to-eat "delicious chop suey" was "available in a shop or restaurant which specializes in this kind of food," chop suey lovers could also "buy prepared chop suey in cans, or to buy several cans of chop suey ingredients." These products included meatless chop suey, even though the Food and Drug Administration (FDA) had deemed chop suey to be a meat dish in 1941.[75] Such companies battled one another for the chop suey market. For example, in 1955 Chun King, a company that had been successful in making chop suey and other Chinese-food products, complained to the FDA that La Choy's new product "New La Choy Mushroom Chop Suey—Just Add Starch" constituted a practice of mislabeling.[76]

Broad participation by non-Chinese corporations and individuals in the production of chop suey as well as the active involvement of the government in regulating the business indicates its extraordinary prevalence. Moreover, these developments also further complicate the question of its authenticity, one that had already fascinated many contemporary observers.

Is chop suey really "not typical of the foods of China," as many believed? People have answered this question differently at various historical moments. At first, many regarded chop suey as a dish entirely and purely Chinese. Some even called it a "national dish" of the Chinese.[77] However, people later started to question its Chinese-ness.[78] Gradually, a new assertion gained currency: chop suey was an American invention. Suggesting it was more American than Chinese, Neal O'Hara wrote in *Life* in 1923 that "The Chinese are responsible for chop suey. But Americans are the only ones that eat it."[79] Calling it an "American dish of Chinese food," Everett Swingle told Chicago's Chinese-food lovers in 1931: "When next you eat chop suey, remember you are eating an American dish, whether it is prepared by American or Chinese chefs."[80] The conclusion that chop suey was an American invention had already been reached by others: the *New York Times* had remarked three years earlier: "That mixture of meat and bean sprouts, bamboo shoots, water chestnuts, celery, onions and what not is about as much Chinese as a concoction mixed in an American bar in Paris is an American cocktail"; and the *Los Angeles Times* characterized it as "a little joke" that China played "on the world" because "it is unknown in China."[81] The persistent belief in chop suey's American origin was magnified by a report in 1968 concerning the visit of Thailand's prime minister, Thanom Kittikachorn, who flew across the country in *Air Force One* as President Lyndon Johnson's guest. Knowing that he liked Chinese food, the White House placed fifty orders of chop suey from a Chinese restaurant for the visitor and his party. The report believed that the White House had made a major faux pas, quoting the restaurant's Chinese proprietor as saying that chop suey was not genuinely Chinese.[82]

Many Chinese Americans would agree that LBJ's White House was wrong in thinking that chop suey was Chinese. J. S. Tow wrote that "Chop Suey by no means represents the real Chinese cuisine. The Chinese themselves never take it because they do not like it."[83] In a cookbook originally published in 1950, Doreen Yen Hung Feng remarked: "Chop suey is known to us Chinese only as an agreeable foreign dish, and as for shark's fin and bird's nest soup lucky are the few who have had the opportunity to taste such delicacies."[84] Two other Chinese-food experts, Johnny Kan and Charles L. Leong, wrote that "*Chop Suey* is no more authentic in Chinese cuisine than Irish stew."[85]

At least two Chinese even claimed to have invented the dish in America. In 1904, Lem Sen, who declared that he was a native of San Francisco and had never been to China, asked a white lawyer in New York to obtain an injunction to stop all the Chinese restaurants from making chop suey. He asserted that he had invented it in San Francisco shortly before the arrival of Viceroy Li Hong-zhang (Li Hung Chang).[86] In 1931, another "inventor" surfaced in Chicago: "a soft-spoken, modest man" named Albert Lee, who avowed that his Tuxedo restaurant in New York was the first chop suey house in America and that he named the food "Li Hung Chang chop suey."[87]

Neither man got any legal or public recognition for their claims, but some Chinese Americans continued to regard chop suey as non-Chinese. Marie Rose Wong, who grew up in Iowa, remembers "a Chinese chop suey restaurant sporting a flashy neon sign that screamed 'serving American and Chinese cuisine.' . . . But the dishes they served were nothing like the food we ate at home."[88]

There have been countless popular accounts of how chop suey came into existence in America. According to one of them, it was a stew that Chinese miners in California cooked from leftovers.[89] A more widespread story associates its creation with Li Hongzhang, who visited the United States in 1896. Different versions of this story have circulated since then. According to the most widely known version, after tasting the dish in New York, Li asked what it was; the cook, who prepared this hurriedly put-together mixture of ingredients, answered "chop suey," meaning "pieces of different things" in Cantonese.[90] Another version placed the incident in San Francisco, which Li actually did not visit.[91]

Clearly, the association of Li with the creation of chop suey is a fiction. Indeed, this particular food had already existed and had been frequently noted by the media before Li set foot in America.[92] In the 1880s, Wong Chin Foo also indicated that chop suey was consumed by the Chinese themselves. He even suggested that it was on the menu of a restaurant in Shanghai, which became a model for a new restaurant planned by Chinese businessmen in New York in 1888.[93] During his visit to New York, Li had chop suey at the banquet hosted by former American ministers to China, but his name was not immediately linked with the dish.[94]

After looking into the origins of chop suey, several authors concluded that its roots lay in South China.[95] Li Shu-fan noted unequivocally in 1964: "Let me set the record straight: chop suey is actually a familiar Chinese dish originating in Toishan, where I spent my childhood."[96] But this has not stopped people from believing that popular dishes like chop suey are not authentically Chinese.

In an otherwise thoughtful and well-researched essay about Chinese Americans' food writings in the 1950s, Sherrie A. Inness characterizes such dishes as "tame" food, which she places in opposition to "authentic" Chinese food. "Chow mein, chop suey, and other tame foods," she declares, "were not Chinese."[97]

Moreover, what chop suey actually is remains largely a mystery. A careful analysis of recipes in early Chinese cookbooks indicates that chop suey in essence is a stir-fry (*chao*). In 1911, Nolton's *Chinese Cookery in the Home Kitchen* discusses the chop suey "kettle," which "is made of steel with a narrow rounded base and a flaring rim, and with small handles riveted on two sides of the rim." To make the best chop suey, "the kettle should be similar in shape, being deeper directly in the center, and sloping up the sides to the rim." Evidently, this is what we call a "wok." And the process is the same as the way we make stir-fry dishes: "The uncooked meat is first put in the kettle with the heated oil, and braised until done, stirring occasionally to prevent burning. . . . When the meat is sufficiently cooked the vegetables and other ingredients are added according to the direction"; when it is ready, there should not be "any separation between the ingredients and the gravy."[98] Shiu Wong Chan, one of the first Chinese American writers of Chinese cooking, used the Chinese words *chao ji pian* (stir-fried chicken slices) for the dish chicken chop suey.[99] In 1945, the famous Chinese cookbook author Buwei Yang Chao defined *chao*, or stir-fry, "as a big-fire-shallow-fat-continual-stirring-quick-frying-of-cut-up material with wet seasoning."[100] Wallace Yee Hong put it plainly in the early 1950s: "The basis of the chow yoke (stir-fry pork) dishes is mixed vegetables. Even the well-known (in America) chop suey is of this family."[101]

In fact, chop suey has never been one specific dish with a strictly set recipe; it is, rather, a method of cooking. The Chinese words for "chop suey" had been romanized in various ways—chop soly, chop sooy, chow chop suey, and chop sui—and its ingredients have varied a great deal. In a word, it was a common Chinese method of cooking a mixture of meat and vegetables, which has been widely adopted in different parts of China. The meat could be pork, beef, or chicken (in the early days, usually chicken gizzards and livers); the commonly used vegetables included bean sprouts, celery, mushrooms, bamboo shoots, water chestnuts, and celery. What Americans may call chop suey constituted a mainstay of my mother's cooking during my childhood in the small city of Enshi in southwestern Hubei Province; the main theme was the meat, a scarce commodity, which had to be chopped or sliced and supplemented with vegetables. A most obvious difference is the American chop suey tends to have more liquid than my mother's *chao* dishes.

When it comes to Chinese food, nothing can be more Chinese than stir-fry, or *chao*—the way to make chop sueys. It is considered the most important of all twenty techniques in Chinese cooking by both Buwei Yang Chao and Kwang-chi Chang, an influential scholar of food in Chinese antiquity.[102] Stir-fry actually has deep historical roots in China. Although there is no consensus on when this technique began, by the Song dynasty it had become quite widespread. In his detailed eyewitness account of everyday life in Kaifeng, the Song capital, Meng Yuanlao mentioned numerous stir-fry dishes such as *chao* chicken, *chao* crab, *chao* rabbit meat, and *chao* clams.[103]

As a cooking method, chop suey is indisputably Chinese in origin. Because of its long history and wide use in China, chop suey was actually more representative of the food of the Chinese than the "treasures" in China's haute cuisine. As a product in the market of mass consumption, though, it was indeed an American innovation. It was only in the United States that this cooking technique evolved into a widely recognized line of dishes. This is similar to the way the Big Mac, a simple hamburger in origin, is regarded as a McDonald's invention. Rather than one individual's creation at a magic moment, chop suey as American Chinese food's most famous dish stemmed from the collective and effective efforts of Chinese Americans in marketing their food. In order to understand such efforts, consider another story of Li Hongzhang's visit to New York City.

Li was the first Chinese visitor to the United States to receive celebrity treatment or "royal reception," in the words of the *New York Times*. Upon his arrival aboard the steamship *St. Louis* in New York on August 28, 1896, he was saluted and welcomed by "war vessels," as "a tremendous crowd flocked" to see him, creating a "great spectacle." His visit became front-page headline news in New York and elsewhere. A reporter even called him "the greatest foreigner and most powerful ruler that has ever visited the United States."[104]

The elated Chinese in the city turned this unprecedented event into an occasion to promote their community and food. To celebrate Li's visit and attract visitors, they decorated Chinatown with hundreds of colorful lanterns strung down the fronts of every building, along with Chinese and American flags. The strategy worked. Reporting the record number of visitors to Chinatown on the day of Li's arrival, the New York *Sun* noted: "Never before in the history of Chinatown was it visited by so many persons in one night as it was last night[105]

Li's visit also drew considerable attention to Chinese food, although not chop suey per se. His food habits came under the microscopic watch of reporters, who wrote at great length that he abstained from Western food and stayed with Chinese meals.[106] In the early twentieth century, many Chinese restaurants, including Wuey Sen Low in Salem, Oregon, named their chop suey after the celebrity visitor, as Renqiu Yu has pointed out.[107] Doing so added another boost for selling a food already widely known. During his visit to the United States in 1903, Liang Qichao observed the popularity of "Li Hongzhang chop suey" in city after city.[108] The name of the dish lived on for decades. Betty S. Goldberg's *Chinese Kosher Cooking* gives the Chinese name for beef chop suey as "Li Gong Za Sui" (Mr. Li [Hongzhang] Chop Suey).[109]

Chinese Americans evidently created the story that chop suey was invented at a banquet that Li attended. The story first circulated among the Chinese, and the New York *Sun* called it "a story in Chinatown."[110] It even reached China. In 1917, Xu Ke, the famous chronicler of life in the Qing dynasty (1644–1911), painted Li as the one who had coined the name "chop suey." According to Xu, during his visit to the United States, Li disliked Western food because of its odor and ordered food from local Chinese restaurants. When Westerners asked him what it was, Li, with no ready answer, simply responded: "chop suey."[111] This folklore has continued in China.[112] The successful creation of the Li Hongzhang–chop suey connection demonstrates Chinese restaurateurs' ingenuity in marketing. It also reminds us that market forces have significantly complicated questions about the authenticity of American Chinese food. As a cooking method, on the one hand, chop suey has a long Chinese tradition. On the other, it was in America that chop suey emerged as the first big brand name of the burgeoning mass-consumer food market. As such, it is quintessentially American. It was, simply put, the Big Mac in the pre-McDonald's era.

Symbolized by chop suey, cheap and convenient Chinese food was an indication and a logical extension of the long Chinese concentration in service industries. Its ascent in popularity marked the empire's domestic expansion, spreading the dining-out experience to the middle class and less privileged groups. This is a social role that McDonald's has continued to carry out since the 1950s. "The McDonald's Corporation has become a powerful symbol of the American service economy," in the words of Eric Schlosser.[113] Such an economy is symptomatic of the American way of life that started to take shape more than a century ago.

Chinese food has continued to evolve under shifting American market conditions. Chinese restaurateurs have always made conscious attempts to adjust the flavor of their dishes to suit the taste buds of non-Chinese consumers, accentuating the sweetness and sometimes sourness of the food, for instance. The American chop sueys for non-Chinese consumers were, almost from the very beginning, soupier than the Chinese versions.[114]

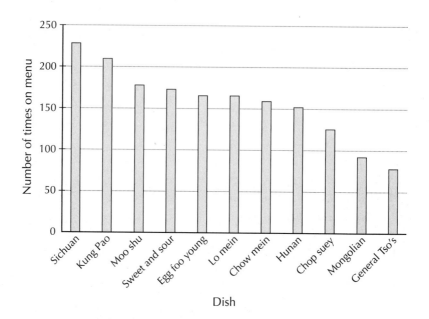

FIGURE 4 The number of times the names of popular dishes appeared on the menus of one hundred Chinese restaurants. (Data from Yong Chen, menu samples)

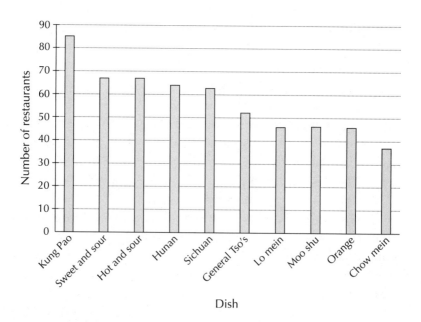

FIGURE 5 The number of Chinese restaurants in which the names of popular dishes appeared at least once on the menu. (Data from Yong Chen, menu samples)

Moreover, chop suey's popularity started to slide gradually but steadily in the postwar years. By the early twenty-first century, it has retained its past prominence only in African American neighborhoods in cities like Detroit and St. Louis. An analysis of menus from one hundred Chinese restaurants in non-Chinese communities in twenty states and Washington, D.C., reveals the diminished presence of chop suey and other traditional popular American Chinese dishes (figure 4).[115] The "big three"—chop suey, chow mein, and egg foo young, the most popular names of food in early-twentieth-century Chinese restaurants—still appear in a large number of dishes.[116] But this is in part because those Chinese restaurants that serve them tend to offer multiple dishes under each of these three names.

When we look at the top ten names among the dishes offered in the one hundred restaurants, it becomes clear that the old "big three" have conceded their predominance to new food names like Kung Pao, Hunan, Sichuan (Szechuan), and General Tso's (figure 5), and chop suey did not even make the list.[117] The national pattern is mirrored locally in southern California. Of the nineteen restaurants I surveyed in non-Chinese communities in Huntington Beach, Tustin, Costa Mesa, Westminster, Newport Beach, and Irvine in 2003, for example, only three served chop suey dishes, a significant drop from 1997, when ten such restaurants in a corresponding sample had offered such food.[118]

In Chinese communities, chop suey has virtually disappeared, as we can tell from an analysis of menus from thirty-eight Chinese restaurants in Los Angeles's Chinatown and Monterey Park (a post-1965 suburban Chinatown) conducted in the summer of 2003: only one of them served chop suey. This is also the case in Chinese communities in other areas, such as the Bay Area, Houston, and Greater New York.

No Chinese Food with Puccini

Despite the menu changes and the emergence of Chinese restaurants in some small towns as reputable dining places along with their continued appeal to the middle class in the postwar years, Chinese food's reputation as "one of the best bargains around" has largely persisted.[119] It has hovered at the lower end of the American restaurant industry and in the minds of many consumers. The food writer Moira Hodgson revealed her understanding of the hierarchical nature of American gastronomy when she wrote in 1982: "Pizza does not seem to go with candlelight, nor Chinese food with Puccini."[120]

Risotto with Sheep-Belly Mushrooms

Serves 4

For many American elites, Chinese food is not high-class enough to be associated with opera. But using what people in Yunnan Province call sheep-belly mushrooms, the following dish may go very well with Puccini.

1 oz dried sheep-belly (morel) mushrooms

8 cups chicken broth

3 tbsp olive oil

½ cup chopped green onion

2 garlic cloves, minced

4 basil leaves

1 tbsp chopped fresh parsley

dash of salt and pepper

¼ stick butter

2 cups Arborio rice

½ cup dry *Shaoxing* Chinese cooking wine

2 oz mascarpone cheese

Soak the mushrooms in cold water for at least 1 hour. Remove the tips of the mushroom roots and rinse several times to clean. Heat the chicken broth in a separate pot. Keep warm over low heat. Heat 1 tbsp olive oil in a wok. Add ¼ cup green onion and 1 garlic clove, and sauté for about 2 minutes. Add the mushrooms. Cook for 2 minutes, add the basil and parsley, and season with salt and pepper. Turn off the heat and mix in the butter.

Heat 2 tbsp olive oil in a saucepan. Add and stir in ¼ cup green onion and 1 garlic clove. Add the rice and stir for 2 minutes until the grains are well coated with oil and are opaque. Pour in the *Shaoxing* wine and cook until it is evaporated. Add the mushrooms to the rice. The next step requires the patience of an opera-goer. Add 1 cup warm chicken broth and keep stirring gently until it is absorbed by the rice. Repeat the process to use all the chicken broth until the rice is al dente. Add the cheese. Stir to mix until the cheese is melted. Turn off the heat and serve.

This is not to say that there is no structural variation among Chinese restaurants in non-Chinese markets. Even in Athens, Georgia, a town of some eighty thousand in the early 1990s, Shun Lu and Gary Allen Fine identified two kinds of restaurants among the eight Chinese establishments there. The first type serves inexpensive and more "American Chinese" menu items; the other type's food was more complicated and more expensive. But neither "has authenticity as its primary goal," as Lu and Fine acknowledged.[121] Neither type had escaped their historically designated role as service and convenience providers. Indeed, throughout the country, eating in a Chinese restaurant is seldom considered a genteel activity of the rich and privileged.

Chinese restaurateurs have never stopped the effort to create upscale establishments. Among them was Tommy Toy, who started the stylish Tommy Toy's Cuisine Chinoise on Montgomery Street in San Francisco in 1985, offering mostly Chinese food with elegant ambience. I went there with relatives in the summer of 2003, and we ordered its seven-course prix-fixe dinner. The second course, seafood bisque baked in fresh coconut, was a novel idea with a memorable taste. The fourth course, Peking duck, was also memorable but for a different reason. As in many other Chinese restaurants, the duck was rolled out on a small cart, but after serving each of us a couple of small pieces the waiters rolled the cart away, and the duck never came back. For the whole evening, I could not stop wondering where the rest of my duck had gone. I had long been used to paying $20 to $30 for the whole duck in a Chinese restaurant, where cost-conscious consumers like me always expect to get more for less than we do in a full-service non-Chinese establishment.[122]

This brings me to another similarity between Chinese food and McDonald's: despite their extensive presence as a class of food, neither has garnered much respect in American society. One of the leading restaurant franchises, McDonald's stands as a salient milestone in the postwar transformation of American society and as an icon of American consumer culture around the world.[123] At the same time, however, it has faced increasingly harsh criticism from Americans. In *The McDonaldization of Society*, for example, George Ritzer condemns the model of production and consumption that McDonald's stands for.[124] McDonald's has also been deplored for serving unhealthy food, which is dramatically represented by Morgan Spurlock's popular documentary, *Super Size Me* (2004). In even more hostile terms, animal-rights activists have denounced the inhumane treatment of animals by the food giant, which has become the world's largest user of beef and second largest user of chicken. The animal-rights group People for the Ethical Treatment of Animals (PETA) painted McDonald's as "the US No. 1 Serial Killer" in a billboard poster campaign in 1999.[125] In *Fast Food Nation*, Eric Schlosser offers an indictment of the business practices of the American fast-food industry that McDonald's symbolizes: "The basic thinking behind fast food has become the operating system of today's retail economy, wiping out small businesses, obliterating regional differences, and spreading identical stores throughout the country like self-replicating code."[126] In 2003, *Merriam-Webster's Collegiate Dictionary* introduced the term "McJob," defining it as "low-paying and dead-end work," which infuriated the corporation and divulged a profound disrespect in American society for the company.

Chinese food has also been disparaged. I described in chapter 1 how this food was constantly assaulted by anti-Chinese forces in the nineteenth century. In recent decades, racism no longer dictates public attitudes toward Chinese food the way it once did. But negative perceptions, including old stereotypes, have persisted, illustrating that Chinese food has not made much progress in altering its status.

Partly because of its image as a nutritionally sound cuisine, however, Chinese food maintained its popularity in the twentieth century.[127] This is captured, for example, in the popular saying that "you rarely see a fat Chinese person." Lyn Stallworth explains that the Chinese "have found that texture, variety, and contrast of flavors please the palate more than sheer abundance."[128] But that image did not necessarily make Chinese food friends with white health experts. In 1993, the Center for Science in the Public Interest (CSPI) launched a series of investigations of nutrition in restaurant food. Chinese restaurants were the first target. When its report came out on August 30, its findings of the unhealthy content of Chinese food became national headline news. *USA Today* published an article, "Chinese Food: Lo Mein, Yes; Low-Fat, No," that cites the report by noting: "Many take-out Chinese dishes are loaded with fat and calories."[129] Stuart Berman, the owner of a Chinese restaurant, called the report "irresponsible and sensationalist," pointing out its various misconceptions, including the confusion between the saturated fats of the Big Mac and the polyunsaturated fats of Chinese food.[130] Many Chinese were also quick to rebuke the report, seeing it as an attempt of the mainstream media to vilify Chinese food. A Chinese nutritionist pointed out the unscientific nature of its sampling, arguing that Chinese dishes with the same name were cooked differently in different restaurants.[131] Others stated that Chinese restaurants would adjust their food according to customers' preferences. In spite of its apparent shortcomings, the report had a chilling effect on the Chinese restaurant industry, especially those in non-Chinese communities. For example, in late September 1993, many Chinese restaurateurs in southern California had to cut prices just to stay afloat.[132] The New York Times also reported that negative publicity hurt Chinese restaurants.[133]

Attempts to harass Chinese restaurants continued. In February 2006, California assemblyman Van Tran introduced the Asian Traditional Food Act (AB 2214), starting what many Chinese dubbed "the defense of the moon cake." For quite some time, including the lunar New Year holiday season, food inspectors in southern California had cited numerous food vendors for keeping moon cakes as well as *banh chung* and *banh tet* (Vietnamese pork and green bean rice cakes) at room temperature for longer than four hours. Their reasoning was that bacteria might build up unless the food was refrigerated. But many Chinese regarded this as another attempt by public-health officials to target Asian food—such "a pounding" that other emblematic Asian foods, such as Peking duck, had taken for similar reasons in the 1980s remains in the memory of people like Michael Woo.[134] I told Lonny Shavelson, a reporter from NPR, in an interview, that "to tell Asian Americans to put the moon cakes in a refrigerator, that's just being culturally insensitive. It's also ignorant of the long history behind it."[135]

A food cherished by the Chinese, the moon cake has been an icon of Chinese cuisine and Chinese identity. This is, in part, because of its close association with the Mid-Autumn Festival. Falling on the fifteenth day of the eighth month in the lunar calendar, the festival probably began as an occasion to worship the god of the earth for a good harvest and has since become one of the most important national holidays in China. National holidays have been widely used to forge national consciousness and identity, as we can see with the celebrations of the Fourth of July and Thanksgiving in the United States. The Mid-Autumn Festival is no exception. According to a popular legend, at the end of the Yuan dynasty, moon cakes were used to distribute a message to synchronize all the uprisings against the Mongolian rulers on the fifteenth day of the eighth month.[136]

In defending the moon cake, the Chinese found a critical ally in Vietnamese Americans, for whom *bahn chung* and *bahn tet* are "as much a part of the Vietnamese Lunar New Year—Tet—as turkey at Thanksgiving."[137] On October 5, 2006, Governor Arnold Schwarzenegger went to the Los Angeles Chinatown district to celebrate the passage of Tran's bill, which required the California Department of Health Services to conduct a study of the sale and consumption of traditional Asian food. Seen in the Chinese world as a rare victory of Chinese Americans in upholding their culinary tradition, the moon cake episode nonetheless discloses again that Chinese food still has a long way to go before it becomes truly acceptable and respected.

In the late 1970s, Michael Freeman summarized a fairly widespread sentiment: "It is usually agreed that Americans are without a cuisine."[138] Two decades later, the famous food scholar Sidney Mintz reiterated the notion that the United States is a country without a national cuisine.[139] As Mintz realized later, some people may strongly disagree with that idea. Whether the United States has a national cuisine is subject to debate, but we can at least say that neither of the nation's two omnipresent food systems—Chinese food and American fast food— has ever received the respect or recognition as the national cuisine.

A few years ago, a newspaper reporter asked me to come up with a top-ten list for the best and worst national cuisines. I politely declined because taste in food is simply too subjective. Moreover, calling a nation's cuisine one of the world's worst would be an unforgivable insult. National cuisines—hard as they are to define—have one thing in common: they have always been an important source of cultural pride. But when it comes to Chinese food or fast food, American society has never exerted the same kind of pride as the French, Italians, and Mexicans do about their national cuisines. The reason is easy in the case of McDonald's or American fast food as a whole, which in fact represents a line of manufactured products rather than a cuisine.[140] As for America's Chinese food, its arrival and spread reflected the division of labor in the modern global political economy, where China has been largely a provider of cheap labor. America has enjoyed Chinese food as a convenient and affordable service but has yet to fully embrace it as a cuisine.

8
THE CHINESE BRILLAT-SAVARIN

Cookbooks tell stories, and so it is fitting to begin this chapter on Chinese cookbooks with a cookbook story.

A few years ago, after learning about my research, my mother showed me her modest cookbook collection. One, in a blue plastic cover, immediately caught my eye. As I opened the book, a few pieces of paper—handwritten recipes and food-ration coupons—slipped out from between the pages, resurfacing from an increasingly distant past.

It was one of the first few cookbooks I had seen my mother use. She got it in the early 1970s, when we had our first real kitchen and no longer had to cook in the passageway in front of our two-room apartment. The book added a few dishes to her repertoire, such as pan-fried eggplant and steamed pork with ground rice, but for the most part my mother used it for her reading pleasure and occasionally for keeping things like recipe notes.[1] In those days of food shortages, many ingredients mentioned in the 496-page book were beyond our reach, and some—such as spaghetti, cream, bear's paw, shark's fin, and deer antler—my mother had never even seen or heard of. In sharp contrast to the asceticism of the Cultural Revolution, which demanded self-sacrifice, the book promotes good eating and gives detailed instructions on such issues as nutrition and food hygiene, which concern the well-being of the individual. Although the authors still had to justify the cookbook in the name of the revolution by inserting five

Chairman Mao quotations on the first page, its publication was a clear sign that ideological radicalism had started to wane.

That book stands as a reminder of the multifaceted meanings of cookbooks as records of history—a uniquely valuable kind of historical record that connects larger socioeconomic currents to our personal experiences and existence.

The focus in this chapter is on Chinese-food cookbooks published in the United States up to the mid-1980s, when Chinese food became America's most ubiquitous ethnic cuisine. Few have taken a comprehensive look at these cookbooks in spite of their apparently wide appeal.[2] When I came to the United States in 1985, almost three hundred Chinese-food cookbooks had been published, many by major presses such as Macmillan, Crown, Doubleday, Grosset & Dunlap, Random House, Harper & Row, and Time-Life Books.[3] Many of these titles saw multiple printings and editions. For example, the Vintage edition of Buwei Yang Chao's *How to Cook and Eat in Chinese*, published in 1972, was the celebrated cookbook's third edition. The restaurateur Wallace Yee Hong's *The Chinese Cook Book*, which focused primarily on the recipes, went through eleven printings in the twelve years after its initial publication in 1952. Lesser known titles sometimes also saw multiple editions, including Clara Tom's *Old Fashioned Method of Cantonese Chinese Cooking*, whose eleventh edition was published in 1983.[4]

Capitalizing on the mounting popularity of Chinese restaurants, the publication of Chinese-food cookbooks was another important vehicle that elevated the visibility of Chinese food differently from the way restaurants did it. Written mostly by Chinese American authors, moreover, these cookbooks serve as a parameter of that visibility and signified the critical role of Chinese Americans in introducing and promoting Chinese food. A close analysis of this style of cookbook writing also helps us better appreciate the meaning that Chinese food held for Chinese Americans. It afforded them a visible platform to speak to the American public. Chinese American authors talked not only about their food but also about Chinese history and culture and, in many cases, about themselves in prominent, proud personal voices. Therefore, Chinese-food cookbooks embody the confluence of important trends in the larger world and matters that are extremely personal to Chinese Americans.

In order to appreciate the value of Chinese-food cookbooks in a historical context, I look at historical cookbook writing in general, especially those in Chinese and American history, both of which significantly influenced cookbook writing by Chinese Americans.

"MUCH MORE THAN A COLLECTION OF RECIPES"

A "humble genre long neglected by professional scholars," cookbooks are not just recipe collections but an especially valuable kind of historical document.[5] They offer fascinating insights into both the private and public spheres, and illustrate the connection between them. This is because cookbook writing and reading are extremely personal endeavors that reflect prevailing ideas and trends in society.

Cookbooks are more than the culinary equivalent of laboratory manuals not because historians or literary scholars can dig out traces of the past or decipher aesthetic value between the lines of a culinary text with their academic tools and occupational idiosyncrasies. Cookbook authors themselves did not merely offer technical tips on cooking but often relayed their individual experiences, their sentiments, and their opinions about important social and political issues in the world around them.

Equally important, in reading cookbooks, readers are not simply looking for cooking advice. In fact, ample evidence suggests that there is no direct correlation between buying or reading cookbooks and cooking at home. The second half of the nineteenth century witnessed a significant increase in the publication of cookbooks in the Anglo-American world. Cookbook writers F. Volant and J. R. Warren wrote in 1860 that "it may be said that the world is inundated with cookery books."[6] There were already so many cookbooks that when publishing *Jennie June's American Cookery Book* (1866), Jane Cunningham Croly felt compelled to ask: "Why another cook-book, when there are already so many?"[7] Yet it was also during this period that dining out emerged as a noticeable recreational activity. Such a non-symbiotic relationship between the volume of cookbook sales and the frequency of home cooking became more pronounced over time. During the late twentieth century, Americans cooked less and less than in earlier decades, a fact confirmed by the numerous focus groups I have conducted and by the continued expansion of the restaurant industry. By the end of the twentieth century, dining out had grown to be the top leisure activity for adults, who spent about half of each food dollar away from home.[8] At the same time, ironically, the sales of cookbooks skyrocketed. In the United States, the world's leading market for cookbooks, about 530 million books on cooking and wine were sold in 2000, representing a 9 percent annual increase from 1996.[9] American consumers' craving for cookbooks has not subsided. "Cookbooks are the second largest category for adult non-fiction," a senior executive of a leading book research company reported recently.[10] This is because the cookbook has been "much more than a collection of recipes," as a leading cookbook publishing company proclaims.[11]

The personal nature of cookbooks is apparent, as manifested in their multifaceted intimate attachment to individual users. Families often have their own cherished books, and many people—ranging from my mother back to Victorian-era Americans—love to compile recipe scrapbooks. Readers also tend to use cookbooks not just in the kitchen but also in the bedroom, where cookbooks have become "a favorite bedtime reading."[12]

For countless authors, writing about food is also an important vehicle to express the self. Traci Marie Kelly identifies three kinds of food writing as "culinary autobiographies": culinary memoirs, autobiographical cookbooks, and autoethnographic cookbooks.[13] In the early years, such writings created precious opportunities for women to share and record their feelings and experiences. Along with diaries and journals, cookbooks have become vehicles for women "to recount and enrich their lives."[14]

Finally, cookbooks are indeed personal because food itself is so essential to each human being. Cookbooks, therefore, often directly address important individual issues, such as health, which remained a prominent theme in historical food writings in both China and the United States.

Cookbooks are also social texts. First, the knowledge in a cookbook reflects the collective wisdom and experiences of communities more than the individual ingenuity of the author. In fact, the very word "recipe," which is from the Latin *recipere* ("take" or "receive"), has connotations of exchange. Cookbooks are repositories of private know-how, making it available to the public. Second, cookbook writing is closely tied to social conditions and trends. In an article published in the magazine *Restaurants USA*, David Belman characterizes American cookbooks as "historical treasures, commercial phenomena and some of the most accurate gauges of the culinary state of the country."[15]

Some Chinese cookbooks, especially those published in the earlier decades of early and the Qing dynasty (1644–1911), further illustrate the importance of cookbooks as historical documents that embody the confluence of the personal and the social. As is the case of food writing in other contexts, early Chinese authors did not write cookbooks with the sole intention of offering cooking advice. Rather, they harbored strong concerns about the well-being of the individual as well as society.

There is no consensus on exactly when the first cookbook appeared in China in part because people have different notions of what constitutes a cookbook. Some regard *Cui Hao Shi Jing* (*Cui Hao's Culinary Classics*), which was attributed to the fifth-century statesman Cui Hao, as the country's first cookbook in part because it "concerned itself mainly with the daily preparation of foods and not with medical application of foodstuffs."[16]

In fact, interest in the health ramifications of food actually constituted a major aspect of ancient Chinese food writings. It reflected the impact of Daoism (or Taoism), which focuses on human individuality, including bodily health. Early Chinese food writing also stemmed from agronomic texts, which were heavily influenced by Confucianism. This influence helps to explain the attention that many early Chinese cookbooks paid to the collective welfare of society.[17] Thus some Chinese American cookbook writers were keenly aware of the impact of Daoism and Confucianism on Chinese cookbook writing.[18] And in many cases, they also invoked early Chinese cookbook authors as a source of inspiration and authority.

In China, the initial drive for recipe writing and collecting came not simply from a preoccupation with cooking technicality per se but from concerns about both the individual and society. The emphasis on food as a means to maintain the health of the individual remained a prominent feature in Chinese cookbooks for centuries. In these cookbooks, considerations about health often outweigh details about cooking. One such book, *Yin Shan Zheng Yao (The Essentials of Food and Beverage)*, is a palace-food handbook written in 1320 during the Yuan dynasty (1271–1368). Its opening chapter details various food-related contraindications, and many of its elaborate recipes focus on the health aspects of the dishes.[19] The book's aim was to use food for *yangsheng*. Meaning "nourish life" in Chinese, this term conveys an understanding among the Chinese of the ultimate purpose of food. And it has persisted as a compelling motif in Chinese cookbook writings since then. Another cookbook, *Yinshi Xu Zhi (All You Must Know About Food)*, written by Jia Ming at the beginning of the Ming dynasty (1368–1644), introduced the medicinal properties of more than three hundred foods. He wrote in the introduction that diet is a way to *yangsheng*. The recipes in the food segment of Gao Lian's *Zun Sheng Ba Jian (Eight Treatises on the Principles of Life)*, written in 1591, were also mainly for the purpose of *yangsheng*. He began the treatise by proclaiming that "food is the foundation of human life.... The movement and function of the body's Yin and Yang as well as and the mutual enforcement of its five elements are based on diet."[20]

Even those that are seen as "pure" cookbooks frequently stressed the importance of food for *yangsheng*. *Yang Xiao Lu (The Little Book on Nurturing Life)* is one such book, written by the Chinese doctor Gu Zhong in 1698 in the early Qing dynasty. In the introduction, the editor Yang Gongjian pointed out that the purpose of diet was to preserve life.[21] Meanwhile, he also exhorted readers to refrain from killing animals excessively and to be frugal. In his own introduction, Gu himself categorized people into three groups: those seeking quantity, for whom more food was better, and those pursuing tasteful and exotic food and vainglory without considering the cost or the harm to others. The third were people who ate to achieve the goal of *yangsheng* and kept their food clean and harmonious without being extravagant. In praising the third type, he was promoting the Confucian lifestyle and the virtue of modesty and self-discipline.[22] Such efforts to encourage proper moral behavior and Confucian social values are also found in other cookbooks.

Also written in the early Qing, Zhu Yizun's *Shi Xian Hong Mi* (*The Grand Secrets of Diets*) is another cookbook with a strong focus on cooking, especially Zhejiang cooking. But in it, readers would find discussions of the medicinal properties of foodstuffs, therapeutic recipes, and a long list of foods to avoid for health reasons. Equally interesting is a statement in the book's introduction, written by a famous general by the name of Nian Xiyao: "[F]ood concerns the morals of society."[23] Edited by his son in the late eighteenth century, Li Huanan's *Xing Yuan Lu* (*Records of the Xing Garden*) also has a clear concentration on food preparation itself. In the introduction, nevertheless, Li reminded readers that reading writings about food could help them avoid food poisoning, and he reiterated the moral teaching in the Confucian text *Liji* (*Book of Rites*) that emphasized the importance of honoring and serving parents as one's social and familial duty.[24]

Chinese cookbooks performed another important historical and social task, which was to develop Chinese food into a culinary system that would transcend local and even regional boundaries—and in so doing, they served to further the cultural coherence of the country. Such an effort became particularly evident in food writings in the mid-Qing. Through the recipes they compiled and constructed, early and mid-Qing writers presented a cuisine not merely for the wealthy alone. The use of vernacular language and the inclusion of ordinary dishes in several early Qing cookbooks demonstrate an apparent attempt to address broad audiences.

A case in point is Yuan Mei's *Suiyuan Shidan* (*Food Menu of the Suiyuan Garden*, 1792), a cookbook mentioned by numerous Chinese American food writers and that embodies a systematic effort to gather and organize culinary knowledge. The author spent forty years traveling to different parts of the country and tasting various foods. The recipes he collected encompass eastern and southern Chinese cooking, and many of them came from his own tasting experiences. The book also shows a thoughtful and deliberate attempt to elevate the appreciation of food to a theoretical level. In the introduction, Yuan cited Chinese classics, including Confucian texts, to illustrate the importance of food. He emphasized the subjectivity in taste and the imperative of personal participation for enhancing one's ability to appreciate food.[25]

In the first part of his cookbook, Yuan theorized principles in dining and cooking, listing twenty things as "must-knows" (xuzhi) and fourteen practices to avoid. The culinary principles he outlined cover topics like the importance of ingredient selection, sauces and seasoning, timing in cooking (huohou), flavor and color, cooking and serving utensils, the sequence in serving food, seasonality of food sources, and cleanliness. Among the things to avoid are animal cruelty and indulgence in drinking alcohol.

Yuan could have not completed Suiyuan Shidan without the extraordinary contributions of his cook, Wang Xiaoyu. When Yuan tasted good food in someone's home, he would send his cook there to learn the recipe. Wang, as master chef in Yuan's kitchen, did all the shopping and cooking, and also demonstrated remarkable knowledge of China's culinary tradition. After Wang's death, Yuan wrote an essay to commemorate him, concluding that his wisdom was useful for elevating both people's lives and learning.[26]

Mid-Qing food writers like Yuan Mei did not fully accomplish the task of articulating Chinese cooking, however. Showing his awareness of the distinctiveness of the cooking of the Han people, Yuan mentioned the differences between Han and Manchu cooking—the Han had a proclivity for soup-style dishes, while the Manchus tended to boil and stew their food.[27] But he did not verbalize what made China's food particularly Chinese, especially in comparison with Western food, in spite of his knowledge of it. Like Yuan Mei, Li Huanan was familiar with Western food and identified it as xi yang (western seas).[28] But the presence of Western food, or any other foreign food, was not significant enough to magnify the Chinese-ness of China's diet. The task of articulating the meaning of Chinese cooking, which had been left unfinished by those early Chinese food writers, would be carried out more comprehensively by Chinese American food writers in the twentieth century. They did so by putting Chinese food in direct comparison with American cooking, a system that they also knew very well.

Resonating with the theme of yangsheng in Chinese food writing, late-nineteenth- and early-twentieth-century American cookbook writers defined food in terms of its importance to bodily health. Fannie Merritt Farmer's The Boston Cooking-School Cook Book (1896), for instance, defined food as "anything that nourishes the body."[29] In her celebrated *The "Settlement" Cook Book* (1901), Lizzie Black Kander reiterated Farmer's definition.[30] What sets American authors apart from their Qing counterparts is that their approach to healthful diet was influenced profoundly by natural sciences. Showing this influence, Farmer offered the following characterization of her book: "It is my wish that it may not only be looked upon as a compilation of tried and tested recipes, but that it may awaken an interest through its condensed scientific knowledge which will lead to deeper thought and broader study of what to eat."[31] This scientific interest in food also triggered mainstream America's first in-depth publications on Chinese food, particularly soy beans and Chinese vegetables.[32]

Scientific perspectives continued to exert a noteworthy influence on food writing. The first edition of *Good Housekeeping Everyday Cook Book* (1903) starts with a classification of food in scientific terms: "All foods are divided into two classes, the nitrogenous, or those which contain nitrogen, and the non-nitrogenous, or those that do not contain nitrogen. The nitrogenous are divided into two classes, the albuminoids or proteids, and the gelatinoids."[33] The opening chapter of the seventh edition, published in 1943, offers extensive nutritional information as the basis on which to prepare healthful meals.[34]

Also like the aforementioned Chinese cookbooks, early American cookbooks reflected prevailing social currents, including Protestant and Victorian notions about family life and gender roles, and the cult of scientific perspectives. In fact, Harriet Beecher Stowe and her sister Catharine Beecher praised and promoted Protestant Victorian values and virtues such as frugality and domesticity in their influential *The American Woman's Home* (1869), calling for "a Christian house; that is, a house contrived for the express purpose of enabling every member of a family to labor with the hands for the common good, and by modes at once healthful, economical, and tasteful."[35]

Such cookbooks conformed to and reinforced the longtime historical reality and idea that home cooking was mainly the responsibility of women. Amelia Simmons's *American Cookery* (1796) was heralded as "the first truly American-written cookbook."[36] It was written for female orphans like herself, forced to work as domestics by "unfortunate circumstances."[37] In time, married women and young brides would become another targeted audience. Kander's cookbook has a telling subtitle: *The Way to a Man's Heart*. In 1918, the *Boston Globe* published *The Boston Globe Cookbook for Brides*, and its opening chapter is titled "How to Cook for a Man." "It takes love," the editor noted.[38]

Cookbooks are not just reflections of existing trends and conditions but have also been used to effect social change and forge communities. Kander published

The "Settlement" Cookbook in order to raise funds to aid Jewish immigrants, and royalties from its sales supported various activities of the first settlement house in Milwaukee. The book exemplified similar fund-raising efforts by various groups, such as women's clubs, religious and political organizations, and ethnic associations in order to promote their causes and build a sense of community.[39]

The community that Kander tried to build was local and ethnic. But cookbooks were also related to creations of national communities in contexts beyond China and the United States. Scholars such as Benedict Anderson have noted the critical role that the printing press played in fashioning modern national consciousness.[40] First appearing in the fifteenth century, cookbooks were among the earliest printed books in Europe. In postcolonial India, Arjun Appadurai writes, the proliferation of cookbooks as "structural devices for organizing a national cuisine is accompanied by the development of a sometimes fairly explicitly nationalist and integrationist ideology."[41] Jeffrey M. Pilcher writes about the role of food in Mexico's search for national identity; he points out that nineteenth-century Mexican cookbook writers frequently resorted to "blatant nationalist language" in an effort to "foment patriotism at home."[42]

ANOTHER MILESTONE IN THE DEVELOPMENT OF AMERICAN CHINESE FOOD

Because of the importance of cookbooks as historical sources, we cannot fully appreciate the saga of Chinese food in America without understanding the cookbooks that articulated and promoted it. Along with the spread of Chinese restaurants, the proliferation of Chinese-food cookbooks stands as another vital milestone in the development of America's Chinese cuisine.

The appearance of Chinese-food cookbooks was not synchronized with the rise of Chinese restaurants. If we do not count the two pamphlets published by the Department of Agriculture, on soy beans and Chinese vegetables, at the end of the nineteenth century,[43] Chinese-food cookbooks did not appear until the 1910s, nor did they attract the same kind of attention as the fast-advancing Chinese restaurants did in the first two decades of the twentieth century. The time lag between the restaurants and the cookbooks is not difficult to understand: American restaurant-goers, who wanted to avoid cooking chores, had no reason to hurry to learn to cook Chinese in their home kitchens. The slow arrival of Chinese-food cookbooks is also consistent with a point made earlier in the book: American visitors to the Chinese restaurant were interested more in its convenient and inexpensive food than in the cuisine of China.

Those early cookbook writers were keenly aware that Chinese-food cook-book writing was closely linked to the rising popularity of the Chinese restau-rant. Jessie Louise Nolton, the author of America's first Chinese-food cookbook, knew that "the favorite dishes of the Orient are rapidly becoming favorite dishes of the Occident."[44] In their *Chinese-Japanese Cook Book* (1914), Sara Bosse and Onoto Watanna remarked: "Chinese cooking in recent years has become very popular in America."[45] As we can see in figure 6, Chinese-cooking cook-book publication started to pick up steam in the 1930s and 1940s, and acceler-ated in the postwar decades, accompanying and fueling the Chinese restaurant boom in the United States.

By 1985, when Chinese restaurants had already become the most dominant force in the "ethnic" dining industry, more than 280 Chinese-food cookbooks had been published in the United States. Besides the voluminous numbers, their prevalence is also evidenced by the wide participation in writing about Chinese cooking. Authors of Chinese recipe books during this period include Chinese and non-Chinese men and women. Among the non-Chinese are well-known au-thors like the Nobel Prize–winning novelist Pearl Buck, who grew up in China,

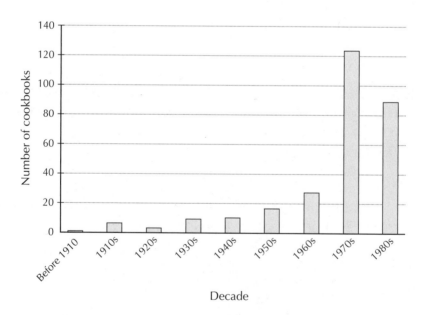

FIGURE 6 The number of Chinese-food cookbooks published in the United States, pre-1910–1985. (Jacqueline M. Newman, *Chinese Cookbooks: An Annotated English Language Compendium/Bibli-ography* [New York: Garland, 1987]; Yong Chen, Chinese-food cookbook collection)

and Emily Hahn, a prolific writer and high-profile figure in the Chinese-U.S. world before the end of World War II.[46] In the postwar years, Chinese cookery publishing was also associated with the names of heavyweights in mainstream American gastronomy like James Beard, dubbed by the *New York Times* "the dean of American cookery" in 1954, and the celebrated food critic and author Craig Claiborne.[47] Major companies that developed prepackaged Chinese food, such as Chun King and La Choy, issued handbooks on Chinese cookery.[48] Even Betty Crocker—a fictitious and iconic personality in food consumption and a long-standing symbol of America's racial identity—had a Chinese-food cookbook published under her name.[49]

CULINARY AMBASSADORS

Studying Chinese-food cookbooks is paramount to understanding the role that individual Chinese Americans played in popularizing Chinese cooking because about 70 percent of these books were written by Chinese Americans.[50] Writers of Chinese-food cookbooks were culinary ambassadors: in bringing Chinese food to mainstream America, they played roles that were quite different from those of Chinese restaurant owners. First of all, while the latter's motivation was largely economic, the former's function was primarily cultural. Second, while the restaurants' clientele always included Chinese diners, the cookbooks' audience in the early decades existed for the most part outside the Chinese community, which remained small and foreign born.[51] Chinese American authors, in particular, made a conscious attempt to address non-Chinese readers. Buwei Yang Chao remarked: "If you live far from Chinese restaurants, roasting your own Peking duck can be very rewarding."[52] Third, while the restaurants remained largely a phenomenon in urban public consumption, the cookbooks promised to carry knowledge of Chinese food to private spaces of readers and remote areas without Chinese restaurants.

Finally, the cookbooks presented more systematic and comprehensive knowledge of Chinese cooking than did the restaurants. Chinese restaurants had to accommodate the preferences of their consumers, especially the repeat customers. Those located outside metropolitan areas, in particular, served a rather predictable set of dishes. Cookbook writers, by comparison, had more autonomy over the content of their work, with the freedom to elaborate on a wide range of dishes and pertinent topics. Some, for example, included discussions of both the cooking and the eating of Chinese food, treating "the arts of eating and cooking as a single subject, each supporting the other," as two Chinese cookbook authors put it.[53] And many provided broader historical contexts of Chinese cuisine.

Nevertheless, Chinese-food cookbooks were by no means isolated from public Chinese-food consumption but were closely related to its trends. Popular dishes like chop suey featured prominently in major Chinese-food cookbooks in the first three decades, when chop suey became the synonym of Chinese food in the restaurant market: the Pacific Trading Company of Chicago even titled its cookbook *Mandarin Chop Suey Cook Book* (1928).[54] Besides eight chop suey dishes, it includes other trendy dishes such as chow mein and egg foo young.

Sometimes cookbook writers anticipated and effected changes in Chinese-food consumption. In the 1940s and 1950s, while chop suey remained quite popular in Chinese restaurants and can be found in writings about Chinese food, some Chinese-cookbook authors started to distance themselves from this iconic food.[55] In Buwei Yang Chao's *How to Cook and Eat in Chinese* (1945), the words "chop suey" disappeared and were replaced by "stir" or "stir-fry." Hu Shih, the "father of the Chinese literary renaissance" and one of the most influential minds of twentieth-century China, credited her as the person to have coined this new culinary phrase in English. The term "stir-fry" thus became the accepted terminology in both Chinese restaurants and cookbooks.

By the late 1950s, Chinese-food writers like Calvin Lee, a third-generation Chinese American owner of a long-standing Chinese restaurant in New York, referred to the "Chop Suey Era" as belonging to the past.[56] And indeed, the Chinese restaurant industry was about to enter a new phase.

Corresponding to the shifts in the market place, Chinese-food writers updated their work, adding new recipes. Changes in duck recipes in Chao's *How to Cook and Eat in Chinese* are a case in point: the second edition (1956) includes a new recipe for "roast duck (Chinese style)"; and the second edition, revised (1968), added more elaborate recipes for "roast duck (Peking style)" and "Szechwan duck." All three were absent in the book's original edition (1945).[57]

The word "Szechwan" is an old-style romanization of Sichuan, a province in the western hinterland of China, known for its highly distinctive (and spicy) style of cooking. Chao's use of the word indicates the emerging attention in the late 1960s to regional variations in what had previously been generalized under the single category of "Chinese food." This new trend is clearly seen in Emily Hahn's *The Cooking of China* (1968), which elaborates on the culinary regions in China. In the opening chapter "An Ancient and Honorable Art," she writes: "Some Chinese still refer to the five early cooking styles of Peking, Honan, Szechwan, Canton and Fukien, but today it is more realistic to speak in terms of four more general schools of cooking: northern (including Peking, Shantung and Honan); coastal (including Shanghai, Hangchow, Soochow and Yangchow); inland (Szechwan and Hunan); and southern (the area around Canton)."[58] The chapter also discusses Chinese geography and history, injecting a lucid lesson in culture into the cookbook.

The 1970s witnessed an explosion in publications on Chinese cooking, when more than 120 new titles appeared. This increase coincided with important historical developments taking place at the time. Most significant was the postwar growth of the Chinese population in the United States, which grew from 150,000 in 1950 to more than 800,000 in 1980. Much of that growth is a result of increased immigration. In the 1960s, 34,764 Chinese immigrants came to the United States, representing a record number since the 1880s and an almost 300 percent jump from the previous decade.[59] Unlike the prewar immigrants, who were primarily Cantonese, the new arrivals came from more varied geographical backgrounds. They not only broadened the customer base and labor force of the Chinese restaurant industry but also brought culinary knowledge from regions other than Guangdong. Another notable event was President Richard Nixon's historic visit to China in 1972. The image of Nixon using chopsticks and eating Chinese food on national television undoubtedly augmented the public interest in Chinese food. It gave a strong boost to the upward trend in Chinese-food cookbook publishing already under way before his trip.[60]

The new cookbook titles significantly expanded the knowledge about Chinese food available to American readers. Several themes—including regional traditions in Chinese cooking, health, and convenience—now received more extensive attention. The 534 pages of *An Encyclopedia of Chinese Food and Cooking* (1970) cover broad topics relevant to Chinese food. Besides recipes, it includes discussions of regional Chinese cooking, a section on instant dishes, and extensive information on diabetic and ulcer diets as well as recipes.[61] While some authors introduced several regional traditions, other focused on specific regions.[62] Cookbook authors also deepened American readers' awareness of Cantonese cooking by introducing dim sum, which Chao had spelled as *tim-sam*, a small-bite type of snack food served in large varieties with tea.[63] The regions that received particular coverage included Beijing, Hunan, and Sichuan, and dishes from these regions began to appear with increasing frequency on restaurant menus.[64] During the 1970s, cookbook writers also made a conscious effort to address the mounting health concerns of American consumers by offering tips on vegetarian and healthful cooking, reflecting and reinforcing the image of Chinese food as a wholesome cuisine.[65] Another theme

Marbled (Tea) Eggs

Many cookbook writers, ranging from the Qing epicurean Yuan Mei to the twentieth-century Chinese American writer Buwei Yang Chao, have offered recipes for this simple dish, which shows that good food does not have to be fancy or difficult.

12 eggs

½ cup light soy sauce

1 tsp dark soy sauce

3 tbsp tea (black, oolong, or *pu er*) or 3 tea bags

1 tsp cinnamon powder

2 star anise

6 small pieces dried tangerine peel

dash of black pepper

Wash the eggs thoroughly. Immerse them in cold water in a pot. Bring to a boil for 2 minutes. Turn to low heat and simmer for 7 minutes, turning the eggs a few times. Then promptly cool the eggs in cold water. Use a dull object (like the back of a spoon) to gently tab the eggs to create cracks on the surface. Put the eggs back in water together with the other ingredients. Bring to a boil and then simmer for 1 hour.

that several authors highlighted is the simplicity or convenience of Chinese cooking.[66]

DEFINING CHINESE FOOD AND EXPRESSING THE SELF

Signifying a dialogue between two cultures, writing about Chinese food was shaped by both Chinese and American cultural influences. The English-language Chinese-food cookbook was wrought as a separate genre by American influence as its initial model came from Anglo-American authors. America's first Chinese-language cookbook, Cui Tongyue's *Hua Ying Chu Shu Da Quan* (*Chinese-English Comprehensive Cookbook*, 1910), contained only Western recipes translated from English-language sources.[67] Such direct translations of English-language cookbooks introduced American cookbook-writing conventions to Chinese readers. Moreover, the first Chinese-food cookbook published in the United States was written by a non-Chinese author, who worked for the *Inter-Ocean*, a newspaper published in Chicago: Jessie Louise Nolton's *Chinese Cookery in the Home Kitchen* (1911).[68] In this as well as subsequent cookbooks, American conventions in recipe format became a model for Chinese-food writers, of which some of them were conscious. M. Sing Au noted in 1936 that Chinese chefs' expertise had to be rendered understandable for non-Chinese readers: "Chinese chefs rely on judgment for their measurements. They have no thermometer to tell degrees of heat, no cup or spoon to measure quantity by, no clock to tell time. Their directions, translated as accurately as possible, are herein set down simply enough for anybody to follow, it is hoped."[69] It is interesting to note, however, that none of the early Chinese-food cookbooks were direct English translations of existing Chinese-language cookbooks.

A more important American influence came from the nature of the readers. As mentioned earlier, Chinese-food writers were writing largely for non-Chinese whose cultural backgrounds compelled these writers to articulate and define Chinese cuisine.

In so doing, Chinese-food cookbook authors greatly advanced Chinese food as a system of cooking while pushing it across cultural boundaries. They felt an urgent need to define Chinese food also because few had clearly or comprehensively done so before. In the foreword to *Chinese Gastronomy* (a cookbook written by his wife and third daughter), Lin Yutang remarked in 1969: "There has been a flood of Chinese cookery books. But there has never been a Chinese Savarin in English."[70] The Chinese-food Brillat-Savarins had a vast vacuum of knowledge to fill, and they had to convince readers that Chinese food was not only desirable to eat but also manageable to cook. The task of articulating and advancing Chinese food fell mostly on the shoulders of Chinese Americans, who wrote most of the Chinese-food cookbooks during this period and provided the first elaborations on Chinese food as a cuisine.

If the model for recipe presentation came from American cookbook writing, the inspiration for Chinese-food cookbooks came from Chinese traditions, which offered a time-honored reservoir of culinary knowledge and experiences; it also afforded Chinese American authors expert authority.

From the very beginning, these authors constantly invoked Chinese history and culture. In *The Chinese Cook Book* (1917), one of the first books on Chinese cooking written by a Chinese, Shiu Wong Chan credited "the Emperor of Pow Hay Se [Pao Xi Shi] in the year 3000 B.C." as the inventor of the "Chinese method of cooking." If Pow Hay Se was unfamiliar to American readers, the next historical figure that Chan mentioned was no stranger.[71] "Confucius," he wrote, "taught how to eat scientifically. The proportion of meat should not be

more than that of vegetable. There ought to be a little ginger in one's food. Confucius would not eat anything which was not chopped properly." Chan linked
contemporary Chinese cooking to the great philosopher: "To-day, uncon-
sciously, the Chinese people are obeying this law."[72] Wallace Yee Hong, another
cookbook author, opened the introduction to his cookbook with a few made-up
Confucius quotes, including one that sounds more Victorian than Confucian:
"To win the heart of your husband—satisfy his stomach."[73] Lee Su Jan and his
wife, May Lee, who taught Chinese cooking lessons in Seattle, also mentioned
the legendary figure Fu Xi Shi/Pow Hay Se and acknowledged the impact of
Daoism on Chinese cooking. But they traced Chinese food's origin to Confucius. "It was Confucius," they wrote, "who set the standard of culinary correct-
ness and who regulated the customs and etiquette of the table."[74]

Proud and elaborate reference to Chinese culture and history remained a
common practice in Chinese-food cookbooks. In the beginning sections of Isabelle C. Chang's cookbook, for instance, the author discussed topics like the
Chinese calendar system, the Chinese kitchen god, a brief history of Chinese
cooking, and Chinese pottery.[75] She also provided an extensive list of recipes
for various Chinese holidays and festivals. Such a practice increased Chinese
Americans' cultural authority and signaled their conscious effort to "change
Western stereotypes of the Chinese as barbarians."[76]

Chinese American writers consistently devoted much energy to delineating
the distinctiveness of Chinese cuisine by clarifying its basics, including the
methods of cooking, ingredients, sauces, utensils, and menu planning. A defining element of cuisines, cooking methods received extensive coverage. Chan's
cookbook includes the section "General Laws of Chinese Cooking," where he
stated: "There are three methods in Chinese cooking: steaming, frying, and
boiling."[77] It was a conclusion accepted by others, such as Au, who wrote: "The
three methods most commonly employed in Chinese cooking are: steaming,
frying, and boiling."[78]

In time, discussions of Chinese cooking methods became more extensive
and more sophisticated. In 1945, Buwei Yang Chao devoted nine pages of her
cookbook to the elaboration of twenty methods of cooking: boiling, steaming,
roasting, red-cooking, clear-simmering, pot-stewing, stir-frying, deep-frying,
shallow-frying, meeting, splashing, plunging, rinsing, cold-mixing, sizzle, salt-
ing, pickling, steeping, drying, and smoking.[79] In addition, she offered lengthy
discussions of chopsticks and other utensils, Chinese culinary terminology,
and basic categories of ingredients, turning the cookbook into an encyclopedic
volume on Chinese cookery. Furthermore, she summarized a conceptual foun-

dation of the Chinese meal system as the dichotomy between *fan*, which is often construed as "rice" in the south, and *tsai* (*cai*) or "dishes." This duality underlines a fundamental characteristic of China's centuries-old starch-centered diet structure, in which starchy foods like rice constituted the main source of calories. That was "the opposite of the American eating system."[80] Nineteenth-century American visitors to southern China duly noticed the centrality of rice in the Chinese diet. Rice, Samuel Wells Williams wrote, "is emphatically the staff of life."[81] In another cookbook originally published five years after Chao's, Doreen Yen Hung Feng identified the seven "most frequently used methods of cooking" in a lengthy chapter on the principal methods of Chinese cooking: *chow* (frying and braising), *mun* (fricasseeing), *jing* (steaming), *hoong sieu* (red-stewing), *sieu* (roasting, barbecuing, or grilling), *ji'aah* (deep-fat frying), and *dunn* (steaming and double-boiling).[82] In the same chapter, she also offered detailed discussions of ingredients, utensils, and important concepts in Chinese cooking.

"What is Chinese food?" The cookbook writers Jonny Kan and his collaborator Charles L. Leong directly confronted that question.[83] In an effort to answer and thus explain the differences between Chinese and American cooking, they covered topics like flavors, cooking and preparation methods and their regional variations, cooking and eating utensils, as well as sauces and other ingredients.

Hsiang-ju Lin and Tsuifeng Lin's *Chinese Gastronomy* (1969) is a milestone in the articulation of Chinese cuisine. A must-read for anyone with serious interest in Chinese food, the book demonstrates and effectively utilizes the authors' extraordinary culinary and historical knowledge. The book discusses the basic characteristics of Chinese food, including the criteria that the Chinese use for appreciating food in terms of flavor and texture as well as the cooking methods and ingredients used to achieve that desired flavor and texture. It also includes an entire chapter on China's regional cooking.

Of particular importance is the chapter on China's ancient cuisine, which constitutes a well-researched treatise on the historical evolution of Chinese cooking. In chronicling changes in cooking methods, utensils, and ingredients, the authors make in-depth references to ancient classics like the *Book of Rites* and the *Shijing* (*Book of Poetry*) as well as mentioning such noted literary figures as the famous Tang poet Du Fu and the Song poet and famous foodie Su Dongpo. The chapter also includes lengthy discussions of ancient Chinese cookbooks and food writers. One cookbook is *Wu Shi Zhong Kui Lu* (*The Cookery of Manager's Records of Ms. Wu*), written in the Song dynasty (960–1279) by an author known to us only by the last name of Wu, whom many believe was a woman from Zhejiang Province.[84] This was also one of the first Chinese cookbooks that include measurements; written in the vernacular, its recipes were for common dishes.[85] Quite expectedly, Hsiang-ju Lin and Tsuifeng Lin also devoted considerable space to discuss "the great gourmet Yuan Mei."[86] Hsiang-ju even tested every recipe in the cookbook of ancient China's culinary giant.

The two authors' inclusion of extensive historical discussions signifies a comprehensive and ambitious attempt to understand and present Chinese cooking as a process. In reference to the classical period, they wrote: "The ancient cuisine was not distinguishably 'Chinese.' . . . By the eighteenth century, Chinese gastronomy had already developed its glories and its pitfalls, had encompassed the tastes of the food snobs, the gourmet, the peasant and the artist. It is very much like that now."[87]

Such a blending of history and culture into food writing was a strategy adopted by other authors, including non-Chinese writers such as Emily Hahn and Gloria Bley Miller.[88] Representing Chinese food as a sophisticated and rich culinary system developed over the centuries, and praising it as art—a word that Chinese-food authors first adopted and frequently used in characterizing Chinese food—undoubtedly helped to promote Chinese food.[89] Grace Zia Chu wrote in 1962 that "the art of Chinese cooking was passed down from generation to generation. . . . The techniques of this art," she continued, "were developed and refined over thousands of years."[90] Such a characterization of Chinese food was especially meaningful for Chinese Americans as it reinforced their authority and the cultural authenticity of their work. Furthermore, the positive representation of Chinese food and culture was an affirmation and a proclamation of this identity. In *The Classic Chinese Cook Book* (1976), Mai Leung acknowledged an intellectual and cultural debt to the people of China, calling them "my people": "To the people and culture of China, I acknowledge my enduring indebtedness. The collective experience of my people has been my teacher and my benefactor. I had the good fortune to be born among them, to participate in their learning and experience."[91]

The cookbooks written by Chinese Americans also reveal the importance of Chinese-food writing as a vehicle for empowerment. For these authors, its meaning extended beyond the realm of gastronomy: it gave Chinese Americans the most significant stage on which to address mainstream audiences. A few Chinese Americans, such as the food promoter and civil-rights fighter Wong Chin Foo and the newspaper editor Ng Poon Chew, occasionally spoke to non-Chinese audiences in speeches or articles in the mainstream print media. But these represented sporadic occurrences. In general, though, Chinese Americans kept silent in public life.

Nonetheless, through cookbook writing Chinese authors created a highly visible and steady venue of public communication that they could claim as their own. In writing about their food, they spoke not as marginalized minorities or victims of discrimination but as experts and teachers of the art of Chinese cuisine, diverging from the racial power structure that prevailed in the larger society.

What is more, cookbook writing gave Chinese American women a particularly meaningful and prominent forum. About three-quarters of the Chinese-food cookbooks published in the first eight decades of the twentieth century were written by women.[92] In public life in the early years, the voices of Chinese American women were seldom heard and their physical presence was rarely seen. This is in part because the number of Chinese women was extremely small in those years. Moreover, they faced not only racial discrimination in American society but also gender prejudice within the Chinese American community. They were even discouraged from going to Chinese restaurants in the early years.

For Chinese American authors, Chinese-food cookbook writing also constituted a form of self-expression. Beginning in the 1940s, Chinese American female cookbook writers outnumbered their male counterparts, and in their writing, the personal voices of Chinese cookbook authors became even more vocal over time. Buwei Yang Chao, for instance, noted how she learned to cook with "an open mind and an open mouth."[93] She also talked about her family's involvement in the production of her book. She mentioned her daughter's contribution in rendering the text into English and, in a humorous tone, her husband's role as a taster and critic. In *Mary Sia's Chinese Cookbook* (1956), Sia discussed her mother's zest for living and hospitality as the inspiration for her own interest in "the art of Chinese cooking."[94] For Hsiang-ju Lin and Tsuifeng Lin, writing a cookbook was also a family affair—a mother–daughter collaboration. As husband and father, Lin Yutang wrote an engaging foreword to the book and also served as a food tester.

The inclusion of family and personal experiences like these is extremely important, illustrating that cookbook writing is in essence a highly personal endeavor. As such, Chinese-food cookbooks did not have the same direct and extensive economic connection to the Chinese community at large as did the Chinese restaurants. Except for those published within a Chinese community, the cookbooks did not play the same role in forging or reinforcing a collective cultural identity, as did Chinese restaurants for Chinese America or Indian cookbooks for India. But this does not diminish the extraordinarily broad social importance of the Chinese-food cookbooks. These publications gave definitive voice to Chinese Americans, who otherwise remained as statistics in government documents or as stereotyped beings in the mass media. These cookbooks functioned as an effective tool in the Chinese struggle against racial prejudice. Cookbooks help us better understand the historic rise of Chinese food in the United States. Finally, they stand as a vivid reminder that the historical forces that shaped American Chinese food and our world are intimately and inseparably linked to our life as individuals.

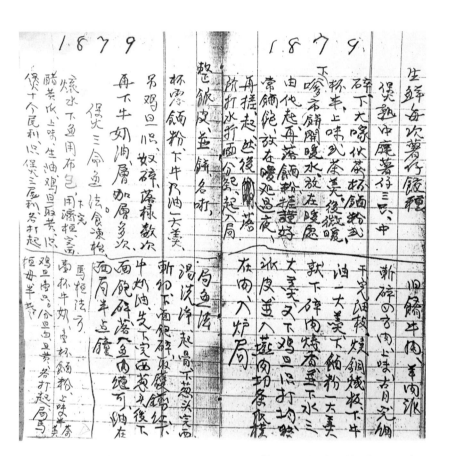

Ah Quin's recipes for potato and salmon dishes, muffins, and beef and lamb pies in his diary, 1879. (*Ah Quin Diary Collection, MS 209, San Diego History Center Document Collection, San Diego, Calif.*)

Nanking Cafe, established by Ah Quin's son, Tom, in San Diego. (*Collection of Yong Chen*)

A CHINESE RECEPTION IN SAN FRANCISCO.—DRAWN BY PAUL FRENZENY.—[SEE PAGE 446.]

© 1999 HARPWEEK®

Paul Frenzeny, "A Chinese Reception in San Francisco," *Harper's Weekly*, June 9, 1877. (*Reprinted by permission of HarpWeek*)

The dining hall of Shanghai Low, in San Francisco, in 1938. Established in 1913, it was proclaimed to be Chinatown's "best" restaurant. (*Collection of Yong Chen*)

Different editions of Buwei Yang Chao's famous cookbook *How to Cook and Eat in Chinese*. (*Photograph by Yong Chen*)

The menu of Yuen Faung Low, in Minneapolis, before World War II. (*Collection of Yong Chen*)

The Hing family's Spring Garden Grocery in Arizona, 1925. (*Courtesy Bill Hing*)

A view of the exhibition "Have You Eaten Yet?" at the Museum of Chinese in America, New York, 2005. (*Photograph by Yong Chen*)

Ming Tsai (*right*), chef/owner of Blue Ginger, one of a new generation of Chinese American restaurateurs who have ventured into fusion cooking. (*Photograph by Yong Chen*)

Panda Drive in Huntington Beach, California, one of the first independently owned drive-through Chinese restaurants, 2004. (*Photograph by Yong Chen*)

Chinese Inn, a take-out restaurant in New Orleans that serves African American customers, 2011. Its menu includes traditional food like chow chow, lo mein, and chow mein, as well as six kinds of Yetcamein dishes. (*Photograph by Yong Chen*)

Golden Bowl Chop Suey, a fortified take-out restaurant in Detroit that serves a predominantly African American clientele. (*Photograph by Yong Chen*)

Ocean Buffet in Brooklyn Center, Minnesota. Often operated by people from Fujian Province, especially Changle County, home to many undocumented immigrants, buffet-style eateries are a new trend in the Chinese restaurant industry across the United States. (*Photograph by Yong Chen*)

The Sichuan-style Cheng Du Tian Fu (Heavenly City of Chengdu) food stall in the basement of the food court at the Golden Mall in Flushing, New York, 2011. (*Photograph by Yong Chen*)

Mr. Lee, a California beef noodle franchise, in Haidian District, Beijing, 2010. (*Photograph by Yong Chen*)

American fast food transported the Chinese way: one of the delivery bicycles in front of a KFC restaurant in Wuhan, 2009. (*Photograph by Yong Chen*)

Panda Express at a rest stop along Interstate 5 in California, 2009. (*Photograph by Yong Chen*)

The first 99 Ranch Market in Irvine, California, which opened in December 1992. Since 1984, this Chinese supermarket chain has established thirty-five stores in four western states, thus becoming an important landmark in the development of new Chinese communities. (*Photograph by Yong Chen*)

Conclusion
THE HOME OF NO RETURN

This book began with my first arrival in the New World from China in 1985. Now I fast-forward to 1997, when I returned to my homeland after a twelve-year odyssey in the United States. Reminding us that "home" helps individuals relate to the larger world, the scholar Aviezer Tucker writes: "Home is the reflection of our subjectivity in the world."[1] Indeed, my long-awaited homecoming not only brought back previous memories but also was a moment of new revelations about the meanings of Chinese food, the "home" that food signified, and the geo-economic order in the modern Pacific world that predicated America's Chinese cuisine as well as my voyage to the United States.

In characterizing my New World journey, I have borrowed the title word of Homer's epic. Food has served as a vital signifier of identity in my American journey, as it did in the adventurous travels of Odysseus, the hero of Homer's *Odyssey*. He referred to unfamiliar people, such as the "Lotus-Eaters," "who live on a flowering food," in terms of their food habits.[2] Moreover, Odysseus harbored an uncompromising desire to return to his beloved home on Ithaka, an island off the coast of Greece. Similarly, when I left China for the New World or, more precisely, the upstate New York college town of Ithaca, I had only one intention: to get my doctorate in American history at Cornell University and return home.

Remembrance of home is a universally perennial motif in the experiences of immigrants and travelers. Ah Quin dreamed about his parents back in Kaiping

County.[3] He never returned to settle in China before his sudden death in San Diego in 1914. Many early Chinese immigrants also dreamed of returning home to China. Even those who could not afford to realize this dream in their lifetime still wished to be buried in their native place, which is why shipping the dead back to China remained an important task of the Chinese American community for decades. An old Chinese saying poetically conveys this desire: "Falling leaves return to their roots."

In the minds of these early Chinese immigrants and others, home represented not only a physical location but the way things used to be in the pre-emigration world as well. While living in the United States, therefore, Chinese Americans also tried to re-create a physical and cultural space that they could call home. In doing so, they formed Chinatowns, transplanted and supported their cuisine, articulated the meaning of Chinese food, and affirmed their identity as Chinese Americans.

Finally returning to his homeland after being away for twenty years, Odysseus reclaimed his home when he destroyed the intruders. But coming back to my native land, "home" became more elusive than ever before. No sooner had I stepped back on Chinese soil than I realized that "you can't go home again," the conclusion also reached by George Webber, the protagonist in Thomas Wolfe's novel.[4]

People have long associated the concept of home with a physical locus. As John Hollander notes, the English word "home" is derived from the Anglo-Saxon *ham*, meaning "village," "town," or "estate."[5] Many early Chinese immigrants kept almost photographic memories of scenes around the village, where their ancestral home resided, such as the small creek with water flowing in a leisurely way and shepherd boys singing joyfully on their way home.[6] Odysseus unwaveringly remembered his physical destination during his two decades of wandering, and even Wolfe's Webber had a hometown to return to. But home for me no longer meant a particular place. I did not return to the home of my childhood. My retired parents had moved from my native town to Wuhan, the capital of Hubei Province. Located in one of the recently built apartment buildings in Wuchang District, their two-bedroom unit hardly fit the image of home that I had longed for.

The country itself was also no longer the homeland of my youth. China had embarked on an unprecedented economic metamorphosis that promised to shatter the geo-economic conditions of our world. In a book published in 2005, Ted C. Fishman captures the astonishing pace and depth of the economic change that was under way in 1997: "No country has ever before made a better run at climbing every step of economic development all at once. . . . No country shocks the global economic hierarchy like China."[7] Figure 7 shows the magni-

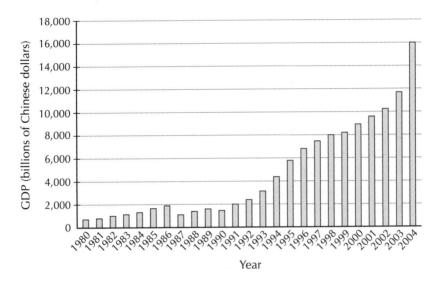

FIGURE 7 The growth of the gross domestic product of China, 1980–2004. (National Bureau of Statistics of China)

tude of this historic transformation of the Chinese economy, which would become the second largest in the world by 2011.

China's economic takeoff was fast narrowing its economic gap with the United States, a gap that has been a fundamental feature in the relationship between the two countries, playing an important role in shaping the character of American Chinese food. In the cities I visited in 1997 during my trip, the landscape was way beyond my recognition. As an indication of the drastic physical transformation under way, one-fifth of all the world's high-rise construction cranes in operation were now located in Greater Shanghai.[8]

Aside from a physical place, we also associate home with food. People often use the word "homemade" to describe the food that we cherish and find familiar. This association between food and home is coded in the Chinese character for "home," 家 (jia). The upper part of the word, 宀, represents a house, and the lower part, 豕, a pig.[9] In other words, home is where we expect to find nourishing, comforting, and familiar food.

Strolling on the streets of China's fast-changing cities, however, I could not even smell the once homey aroma of food. New eateries, including KFC and McDonald's, and often more upscale restaurants had replaced old food places. Back in 1985, there was no American fast food in China's food market. To get a hamburger in Beijing at that time, one had to go to the few exclusive hotels that were off-limits to ordinary Chinese, and it cost my American friends Bruce and Sandra 8 yuan, or about one-third of a common worker's monthly income, to buy my first American hamburger in the Great Wall Hotel. The rapidly expanding presence of the Golden Arches and Colonel Sanders in urban China now epitomizes a country in drastic metamorphosis.

American fast food's swift advance in China stands in sharp contrast to the development of Chinese food in America, which traveled on a long and winding road to mainstream America and consisted largely of small family operations. Backed by big capital, the Big Mac, by comparison, was an instant, spectacular success. The opening of China's first McDonald's in Beijing on April 23, 1992, shattered the Moscow opening-day record, attracting some 40,000 Chinese customers to the 28,000-square-foot restaurant, which had twenty-nine cash-register stations to handle the flow of customers.

Chinese restaurants rose to serve cheap food largely to underprivileged American consumers. Coming to China a century later, however, American fast food became an important part of the lifestyle of young and affluent consumers. In 1994, according to the anthropologist Yunxiang Yan, "a dinner at McDonald's for a family of three normally cost one-sixth of a worker's monthly salary."[10] In 2004, a relative of mine, who worked at a local bank in Wuhan, spent almost one-fifth of her monthly salary to take both our families to a KFC. In 1987, KFC was the first American fast-food company to arrive in China, and it has been the most successful.[11] The number of its stores broke the one thousand mark in 2004 and exceeded four thousand in 2012, almost three times the number of McDonald's outlets in the country, making KFC the largest restaurant franchise in China. When the four thousandth KFC store opened its doors in the coastal city of Dalian on September 25, 2012, the restaurant was serving at least 700,000 Chinese customers daily, or more than 250 million a year.

As in the case of American Chinese food, the spread of American fast food in China is also a socioeconomic, rather than a gastronomic, story. In other words, its success bespeaks the global dominance of America as an empire of mass consumption more than the supremacy of its food. Since 1997, the power of the American empire of mass consumption has been ever more evident in China, where the desire to live like Americans continues to expand. Even the Chinese premier wanted every Chinese to be able to have half a quart of milk every day.[12] At the same time, the consumption appetites of the more affluent consumers have made China's real estate red hot and turned the country into the world's largest automobile market in 2009. In terms of consumer desires and physical appearance, China increasingly looks more like America than the country where I grew up.

Everywhere I went in China in 1997 and in subsequent years, family and friends showered me with touching affection and generous hospitality. Many were eager to show me the good and real food of China. The food I tasted in glitzy restaurants, in little mom-and-pop places on crowded streets, or at the chaotic and dirty *da pai dang* (cooked-food stalls) opened my eyes to the diverse and dynamic world of Chinese cooking that I had not fully known before. It also reveals the complexities of questions about culinary authenticity, prompting me to wonder: Which is more authentic, the food of China in 1985 or that in 1997 and after?

Odysseus's odyssey concluded with his eventual homecoming, but mine has continued. Coming home to China, I realized that I could no longer return to the native land of my childhood, and I have become a temporary visitor and, quite often, a stranger. For all the years in the United States, I had been a Chinese in the minds of myself and others, but old Chinese friends in China saw and treated me more as an American than as a Chinese.

Where is home? I asked myself over and over. That question has attracted much scholarly interest in recent years. As Shelley Mallett points out, "There has been a proliferation of writing on the meaning of home" in a multitude of disciplines.[13] For me, though, it is not just an academic question but also an existential one about my selfhood in a fast-changing world, which sometimes makes me wonder which has changed more, China or myself.

Unlike Odysseus, who overcame many ordeals and temptations in his steadfast resolve to return to his home, I have eaten and have learned to enjoy many of the different cuisines that America has to offer, such as Indian, Japanese, French, Thai, Greek, Mexican, Korean, and Vietnamese. I have acquired a house and a job in southern California, where the climate turns people into lotus eaters, as the British thinker Bertrand Russell was once told.[14] As Odysseus knew, those who had eaten this "honey-sweet fruit" would forget their homes and want to stay with "the lotus-eating people."

Many early Chinese immigrants kept strong memories of China as their homeland but not just because they continued to uphold their traditional diet. There was another reason: the anti-Chinese racism they suffered in the United States, which repeatedly banned the entry of the Chinese, took away the rights of those visiting China to return to America, denied Chinese immigrants the right to become citizens, and even prohibited them to own real estate or marry a white person. In reference to such racial prejudice, Lee Chew remarked more than a century ago: "Under the circumstances, how can I call this my home, and how can any one blame me if I take my money and go back to my village in China?"[15]

The transformation of American society since then has fundamentally altered the meaning of being American. I have never had to face the same kind of racism that early Chinese Americans like Lee Chew did. Spending a majority of my half-century-long journey on earth in the United States, I have come to know the gastronomic landscape in American cities like Irvine, Los Angeles, San Francisco, and New York better than in Beijing, Shanghai, Nanjing, and Wuhan. Important changes in the socioeconomic conditions within China and America and in the U.S.-China equation during the past quarter-century have quietly but drastically shifted the meaning of home for Chinese Americans.

These changes have also broadened the meaning of Chinese food in China. A dazzling array of diverse regional and local foods from different provinces as well as Taiwan, Hong Kong, and ethnic Chinese communities in Southeast Asia has become a constant feature of the Chinese-food markets in major cities. Even American fast food in China has started to offer Chinese breakfast and lunch meals with increasing zest. Around 2004, the two giants, McDonald's and KFC, started a fierce war, each offering different Chinese breakfast items. Now, even traditional items like KFC's chicken popcorn sometimes tastes different from its version in America, as my two young sons found out in Wuhan in 2004—"It is so spicy!" they screamed. In January 2013, Yum! Brands—a restaurant company whose brands are KFC, Taco Bell, and Pizza Hut—received the Chinese government's permission to acquire, for $566 million, Little Sheep, a Mongolian hot-pot restaurant chain that first started in Inner Mongolia in 1999.[16]

As an illustration of how complex questions about the meaning of Chinese food have become, Chinese Americans have opened two restaurant franchises in China, selling food that is apparently Chinese but claiming it to be American in origin. Both offer "California beef noodles" (*jiazhou niu rou mian*). The founder of one of them, Wu Jinghong, started China's earliest California Beef Noodle King U.S.A. restaurant in 1986. By 2006, the franchise had more than three hundred stores nationwide. In spite of its name, this is, in reality, a brand made in China, not California or anywhere else in the United States. She did not even register the company in the United States until 1996, as she admitted to a reporter of *Beijing Chen Bao* (*Beijing Morning News*) in 2004.[17] Another California beef noodle restaurant franchise was started in 1987 by Li Beiqi, a China-born, Taiwan-educated Chinese immigrant. In 2008, Li changed the name of the more than four hundred restaurants from California Beef Noodle King to Mr. Lee. But as I have found out during my visits to several Mr. Lee outlets in recent years, reference to California Beef Noodle King remains visible in various places, including on its napkins. During a conversation with me in 2010, a customer in a Mr. Lee restaurant near Peking University was surprised to learn that the food was not American.

Changes in the China-U.S. Pacific world are also exerting a transformative impact on the Chinese-food industry in the United States. New waves of immigrants from far more diverse geographical regions in both China and the Chinese diaspora have added an extensive array of new dishes to the menus of Chinese restaurants. While some traditional American Chinese foods like chow mein and egg foo young have stayed quite noticeable, chop suey has long lost its prominence, eclipsed by Kung Pao, Sichuan, Hunan, and moo shu dishes. A few new dishes—most notably General Tso's chicken, which was adapted from a Hunan-style dish by a Taiwanese immigrant named Peng Chang-kuei—have evolved in the United States.[18] A growing number of Chinese restaurants, especially those in non-Chinese neighborhoods, offer dishes from non-Chinese cuisines, such as Japanese, Thai, Korean, and Malaysian. Many all-you-can-eat Chinese buffets, which have mushroomed across the nation in recent years, also prominently feature sushi, Thai-style noodles, and American desserts. Recent immigrants, especially ethnic Chinese from Cambodia, have opened restaurants that offer both Chinese food and donuts in California, where immigrants from Cambodia had owned 80 percent of the independent donut shops by the early twentieth century.[19] In such establishments as Jolly Chan's Chinese Food & Donuts in San Francisco, Chinese foods like orange chicken and fried rice with a "rainbow of donuts" combine to make a statement of cultural hybridity.[20]

Established food companies in mainland China as well as Taiwan, such as the legendary restaurant group Quanjude Roast Duck (famous for its Peking duck), have opened branches in the United States. Compared with the early Chinese-food establishments, which remained small operations, these new enterprises have far more resources and expertise, and can expand much more quickly. Little Sheep now operates in eleven cities in the United States, including Dallas, Irvine, New York, San Diego, San Gabriel, and San Mateo. The Little Sheep in San Mateo has already been recognized by CNN as one of the fifty best Chinese restaurants in the United States.[21]

More important, a continually improving Chinese economy will further shorten the economic distance between the United States and China. In doing so, it will significantly change the image and reality of the Chinese as a source of cheap labor. Such a change, in turn, will alter the century-long trajectory of American Chinese restaurants which have relied on Chinese labor.

Moon Cakes

Yields 16 cakes

It is time for dessert. Like our personal experiences, the development of foods, such as moon cakes, is also entangled with historical currents, as I have shown in chapter 7.

FILLING

8 pkg Green Max (Ma Yu Shan) Black Sesame Cereal
1 cup ground black sesame (or ground almond)
1¼ cup powdered sugar
¾ cup multigrain baking and pancake mix
½ cup nuts: pine nuts, walnuts, or pecans
1½ stick butter, at room temperature

CRUST

3¾ cups flour
1 tsp salt
2 tbsp sugar
14 tbsp shortening
11 oz heavy cream

For the filling, put the ingredients in a bowl. Use a pastry blender or fork to cut the butter into small pieces or until crumbled. Mix the ingredients thoroughly. Divide into 16 portions. Press and make 16 balls.

For the crust, place the flour, salt, sugar, and shortening in a bowl. Use a pastry blender or fork to cut the shortening into small pieces. Pour in the heavy cream and make a dough. Add extra heavy cream if needed. Divide into 16 pieces.

Roll out the dough and wrap the filling inside each. Lightly flatten the cake. Refrigerate for 30 minutes. Bake at 350°F for 30 minutes.

Set off by the overwhelmingly foreign environment that I entered more a quarter-century ago, my longing for things palatable to eat was the genesis of this book. The search for Chinese food has led me to towns and cities across the nation. It eventually brought me to California, home to America's first Chinatowns, and later all the way back to China. It was also a search for "home" in the fast-changing and globalizing world. But the exploration has also spawned new questions, including: Why there are so many Chinese restaurants in the United States? People in China and America have grappled with that question for more than a century. The ultimate answer lies not in the realm of gastronomy but in the geo-economic context in modern history, in which the United States has become a dominant power with incredible material abundance and China remained a land of scarcity and supplier of cheap labor. This context explains the exodus of Chinese immigrant laborers, who satisfied the budding consumption empire's needs—first in private kitchens and laundries, and later in affordable and convenient Chinese restaurants. The labor of the Chinese as well as other minorities and immigrants has helped America maintain its attraction as a land of material abundance.

The world order of the past two centuries is now seriously challenged in the Pacific region. When Americans can no longer get a Chinese lunch special for as little as the price for a Starbucks coffee, when customers no longer expect the entire Peking duck for less than $30, and when opera-goers regularly dine in a Chinese restaurant before going to a theater for Puccini, then a new geo-economic order will be just around the corner. Then, perhaps, I will finally find the home that I have been searching for. Then there will no longer be the American Chinese food as we know it.

Afterword
WHY STUDY FOOD?

In recent years, studies of food have proliferated and are reaching increasingly large audiences. This is in part because of the participation of popular writers and public intellectuals, who have extensive experience in writing for the general public. Written in lucid prose, their work tends to focus strategically on common individual foodstuffs;[1] some of them provocatively engage with fundamental socioeconomic, cultural, and moral matters that concern the well-being of society and individuals.[2] Many scholars have also adopted the approach of addressing large issues through the lens of a singular food item or system.[3]

There has been a marked increase in scholarly research on food within various academic disciplines, such as public health, literary studies, sociology, and anthropology, touching on a wide variety of topics ranging from culture to policies.[4] As latecomers to the table, as it were, historians are looking at food with newfound energy. In the area of American history, researchers have made fruitful efforts in chronicling food consumption in the United States.[5] Among them, Harvey A. Levenstein's work on nineteenth- and twentieth-century American foodways stands as still-unrivaled social history, combining his passion for food with meticulous research.[6] New research since then has significantly furthered our knowledge of food in American history and society, covering issues that did not receive sufficient attention from earlier scholars like Levenstein.[7]

One such issue is gender. Representing the fast-growing scholarship on this issue is the work of Sherrie A. Inness, a literary scholar by training, who has done a great deal in illuminating the importance of women in American food history. The essays in her anthology *Kitchen Culture in America* explore the critical roles of women in American food consumption.[8] Expanding her study of the ways in which American cooking literature served to keep women in the kitchen during the first half of the twentieth century in *Dinner Roles*, Inness wrote another book about the 1950s, *Secret Ingredients*, exploring not only gender but also race and class in cooking literature.[9]

Ethnic food, largely a misnomer for non-Anglo food, is another topic that has generated growing intellectual interest, and it has been used as a vehicle for studying racial minorities and immigrants in the world of gastronomy. The geographer Wilbur Zelinsky was one of the first to systematically survey America's ethnic-food landscape in his pioneering work in the 1980s.[10] Published around the same time, the anthology *Ethnic and Regional Foodways in the United States*, includes nine case studies of different minority and immigrant groups in an effort to explore the meaning and practice of traditional food in their lives.[11] Donna Gabaccia's pathbreaking book offers a comprehensive examination of the history of America's gastronomic diversity.[12] In an engagingly accessible study, Joel Denker, a longtime food writer, chronicles how different immigrant groups brought their food to the New World.[13]

A great amount of work has been done in understanding the connection between food and race in recent years, as evidenced in my essay "Food, Race, and Ethnicity."[14] For example, Frederick Douglass Opie highlights the immigrant presence in soul food, noting not only the influence of Caribbean cooking in the 1960s and 1970s but also the growing importance of ethnic succession as Harlem soul food restaurants have been taken over by recent immigrants.[15] Psyche A. Williams-Forson investigates the importance of chicken in the lives of African Americans, especially African American women. She acknowledges the racial stereotypes of African Americans that developed in connection with chicken, but she also shows its significance as a source of empowerment and income for them.[16]

Mexican food is another important ethnic cuisine. By 1980, it had become one of the "big three"—along with Chinese and Italian food—in the quickly expanding ethnic restaurant industry in the United States. Its history "has bubbled up in articles and chapters in books." Yet few have attempted a book-length study that "tracks each foodstuff, each craze, each pioneer, each controversy," as Gustavo Arellano notes in *Taco USA*, a provocative account of Mexican food's journey to American mass consumption.[17] Scholarly research on Mexican food remains disproportionately inadequate in light of its enormous presence in the marketplace and its extraordinary roles in facilitating immigration and cultural interactions.

Similarly, Americans have relished the food and convenience in Chinese restaurants for more than a century, but mainstream America paid strikingly scanty attention to the historical and cultural meaning of Chinese-food consumption. Since the 1990s, though, several essays have appeared in scholarly publications. In 1993, Gaye Tuchman and Harry Gene Levine drew attention to an extraordinary phenomenon: the long-standing Jewish connection to Chinese food.[18]

Shun Lu and Gary Alan Fine look into a question that many American Chinese restaurant-goers and commentators have wondered about: How authentically Chinese *is* the food in such restaurants? Chinese restaurateurs, the authors note, understood that "novel culinary traditions must be situated so as to seem simultaneously exotic and familiar: distinguishable from mainstream cuisine (and thus desirable) yet able to be assimilated as edible creations."[19] In a chapter in *Secret Ingredients*, Inness also explores the issue of culinary authenticity faced by Chinese American cookbook writers as they tried to appeal to non-Chinese audiences.[20]

Scholars have reminded us of the importance of transnational interactions as a context in which to understand the history of American Chinese food. For example, J. A. G. Roberts's *China to Chinatown* chronicles the spread of Chinese food in the West, including the United States, during the nineteenth and twentieth centuries. He also discusses writings about Chinese food by Americans living in China.[21] In an essay about the evolving Chinese restaurant industry in southern California, Haiming Liu and Lianlian Lin consider the role of immigration in the development of Chinese food and its importance to the Chinese community.[22]

The first decade of the twentieth-first century witnessed the publication of three books devoted to America's Chinese food: Jennifer 8 Lee's *The Fortune Cookie Chronicles*, Andrew Coe's *Chop Suey*, and John Jung's *Sweet and Sour*.[23] Lee provides captivating accounts of important episodes in the development of Chinese food in the United States, such as General Tso's chicken, the fortune cookie, and the experiences of illegal immigrants working in Chinese restaurants. As the first book-length study of the topic in English, Lee's book has garnered widespread attention. Coming from the world of food writing, Coe brings greater historical depth to the topics he covers. His extensive discussions of China's culinary tradition and the reactions to it from American travelers there help us understand the background of its development in the United States. Jung, a retired psychology professor, has successfully reinvented himself as an insightful and prolific scholar of the Chinese American experience. *Sweet and Sour* contains valuable stories, many told directly by Chinese restaurateurs, that shed important insights into the saga of American Chinese food. These publications pave the way for us to more directly and systematically investigate that fundamental question: How and why did Chinese food become so popular in the United States?

Indeed, the new research and publications about food mark only the beginning, and much more lies ahead. Of particular importance are two challenges. First, while participation by scholars and writers from a wide range of disciplines has significantly broadened our comprehension of the importance of food in different aspects of life, food as a topic has yet to become a coherent field of intellectual inquiry. Second, and more important, in spite of the fruitful efforts and insights of numerous food writers and scholars in this regard, the scholarship on food as a whole has not sufficiently helped society recognize the centrality of food in human experience and history.[24]

Confucius proclaimed in the *Book of Rites* that the pleasures in food and sex embody the great human desires.[25] Two centuries later, a young philosopher named Gao Zi expressed the same idea in a conversation with Mencius, declaring that the desires for food and for sexual pleasures represented human nature.[26] The United States and other Western societies have, since Freud, significantly advanced an appreciation of the far-reaching importance of human sexuality. But the role of food remains underappreciated, and the field of food studies has yet to produce Freud-like giants to comprehensively theorize and widely disseminate the centrality of food in human experience and history. Symptomatic of this underappreciation, many people have harbored deep and undisguised doubts of the intellectual legitimacy of such a seemingly mundane topic. After moving to the United States in 1959 and earning a master's degree in 1972 in eighteenth-century French literature, Jacques Pepin hoped to write a dissertation on the history of French food. But his hope was crushed by his adviser at Columbia University, a Frenchman, who said that "cuisine is not a serious art form. It's far too trivial for academic study." It was, the professor added, "not intellectual enough to form the basis of a Ph.D. thesis."[27] Over the decades, food researchers and writers often have to explain or even defend the significance of their topic. For example, the famous American food writer M. F. K. Fisher faced such questions as "Why do you write about food, and eating and drinking? Why don't you write about the struggle for power and security, and about love, the way others do?"[28] Other American food authors, such as Hasia Diner, have encountered similar suspicions about the academic validity of their topic.[29]

The failure of many Americans to fully appreciate the importance of food can be traced to four sources. First, in both the United States and China, there is a tendency to regard food as something sensual. A popular early-twentieth-century Chinese writer, Lin Yutang, wrote fondly that food is one of the "keen sensual pleasures of our childhood."[30] The American art historian Bernard Berenson also saw food as belonging to the realm of "sensual pleasures."[31] In both countries, eating is associated more with our emotions and bodily needs than with our minds.

Second, food, especially food preparation, is often seen as belonging to the private sphere of "women's work," whereas society tends to privilege men's activities and the public sphere. In the United States, historically, home cooking was considered to be women's responsibility, and white working-class men tended to stay away from jobs in the kitchen. This is why cooking quickly became an important occupation of marginalized and feminized Chinese immigrant men after their arrival in the mid-nineteenth century.

Third, prevailing social currents, such as the Puritan outlook, strongly discouraged attention to things gastronomic. The Bible extorts Christians not to focus on their bodily desires because "your body is the temple of the Holy Ghost which is in you" (1 Corinthians 6:19 [KJV]). And it warns: "[P]ut a knife to thy throat, if thou be a man given to appetite" (Proverbs 23:2 [KJV]). In the late nineteenth and early twentieth centuries, white Protestant reformers and home economists made a concerted effort to streamline American foodways in a dispassionately utilitarian approach. An important leader of the home economics movement was Ellen Henrietta Richards, a native of New England, who founded the American Home Economics Association in 1909. In 1870, she was the first woman to be admitted to the Massachusetts Institute of Technology, and she was also its first female graduate and instructor. As a chemist, she applied scientific concepts and principles to food, and in 1890 she opened the New England Kitchen, a demonstration workplace designed to provide scientifically prepared and low-cost food to the working class. Nonetheless, she could hardly have been called a foodie. For her, the value of food was determined in terms of calories, nutrition, and economics; it was not to be enjoyed in terms of taste or aesthetics. In her widely read *The Cost of Food* (1902), she cautioned against indulgence in food: "The man who has his eyes fixed on a good for which he is willing to subordinate everything else can maintain health without the luxuries of the table. He finds that food which will serve him best, and is not tempted by that which is useless."[32] In her mind, anything beyond what was necessary was bad not just for her individual Anglo readers but also for their race: "We take no warning from other animals and from plants, all of which fail of their best end when overfed. Nature does not make an exception in favor of man. . . . In all the discussions of the infertility of the higher branches of the human race, how little attention is paid to the weakening effect of the pampered appetite."[33] Apparently, her focus was not on food itself but on its social and moral ramifications.

Fourth, we have a tendency to take for granted things that are obvious and easily reachable. In affluent societies like the United States, food is numbingly abundant, making it seem mundane. In 2009, the average store (among the 35,612 large supermarkets) carried more than 48,000 food and food-related items, all of which are also available in other places, including retail giants like Wal-Mart and Target.[34] In addition, the plentitude of food is also measured by its accessibility and affordability. The percentage of income the average American has to spend on food has fallen from more than 42 percent in 1901 to about 13 percent in 2003.[35] Evidently, the more we are removed from hunger as a society, the less we remember the centrality of food in our existence as individuals and communities.

We must remember, though, that such extraordinary food abundance represents only an exception. As the economist John Kenneth Galbraith pointed out, throughout history most societies have been poor, and with poverty comes hunger. For most human beings, food scarcity has been a very common experience.

To more appropriately appreciate the significance of food, we have to recognize not only its intimate connection to every facet of our socioeconomic, cultural, and political life but also its central importance to our physical well-being and existence. To do so, we must study and understand food from perspectives that transcend the boundaries of traditional disciplines. This is a daunting task, but it also makes the study of food an exciting intellectual endeavor.

Notes

PREFACE

1. Fernand Braudel, *Civilization and Capitalism, 15th-18th Century*, vol. 2, *The Wheels of Commerce*, trans. Siân Reynolds (New York: Harper & Row, 1982), 134.

2. Alexis de Tocqueville, *Democracy in America* (1835, 1840; repr., New York: Walker, 1947), 346.

3. William Speer, *The Oldest and the Newest Empire: China and the United States* (Cincinnati: National Publishing, 1870).

4. Cynthia L. Chou, *My Life in the United States* (North Quincy, Mass.: Christopher, 1970), 18.

5. Kristin Hoganson, "Food and Entertainment from Every Corner of the Globe: Bourgeois U.S. Households as Points of Encounter, 1870-1920," *Amerikastudien* 48, no. 1 (2003): 115-135.

6. Lin Yutang, *My Country and My People* (1936; London: Heinemann, 1939), 318.

7. Wei Cheng, "My Chinese Stomach," *People's Daily*, January 26, 2005, 3, overseas edition.

ACKNOWLEDGMENTS

1. Arlie Hochschild, with Anne Machung, *The Second Shift: Working Families and the Revolution at Home* (New York: Penguin, 2012).

2. Frank Dikötter translates the quote as "Revolution is not a dinner party," in *Mao's Great Famine: The History of China's Most Devastating Catastrophe, 1958-1962* (New York: Walker, 2010).

3. The phrase is borrowed from Gang Yue, *The Mouth That Begs: Hunger, Cannibalism, and the Politics of Eating in Modern China* (Durham, N.C.: Duke University Press, 1999), 150.

INTRODUCTION

1. In their famous cookbook, the Beecher sisters characterized American cooking as representing "a fine abundance of material, carelessly and poorly treated" (Harriet Beecher Stowe and Catharine Esther Beecher, *The American Woman's Home: or, Principles of Domestic Science; Being a Guide to the Formation and Maintenance of Economical, Healthful, Beautiful, and Christian Homes* [New York: Ford, 1869], 168). For contemporary remarks on the topic, see Harvey A. Levenstein, *Revolution at the Table: The Transformation of the American Diet* (New York: Oxford University Press, 1988), 4; and Andrew P. Haley, *Turning the Tables: Restaurants and the Rise of the American Middle Class, 1880-1920* (Chapel Hill: University of North Carolina Press, 2011), 94. The mainstream American foodways came from the English, about whom Lin Yutang remarked: "The danger of not taking food seriously and allowing it to degenerate into a slipshod business may be studies in the English national life" (*My Country and My People* [1936; London: Heinemann, 1939], 319).

2. Bryan R. Johnson, "Let's Eat Chinese Tonight," *American Heritage*, December 1987, 98-107. A line below the title states: "Americans have been doing just that since the days of the California gold rush—and we're still not full."

1. WHY IS CHINESE FOOD SO POPULAR?

1. "Odd Chinese Dishes," *New York Tribune*, August 30, 1903, B2.

2. Xiang Dingrong, *Guofu Qi Fang Mei Tan Kao Shu* (*The Founding Father's Seven Visits to the Continental United States and Hawaii*) (Taipei: Shibao, 1982), 281.

3. Sun Yat-sen, *Memoirs of a Chinese Revolutionary: A Program of National Reconstruction for China* (1918; rept., Taipei: Sino-American, 1953), 24.

4. Tang Fuxiang, "The Crisis Facing Chinese Restaurants and the Solution," *Zhongguo Pengren* (*Chinese Cooking*) 8 (1988): 43.

5. Ronald Reagan to Ben J. Chen, November 29, 1982, in Ben John Chen (Chen Benchang), *Chen Benchang Wen Ji* (*Selected Works of Ben John Chen*) (New York: Asian American Republican National Federation, 1998), 3.

6. Chen Benchang (Ben John Chen), *Meiguo Huaqiao Canguan Gongye* (*The Chinese Restaurant Industry*) (Taipei: Yuandong Books, 1971), 216.

7. Paul Chan and Kenneth Baker, *How to Order a Real Chinese Meal* (New York: Guild Books, 1976), 3.

8. Wilbur Zelinsky, "The Roving Palate: North America's Ethnic Cuisines," *Geoforum* 16, no. 1 (1985): 56, 60. A survey conducted in 1989 of nineteen cuisines—including

Indian, German, Mexican, Italian, as well as Caribbean, Eastern European, Middle Eastern, Scandinavian, African, and Russian—showed that Chinese cuisine remained as the most frequently consumed. See National Restaurant Association, *The Market for Ethnic Foods: A Consumer Attitude and Behavior Study* (Washington, D.C.: National Restaurant Association, 1989), 9.

9. Tang, "Crisis Facing Chinese Restaurants and the Solution," 43.

10. Jennifer 8 Lee, *The Fortune Cookie Chronicles: Adventures in the World of Chinese Food* (New York: Twelve, 2008), 9. Lee's number comes from *Chinese Restaurant News*, an industry magazine, which did not provide details about how the number was determined.

11. The extensive survey, carried out with the help from a research assistant, was to get an estimate of the number of Chinese restaurants in the continental United States. The sixty-two cities in my sample were selected from different regions of the country. The total population size of the cities was more than 29 million, roughly 10 percent of the national population. The total number of Chinese restaurants that resulted from Yahoo Yellow Pages searches was 3,059. Assuming that this number represents 10 percent of the nation's total Chinese restaurants, there were more than 30,000 throughout the country. This, however, is likely to be an underestimate for two reasons. First, the tendency of Internet listings to be incomplete was common knowledge and was confirmed through a few sample cities. For example, in the city of Monterey Park, we found only twenty-one Chinese restaurants in the Yahoo Yellow Pages, but we located fifty-four in the 2006/2007 California Yellow Pages (Jiazhou caiye [published by the Chinese Overseas Company]).

12. Alexander Young, "Chinese Food and Cookery," *Appleton's Journal of Literature, Science and Art*, September 14, 1872, 293.

13. "Maxims of a Chinese Gourmand," *New York Times*, October 25, 1885, 4.

14. "Ways and Means," *Independent*, November 17, 1917, 343.

15. See, for example, "The Chinese to the President" [open letter], *Record of the Year* 1, no. 6 (1876): 601; and American Federation of Labor, *Some Reasons for Chinese Exclusion. Meat vs. Rice. American Manhood Against Asiatic Coolieism: Which Shall Survive?* (Washington, D.C.: American Federation of Labor, 1901).

16. Walter Francis Willcox et al., *Supplementary Analysis and Derivative Tables: Twelfth Census of the United States, 1900* (Washington, D.C.: Government Printing Office, 1906), 184; U.S. Bureau of the Census, *Abstract of the Fourteenth Census of the United States, 1920* (Washington, D.C.: Government Printing Office, 1923), 104.

17. U.S. Census Office, *Abstract of the Twelfth Census of the United States, 1900* (Washington, D.C.: Government Printing Office, 1902), 8.

18. The country's first naturalization act stipulates that only "a free white person" could become naturalized. See Richard Peters, ed., *The Public Statutes at Large of the United States of America* (Boston: Little and Brown, 1845), 1:103. Section 14 of the country's first

Chinese Exclusion Act (1882) expressly denies the right of the Chinese to be naturalized. See *The Statutes at Large of the United States of America* (Washington, D.C.: Government Printing Office, 1883), 22:61.

19. "Chinese Restaurants," *New York Tribune*, February 3, 1901, B6.

20. Arthur Chapman, "Why All the Chinese Restaurants?" *New York Tribune*, December 25, 1921, 6.

21. Sun Yat-sen, *Sun Wen Wueshuo* (*The Treatises of Sun Yat-sen*), facsimile of the 1918 manuscript (Taipei: Yangming, 1988). I did not use the text from the book's English-language version, *Memoirs of a Chinese Revolutionary*, because it contains significant differences from the Chinese version.

22. L'Enfant, "Odds and Ends from a Barrel of Shakings," *Spirit of the Times: A Chronicle of the Turf, Agriculture, Field Sports, Literature, and the Stage*, June 25, 1853, 217.

23. "A Chinese Banquet," *New York Times*, March 15, 1877, 2.

24. Cui Tongyue, *Hua Ying Chu Shu Da Quan* (*Chinese-English Comprehensive Cookbook*) (San Francisco: Fa Ming Gong Si, 1910).

25. Shiu Wong Chan, preface to *The Chinese Cook Book* (New York: Stokes, 1917).

26. Chen, *Meiguo Huaqiao Canguan Gongye*, 217.

27. Gregory C. Chow, *Knowing China* (River Edge, N.J.: World Scientific, 2004), 32.

28. "King Joy: The Finest Chinese-American Restaurant in the World," *Chicago Daily Tribune*, December 22, 1906, 20. Others had praised China's culinary tradition in like fashion. In 1893, Don Seitz wrote that the "Chinese are the epicures of the earth" ("A Celestial Farm on Long Island," *Frank Leslie's Popular Monthly* 35, no. 4 [1893]: 489).

29. Kenneth W. Andrew, *Chop Suey* (Elms Court Ilfracombe, Eng.: Stockwell, 1975), 76.

30. Fernand Braudel, *Civilization and Capitalism, 15th–18th Century*, vol. 1, *The Structures of Everyday Life*, trans. Siân Reynolds (1981; repr., Berkeley: University of California Press, 1992), 187.

31. Juliet Corson, "Chinese Cookery," *Harper's Bazaar*, July 17, 1897, 593.

32. "King Wah Lo," *Chicago Daily Tribune*, December 18, 1909, 24.

33. Wong Chin Foo, "Chinese Cooking," *Brooklyn Daily Eagle*, July 6, 1884, 4. Wong's article also appeared elsewhere, such as *Galveston (Tex.) Daily News*, July 27 1884, 10.

34. Emily Hahn, with editors of Time-Life Books, *The Cooking of China* (New York: Time-Life Books, 1968), 11.

35. Zelinsky, "Roving Palate," 53. Subsequently, other scholars have also looked at social factors as reasons to explain the popularity of ethnic food. See, for example, Krishnendu Ray, "Ethnic Succession and the New American Restaurant Cuisine," in

The Restaurants Book: Ethnographies of Where We Eat, ed. David Beriss and David Sutton (Oxford: Berg, 2007), 97–114.

36. For further discussions of this issue, see Murray A. Rubinstein, "American Board Missionaries and the Formation of American Opinion Toward China, 1830–1860," in *America Views China: American Images of China Then and Now*, ed. Jonathan Goldstein, Jerry Israel, and Hilary Conroy (Bethlehem, Pa.: Associated University Presses, 1991), 67–79. J. A. G. Roberts offers a survey of descriptions of Chinese food by Westerners, including American missionaries, in *China to Chinatown: Chinese Food in the West* (London: Reaktion, 2002), chaps. 2 and 3.

37. Warren I. Cohen, *Pacific Passage: The Study of American–East Asian Relations on the Eve of the Twenty-first Century* (New York: Columbia University Press, 1996), 10.

38. Samuel Wells Williams, *The Middle Kingdom: A Survey of the Geography, Government, Literature, Social Life, Arts, and History of the Chinese Empire and Its Inhabitants* (1848; repr., New York: Paragon Book, 1966), 1:771.

39. Ibid., 779.

40. Ibid., 781.

41. Immigration has continued to play an important role in the transplantation of new regional Chinese foodways to the United States. See Haiming Liu and Lianlian Lin, "Food, Culinary Identity, and Transnational Culture: Chinese Restaurant Business in Southern California," *Journal of Asian American Studies* 12, no. 2 (2009): 135–162.

42. Brian Greenberg and Linda S. Watts, *Social History of the United States: The 1990s* (Santa Barbara, Calif.: ABC-CLIO, 2009), 337.

43. U.S. Bureau of the Census, *1980 Census of Population: Subject Reports. Asian and Pacific Islander Population in the United States, 1980* (Washington, D.C.: Bureau of the Census, 1988), 2.

44. Terrance J. Reeves and Claudette E. Bennett, *We the People: Asians in the United States*, Census 2000 Special Reports (CENSR-17) (Washington, D.C.: U.S. Economics and Statistics Administration and U.S. Bureau of the Census, December 2004), 1.

45. *Wayside, Gleason's Pictorial Drawing-Room Companion*, January 21, 1854, 47.

46. *Saturday Evening Post*, August 25, 1860, 8.

47. Thomas W. Cox, "The Coming Man," *Frank Leslie's Illustrated Newspaper*, May 21, 1870, 154.

48. "Chinese Cookery," *Daily Arkansas Gazette* (Little Rock), June 10, 1880.

49. "The Chinese in San Francisco: How to Cook and Eat in Their Theatres," *Frank Leslie's Illustrated Newspaper*, June 14, 1879, 248.

50. *Monroe City (Mo.) Democrat*, October 18, 1906, 3.

51. Joseph Carey, *By the Golden Gate: Or, San Francisco, the Queen City of the Pacific Coast; with Scenes and Incidents Characteristic of Its Life* (Albany, N.Y.: Albany Diocesan Press, 1902), 196.

52. Louis Joseph Beck, *New York's Chinatown: An Historical Presentation of Its People and Places* (New York: Bohemia, 1898), 296.

53. "Mott-Street Chinamen Angry," *New York Times*, August 1, 1883, 8.

54. Mary H. Krout, "Cookery Among the Chinese," *New York Tribune*, October 30, 1904, 10.

55. Paul C. P. Siu, *The Chinese Laundryman: A Study of Social Isolation*, ed. John Kuo Wei Tchen (New York: New York University Press, 1988), 8.

56. *People's Daily*, March 2, 2007, 6, overseas edition.

57. Xu Ke, *Qing Bai Lei Chao (Qing Unofficial History Categorized Extracts)* (Shanghai: Shangwu, 1917). This forty-eight-volume book provides an encyclopedic coverage of Chinese life during the Qing dynasty. For the original text in Chinese, see http://www.guoxue123.com/zhibu/0201/03qblc/ (accessed June 16, 2014).

58. Jia Ming, *Yingshi Xu Zhi (All You Must Know About Food)*, in *Yin Zhuan Pu Lu (A Collection of Writings on Drinks and Food)*, ed. Yang Jialuo (Taipei: Shijie shuju, 1992), 103. For the original text in Chinese, see http://www.tcm100.com/user/ysxz/zzbook7.htm (accessed February 9, 2014).

59. Frank Morton Todd, *Eradicating Plague from San Francisco: Report of the Citizens' Health Committee and the Account of Its Work* (San Francisco: Murdock, 1909), 19, 25, 38, 21.

60. Lee Chew, "The Life Story of a Chinaman," *Independent*, February 19, 1903, 421.

2. THE EMPIRE AND EMPIRE FOOD

1. M. C. Briggs, introduction to Otis Gibson, *The Chinese in America* (Cincinnati: Hitchcock & Walden, 1877), 11.

2. See, for example, Sidney Wilfred Mintz, *Sweetness and Power: The Place of Sugar in Modern History* (New York: Viking, 1986); James Walvin, *Fruits of Empire: Exotic Produce and British Taste, 1660–1800* (New York: New York University Press, 1997); and Gary Y. Okihiro, *Pineapple Culture: A History of the Tropical and Temperate Zones* (Berkeley: University of California Press, 2009).

3. Mintz, *Sweetness and Power*, 14.

4. Richard Street, *Beasts of the Field: A Narrative History of California Farmworkers, 1769–1913* (Stanford, Calif.: Stanford University Press, 2004), 246.

5. Cecilia Leong-Salobir, *Food Culture in Colonial Asia: A Taste of Empire* (New York: Routledge, 2011), 1.

6. See, for example, Charles J. McClain and Laurene Wu McClain, "The Chinese Contribution to the Development of American Law," in *Entry Denied: Exclusion and the Chinese Community in America, 1882–1943*, ed. Sucheng Chan (Philadelphia: Temple University Press, 1991), 3–24.

7. Ching Chao Wu, "Chinatowns: A Study of Symbiosis and Assimilation" (Ph.D. diss., University of Chicago, 1928), 22.

8. "Chop Suey Best of All," *Guthrie (Okla.) Daily Leader*, July 8, 1907, 5.

9. Norman Douglas, *Good-bye to Western Culture: Some Footnotes on East and West* (New York: Harper, 1930), 19.

10. Ronald Reagan called the Soviet Union "an evil empire" with "aggressive impulses" (Remarks at the Annual Convention of the National Association of Evangelicals [Orlando, Fla., March 8, 1983], TeachingAmericanHistory.org, http://teachingamer icanhistory.org/library/index.asp?document=961 [accessed July 2, 2010]).

11. Walter Lippmann, *Men of Destiny*, with a new introduction by Paul Roazen (1927; repr., Piscataway, N.J.: Transaction, 2003), 215.

12. William Appleman Williams, *Empire as a Way of Life: An Essay on the Causes and Character of America's Present Predicament, Along with a Few Thoughts About an Alternative*, with an introduction by Andrew Bacevich (1980; repr., New York: Ig, 2007), 4.

13. Niall Ferguson, *Colossus: The Rise and Fall of the American Empire* (New York: Penguin, 2004), 6.

14. Charles S. Maier, *Among Empires: American Ascendancy and Its Predecessors* (Cambridge, Mass.: Harvard University Press, 2006), 3.

15. John Gallagher and Ronald E. Robinson, "The Imperialism of Free Trade," *Economic History Review*, 2nd ser., 6, no. 1 (1953): 1–15.

16. Andrew Dalby, *Empire of Pleasures: Luxury and Indulgence in the Roman World* (New York: Routledge, 2000), 248.

17. Jerome Carcopino, *Daily Life in Ancient Rome: The People and the City at the Height* (New Haven, Conn.: Yale University Press, 1960), 17.

18. C. R. L. Fletcher and Rudyard Kipling, *A School History of England* (Oxford: Clarendon Press, 1911), 235–236. At the time, Britain relied on imports for more than half of its food supplies. See Rachel Laudan, *Cuisine and Empire: Cooking in World History* (Berkeley: University of California Press, 2013), 307.

19. Okihiro, *Pineapple Culture*, 5.

20. Lenin is one of those who saw empires as representing a different phase in human history. While noting the economic nature of imperial expansions, he branded imperialism as the highest and last stage of capitalism before the victory of Communism. Some scholars have insisted that "an empire must be distinguished from a state" (Michael Hardt, *Empire* [Cambridge, Mass.: Harvard University Press, 2000], 1).

21. Ferguson, *Colossus*, 14.

22. Stuart Banner, *How the Indians Lost Their Land: Law and Power on the Frontier* (Cambridge, Mass.: Belknap Press of Harvard University Press, 2005).

23. J. D. B. Debow, *Statistical View of the United States* (Washington, D.C.: Beverley Tucker, Senate Printer, 1854), 32.

24. Ellen C. Collier, "Instances of Use of United States Forces Abroad, 1798–1993" (1993), Naval History and Heritage Command, http://www.history.navy.mil/wars /foabroad.htm (accessed May 7, 2012). Williams listed 130 instances of American interventionist activities from 1798 to 1941, in *Empire as a Way of Life*, 71–74, 97–106, 130–136, 156–159.

25. Herfried Münkler, *Empires: The Logic of World Domination from Ancient Rome to the United States*, trans. Patrick Camiller (Cambridge: Polity, 2007).

26. Woodrow Wilson, "Address on International Trade, Before the Salesmanship Congress," in *President Wilson's Foreign Policy: Messages, Addresses, Papers*, ed. *James Brown Scott* (New York: Oxford University Press, 1918), 224.

27. One of the most influential and perceptive critics of the American empire on the Left is William Appleman Williams, author of *The Tragedy of American Diplomacy*, rev. ed. (New York: Dell, 1962). An example of its recent critics, on the Right, is Patrick Buchanan, *A Republic, Not an Empire: Reclaiming America's Destiny* (Washington, D.C.: Regnery, 1999).

28. Ronald Steel, "When Worlds Collide," *New York Times*, July 21, 1996, E15.

29. U.S. Bureau of the Census, *Historical Statistics of the United States: Colonial Times to 1970* (Washington, D.C.: Government Printing Office, 1975), pt. I, 10, 105–106.

30. John Galbraith, *The Affluent Society* (Boston: Houghton Mifflin, 1958), I.

31. Robin Archer, *Why Is There No Labor Party in the United States?* (Princeton, N.J.: Princeton University Press, 2010), 25.

32. Alan Thein Durning, *How Much Is Enough? The Consumer Society and the Future of the Earth* (New York: Norton, 1992), 8.

33. Lawrence B. Glickman, "Introduction: Born to Shop? Consumer History and American History," in *Consumer Society in American History: A Reader*, ed. Lawrence B. Glickman (Ithaca, N.Y.: Cornell University Press, 1999), I.

34. Marshall Sahlins, *Stone Age Economics* (Chicago: Aldine-Atherton, 1972), 13–14.

35. "Richard M. Nixon & Nikita Khrushchev: The Kitchen Debate," YouTube, http://www.youtube.com/watch?v=VPWGIi6YqVo (accessed May 11, 2012).

36. Jung Chang and Jon Holiday, *Mao: The Unknown Story* (New York: Knopf, 2005).

37. Williams, *Empire as a Way of Life*, 7.

38. George H. Hildebrand, "Consumer Sovereignty in Modern Times," *American Economic Review* 41, no. 2 (1951): 33.

39. John Burnett, *A History of the Cost of Living* (New York: Penguin, 1969); Zygmunt Bauman, *Work, Consumerism, and the New Poor* (Milton Keynes, Eng.: Open University Press, 1998).

40. William Grimes, "American Culture Examined as a Force That Grips the World," *New York Times*, March 11, 1992, C17.

41. Gary Cross, *An All-Consuming Century: Why Commercialism Won in Modern America* (New York: Columbia University Press, 2000), 3. At the same time, however, we must not overstate the democratic nature of mass consumption. We will see later that class status still matters significantly in the American mass consumer society. Cross also points out that in some ways consumerism poses a threat to political democracy. Pierre Bourdieu has remarked that individuals' taste in consumption choices is not as individualistic as it seems, but has much to do with class distinction, in *Distinction: A Social Critique of the Judgment of Taste* (Cambridge, Mass.: Harvard University Press, 1984), chap. 3. Thoughtful and more recent critiques of mass consumer culture and its class dimension are Josée Johnston, "The Citizen–Consumer Hybrid: Ideological Tensions and the Case of Whole Foods Market," *Theory and Society* 37, no. 3 (2008): 229–270; and Juliet B. Schor, "In Defense of Consumer Critique: Revisiting the Consumption Debates of the Twentieth Century," *Annals of the American Academy of Political and Social Science* 611 (2007): 16–30.

42. James Madison, "Letter to Spencer Roane," September 2, 1819, in *The Writings of James Madison*, ed. Gaillard Hunt (New York: Putnam, 1908), 3:448.

43. James Madison, "Letter to Thomas Jefferson," October 24, 1787, in *The Writings of James Madison*, ed. Gaillard Hunt (New York: Putnam, 1904), 5:28.

44. Alexander Hamilton, James Madison, and John Jay, *The Federalist Papers*, ed. Clinton Rossiter (New York: New American Library, 1961), 83.

45. Jeremy D. Bailey, *Thomas Jefferson and Executive Power* (Cambridge: Cambridge University Press, 2007), 172.

46. Alexander DeConde, *This Affair of Louisiana* (New York: Scribner, 1976), 185.

47. Thomas Jefferson, "The President to the Territorial Legislature," December 28, 1805, Indiana Historical Bureau, http://www.in.gov/history/2893.htm (accessed May 8, 2012).

48. Barry J. Balleck, "When the Ends Justify the Means: Thomas Jefferson and the Louisiana Purchase," *Presidential Studies Quarterly* 22, no. 4 (1992): 687.

49. Francis Higginson, *New-England's Plantation: With the Sea Journal and Other Writings* (1630; repr., Salem, Mass.: Essex Book and Print Club, 1908), 93–94.

50. Timothy H. Breen, "Narrative of Commercial Life: Consumption, Ideology, and Community on the Eve of the American Revolution," *William and Mary Quarterly* 50, no. 3 (1993): 483–484.

51. Timothy H. Breen, *The Marketplace of Revolution: How Consumer Politics Shaped American Independence* (Oxford: Oxford University Press, 2004), 72.

52. Alexis de Tocqueville, *Democracy in America* (1835, 1840; repr., New York: Walker, 1947), 251.

53. Michael Schudson, "Delectable Materialism: Second Thoughts on Consumer Culture," in Glickman, *Consumer Society in American History*, 341–358.

54. Ibid.

55. *Zuo Zhuan* (*Tso Chuan*), "Zhuanggong Shinian" (The Tenth Year of Duke Zhuang), quoted and translated from Chinese Text Project, http://ctext.org/chun-qiu-zuo-zhuan/zhuang-gong. Also known as the *Chronicle of Zuo* and allegedly written by Zuo Qiuming in the fourth century B.C.E, *Zuo Zhuan* is an ancient Chinese historical text covering the years 722 to 468 B.C.E.

56. *Zuo Zhuan*, "Aigong Shinian" (The Tenth Year of Duke Ai), quoted and translated from Chinese Text Project, http://ctext.org/chun-qiu-zuo-zhuan/ai-gong.

57. "Eating in China," *New York Times*, March 16, 1873, 2.

58. *China and the Chinese: A Compend of Missionary Information from Various Sources* (Toronto: Methodist Society, 1892), 7.

59. Charles Dickens, "The Italian Peasant," *All the Year Round* 4, no. 97 (1870): 442.

60. Vaclav Smil, *Feeding the World: A Challenge for the Twenty-first Century* (Cambridge, Mass.: MIT Press, 2001), 262. It is likely that Fernand Braudel's notion of "carnivorous Europe" in the two centuries before the 1650s may have significantly overstated the amount of meat that was generally available. After mentioning a six-course meal from late-fourteenth-century French cookbooks, which included a dish with pâtés of beef, rissoles, lamprey, and two broths with meat, he notes that "consumption of meat on this scale does not seem to have been a luxury reserved to the very rich in the fifteenth and sixteenth centuries" (*Civilization and Capitalism, 15th–18th Century*, vol. 1, *The Structures of Everyday Life*, trans. Siân Reynolds [1981; repr., Berkeley: University of California Press, 1992], 190). In the agricultural age, both yields of grain and efficiency of animal meat production were very low, making it difficult to believe that sufficient quantities of meat could be generated for munificent consumptions of the general population. Game could not be a reliable source of regular meat supply.

61. Quoted in Hasia R. Diner, *Hungering for America: Italian, Irish, and Jewish Foodways in the Age of Migration* (Cambridge, Mass.: Harvard University Press, 2002), 13.

62. "Consumption of Meat," *Southern Planter* 1, no. 6 (1841): 119.

63. Alan Beardsworth and Teresa Keil, *Sociology on the Menu: An Invitation to the Study of Food and Society* (New York: Routledge, 1997), 211.

64. Jeremy Rifkin, *Beyond Beef: The Rise and Fall of the Cattle Culture* (New York: Plume, 1992), 244.

65. American Federation of Labor, *Some Reasons for Chinese Exclusion. Meat vs. Rice. American Manhood Against Asiatic Coolieism. Which Shall Survive?* (Washington, D.C.: American Federation of Labor, 1901).

66. Peter Dauvergne, *The Shadows of Consumption: Consequences for the Global Environment* (Cambridge, Mass.: MIT Press, 2008), 140. See also Marvin Harris and Eric B. Ross, "How Beef Became King," *Psychology Today* 12, no. 5 (1978): 88–94; and C. E. Ball, "Historical Overview of Beef Production and Beef Organizations in the United States," *Journal of Animal Science* 79 (2000): 1–8.

67. *Daily Picayune* (New Orleans, La.), May 22, 1898, 5.

68. John H. Dyck and Kenneth E. Nelson, *Structure of the Global Markets for Meat*, Agriculture Information Bulletin, no. 785 (Washington, D.C.: Market and Trade Economics Division, Economic Research Service, U.S. Department of Agriculture, 2003), 5. Estimates of feed-meat conversion efficiency fluctuate quite a bit because the calculation involves several variables, such as feed quality and levels of concentrates and moisture contained in it. People have also defined "meat" differently in their calculations. The calculations also vary from country to country.

69. Allan G. Bogue, "Farming in the Prairie Peninsula, 1830–1890," *Journal of Economic History* 23, no. 1 (1963): 3.

70. Frederick A. P. Barnard, ed., *Johnson's (Revised) Universal Cyclopaedia* (New York: Johnson, 1886), 8:759, s.v., "United States Meat Production."

71. Tocqueville, *Democracy in America*, 464.

72. U.S. Congress, House of Representatives, *Hearings Before the Committee on Banking and Currency*, 53rd Cong., 3rd sess. (Washington. D.C.: Government Printing Office, 1894), 5.

73. Williams, *Tragedy of American Diplomacy*, 15.

74. Andrew J. Bacevich, *The Limits of Power: The End of American Exceptionalism* (New York: Metropolitan Books, 2008), 22.

75. Münkler, *Empires*, 27.

76. Tocqueville, *Democracy in America*, 325.

77. Such deficiencies have been pointed out by an increasing number of scholars, including the Western historian Patricia Limerick, in introduction to *The Legacy of Conquest: The Unbroken Past of the American West* (New York: Norton, 1987).

78. Frederick Jackson Turner, *The Frontier in American History* (New York: Holt, 1921), 293. This book includes his seminal essay "The Significance of the Frontier in American History," which he delivered at the World's Columbian Exposition in Chicago in 1893.

79. David Potter, *People of Plenty: Economic Abundance and the American Character* (Chicago: University of Chicago Press, 1954), 112.

80. Lizabeth Cohen, *A Consumers' Republic: The Politics of Mass Consumption in Post-war America* (New York: Vintage, 2003), 126.

81. Reinhold Niebuhr, *The Irony of American History*, with a new introduction by Andrew J. Bacevich (1952; repr., Chicago: University of Chicago Press, 2008), 55.

82. Werner Sombart, *Why There Is No Socialism in the United States*, trans. Patricia M. Hocking and C. T. Husbands (1906; repr., White Plains, N.Y.: International Arts and Sciences Press, 1976), 106. The question has generated "endless debates among historians" and many others, as Eric Foner pointed out in "Why Is There No Socialism in the United States?" *History Workshop*, no. 17 (1984): 57.

83. "Uncle Sam's Thanksgiving Dinner," *Harper's Weekly*, November 20, 1869, 745.

84. Gordon Lloyd, *The Two Faces of Liberalism: How the Hoover-Roosevelt Debate Shapes the 21st Century* (Salem, Mass.: Scrivener Press, 2006), 31.

85. Ibid., 37.

86. Franklin D. Roosevelt, "Address of Governor Franklin D. Roosevelt in Forbes Field, Pittsburgh, Pennsylvania, October 19, 1932," FDR Presidential Library, http://www.fdrlibrary.marist.edu/aboutfdr/pdfs/smCampaign_10-19-1932.pdf (accessed May 17, 2012).

87. Gardiner C. Means, "The Consumer and the New Deal," *Annals of the American Academy of Political and Social Science* 173 (1934): 7.

88. Walter LaFeber, *The American Century: A History of the United States Since the 1890s*, 2nd ed. (New York: Wiley, 1979), 210.

89. Stuart Blumin, *The Emergence of the Middle Class: Social Experience in the American City, 1760-1900* (Cambridge: Cambridge University Press, 1989), 185.

90. Kathryn Grover, *Dining in America, 1850-1900* (Amherst: University of Massachusetts Press, 1987), 155.

91. Many scholars of the emerging American middle class have focused on women, including their household managerial roles. See, for example, Mary Ryan, *Cradle of the Middle Class: The Family in Oneida County, New York, 1790-1865* (Cambridge: Cambridge University Press, 1981); Nancy Cott, *The Bonds of Womanhood: "Woman's Sphere" in New England, 1780-1835* (New Haven, Conn.: Yale University Press, 1977); and Reva B. Siegel, "Home as Work: The First Woman's Rights Claims Concerning Wives' Household Labor, 1850-1880," *Yale Law Journal* 103, no. 5 (1994): 1073-1217.

92. Francis A. Walker, *Compendium of the Ninth Census* (Washington, D.C.: Government Printing Office, 1872), 605; J. D. B. Debow, *The Seventh Census of the United States* (Washington, D.C.: Robert Armstrong, Public Printer, 1853), lxxvi; U.S. Census Office, *Compendium of the Tenth Census* (Washington, D.C.: Government Printing Office, 1883), pt. 2, 1378.

93. U.S. Bureau of the Census, *Thirteenth Census of the United States*, vol. 4, *Population 1910: Occupational Statistics* (Washington, D.C.: Government Printing Office, 1914), 41.

94. Daniel J. Boorstin, *The Americans*, vol. 3, *The Democratic Experience* (New York: Random House, 1973), 91.

95. Alexander Hamilton, *Itinerarium*, quoted in Breen, *Marketplace of Revolution*, 34.

96. Glenna Matthews, *"Just a Housewife": The Rise and Fall of Domesticity in America* (New York: Oxford University Press, 1987), 100.

97. Edward Bellamy, *Looking Backward: 2000–1887* (1887; repr., Bedford, Mass.: Applewood Books, 2000), 74–75.

98. Alice A. Deck, "'Now Then—Who Said Biscuits'? The Black Woman Cook as Fetish in American Advertising, 1905–1953," in *Kitchen Culture in America: Popular Representations of Food, Gender, and Race*, ed. Sherrie Inness (Philadelphia: University of Pennsylvania Press, 2001), 89.

99. For a survey of historical changes in the complex notion of work, see Herbert A. Applebaum, *The Concept of Work: Ancient, Medieval, and Modern* (Albany: State University of New York Press, 1992).

100. Karl Marx, *Critique of the Gotha Program* (1875; repr., Rockville, Md.: Wildside Press, 2008), 27.

101. Others have also paid attention to such efficacies in Marx's understanding of human nature. See, for example, Mark A. Lutz, "The Limitations of Karl Marx's Social Economics," *Review of Social Economy* 37, no. 3 (1979): 329–344.

102. Thorstein Veblen, *The Theory of the Leisure Class* (1899; repr., New York: Kelley, 1965), 56.

103. Catherine Selden, "The Tyranny of the Kitchen," *North American Review* 157, no. 4 (1893): 431–440.

104. Minna Wright, "My Chinese Cook," *Ladies' Repository*, April 1870, 301.

105. *The Good Housekeeping Cook Book* (New York: Farrar & Rinehart, 1943), 3.

106. Peg Bracken, *I Hate to Cook Book* (Greenwich, Conn.: Fawcett Crest, 1960), vii.

107. Bracken passed away in 2007. See Adam Bernstein, "Peg Bracken: Eased the Path to Dinner," *Washington Post*, October 23, 2007, http://www.washingtonpost.com/wp-dyn/content/article/2007/10/22/AR2007102202204.html (accessed November 6, 2012).

108. Toni Morrison, "What the Black Woman Thinks About Women's Lib," *New York Times Magazine*, August 22, 1971, 63.

109. Confucius, *Confucian Analects* (*Lunyu-Shuer*). James Legge translated the statement as "From the man bringing him a bundle of dried flesh for my teaching upwards, I have never refused instruction to any one" (Chinese Text Project, http://ctext.org

/analects/shu-er [accessed June 7, 2012]). Frequently cited as evidence of his egalitarian education philosophy, this statement has received different interpretations over the centuries, as the Chinese scholar Yu Zhihui has shown in "Lunyu-Shuer 'Zi Xing Shu Xiu Yi Shang, Wu Wei Xhang Wu Hui Yan'" (On the Statement "From the man bringing him a bundle of dried flesh for my teaching upward, I have never refused instruction to any one," in *Confucian Analects*), *Kong Meng Yue Kan* (*Confucius and Mencius Studies Monthly*) 37, no. 5 (1999). This statement nonetheless reveals his love for meat, which was known to his contemporaries. A high-ranking official, whom Confucius strongly disliked, sent him a small cooked pig, in order to see him. See *Confucian Analects*.

110. *Book of Rites* (*Liji-Yuzao*). Later, Mencius repeated the statement in *Mengzi-Liang Hui Wang*. Both Confucius and Mencius appear to have been referring to the killing of animals, but many have since read the statement also as expressing a desire to stay away from kitchen work.

111. Bureau of the Census, *Thirteenth Census of the United States*, 4:23, and *Fourteenth Census of the United States*, vol. 4, *Population 1920: Occupations* (Washington, D.C.: Government Printing Office, 1923), 16.

112. In re Ah Yow, *The Federal Reporter*, vol. 59, *Cases Argued and Determined in the Circuit Courts of Appeals and Circuit and District Courts of the United States* (St. Paul: West, 1894), 561.

113. Bellamy, *Looking Backward*, 74.

114. More detailed recommendations of daily calorie intake for different groups can be found in U.S. Department of Agriculture and U.S. Department of Health and Human Services, *Dietary Guidelines for Americans, 2010* (Washington, D.C.: Government Printing Office, 2010), 78.

115. W. E. Burghardt Du Bois, *The Philadelphia Negro: A Social Study, Together with A Special Report on Domestic Service by Isabel Eaton* (Philadelphia: University of Pennsylvania, 1899), 136.

116. Judith Rollins, *Between Women: Domestics and Their Employers* (Philadelphia: Temple University Press, 1985), 51. Rollins's assumption that from the mid-nineteenth century to World War I, immigrants replaced native-born whites as the dominant group in domestic service underestimates the continued presence of native whites in this area. See Bureau of the Census, *Thirteenth Census of the United States*, 4:433.

117. U.S. Census Office, *Report on Population of the United States at the Eleventh Census: 1890* (Washington, D.C.: Government Printing Office, 1897), pt. 2, cxlvi.

118. William Leach, *Land of Desire: Merchants, Power, and the Rise of a New American Culture* (New York: Vintage, 1992), 131.

119. Andrew P. Haley, *Turning the Tables: Restaurants and the Rise of the American Middle Class, 1880–1920* (Chapel Hill: University of North Carolina Press, 2011), 71.

120. Gary Y. Okihiro, *Margins and Mainstreams: Asians in American History and Culture* (Seattle: University of Washington Press, 1994), ix.

3. Chinese Cooks as Stewards of Empire

1. "The Chinaman's Conquest," *Youth's Companion*, March 18, 1909, 136.

2. Peter Lampe, *Christians at Rome in the First Two Centuries: From Paul to Valentinus* (London: Continuum, 2006), 172.

3. "The Cooleys," *Sacramento Union*, May 1, 1852.

4. *Alta California* (San Francisco), August 1, 1853.

5. Rodman W. Paul, "The Origin of the Chinese Issue in California," *Mississippi Valley Historical Review* 25, no. 2 (1938): 196.

6. William Speer, "The First Stone in the Foundation of the Synod of China," *Chinese Recorder and Missionary Journal* 30 (1899): 479.

7. William Speer, *China and California: Their Relations, Past and Present* (San Francisco: Marvin & Hitchcock, 1853), 11.

8. Ibid., 15.

9. William Speer, *An Humble Plea, Addressed to the Legislature of California, in Behalf of the Immigrants from the Empire of China to This State* (San Francisco: Oriental, 1856), 28.

10. "A Soothing View of That Terrible Individual," *San Francisco Daily Chronicle*, May 15, 1869, 2.

11. George Frederick Seward, *Chinese Immigration in Its Social and Economical Aspects* (New York: Scribner, 1881), 124, 334.

12. Clara E. Hamilton, "A Woman's View of Chinese Exclusion," *Independent* 54, no. 2781 (1902): 692.

13. Sunyowe Pang, "The Chinese in America," *Forum* 32, no. 5 (1902): 605.

14. "The Chinese in New York," *New York Tribune*, October 8, 1870, 11.

15. Robert Henry Cobbold, *Pictures of the Chinese, Drawn by Themselves* (London: Murray, 1860), 206.

16. *Lippincott's Monthly Magazine*, February 1892, 262.

17. "Chinese Cooks," *Current Literature* 31, no. 3 (1901): 315.

18. Alice A. Harrison, "Chinese Food and Restaurant," *Overland*, June 1917, 527. The notion of Chinese as good cooks has continued over the decades. See, for example, Gaye Tuchman and Harry Gene Levine, "New York Jews and Chinese Food: The Social Construction of an Ethnic Pattern," in *The Taste of American Place: A Reader on Regional and Ethnic Foods*, ed. Barbara Gimla Shortridge and James R. Shortridge (Lanham, Md.: Rowman & Littlefield, 1998), 165.

19. "China as Affected by Protestant Missions," *Biblical Repertory and Princeton Review* 42, no. 4 (1870): 620.

20. Mary Stewart Daggett, "The Lion and the Lamb," *Outlook*, July 28, 1906, 761.

21. Arnold Genthe, *Pictures of Old Chinatown*, with text by Will Irwin (New York: Moffat, Yard, 1909), 7.

22. Jane Faison, "The Virtues of the Chinese Servant," *Good Housekeeping*, March 1906, 279.

23. Canada Royal Commission on Chinese Immigration, *Report of the Royal Commission on Chinese Immigration: Report and Evidence* (Ottawa: Printed by order of the Commission, 1885), xxxvii.

24. See, for example, "Just One Chinese Servant," *New York Evangelist*, July 29, 1886, 7.

25. "A California Housekeeper on Chinese Servants," *Harper's Bazaar*, May 8, 1880, 290.

26. "The Attitude of the United States Towards the Chinese," *Forum*, June 1900, 392.

27. David Igler, *Industrial Cowboys: Miller & Lux and the Transformation of the Far West, 1850–1920* (Berkeley: University of California Press, 2001), 133.

28. Alice Louise Lee, "'Ma' Staples and Her 'Boys,'" *Youth's Companion*, November 18, 1909, 597.

29. *San Francisco Chronicle*, August 25, 1902, 6.

30. *Oregonian* (Portland), October 14, 1886.

31. *San Diego Union*, June 10, 1884, 3.

32. *Riverside (Calif.) Daily Press*, October 2, 1893, 3.

33. Quoted in Seward, *Chinese Immigration in Its Social and Economical Aspects*, 124, 334.

34. "White Cooks Must Keep Sober or Go," *New York Times*, November 7, 1885, 3.

35. Hamilton, "Woman's View of Chinese Exclusion," 693.

36. Charles Dobie, *San Francisco's Chinatown* (New York: Appleton-Century, 1936), 93.

37. "The Chinese as Servants: What Happened When Bridget and Maggie Retired, and Ching Took Charge of the House," *New York Times*, April 4, 1880, 5.

38. U.S. Congress, *Report of the Joint Special Committee to Investigate Chinese Immigration* (Washington, D.C.: Government Printing Office, 1877).

39. James Beard, *The Essential James Beard Cookbook: 450 Recipes That Shaped the Tradition of American Cooking* (New York: Macmillan, 2012), 1.

40. In 1870, the 143,956 Irish domestic servants represented 15 percent, as well as the single most important segment, of the Irish labor force. See Francis A. Walker, *Compendium of the Ninth Census* (Washington, D.C.: Government Printing Office, 1872), 605.

41. Only 3,835 African Americans and less than 3 percent of the Irish immigrants lived in California.

42. Walker, *Compendium of the Ninth Census*, 605-615. Kwang Chang Ling (the pseudonym of Alexander del Mar) estimated that there were 7,200 Chinese in domestic service and the laundry business, in *Why Should the Chinese Go? A Pertinent Inquiry from a Mandarin High in Authority* (San Francisco: Bruce's, 1878), 14.

43. J. S. Tow, *The Real Chinese in America* (New York: Academy Press, 1923), 75.

44. Federal census manuscript schedules for 1870 from the Second through the Fifth Wards of San Francisco, National Archives.

45. Lee Chew, "The Life Story of a Chinaman," *Independent*, February 19, 1903, 420.

46. Ping Chiu, *Chinese Labor in California, 1850-1880: An Economic Study* (Madison: State Historical Society of Wisconsin for the Department of History, University of Wisconsin, 1963), 65.

47. Letter to the editor, *Oregonian*, October 14, 1886.

48. *San Francisco Bulletin*, August 1, 1885, 1.

49. J. H. Russell, *Cattle on the Conejo* (Pasadena, Calif.: Ward Ritchie Press, 1959), 13.

50. Richard Street, *Beasts of the Field: A Narrative History of California Farmworkers, 1769-1913* (Stanford, Calif.: Stanford University Press, 2004), 243.

51. Stewart Edward White, "The Mountains," *Outlook*, July 30, 1904, 746.

52. Arthur Chapman, "Why All the Chinese Restaurants?" *New York Tribune*, December 25, 1921, 6.

53. John David Borthwick, *Three Years in California* (Edinburgh: Blackwood, 1857), 75-76.

54. Olivier Zunz, *The Changing Face of Inequality: Urbanization, Industrial Development, and Immigrants in Detroit, 1880-1920* (Chicago: University of Chicago Press, 2000), 16.

55. U.S. Bureau of the Census, *Fifteenth Census of the United States: 1930. Population* (Washington, D.C.: Government Printing Office, 1930), 932.

56. G. H. Thurston and J. H Diffenbacher, comps., *Directory of Pittsburgh and Allegheny Cities for 1875-1876* (Pittsburgh: Anderson, 1875).

57. R. L. Polk & Co., comp., *Michigan State Gazetteer and Business Directory* (Detroit: Tribune, 1875), 815.

58. Paul C. P. Siu, *The Chinese Laundryman: A Study of Social Isolation*, ed. John Kuo Wei Tchen (New York: New York University Press, 1988), 23.

59. Huping Ling, *Chinese St. Louis: From Enclave to Cultural Community* (Philadelphia: Temple University Press, 2004), 35.

60. Sampson, Davenport & Co., *The Boston Directory, Embracing the City Record, a General Directory of the Citizens, and a Business Directory for the Year Commencing July 1, 1875*, Boston Streets: Mapping Director Data, http://bcd.lib.tufts.edu/view_text.jsp?urn=tufts:central:dca:UA069:UA069.005.DO.00020&chapter=d.1875.su.Wah (accessed January 5, 2014).

61. For more detailed discussions of the early Chinese presence in New York, see John Kuo Wei Tchen, *New York Before Chinatown: Orientalism and the Shaping of American Culture, 1776–1882* (Baltimore: Johns Hopkins University Press, 1999).

62. "Chinese in New York," *New York Tribune*, 11. In 1875, C. P. Bush estimated that of the two hundred Chinese in the city, more worked as cigar makers than as servants, in "The Chinese in New York," *New York Evangelist*, August 5, 1875, 1.

63. "The Chinese in New York," *New York Times*, March 6, 1880, 8.

64. Ibid.; "Chinese New Year Festivity," *New York Times*, February 8, 1883, 10.

65. "Queer Chinese Traits," *York Tribune*, May 22, 1887, 13.

66. Stewart Culin, *China in America: A Study in the Social Life of the Chinese in the Eastern Cities of the United States* (Philadelphia, 1887); Wong Chin Foo, "The Chinese in New York," *Cosmopolitan*, June 1888, 298.

67. *Providence Directory* (Providence: Sampson, Davenport, 1878), 392.

68. *Providence Directory and Rhode Island Business Directory* (Providence: Sampson, Murdock, 1900), 935–936.

69. *Chicago City Directory* (Chicago: Chicago Directory Company, 1900), 2419.

70. *Boyd's Copartnership and Residence: Business Directory of Philadelphia City* (Philadelphia: Boyd's Directory Office, 1900).

71. "Our Chinese Colony," *Harper's Weekly*, November 22, 1890, 910.

72. Chiu, *Chinese Labor in California*, 65.

73. Quoted in Seward, *Chinese Immigration in Its Social and Economical Aspects*, 115.

74. U.S. Bureau of the Census, *Thirteenth Census of the United States*, vol. 4, *Population 1910: Occupational Statistics* (Washington, D.C.: Government Printing Office, 1914). This volume lists Chinese together with Indians and Japanese.

75. Ibid., 433.

76. "My Chinese Cook," *Ladies' Repository*, April 1870, 1.

77. *Chinese Nationalist Daily*, July 4, 1903, 8.

78. Liu Zongren, *Two Years in the Melting Pot* (1984; repr., San Francisco: China Books, 1988), 178.

79. Lewis Coser, "Servants: The Obsolescence of an Occupational Role," *Social Forces* 52, no. 1 (1973): 31–40.

80. David M. Katzman, *Seven Days a Week: Women and Domestic Service in Industrializing America* (1978; repr., Urbana: University of Illinois Press, 1981), 55.

81. David Held, Anthony McGrew, David Goldblatt, and Jonathan Perraton, *Global Transformations: Politics, Economics, and Culture* (Stanford, Calif.: Stanford University Press, 1999), 415.

82. Sucheng Chan, "Chinese Livelihood in Rural California: The Impact of Economic Change, 1860–1880," *Pacific Historical Review* 53, no. 3 (1984): 185.

83. Roi Ottley, "Hectic Harlem," *New York Amsterdam News*, April 25, 1936, 13.

84. Rebecca Sharpless, *Cooking in Other Women's Kitchens: Domestic Workers in the South, 1865–1960* (Chapel Hill: University of North Carolina Press, 2010), 3.

85. Prentice Mulford, "California Culinary Experiences," *Overland Monthly*, June 1869, 557.

86. "Over the Mountains," *Daily Morning Chronicle* (Washington, D.C.), October 1, 1868, 3.

87. *Independent*, February 14, 1878, 7.

88. Ah Quin, diary entry, June 1, 1878.

89. Pang, "Chinese in America," 604.

90. Street, *Beasts of the Field*, 246.

91. I am deeply grateful to Frank Low, grandson of Kee Low, for sharing his memory and knowledge about his grandfather and his family.

92. Russell, *Cattle on the Conejo*, 13.

93. Susie Lan Cassel, "To Inscribe the Self Daily: The Discovery of the Ah Quin Diary," in *The Chinese in America: A History from Gold Mountain to the New Millennium*, ed. Susie Lan Cassel (Walnut Creek, Calif.: AltaMira Press, 2002), 60.

94. My discussions here are based on Richard Wing, interview with the author, March 2001.

95. Gerald M. Pops, *Ethical Leadership in Turbulent Times: Modeling the Public Career of George C. Marshall* (Lanham, Md.: Lexington Books, 2009), 272. Richard Wing recalled instances that indicate his close personal relationship with the general, in "General George Marshall and I," *Gum Saan Journal* 30 (2007): 33–34.

96. Robin Michael Roberts, *Hanford: 1900–2000* (San Francisco: Arcadia, 2007), 62.

97. Eunice Ward, "Ah Gin," *Overland Monthly and Out West Magazine*, May 1907, 393–396.

98. "The Situation in China," *Outlook*, October 13, 1915, 352.

99. *Manford's New Monthly Magazine* 39, no. 6 (1895): 382.

100. *Current Literature* 36, no. 6 (1904): 676; *Anderson (S.C.) Intelligencer*, March 13, 1901, 6

101. "The Heathen Husband," *Riverside Independent Enterprise*, October 5, 1894, 1.

102. "Loved Her Chinese Cook," *National Police Gazette*, May 25, 1895, 6.

103. "Chinese in New York," *New York Tribune*, 11. In the 1870s in San Francisco, the rate for domestics was $25 to $30 a month, according to Benjamin S. Brooks, *The Chinese in California: To the Committee on Foreign Relations of the United State Senate* (1876), 12.

104. Lee, "Life Story of a Chinaman," 420. Comparable wage numbers were reported elsewhere. See, for example, "Chinese in New York," *New York Times*, 8.

105. See, for example, John Bonner, "The Labor Question of the Pacific Coast," *Californian Illustrated Magazine*, April 1892, 415.

106. Charles H. Shinn, "Another Word on That Chinese Question," *Outlook*, June 14, 1902, 475; "Reviving San Francisco," *Congregationalist and Christian World*, August 18, 1906, 197.

107. Russell Herman Conwell, *Why and How: Why the Chinese Emigrate, and the Means They Adopt for the Purpose of Reaching America* (Boston: Lee & Shepard, 1871), 62.

108. Dora E. W. Spratt, "Earning a Living in China," *Lippincott's Monthly Magazine*, May 1, 1897, 670.

109. Gunther Paul Barth, *Bitter Strength: A History of the Chinese in the U.S., 1850–1970* (Cambridge, Mass.: Harvard University Press, 1974), 196. The two thousand or so Chinese who went to work in the South were actually paid $13 to $18, plus room and board as well as a free return passage. See Sucheng Chan, *Asian Americans: An Interpretive History* (Boston: Twayne, 1991), 82.

110. Chiu, *Chinese Labor in California*, 45, 72.

111. "Must the Chinese Go?" *Christian Union*, August 2, 1888, 118.

112. *Alta California*, June 4, 1856, col. E.

113. Rose Hum Lee, *The Chinese in the United States of America* (Hong Kong: Hong Kong University Press, 1960), 357.

114. Liping Zhu, *A Chinaman's Chance: The Chinese on the Rocky Mountain Mining Frontier* (Niwot: University Press of Colorado, 1997), 119.

115. Beard, *Essential James Beard Cookbook*, 1.

116. "California Housekeeper on Chinese Servants," 290.

117. Lee, "Life Story of a Chinaman," 420.

118. "California Culinary Experiences," *Overland Monthly and Out West Magazine*, June 1869, 557.

119. See, for example, Ah Quin, diary entry, January 20, 1879.

120. Cui Tongyue, ed., *Hua Ying Chu Shu Da Quan* (*Chinese-English Comprehensive Cookbook*) (San Francisco: Fa Ming Gong Si, 1910), conversation handbook, 1–2.

121. Ibid., 13, 14, 18, 20–24.

122. *Oriental*, February 12, 1875.

123. Barbara Thuro, *Gardening in Spanish: How to Communicate Effectively with Your Spanish Speaking Gardener* [audio cassette] (Carlsbad, Calif.: Penton Overseas, 1995); Jardinera Feliz, *Gardening in Spanish: Useful Spanish Terms and Expressions for Gardeners, Landscaper Professionals, Horticulturalists, and Produce Growers* (Fallbrook, Calif.: Ammie, 2010).

124. Benoni Lanctot, *Chinese and English Phrase Book, with the Chinese Pronunciation Indicated in English, Specially Adapted for the Use of Merchants, Travelers, and Families* (San Francisco: Roman, 1867), 23, 30, 34.

125. Wong Sam and Assistants, *An English–Chinese Phrase Book*, in *The Big Aiiieeeee! An Anthology of Chinese American and Japanese American Literature*, ed. Jeffery Paul Chan, Frank Chin, Lawson Fusao Inada, and Shawn Wong (New York: Penguin, 1991), 93.

126. Ibid., 101.

127. Thomas Lathrop Stedman and K. P. Lee, *A Chinese and English Phrase Book in the Canton Dialect: Or, Dialogues on Ordinary and Familiar Subjects for the Use of the Chinese Resident in America, and of Americans Desirous of Learning the Chinese Language; with the Pronunciation of Each Word Indicated in Chinese and Roman Characters* (New York: Jenkins, 1888). The conversational sentences appear in both Chinese and English with corresponding transliterations in both languages. Clearly, the book was not intended only for Chinese immigrants.

128. Wolfgang Mieder, *Politics of Proverbs: From Traditional Wisdom to Proverbial Stereotypes* (Madison: University of Wisconsin Press, 1997), 161.

129. In 1994, a Chinese scientist sued his white colleague for using this slur toward him. See Wolfgang Mieder, "'No Tickee, No Washee': Subtleties of a Proverbial Slur," *Western Folklore* 55, no. 1 (1996): 1–40.

130. Stedman and Lee, *Chinese and English Phrase Book*, 108.

131. Ibid., 114.

132. Ibid., 116, 118, 120.

133. Cui Tongyue, ed., *Hua Ying Chu Shu Da Quan*, preface.

134. Russell, *Cattle on the Conejo*, 15.

135. U.S. Bureau of the Census, *Statistical Brief* (November 1995).

136. U.S. Bureau of the Census, *We, the American Asians* (Washington, D.C.: Government Printing Office, 1993), 7.

137. "Filipinos Feed 4,800 Navy Cadets," *Filipino Reporter*, March 28, 2002, 46.

138. Edmund M. Silvestre, "Survey: Filipino Food Going Nowhere," *Filipino Reporter*, September 22, 1994, 20.

139. Ibid.

4. THE CRADLE OF CHINESE FOOD

1. Jerome A. Hart, "The New Chinatown in San Francisco," *Bohemian Magazine*, May 1909, 604.

2. "Voice of Wisdom and Age," *Friends' Weekly Intelligencer*, January 26, 1850, 349.

3. "Meeting of the Chinese Residents of San Francisco," *Alta California* (San Francisco), December, 10, 1849.

4. Bayard Taylor, *Eldorado, or, Adventures in the Path of Empire, Comprising a Voyage to California, via Panama; Life in San Francisco and Monterey; Pictures of the Gold Region; and Experiences of Mexican Travel* (New York: Putnam, 1894), 117, 165.

5. Ibid., 95, 165.

6. Mary Beth Norton et al., *A People and a Nation: A History of the United States*, 9th ed. (Boston: Wadsworth, 2011), 355.

7. Philip J. Ethington, *The Public City: The Political Construction of Urban Life in San Francisco, 1850–1900* (Berkeley: University of California Press, 2001), 47.

8. *Alta California*, August 15, 1851, 3.

9. William Shaw, *Golden Dream and Waking Realities* (London: Smith, Elder, 1851), quoted in *Literary Gazette and Journal of the Belles Letters*, September 20, 1951, 634.

10. James O'Meara, "The Chinese in Early Days," *Overland Monthly*, May 1884, 477.

11. *Alta California*, October 1, 1850.

12. *Alta California*, March 1, 1852.

13. *Golden Hill's News* (San Francisco), June 24, 1854.

14. "Chinese Directory," *Oriental* (San Francisco), February 8, 1856.

15. Charles P. Kimball, *San Francisco City Directory* (San Francisco: Journal of Commerce Press, 1850), 8, 24.

16. For more detailed discussion of French origins of the restaurant in the West, see Rebecca Spang, *The Invention of the Restaurant: Paris and Modern Gastronomic Culture* (Cambridge, Mass.: Harvard University Press, 2000).

17. Several scholars have written about him, including Gunther Paul Barth, *Bitter Strength: A History of the Chinese in the United States, 1850–1870* (Cambridge, Mass.: Harvard University Press, 1964), 82–85; H. Mark Lai, *Becoming Chinese American: A History of Communities and Institutions* (Walnut Creek, Calif.: AltaMira Press, 2004); and David Brion Davis, *Antebellum American Culture: An Interpretive Anthology* (University Park: Penn State University Press, 1979).

18. Lai, *Becoming Chinese American*, 179.

19. Yuk Ow, H. Mark Lai, and P. Choy, eds., *Lumei Sanyi Zonghuiguan Jianshi (A Brief History of the Three-District Association)* (San Francisco, 1975), 58.

20. *Alta California*, October 31, 1850.

21. "To His Excellency Gov. Bigler," *Daily Alta California*, May 5, 1852.

22. Ow, Lai, and Choy, *Yumei Sanyi Zonghuiguan Jianshi*, 58.

23. *Alta California*, October 15, 1850.

24. *LeCount and Strong's San Francisco City Directory for the Year 1854* (San Francisco: San Francisco Herald Office, 1854), 228.

25. Barth, *Bitter Strength*, 82–83.

26. Ibid., 82.

27. James O'Meara, "Pioneer Sketches–4. To California by Sea," *Overland Monthly*, April 1884, 380.

28. Mary Floyd Williams, *History of the San Francisco Committee of Vigilance of 1851: A Study of Social Control on the California Frontier in the Days of the Gold Rush* (Berkeley: University of California Press, 1921).

29. *Daily Alta California*, March 8, 1851.

30. Ibid., June 16, 1852.

31. *Sacramento Daily Union*, February 10, 1855.

32. *The Constitution of Oregon* (Portland: McCormick, 1857).

33. *Evening Bulletin* (San Francisco), October 13, 1858.

34. William Speer, *An Humble Plea, Addressed to the Legislature of California, in Behalf of the Immigrants from the Empire of China to This State* (San Francisco: Oriental, 1856), 24.

35. *Hale and Emory's Marysville City Directory* (Marysville, Calif.: Printed at the Marysville Herald Office, 1853), 49, 52.

36. Sucheng Chan, "Chinese Livelihood in Rural California: The Impact of Economic Change, 1860–1880," *Pacific Historical Review* 53, no. 3 (1984): 300–303.

37. Wells Fargo, *Directory of Principal Chinese Business Firms* [San Francisco, Sacramento, Marysville, Portland (Oregon), Stockton, San Jose, and Virginia City (Nevada)] (San Francisco, 1878), and *Directory of Principal Chinese Business Firms* [San Francisco, Oakland, Los Angeles, Virginia City, Victoria, and Denver] (San Francisco, 1882).

38. Chan, "Chinese Livelihood in Rural California," 302, 304.

39. Ibid., 301, 303, 306.

40. Wells Fargo, *Directory of Principal Chinese Business Firms* (1878).

41. Chan, "Chinese Livelihood in Rural California," 304–305.

42. Speer, *Humble Plea*, 24.

43. Wells Fargo, *Directory of Principal Chinese Business Firms* (1882); Henry G. Langley, comp., *San Francisco Directory* (San Francisco, 1878, 1882).

44. *Oriental*, October 23, 1875, 1.

45. Richard Wing, interview with the author, March 12, 2001; Sasha Khokha, "In Rural California, an Imperial Dynasty Ends," NPR, March 24, 2006, http://www.npr.org/templates/story/story.php?storyId=5298206 (accessed August 19, 2012); Lai, *Becoming Chinese American*, 154.

46. Marie Rose Wong, *Sweet Cakes, Long Journey: The Chinatowns of Portland, Oregon* (Seattle: University of Washington Press, 2004). Her exact count of service workers in 1880 was eight (under the category of "servant/housekeeper"), thirty-five (under "cook"), and sixty-nine (under "domestics").

47. Wells Fargo, *Directory of Principal Chinese Business Firms* (1878).

48. Lou Chenghao and Xue Shunsheng, *Xiao Shi De Shanghai Lao Jian Zhu* (*Disappearing Historical Buildings in Shanghai*) (Shanghai: Tongji University Press, 2002), 56.

49. Andrew Coe, *Chop Suey: A Cultural History of Chinese Food in the United States* (New York: Oxford University Press, 2009), 123.

50. "Pagan Gods Scotched," *Morning Call* (San Francisco), October 27, 1892, 3.

51. Huping Ling, *Chinese St. Louis: From Enclave to Cultural Community* (Philadelphia: Temple University Press, 2004), 26; U.S. Census Office, *Ninth Census of the United States: Statistics of Population* (Washington, D.C.: Government Printing Office, 1872).

52. The city had 170 Chinese in 1900, according to Ling, *Chinese St. Louis*, 30, 35. There were also Chinese servants in the city, but they were likely fewer than the laundrymen. In 1910, for instance, there were only twenty-seven "Indian, Chinese, and Japanese" servants. See U.S. Bureau of the Census, *Thirteenth Census of the United States*, vol. 4, *Population 1910: Occupational Statistics* (Washington, D.C.: Government Printing Office, 1914), 598.

53. Stewart Culin, *China in America: A Study in the Social Life of the Chinese in the Eastern Cities of the United States* (Philadelphia, 1887), 10, 11.

54. G. B. Densmore, *The Chinese in California: Descriptions of Chinese Life in San Francisco, Their Habits, Morals and Manners* (San Francisco: Pettit & Russ, 1880), 31.

55. William A. Cohen, *Filth: Dirt, Disgust, and Modern Life* (Minneapolis: University of Minnesota Press, 2004).

56. Trygg Engen, *Odor Sensation, and Memory* (New York: Praeger, 1991), 1; Richard Palmer, "In Bad Odour: Smell and Its Significance in Medicine from Antiquity to the Seventeenth Century," in *Medicine and the Five Senses*, ed. W. F. Bynum and Roy Porter (New York: Cambridge University Press, 1993), 61–68.

57. Marcia Barinaga, "Salmon Follow Watery Odors Home," *Science*, October 22, 1999, 705–706.

58. Lin Yutang, *The Importance of Living* (New York: Day, 1937), 221.

59. David E. Sutton, *Remembrance of Repasts: An Anthropology of Food and Memory* (New York: Berg, 2001), 89.

60. Ibid., 94.

61. Wah-chung Leung, diary entry, February 10, 1922. I am grateful to Sandy Yee Man Leung for permission to use her family documents.

62. John David Borthwick, *Three Years in California* (Edinburgh: Blackwood, 1857), 75.

63. Alain Corbin, *The Foul and the Fragrant: Odor and the French Social Imagination* (New York: Berg, 1986).

64. Mark M. Smith, "Producing Sense, Consuming Sense, Making Sense: Perils and Prospects for Sensory History," *Journal of Social History* 40, no. 4 (2007): 852.

65. Otis Gibson, *The Chinese in America* (Cincinnati: Hitchcock & Walden, 1877), 63–64.

66. William H. Brewer, "In and About San Francisco," in *Up and Down California in 1860–1864: The Journal of William H. Brewer*, ed. Francis P. Farquhar (1933; repr., Berkeley: University of California Press, 1966), 367. See also William Brown Meloney, "Slumming in New York's Chinatown," *Munsey's Magazine*, September 1909, 821.

67. *Chinatown Declared a Nuisance!* (San Francisco, 1880), 15; Densmore, *Chinese in California*, 47.

68. Samuel Bowles, *Our New West: Records of Travel Between the Mississippi River and the Pacific Ocean* (New York: Dennison, 1869), 412–413.

69. Iza Duffus Hardy, *Between Two Oceans: Or, Sketches of American Travel* (London: Hurst & Blackett, 1884), 153.

70. "Luxuries at a Chinese Restaurant," *New York Tribune*, October 23, 1887, 12.

71. "Chicago Chinamen," *Wisconsin State Register* (Portage), August 24, 1889, col. C.

72. "Chinese Restaurants," *Atchison (Kan.) Daily Champion*, December 23, 1890, 6.

73. "Bits of Chinatown," *New York Tribune*, May 2, 1880, 2.

74. "Hop Alley," *St. Louis Republic*, January 29, 1905, sec. 2.

75. For more discussion of this subject, see Thomas Hummel and Antje Welge-Lüssen, eds., *Taste and Smell: An Update* (Basel: Karger, 2006).

76. Connie Y. Chang, "Monterey-by-the-Smell: Odors and Social Conflict on the California Coastline," *Pacific Historical Review* 73 (2004): 183–214.

77. "Mott-Street Chinamen Angry," *New York Times*, August 1, 1883, 8.

78. Guenter B. Risse, *Plague, Fear, and Politics in San Francisco's Chinatown* (Baltimore: Johns Hopkins University Press, 2012), 71.

79. *Chinatown Declared a Nuisance!*, 15.

80. "Chinese Restaurants," 6.

81. Virgil C. Hart, *Western China: A Journey to the Great Buddhist Centre of Mount Omei* (Boston: Ticknor, 1888), 40. Hart and many other Westerners railed about odors in China. See Diana Preston, *The Boxer Rebellion: The Dramatic Story of China's War on Foreigners That Shook the World in the Summer of 1900* (New York: Walker, 2000).

82. Jean Anthelme Brillat-Savarin, *The Physiology of Taste or Transcendental Gastronomy*, trans. Fayette Robinson (Philadelphia: Lindsay & Blakiston, 1854), 25.

83. *Scribner's Magazine*, January 1910, 14.

84. Arthur Henderson Smith, *Chinese Characteristics* (New York: Revell, 1894), 19.

85. Samuel Wells Williams, *The Middle Kingdom: A Survey of the Geography, Government, Literature, Social Life, Arts, and History of the Chinese Empire and Its Inhabitants* (1848; repr., New York: Paragon Book, 1966), 1:771.

86. Charles M. Dyce, *Personal Reminiscences of Thirty Years' Residence in the Model Settlement Shanghai, 1870–1900* (London: Chapman & Hall, 1906), 98.

87. Osmond Tiffany, *The Canton Chinese: Or, the American's Sojourn in the Celestial Empire* (Boston: Munroe, 1849).

88. James Harrison Wilson, *China Travels and Investigations in the "Middle Kingdom": A Study of Its Civilization and Possibilities* (New York: Appleton, 1887), 238.

89. Robert Bickers, *Britain in China: Community, Culture, and Colonialism, 1900–49* (New York: St. Martin's Press, 1999), 102.

90. *Christian Index*, January 26, 1899, 11.

91. Emma Inveen, "Up the Yangtze River," *Baptist Missionary Magazine*, September 1894, 445.

92. Alvyn Austin, *China's Millions: The China Inland Mission and Late Qing Society, 1832–1905* (Grand Rapids, Mich.: Eerdmans, 2007), 2.

93. Stephen Bonsal, "Champions of Christendom," *Independent*, April 11, 1901, 829.

94. "The Last Tour of Miss Fannie Wright," *New York Evangelist*, August 4, 1898, 27.

95. *Zhao Yang Fan Shu (Foreign Cookery in Chinese)* (1866; repr., Shanghai: American Presbyterian Mission Press, 1909). This is the second Western cookbook published by the American Presbyterian Mission Press in Shanghai. Xia Xiaohong offers detailed discussions of *Foreign Cookery in Chinese* and two other Western cookbooks published during the late Qing, in "Wan Qing De Xican Shipu Jiqi Wenhua Yihan" (The Western Cookbooks of the Late Qing and Their Cultural Meaning), *Xueshu Yanjiu (Academic Research)* 1 (2009): 138–146. Her otherwise thoughtful analysis overestimates the extent of localization in *Foreign Cookery in Chinese*. For example, she argues that the cookbook completely ignored salad (142), but there is a recipe for chicken salad. And the ingredients in the recipes of the book are predominantly Western.

96. Margaret Mead, "Ethnicity and Anthropology in America," in *Ethnic Identity: Cultural Continuity and Change*, ed. George A. DeVos and Lola Romanucci-Ross (Palo Alto, Calif.: AltaMira Press, 1995), 313.

97. "The Joy of Growing Up Italian," in *Raising Humanity*, ed. Robin Alexis (Bloomington, Ind.: AuthorHouse, 2007).

98. Netta Davis, "To Serve the 'Other': Chinese-American Immigrants in the Restaurant Business," *Journal for the Study of Food and Society* 6, no.1 (2002): 71.

99. "Six Chinese Students Sent to New Bedford," *Friend: A Religious and Literary Journal*, November 4, 1905, 131.

100. Blanche Ching-Yi Wu, *East Meets West* (Baltimore: Huang, 1985), 43.

101. ZhangYinhuan, *Sanzhou Riji (Journal of the Journey to Three Continents)* (Beijing: Yuedong xinguan, 1896), I:11.

102. Cui Guoyin, *Chushi Meirimiguo Riji (Journal of Chinese Minister to the United States, Spain, and Peru)* (1894; repr., Taipei: Wen Hai), 2.

103. "The Viceroy Their Guest: Ex-Ministers to China Entertain Li Hung Chang," *New York Times*, August 30, 1896, 2.

104. J. Y. Wong, *Yeh Ming-Ch'en: Viceroy of Liang Kuang, 1852–58* (Cambridge: Cambridge University Press, 1976), xviii.

105. Li Gui, *Huan You Diqiu Xin Lu (New Accounts of Travels Around the Globe)*, in *Wang Tao: Man You Sui Lu (Accounts of Travels)*, ed. Zhong Shuhe (Shangsha: Yue lu shushe, 1985), 323–324.

106. American Mail Line, Chinese Third-Class Menu, collection of Yong Chen. For more information about the American Mail Line, see E. Mowbray Tate, *Transpacific Steam: The Story of Steam Navigation from the Pacific Coast of North America to the Far East and the Antipodes, 1867–1941* (Cranbury, N.J.: Cornwall Books, 1986), 128–131.

107. Archaeological evidence from the Lower China Store, which supplied the Chinese miners in Madera County, California, from the 1860s to 1885, shows that the "foods, culinary wares, implements and techniques of production are traditionally Chinese with few exceptions" (Paul E. Langenwalter II, "The Archaeology of 19th-Century Chinese Subsistence at the Lower China Store, Madera County, California," in *Archaeological Perspectives on Ethnicity in America: Afro-American and Asian American Culture History*, ed. Robert L. Schuyler [Farmingdale, N.Y.: Baywood, 1980], 110). I do not suggest that the diet of the Chinese remained entirely intact. Early Chinese immigrants added new foods from coffee to beef to their meals. Their postwar counterparts also made culinary adaptations. See, for example, Grace I-Ping Yang and Hazel M. Fox, "Food Habit Changes of Chinese Persons Living in Lincoln, Nebraska," *Journal of the American Dietary Association* 75, no. 10 (1979): 420–424. In spite of the changes, Chinese food remained a primary source of comfort for many immigrants, especially in the early decades.

108. "The Chinese to the President" [open letter], *Record of the Year* 1, no. 6 (1876): 601.

109. For discussions of invoices of such importations, see Robert F. G. Spier, "Food Habits of Nineteenth-Century California Chinese," *California Historical Society Quarterly* 37, no. 1 (1958): 79–84. Many observers also mentioned that many things used in Chinese cooking were imported from China.

110. Charles Nordhoff, *California: For Health, Pleasure and Residence, a Book for Travellers and Settlers* (New York: Harper, 1873), 190.

111. Willard B. Farwell and San Francisco Board of Supervisors, *The Chinese at Home and Abroad: Together with the Report of the Special Committee of the Board of Supervisors of San Francisco, on the Condition of the Chinese Quarter of That City* (San Francisco: Bancroft, 1885).

112. "Heathen Cuisine," *Daily Inter-Ocean* (Chicago), September 27, 1874, 3.

113. Otis Gibson, *The Chinese in America* (Cincinnati: Hitchcock & Walden, 1877), 71.

114. Ah Qui, diary entries, December 12 and 18, 1878.

115. "Like Oriental Cuisine," *Washington Post*, November 30, 1902, 28.

116. "A Chinese Dinner," *St. Louis Daily Globe-Democrat*, June 1885, 9. See also Joseph Carey, *By the Golden Gate: Or, San Francisco, the Queen City of the Pacific Coast; with Scenes and Incidents Characteristic of Its Life* (Albany, N.Y.: Albany Diocesan Press, 1902), 187.

117. Noah Brooks, "Restaurant Life in San Francisco," *Overland Monthly*, November 1868, 472.

118. Wong Ching Foo, "The Chinese in New York," *Cosmopolitan*, June 1888, 304.

119. Paul C. P. Siu, *The Chinese Laundryman: A Study of Social Isolation*, ed. John Kuo Wei Tchen (New York: New York University Press, 1988), 145.

120. Walter Charles Blasdale, *A Description of Some Chinese Vegetable Food Materials and Their Nutritive and Economic Value* (Washington, D.C.: Government Printing Office, 1899).

5. THE RISE OF CHINESE RESTAURANTS

1. "Onward March of Chop Suey," *Sun* (New York), November 29, 1908, sec. 2, 2.

2. Carlos Sabillon, *On the Causes of Economic Growth: The Lessons of History* (New York: Algora, 2008), 139.

3. Robin Archer, *Why Is There No Labor Party in the United States?* (Princeton, N.J.: Princeton University Press, 2010), 25. For the rise of personal income, see also U.S. Bureau of Economic Analysis and U.S. Bureau of the Census, *Long-Term Economic Growth* (Washington, D.C.: Government Printing Office, 1973).

4. Michael Lind, *Land of Promise: An Economic History of the United States* (New York: HarperCollins, 2012), 263.

5. Brian Gratton, "The Poverty of Impoverishment Theory: The Economic Well-Being of the Elderly, 1890–1950," *Journal of Economic History* 56, no. 1 (1996): 39–61.

6. Charles S. Maier, *Among Empires: American Ascendancy and Its Predecessors* (Cambridge, Mass.: Harvard University Press, 2006), 239.

7. Maureen E. Montgomery, "'Natural Distinction': The American Bourgeois Search for Distinctive Signs in Europe," in *The American Bourgeoisie: Distinction and Identity in the Nineteenth Century*, ed. Sven Beckert (New York: Palgrave Macmillan, 2010), 27.

8. Dean MacCannell, *The Tourist: A New Theory of the Leisure Class* (New York: Schocken, 1976), 5.

9. Catherine Cocks, *Doing the Town: The Rise of Urban Tourism in the United States, 1850–1915* (Berkeley: University of California Press, 2001), 5.

10. For more discussions of the topic, see Sabine Haenni, *The Immigrant Scene: Ethnic Amusements in New York, 1880–1920* (Minneapolis: University of Minnesota Press, 2008).

11. Forest Morgan, "The Towers of Babel," *Rich Hill (Mo.) Tribune*, March 17, 1910, 6.

12. For more detailed discussions of such attacks, see Elmer Clarence Sandmeyer, *The Anti-Chinese Movement in California* (Urbana: University of Illinois Press, 1991); and Jean Pfaelzer, *Driven Out: The Forgotten War Against Chinese Americans* (New York: Random House, 2007).

13. Pfaelzer, *Driven Out*, 253.

14. Craig Storti, *Incident at Bitter Creek: The Story of the Rock Springs Chinese Massacre* (Ames: Iowa State University Press, 1991), 142.

15. Roger Daniels, *Asian America: Chinese and Japanese in the United States Since 1850* (Seattle: University of Washington Press, 1995), 64.

16. Rose Hum Lee, "The Decline of Chinatowns in the United States," *American Journal of Sociology* 54, no. 5 (1949): 427.

17. Arthur B. Stout, *Chinese Immigration and the Physiological Causes of the Decay of the Nation* (San Francisco: Agnew & Deffebach, 1862).

18. In 1876, Dr. Hugh H. Toland asserted that Chinese prostitutes were responsible for nine-tenths of the syphilis cases in San Francisco. That famous medical doctor even claimed that his white patients "think diseases contracted from Chinawomen are harder to cure than those contracted elsewhere" (quoted in Special Committee on Chinese Immigration, Senate of California Legislature, *Chinese Immigration: The Social, Moral, and Political Effect of Chinese Immigration* [Sacramento, 1876; repr., San Francisco, 1970], 104). See also Susan Craddock, "Embodying Place: Pathologizing Chinese and Chinatown in Nineteenth-Century San Francisco," *Antipode* 31, no. 4 (1999): 351–371; and Nayan Shah, *Contagious Divides: Epidemics and Race in San Francisco's Chinatown* (Berkeley: University of California Press, 2001).

19. Cocks, *Doing the Town*, 5.

20. Iza Duffus Hardy, *Between Two Oceans: Or, Sketches of American Travel* (London: Hurst & Blackett, 1884), 154. See also J. W. Buel, *Metropolitan Life Unveiled; Or the Mysteries and Miseries of America's Cities* (St. Louis: Linahan, 1882), 276.

21. E. Lyell Earle, "Character Studies in New York's Foreign Quarters," *Catholic World* 68, no. 408 (1899): 790.

22. Mary Coolidge, *Chinese Immigration* (New York: Holt, 1909), 252–253.

23. John Kuo Wei Tchen informs us of the long historical roots of this curiosity in *New York Before Chinatown: Orientalism and the Shaping of American Culture, 1776–1882* (Baltimore: Johns Hopkins University Press, 1999).

24. A. W. Loomis, "The Old East in the New West," *Overland Monthly*, October 1868, 363.

25. "The Movements of the Philadelphians," *Daily Alta California* (San Francisco), August 20, 1873.

26. "Chinese Now Tolerated," *New York Tribune Illustrated Supplement*, July 30, 1899, 4.

27. "The French Visitors in Chinatown," *Sacramento Daily Record-Union*, November 29, 1881, 4.

28. "Lorne and Louise in Chinatown," *New York Times*, September 29, 1882, 3.

29. *Sacramento Daily Record-Union*, June 12, 1885, 1.

30. This was the image of Chinatown projected by publicists during the Panama-Pacific International Exposition, held in San Francisco in 1915. See Abigail Markwyn, "Economic Partner and Exotic Other: China and Japan at San Francisco's Panama-Pacific International Exposition," *Western Historical Quarterly* 39, no. 4 (2008): 485.

31. M. H. Cross, "Seeing Chinatown," *New York Times*, April 28, 1905, 8.

32. William Norr, *The Romance of "Chuck" Connors, Stories of Chinatown* (New York: Norr, 1892), 5–13; Mary Ting Yi Lui, *The Chinatown Trunk Mystery: Murder, Miscegenation, and Other Dangerous Encounters in Turn-of-the-Century New York City* (Princeton, N.J.: Princeton University Press, 2004), chap. 1.

33. Alfred Robinson, *Doxey's Guide to San Francisco and the Pleasure Resorts of California* (San Francisco: Doxey, 1897), 116.

34. Ivan Light, "From Vice District to Tourist Attraction: The Moral Career of American Chinatowns, 1880–1940," *Pacific Historical Review* 43 (1974): 367–394.

35. Elizabeth C. MacPhail, "When the Red Lights Went Out in San Diego: The Little Known Story of San Diego's 'Restricted' District," *Journal of San Diego History* 22, no. 2 (1974): 2, 7.

36. "The French Visitors in Chinatown," *Sacramento Daily Record-Union*, November 29, 1881, 4.

37. Alexander Wallace, "Seeing Chinatown," *New York Times*, April 28, 1905, 8.

38. "Chinatown," *New York Times*, October 25, 1910, 10.

39. "No More Bowery Thrills for Sightseers," *Sun*, February 25, 1912, sec. 4, 14.

40. "Party Sees Sights in Chinese District," *St. Louis Republic*, January 5, 1904, 2.

41. Light, one of the pioneer scholars in studying the Chinatown as a tourist site, for example, does not fully recognize this role of restaurants in "From Vice District to Tourist Attraction."

42. "Like Oriental Cuisine," *Washington Post*, November 30, 1902, 28.

43. "Seen in Chinatown," *Atchison (Kan.) Daily Champion*, October 25, 1888, 7.

44. Peter Kwong, *The New Chinatown*, rev. ed. (New York: Hill & Wang, 1996), 140.

45. Ross C. Brownson, Graham A. Colditz, and Enola K. Proctor, *Dissemination and Implementation Research in Health: Translating Science to Practice* (New York: Oxford University Press, 2012).

46. Helen Worden, *The Real New York: A Guide for the Adventurous Shopper, the Exploratory Eater and the Know-it-all Sightseer Who Ain't Seen Nothin' Yet* (Indianapolis: Bobbs-Merrill, 1933).

47. Craig Claiborne, "The Food of China," in Craig Claiborne and Virginia Lee, *The Chinese Cookbook* (Philadelphia: Lippincott, 1972), xiii.

48. Randy Schnepf and Joe Richardson, "Consumers and Food Price Inflation," Congressional Research Service, April 14, 2011, R40545, 10, Congressional Research Service, http://www.fas.org/sgp/crs/misc/R40545.pdf (accessed August 4, 2012).

49. Richard Pillsbury, *No Foreign Food: The American Diet in Time and Place* (Boulder, Colo.: Westview Press, 1998), 176.

50. For more detailed discussions of the American diner, see Richard J. S. Gutman, *American Diner Then and Now* (Baltimore: Johns Hopkins University Press, 2000).

6. THE MAKERS OF AMERICAN CHINESE FOOD

1. Andrew P. Haley, *Turning the Tables: Restaurants and the Rise of the American Middle Class, 1880–1920* (Chapel Hill: University of North Carolina Press, 2011), 12.

2. Louis Joseph Beck, *New York's Chinatown: An Historical Presentation of Its People and Places* (New York: Bohemia, 1898), 48–49.

3. "The Real Chinatown," *Sun* (New York), May 14, 1905, 5.

4. Steven A. Shaw, *Turning the Tables: Restaurants from the Inside Out* (New York: HarperCollins, 2005).

5. "Chinese Restaurants," *New York Tribune*, February 3, 1901, B6.

6. Arthur Chapman, "Why All the Chinese Restaurants?" *New York Tribune*, December 25, 1921, 6.

7. "Chinatown 'Slumming' Parties Are Now the Fad," *Washington Times*, March 29, 1903, 6.

8. Gaye Tuchman and Harry Gene Levine, "New York Jews and Chinese Food: The Social Construction of an Ethnic Pattern," in *The Taste of American Place: A Reader on Regional and Ethnic Foods*, ed. Barbara Shortridge and James R. Shortridge (Lanham, Md.: Rowman & Littlefield, 1998), 173.

9. "Seen in Chinatown," *Atchison (Kan.) Daily Champion*, October 25, 1888, 7; "Five Topics About Town," *Sun*, July 27, 1896, 7.

10. William Brown Meloney, "Slumming in New York's Chinatown," *Munsey's Magazine*, September 1909, 823.

11. "300 Captured in Chop Suey Raids," *Sun*, April 15, 1918, 14. For more discussions of slumming in New York, see Mary Ting Yi Lui, *The Chinatown Trunk Mystery: Murder, Miscegenation, and Other Dangerous Encounters in Turn-of-the-Century New York City* (Princeton, N.J.: Princeton University Press, 2004).

12. "300 Captured in Chop Suey Raids."

13. "A Drastic Remedy," *St. Joseph (Mo.) Observer*, June 22, 1918, 3.

14. "Chinese Mix Sin with Chop Suey," *Chicago Daily Tribune*, March 27, 1910, 3.

15. "Two Girls Show How Easy It Is to Buy Dope Here," *Evening Public Ledger* (Philadelphia), September 12, 1916, 1, night extra.

16. "Chinatowns Compared," *Evening Public Ledger*, July 25, 1916, 8, night extra.

17. "Chinatown 'Slumming' Parties Are Now the Fad."

18. Gary W. Libby, "Historical Notes on Chinese Restaurants in Portland, Maine," *Chinese America: History and Perspectives* 20 (2006): 49.

19. "The Chinese Restaurants," *Boston Daily Advertiser*, August 12, 1899, 4.

20. "Chinese Restaurants," *Atchison Daily Champion*, December 23, 1890, 6.

21. "How a Great City Feeds Night Hawks," *Rising Son* (Brooklyn, N.Y.), August 30, 1906, 3.

22. "Chief's Pleadings in Vain," *Los Angeles Herald*, June 6, 1906, 14.

23. "Chinese Restaurants," *New York Tribune*, February 3, 1901, B6.

24. "Chopstick Dinner: A Fad with Would Be Bohemians in New York," *Evening Tribune*, April 1, 1901, 7. See also *Riverside (Calif.) Daily Press*, April 4, 1901, 7.

25. "Odd Chinese Dishes," *New York Tribune*, August 30, 1903, B2.

26. "Young Swindlers," *Sacramento Record-Union*, July 22, 1898, 3.

27. "Donnelly's Dinner," *Sacramento Record-Union*, November 25, 1899, 5.

28. "Chinatown of the Present a Sad Shadow of the Past," *Sun*, January 27, 1918, sec. 5, 10, Special Feature Supplement.

29. "Chinese Restaurants," *New York Tribune*, February 3, 1901, B6.

30. Bancroft-Whitney and Edward Thompson Co., comps., *American Annotated Cases* (San Francisco: Bancroft-Whitney, 1916), 726. For further discussions of the law and relevant cases, see John E. H. Sherry, *The Laws of Innkeepers: For Hotels, Motels, Restaurants, and Clubs* (Ithaca, N.Y.: Cornell University Press, 1993).

31. "'Equal Rights' in New York," *Outlook*, September 13, 1913, 56.

32. Louis Chu, "The Chinese Restaurants in New York" (master's thesis, New York University, 1939). 55.

33. Monroe N. Work, ed., *Negro Year Book* (Tuskegee, Ala.: Negro Year Book, 1919).

34. "Chop Suey and the Color Line," *New York Tribune*, December 16, 1904, 4. For reports of Chinese refusing to serve African Americans, see also Harold Robert Isaacs, *Scratches on Our Minds: American Views of China and India* (New York: Day, 1958).

35. "Hop Alley," *St. Louis Republic*, January 29, 1905, sec. 2.

36. Huping Ling, *Chinese St. Louis: From Enclave to Cultural Community* (Philadelphia: Temple University Press, 2004). John Jung also discusses the African American–Chinese food connection in several cities in *Sweet and Sour: Life in Chinese Family Restaurants* (Cypress, Calif.: Yin & Yang Press, 2010).

37. Wallace Thurman, "Negro Life in New York's Harlem: A Lively Picture of a Popular and Interesting Section," in *The Collected Writings of Wallace Thurman: A Harlem Renaissance Reader*, ed. Amritjit Singh and Daniel M. Scott III (New Brunswick, N.J.: Rutgers University Press, 2003), 49.

38. Malcolm Gay, "St. Louie Chop Suey," *River Front Times*, November 15, 2006, http://www.riverfronttimes.com/2006-11-15/news/st-louie-chop-suey/ (accessed February 9, 2014).

39. Ben Austen, "End of the Road: After Detroit, the Wreck of an American Dream," *Harper's Magazine*, August 2009, 26–36.

40. Daniel Okrent, "Detroit: The Death—and Possible Life—of a Great City," *Time*, September 24, 2009, http://www.time.com/time/magazine/article/0,9171,1926017,00.html (accessed August 27, 2012).

41. For a brief discussion of Detroit's Chinatown, see Harley Spiller, "On Menus in Motown, Detroit's Chinatown," *Flavor and Fortune* 11, no. 3 (2004): 17–18.

42. Wallace Yee Hong, "Recommended Chinese Restaurants," in *The Chinese Cook Book* (New York: Crown, 1952).

43. Roberta Chang and Wayne Patterson, *The Koreans in Hawai'i: A Pictorial History, 1903–2003* (Honolulu: University of Hawai'i Press, 2003), 61; *Polk's Detroit City Directory, 1928–1929* (Detroit: Polk, 1929), 1156.

44. Alan J. Pollock, *Barnstorming to Heaven: Syd Pollock and His Great Black Teams* (Tuscaloosa: University of Alabama Press, 2012), 249.

45. Changle has been an important originating place of illegal immigration, and newcomers from it in the past two decades have constituted a major labor force in the Chinese restaurant industry.

46. U.S. Bureau of the Census, State and County Quick Facts, http://quickfacts.census.gov/qfd/states/26/2679000.html (accessed February 9, 2014).

47. Tê-chao Chêng, *Acculturation of the Chinese in the United States: A Philadelphia Story* (Foochow [Fuzhou]: Fukien Christian University Press, 1948), 92.

48. Ruth Gay, *Unfinished People: Eastern European Jews Encounter America* (New York: Norton, 2001), 3.

49. Nathan Glazer and Daniel Moynihan, *Beyond the Melting Pot: The Negroes, Puerto Ricans, Jews, Italians, and Irish of New York City* (Cambridge, Mass.: MIT Press, 1992), 138–139.

50. *American Hebrew,* June 2, 1899, editorial notes. I am grateful to Hasia Diner for alerting me to the source.

51. Hasia Diner, *Hungering for America: Italian, Irish, and Jewish Foodways in the Age of Migration* (Cambridge, Mass.: Harvard University Press, 2001), 205–206.

52. Patricia Volk, "A Love Affair, Dumplings on the Side," *New York Times,* March 26, 2006, CY4.

53. Vicky, interview with the author, July 31, 2003.

54. Sandye, interview with the author, November 24, 2003.

55. Ibid.

56. Lizzie Black Kander, *The "Settlement" Cook Book: The Way to a Man's Heart* (Milwaukee, 1901), 227.

57. Betty Dean, *The New Jewish Cook Book* (New York: Hebrew Publishing, 1947), 139, 325–329.

58. Janet Theophano, *Eat My Words: Reading Women's Lives Through the Cookbooks They Wrote* (New York: Palgrave, 2002), 68.

59. Sandye, interviews with the author September 11, 2011, and November 24, 2003.

60. Tuchman and Levine, "New York Jews and Chinese Food," 164; Matthew Goodman, "'Safe Treyf,' or When Won-Tons Were Called Kreplach," *Forward,* April 2, 1999, 19; Volk, "Love Affair, Dumplings on the Side."

61. Goodman, "Safe Treyf."

62. Stuart Schoffman, "Jews, Christmas, and Chinese Food," *Jewish Journal,* December 19, 2011, http://www.jewishjournal.com/opinion/article/jews_christmas_and_chinese_food_20111219/ (accessed August 30, 2012).

63. Tuchman and Levine, "New York Jews and Chinese Food," 175.

64. Eleanor, interview with the author, October 24, 2000.

65. Mimi Sheraton, "A Jewish Yen for Chinese," *New York Times Magazine,* September 23, 1990, 71.

66. Volk, "Love Affair, Dumplings on the Side."

67. Tuchman and Levine, "New York Jews and Chinese Food," 167.

68. In an interesting article, Hanna Miller regards Chinatown's proximity to Jewish settlement in the Lower East Side as the most important reason for the Jews' Chinese food connection: "Identity Takeout: How American Jews Made Chinese Food Their Ethnic Cuisine," *Journal of Popular Culture* 39, no. 3 (2006): 457. But this geographic proximity explanation leaves many questions unanswered. For example, it does not explain why such a connection did not take place between Chinese and other ethnic groups, such as Italians in Little Italy. Nor does it sufficiently explain the extensive and long-standing Jewish attachment to Chinese food elsewhere.

69. Sandye, interview with the author, September 11, 2011.

70. Alen Kraut, *The Huddled Masses: The Immigrant in American Society, 1880–1921* (Wheeling, Ill.: Harlan Davidson, 1982), 105.

71. New York Chamber of Commerce, *Fifty-sixth Annual Report* (New York: Press of the Chamber of Commerce, 1914), 225; Ira Rosenwaike, *Population History of New York City* (Syracuse, N.Y.: Syracuse University Press, 1972), 95, 141. The city's total Chinese population was 4,614 at the time.

72. Liang Qichao, *Xindalu Youji (My Journey to the New Continent*, 1904), in *Jindai Zhongguo Zhiliao Congkan (Historical Documents Concerning Modern China)*, ed. Shen Yun-long (Shanghai: Wen-hai, 1967), 10:383. Liang was an important political and intellectual figure in modern China. During his visit to the United States, he also did an extensive survey of Chinese America.

73. Chapman, "Why All the Chinese Restaurants?"

74. For discussions of this topic, see David R. Roediger, *The Wages of Whiteness: Race and the Making of the American Working Class* (New York: Verso, 1991); and Noel Ignatiev, *How the Irish Became White* (New York: Routledge, 1995).

75. Tuchman and Levine, "New York Jews and Chinese Food," 168.

76. Philip Roth, *Portnoy's Complaint* (New York: Random House, 1969), 90.

77. Diner, *Hungering for America*, 205.

78. Chêng, *Acculturation of the Chinese in the United States*, 93.

79. "Yule Stirs Chinese to Aid Jewish Home," *New York Times*, December 26, 1935, 15.

80. *Morning Oregonian* (Portland), September 8, 1888, 5.

81. Wong first came to the United States in 1868 as a student sponsored by "an American lady philanthropist." After graduating from college, he returned to China, where he got into political trouble because of his activism against opium use, forcing him to return to America. For an account of his early life, see "Wong Chin Foo," *New York Times*, October 4, 1873, 4.

82. "To Produce the Chinese Drama," *New York Tribune*, September 2, 1883, 4; "Wong Chin Foo Assaulted," *New York Times*, May 21, 1885, 1; "Wong Chin Foo Sued for Libel," *New York Tribune*, June 20, 1883, 8.

83. "Wong Chin Foo Assaulted," *New York Times*, June 10, 1883, 9 (the New York Times articles are different reports of the initial assault); Wong Chin Foo, "The Chinese Equal Rights League," *Washington Post*, December 29, 1892, 4; "Wong Chin Foo in Danger," *New York Times*, March 7, 1888, 8; "A Chinese Detective," *Washington Post*, July 23, 1894, 2.

84. He was physically assaulted by whites and was denied a U.S. passport. See "Wong Foo's Citizenship," *San Francisco Chronicle*, September 29, 1891, 1.

85. "Wong Chin Foo and Denis," *Chicago Daily Tribune*, October 23, 1887, 26.

86. "Chinese American Hero: Wong Chin Foo," *Asian Week*, August 20, 2009, http://www.asianweek.com/2009/08/20/chinese-american-hero-wong-chin-foo/ (accessed September 4, 2012); Qingsong Zhang, "The Origins of the Chinese Americanization Movement: Wong Chin Foo and the Chinese Equal Rights League," in *Claiming America: Constructing Chinese American Identities During the Exclusion Era*, ed. K. Scott Wong and Sucheng Chan (Philadelphia: Temple University Press, 1998), 58.

87. "Wong Chin Foo and Denis."

88. "A Chinese Reception," *Harper's Weekly*, June 9, 1877, 446.

89. Andrew Coe, *Chop Suey: A Cultural History of Chinese Food in the United States* (New York: Oxford University Press, 2009), 152–153.

90. Samuel Bowles, *Our New West: Records of Travel Between the Mississippi River and the Pacific Ocean* (New York: Dennison, 1869), 412–413.

91. Menu of the banquet, March 20, 1907, Menu Collection, New York Public Library, New York.

92. "A Chinese Banquet," *New York Times*, March 15, 1877, 2.

93. C. J. W. R., "A Dinner with Chinese," *Hutchings' Illustrated California Magazine*, May 1857, 512–513.

94. "Mayor Strong in Chinatown," *Sun*, April 5, 1895, 1.

95. "A Chinese New Year's Day in Santa Barbara," *St. Nichola*, January 1883, 201.

96. *New York Tribune*, May 28, 1899, 12.

97. *Popular Science*, June 1899, 3.

98. "'Chow' of Many Kinds," *New York Tribune*, June 11, 1899, C9. A Chinese restaurant appears to have been a sponsor of the fair.

99. G. B. Densmore, *The Chinese in California: Descriptions of Chinese Life in San Francisco, Their Habits, Morals and Manners* (San Francisco: Pettit & Russ, 1880), 31.

100. Beck, *New York's Chinatown*, 47.

101. Ibid.

102. "Onward March of Chop Suey," *Sun*, November 29, 1908, 2.

103. Arthur Bonner, *Alas! What Brought Thee Hither? The Chinese in New York, 1800–1950* (Madison, N.J.: Fairleigh Dickinson University Press, 1997), 105.

104. Otis Gibson, *The Chinese in America* (Cincinnati: Hitchcock & Walden, 1877), 69–70.

105. Ira Miller Condit, *The Chinaman as We See Him and Fifty Years of Work for Him* (Chicago: Revell, 1900), 42.

106. "'China Town' in San Francisco," *Cornhill Magazine*, n.s., 7 (1886): 51.

107. "Chinese Reception," 444–445.

108. "Pagan Gods Scotched," *Morning Call* (Allentown, Pa.), October 27, 1892, 3.

109. "Chinese Restaurants," *Atchison Daily Champion*, 6.

110. Henry Burden McDowell, "A New Light of the Chinese," *Harper's New Monthly Magazine*, December 1892, 6.

111. Chêng, *Acculturation of the Chinese in the United States*, 93.

112. "Chinese Restaurants," *New York Tribune*, August 17, 1919, 12.

113. "Chinese Restaurants," *New York Tribune*, February 3, 1901, B6.

114. Scholars generally agree that large American cities at this time were dirty places. See, for example, Rachelle A. Dorfman, "Clinical Social Work: The Development of a Discipline," in *Paradigms of Clinical Social Work*, ed. Rachelle A. Dorfman (New York: Brunner/Mazel, 1988), 1:7. Jacob August Riis's most influential work is *How the Other Half Lives: Studies Among the Tenements of New York* (New York: Scribner, 1890).

115. "Five Topics About Town."

116. Quoted in Bryan R. Johnson, "Let's Eat Chinese Tonight," *American Heritage*, December 1987, 102.

117. Beck, *New York's Chinatown*, 47.

118. "Chinese Restaurants in New York," *Atchison Daily Champion*, June 16, 1887, 7.

119. "Chinese Restaurants," *New York Tribune*, February 3, 1901, B6.

120. "Odd Chinese Dishes."

121. *San Diego Union*, December 7, 1887, 5.

122. "Chicago Chinamen," *Wisconsin State Register*, August 24, 1889, col. C; Densmore, *Chinese in California*, 46; "Fad for Chinese Food," *Washington Post*, July 21, 1901, 28

123. George Chappell, *The Restaurants of New York* (New York: Greenberg, 1925), 159.

124. J. S. Tow, *The Real Chinese in America* (New York: Academy Press, 1923), 91.

7. "CHINESE-AMERICAN CUISINE" AND THE AUTHENTICITY OF CHOP SUEY

1. "Luxuries at a Chinese Restaurant," *New York Tribune*, October 23, 1887, 12.

2. *Appleton's Dictionary of New York and Vicinity* (New York: Appleton, 1892), 221.

3. "Chinese Restaurants in New York," *Atchison (Kan.) Daily Champion*, June 16, 1887, 7; "Queer Chinese Traits," *New York Tribune*, May 22, 1887, 13.

4. "Seen in Chinatown," *Atchison Daily Champion*, October 25, 1888, 7.

5. Bayard Taylor, *Eldorado: or, Adventures in the Path of Empire, Comprising a Voyage to California, via Panama; Life in San Francisco and Monterey; Pictures of the Gold Region; and Experiences of Mexican Travel* (New York: Putnam, 1894), 115, 116.

6. James O'Meara, "The Chinese in Early Days," *Overland Monthly*, May 1884, 477. Andrew Coe writes, "The chief attraction of the first Chinese restaurants in North America was clearly the price—you could eat for $1.00, in the city where food probably cost more than anywhere else on the planet" (*Chop Suey: A Cultural History of Chinese Food in the United States* [New York: Oxford University Press, 2009], 110).

7. Wong Chin Foo, "The Chinese in New York," *Cosmopolitan*, June 1888, 304.

8. "Increase in Chinese Restaurants," *New York Tribune*, May 27, 1901, 4. In newspapers and on restaurant menus, the name of the noodle dish has been spelled in many different ways, including "Yockaman," "yet quo mein," "yakuman," "yockaman," yok su meen," "yat ko main," "yet quo mein," "yat gaw mein," and "yakami." This may be a reason why it did not acquire the level of national recognition that chop suey did. But the noodle dish has remained popular in various regions, especially in New Orleans, where it has been regarded as a local dish and hangover cure known as "yakamein" or Old Sober. In prewar Philadelphia, it was spelled "it-ko-mein" and was a favorite among African Americans, as Tê-chao Chêng mentions in *Acculturation of the Chinese in the United States: A Philadelphia Study* (Foochow [Fuzhou]: Fukien Christian University Press, 1948), 92.

9. "Like Oriental Cuisine," *Washington Post*, November 30, 1902, 28.

10. "Chinese Restaurants," *New York Tribune*, February 3, 1901, B6.

11. *Independent*, November 17, 1917, 343.

12. "Chop Suey Resorts," *New York Times*, November 15, 1903, 20.

13. "Chinese Restaurants," *Atchison Daily Champion*, December 23, 1890, 6.

14. "What to Eat in 'Chop Suey' Restaurants," *San Diego Union*, August 14, 1904, 19.

15. "Chow Chop Suey," *Daily Inter Ocean* (Chicago), March 23, 1896, 4.

16. *Coconino Sun* (Flagstaff, Ariz.), September 18, 1914, 5.

17. *Daily Ardmoreite* (Ardmore, Okla.), March 23, 1904, 6.

18. *Washington Times*, August 16, 1917, 7.

19. Chêng, *Acculturation of the Chinese in the United States*, 96.

20. *Waco (Tex.) Evening News*, April 12, 1894, 8.

21. Alexander Cockburn, *Corruptions of Empire: Life Studies and the Reagan Era* (New York: Verso, 1988).

22. Michael Freeman, "Sung," in *Food in Chinese Culture: Anthropological and Historical Perspectives*, ed. Kwang-chih Chang (New Haven, Conn.: Yale University Press, 1977), 144–145.

23. Wong Chin Foo, "Chinese Cooking," *Brooklyn Daily Eagle*, July 6, 1884, 4.

24. W. C. Hunter, *The "Fan Kwae" at Canton Before Treaty Years, 1825–1844* (London: Paul, Trench, 1882), 24.

25. Juliet Corson, "Chinese Cookery," *Harper's Bazaar*, July 17, 1897, 593.

26. Alexander Young, "Chinese Food and Cookery," *Appleton's Journal of Literature, Science and Art*, September 14, 1872, 291. Sophie Song estimates that bird's nests now sell for up to $2,500 per kilogram (2.2 lbs.), in "Asia's Increasingly Wealthy Population Demands More Edible Bird's Nests and Vietnam Is Keen to Become a Major Producer of the Delicacy," *International Business Times*, August 20, 2013, www.ibtimes.com /asias-increasingly-wealthy-population-demands-more- edible-birds-nests-vietnam-

keen-become-major (accessed February 9, 2014). It is banned in official banquets in Hong Kong and in China as well.

27. For more detailed information on the source of this food, see Frederick J. Simoons, *Food in China: A Cultural and Historical Inquiry* (Roca Raton, Fla.: CRC Press, 1991), 427.

28. Fu Rong and Cong Shi, *Hongloumeng Yu Meishi Wenhua (The "Dream of the Red Chamber" and Culinary Culture)* (Beijing: Beijing Economics College Press, 1994), 165; Jia Ming, a writer during the Yuan dynasty (1271–1368), discussed the medicinal properties of both bird's nest and sea cucumber, along with more than three hundred other foods, in his diet manual, *Yinshi Xu Zhi (All You Must Know About Food)*, in *Yin Zhuan Pu Lu (A Collection of Writings on Drinks and Food)*, ed. Yang Jialuo (Taipei: Shijie shuju, 1992). For the original text in Chinese, see http://www.tcm100.com/user/ysxz/zzbook7.htm (accessed February 9, 2014).

29. C. J. W. R., "A Dinner with Chinese," *Hutchings' Illustrated California Magazine*, May 1857, 513.

30. Samuel Bowles, *Our New West: Records of Travel Between the Mississippi River and the Pacific Ocean* (New York: Dennison, 1869), 410–411.

31. B. W. Higman, *How Food Made History* (Malden, Mass.: Wiley-Blackwell, 2012), 165.

32. Jerome A. Hart, "The New Chinatown in San Francisco," *Bohemian Magazine*, May 1909, 604.

33. Harriet Beecher Stowe and Catharine Esther Beecher, *The American Woman's Home: or, Principles of Domestic Science; Being a Guide to the Formation and Maintenance of Economical, Healthful, Beautiful, and Christian Homes* (New York: Ford, 1869), 168.

34. Michel Chevalier, *Society, Manners and Politics in the United States: Being a Series of Letters on North America* (Boston: Weeks, Jordan, 1839), 284.

35. Fannie Merritt Farmer, *The Boston Cooking-School Cook Book* (Boston: Little, Brown, 1896), 1.

36. Ellen Henrietta Richards, *The Cost of Food: A Study in Dietaries* (New York: Wiley, 1902), 2–3.

37. Menu, Mann Fang Lowe, April 19, 1900, Menu Collection, New York Public Library, New York.

38. Arthur Waley, *Yuan Mei: Eighteenth Century Chinese Poet* (Stanford, Calif.: Stanford University Press, 1956), 48.

39. Yuan Mei, *Suiyuan Shidan (Food Menu of the Suiyuan Garden, 1792)*, in *Yuan Mei Quan Ji (Complete Works of Yuan Mei)*, ed. Wang Yingzhong, vol. 5 (Nanjing: Jiangsu gu ji chu ban she, 1993).

40. Wong Chin Foo, "Chinese in New York"; "Seen in Chinatown."

41. "Chinese Restaurants," *New York Tribune*, B6.

42. Roi Ottley, "Hectic Harlem," *New York Amsterdam News*, April 25, 1936, 13.

43. Richard Wing, interview with the author, March 12, 2001.

44. Otis Gibson, *The Chinese in America* (Cincinnati: Hitchcock & Walden, 1877), 71.

45. "Chop Suey Resorts."

46. *Evening Public Ledger* (Philadelphia), October 16, 1919, 15.

47. *Washington Post*, December 6, 1942, S11.

48. *Evening Public Ledger* (Philadelphia), November 26, 1914, 12.

49. Ibid., November 24, 1921, 3.

50. All the menus discussed here are from the author's collection, unless noted otherwise.

51. Lily Cho, *Eating Chinese: Culture on the Menu in Small Town Canada* (Toronto: University of Toronto Press, 2010).

52. It is probably from the 1940s or early 1950s. In format and content, it is similar to the menu of Ruby Foo's in New York, in 1939. Its food price was just slightly higher than that of Ruby Foo's.

53. Charles Choy Wong, "The Continuity of Chinese Grocers in Southern California," *Journal of Ethnic Studies* 8 (1980): 64.

54. Alfred Yee chronicles the Chinese grocery business in the Sacramento area in *Shopping at Giant Foods: Chinese American Supermarkets in Northern California* (Seattle: University of Washington Press, 2003). Chinese immigrants in towns in other western states also operated grocery stores. One such a town is Superior, Arizona, where Ong Choon Hing started the Spring Garden Grocery a few years after his arrival in America in 1912. Besides serving non-Chinese customers in the store, he and his employees delivered groceries to them. See Bill Ong Hing, "No Place for Angels: In Reaction to Kevin Johnson," *University of Illinois Law Review* 2 (2000): 559–601. I am grateful to Bill Hing for sharing his family history with me on March 17, 2005.

55. Paul Chan and Kenneth Baker, *How to Order a Real Chinese Meal* (New York: Guild Books, 1976), 5.

56. Betty S. Goldberg, *Chinese Kosher Cooking* (Middle Village, N.Y.: Jonathan David, 1984), 193.

57. According to "In Search of Baltimore's Chinatown: What It Was Like to Be Chinese in Jim Crow Baltimore," a law-school-student project at the University of Maryland in 1998, there were only four hundred Chinese in the city in 1941. See http://www.law.umaryland.edu/faculty/tbanks/chinatown/history.htm (accessed October 23, 2010).

58. Fred Ferretti, "Beyond Columns A and B," *New York Times*, March 27, 1983, A41.

59. Jeffrey M. Pilcher, *Planet Taco: A Global History of Mexican Food* (New York: Oxford University Press, 2012), xiii.

60. "Dinners à la Mongolian," *Kansas City (Mo.) Journal*, February 26, 1899, 13.

61. "Chop Suey Resorts."

62. See, for example, the advertisement posted by Wuey Sen Low and Company of Salem, Oregon, for "Chop Suey at the Chinese Restaurant," *Daily Capital Journal*, October 12, 1905, 5.

63. J. S. Tow, *The Real Chinese in America* (New York: Academy Press, 1923), 91.

64. Jessie Louise Nolton, *Chinese Cookery in the Home Kitchen: Being Recipes for the Preparation of the Most Popular Chinese Dishes at Home* (Detroit: Chino-American, 1911).

65. *Holt County Sentinel* (Oregon, Mo.), September 22, 1905.

66. *New York Tribune*, July 24, 1908, 6.

67. *St. Paul Globe*, May 8, 1904, 42.

68. "Party Sees Sights in Chinese District," *St. Louis Republic*, January 5, 1904, 2.

69. "New Divorcees Eat Chop Suey to Show Their Emancipation," *Columbia Evening Missourian*, February 24, 1922, 4.

70. "To Put on Irwin's First Burlesque," *San Francisco Chronicle*, March 10, 1903, 8.

71. "Chop Suey Will Be Investigated," *Minneapolis Journal*, August 22, 1906, 7.

72. "Law Will Check Chinese," *Chicago Daily Tribune*, Apr 28, 1906, 5.

73. "Onward March of Chop Suey," *Sun* (New York), November 29, 1908, 2.

74. Brent, interview with the author, November 27, 2013. I am grateful to Brent for sharing his grandmother's recipes with me.

75. *Chicago Daily Tribune*, October 31, 1941; Beatrice Foods Company, *The Art and Secrets of Chinese Cookery* (Archbold, Ohio: Beatrice Foods, 1941); Mary Meade, "Chop Suey Is Basic Dish in Quick Dinner," *Chicago Daily Tribune*, October 11, 1939, 23; Memorandum, March 14, 1955, FDA Records, Record Group 88, File 491.2-11, AF 26-474, National Archives.

76. Memorandum of interview, February 14, 1955, FDA Records, Record Group 88, File 491.2-11, AF 1-82, National Archives.

77. See, for example "Onward March of Chop Suey"; Wong Chin Foo, "Chinese Cooking"; "How Chop Suey Is Made," *Grand Valley Times* (Moab, Utah), October 10, 1902, 3.

78. Jeanette Norton, "Peculiarities of Chinese Cooking," *San Francisco Chronicle*, November 3, 1918, 7.

79. *Life*, June 14, 1923, 16.

80. Everett Swingle, "Chop Suey? It's Many Things in Small Pieces," *Chicago Daily Tribune*, March 20, 1931.

81. "Chop Suey, Popular Here, Is Hardly Known in China," *New York Times*, November 11, 1928, 151; "China Has Most Things Chinese but Chop Suey Isn't to Be Found There," *Los Angeles Times*, May 25, 1924, 12.

82. "LBJ and Chop Suey," *Hutchinson (Kan.) News*, June 16, 1968, 5.

83. Tow, *Real Chinese in America*, 92.

84. Doreen Yen Hung Feng, *The Joy of Chinese Cooking*, 3rd ed. (New York: Grosset & Dunlap, 1977), 12.

85. Johnny Kan, with Charles L. Leong, *Eight Immortal Flavors: Secrets of Cantonese Cookery from San Francisco's Chinatown* (Berkeley, Calif.: Howell-North Book, 1963), 11.

86. "Chop Suey Injunction," *New York Times*, June 15, 1904, 7.

87. Virginia Gardner, "The Inventor of U.S. Chop Suey Tells His Story," *Chicago Daily Tribune*, November 20, 1931, 21.

88. Marie Rose Wong, *Sweet Cakes, Long Journey: The Chinatowns of Portland, Oregon* (Seattle: University of Washington Press, 2004), xiii.

89. Joey Green, *Contrary to Popular Belief: More Than 250 False Facts Revealed* (New York: Random House, 2005), 111. See also Dorothy Hoobler and Thomas Hoobler, *The Chinese American Family Album* (New York: Oxford University Press, 1998), 96.

90. Tow, *Real Chinese in America*, 91.

91. "Six Chinese Students Sent to New Bedford," *Friend: A Religious and Literary Journal*, November 4, 1905, 131.

92. Wong Chin Foo, "Chinese Cooking"; "A Chinese Dinner," *St. Louis Daily Globe-Democrat*, June 1885, 9; "Gotham's Chinese," *Sentinel: Milwaukee*, July 25, 1886, 10; "Seen in Chinatown"; "Verdenal's Chat," *San Francisco Chronicle*, March 27, 1892, 11.

93. Wong Chin Foo, "Chinese in New York," 304; Wong Chin Foo, "Chinese Food for New Yorkers," *Sun*, March 19, 1888, 2.

94. "Presents His Letter," *Washington Post*, August 30, 1896, 5.

95. Eugene Anderson, *The Food of China* (New Haven, Conn.: Yale University Press, 1988), 212–213; Coe, *Chop Suey*, 161.

96. Li Shu-fan, *Hong Kong Surgeon* (New York: Dutton, 1964), 211.

97. Sherrie A. Inness, *Secret Ingredients: Race, Gender, and Class at the Dinner Table* (New York: Palgrave Macmillan, 2006), 51, 53, 59.

98. Nolton, *Chinese Cookery in the Home Kitchen*.

99. Shiu Wong Chan, *The Chinese Cook Book* (New York: Stokes, 1917), 37.

100. Buwei Yang Chao, *How to Cook and Eat in Chinese* (1945; repr., New York: Vintage, 1972), 43.

101. Wallace Yee Hong, *The Chinese Cook Book* (New York: Crown, 1952), 61.

102. Chao, *How to Cook and Eat in Chinese*, 43; Zhang Guangzhi (Kwang-chih Chang), *Zhongguo Qingtong Ahidai* (*The Bronze Age of China*) (Hong Kong: Chinese University of Hong Kong Press, 1982), 140.

103. Meng Yuanlao, *Dongjing Meng Hua Lu* (*A Reminiscence of the Glory of Bianjin*) (repr., Beijing: Zhonghua, 1962), 17.

104. "Royal Reception in the Bay," *New York Times*, August 29, 1896, 1; "Welcome to Earl Li," *New York Times*, August 29, 1896, 1.

105. "Crowds in Chinatown," *New York Tribune*, August 30, 1896, 3; "Li Comes in State," *Sun*, August 29, 1896, 2.

106. "The Viceroy Their Guest: Ex-Ministers to China Entertain Li Hung Chang," *New York Times*, August 30, 1896, 2.

107. Renqiu Yu, "Chop Suey: From Chinese Food to Chinese American Food," *Chinese America: History and Perspectives* 1 (1987): 94.

108. Liang Qichao, *Xindalu Youji* (*My Journey to the New Continent*, 1904), in *Jindai Zhongguo Zhiliao Congkan* (*Historical Documents Concerning Modern China*), ed. Shen Yunlong (Shanghai: Wen-hai, 1967), 10:385.

109. Goldberg, *Chinese Kosher Cooking*, 193.

110. "Onward March of Chop Suey."

111. Xu Ke also reported the popularity of chop suey restaurants in U.S. cities, which served Li Hongzhang chop suey as well as Li Hongzhang rice and Li Hongzhang noodle dishes, in *Qing Bai Lei Chao* (*Qing Unofficial History Categorized Extracts*) (Shanghai: Shangwu, 1917). This forty-eight-volume book provides an encyclopedic coverage of life during the Qing dynasty.

112. A more recent version of this story recounts that when food ran out at a banquet that Li hosted for foreigners, Li ordered the chefs to cook the leftovers in a pot. Jing Hong and Wu Hua, *Chi shen* (*The Eating Gods*) (Shanghai: Shanghai University of Chinese Medicine, 2006), 145.

113. Eric Schlosser, *Fast Food Nation: The Dark Side of the All-American Meal* (New York: Houghton Mifflin, 2001), 4.

114. For a comparison between "Chinese" and "American" chop sueys, see Vernon Galster, *Chinese Cook Book, in Plain English* (Morris, Ill.: Galster, 1917), 3.

115. These states are Alabama, California, Colorado, Indiana, Louisiana, Massachusetts, Michigan, Missouri, Montana, Nevada, New Mexico, New York, North Carolina, Ohio, Oregon, Pennsylvania, South Dakota, Tennessee, Texas, and Virginia. The menus are from two samples collected in 2006 and 2011, respectively. Certain foods such as rice, including fried rice, are not included in this tally.

116. For an interesting story about egg foo young, see Mei Chin, "Oriental Express," *Saveur*, April 2013, 30–32.

117. Of the one hundred Chinese restaurants, only nineteen offered chop suey dishes.

118. The items include names of dishes, ingredients, and sauces on the menus. The restaurants in the 2003 sample do not overlap with those in the national samples. The 1997 survey of similar restaurants were conducted by Christopher Spiro in a research project under my supervision. Figure 4 is based on national samples; the 1997 and

2003 surveys are local; the 1997 survey was done by a student. In 2003, I surveyed the same restaurants.

119. Valerie Sinclair, "Chinese Dining with a Difference," *New York Times*, March 27, 1983, NJ29. I am grateful to Emily Rosenberg for reminding me of the postwar development in some small towns, such as her native Billings, Montana, where the best restaurant in the 1950s was Wong Village.

120. Moira Hodgson, "The Setting Can Be as Important as the Food," *New York Times*, February 3, 1982, C1.

121. Shun Lu and Gary Allen Fine, "The Presentation of Ethnic Authenticity: Chinese Food as a Social Accomplishment," *Sociological Quarterly* 36, no. 3 (1995): 545–547.

122. Tommy Toy's announced that it would close its doors at the end of March 2013. The end of its twenty-seven-year run is another setback in the efforts by Chinese restaurateurs to climb up the gastronomical hierarchy.

123. According to Franchise Direct, Subway has become the foremost restaurant franchise with 37,335 stores. See http://www.franchisedirect.com/directory/subway/ufoc/915/ (accessed September 30, 2012). See also Subway Timeline at http://www.subway.com/subwayroot/about_us/TimeLine.aspx (accessed September 30, 2012).

124. George Ritzer, *The McDonaldization of Society: An Investigation into the Changing Character of Contemporary Social Life*, rev. ed. (Thousand Oaks, Calif.: Pine Forge Press, 1996).

125. John Madeley, *A People's World: Alternatives to Economic Globalization* (London: Zed Books, 2003), 127.

126. Schlosser, *Fast Food Nation*, 5.

127. Martha Ellyn, "Chinese Food Good, Non-Fattening," *Washington Post*, September 19, 1942, B3; Marian Burros, "Eating Well: A Reversal of the Kind of Chinese Food Americans Eat," *New York Times*, September 15, 1993, C1.

128. Lyn Stallworth, "Woks, Steamers, and Fire Pots," in *The Great Cooks' Guide to Woks, Steamers, and Fire Pots: America's Leading Food Authorities Share Their Home-Tested Recipes and Expertise on Cooking Equipment and Techniques*, ed. Arnold Goldman, Barbara Spiegel, and Lyn Stallworth (New York: Random House, 1977), 1.

129. Nanci Hellmich, "Chinese Food: Lo Mein, Yes; Low-Fat, No," *USA Today*, September 1, 1993, 1D.

130. Stuart Berman, "Moo Shu Is Good for You," *Washington Post*, October 2, 1993, A18.

131. "Is Chinese Food High in Fat and Cholesterol and Excessive in Sodium?" *Shijie Ribao (World Journal)*, September 1, 1993, A1. Other studies that came out later contradicted the claims of the CSPI's report. See, for example, "Chinese Food Vindicated," *UC Berkeley Wellness Letter*, December 1994, 5.

132. "Mainstream Media Vilifies Chinese Food," *Shijie Ribao*, September 1, 1993, C1.

133. Lena Williams, "Chinese Say Study Hurts Restaurants," *New York Times*, September 29, 1993, C1, C6.

134. Charles Proctor, "Asian Pastries Take a Pounding," *Orange County Register* (Santa Ana, Calif.), August 19, 2006, http://www.ocregister.com/ocregister/news /state/article_1248449.php (accessed November 2, 2012); Michael Woo, conversation with the author, October 30, 2010. Woo, a former Los Angeles city councilman, became the first Asian American to run for mayor in the city.

135. Lonny Shavelson, "Moon Cakes Prompt American Culture Clash," NPR, February 18, 2007, http://www.npr.org/templates/story/story.php?storyId=7480086 (accessed February 9, 2014). See also Lonny Shavelson, "Not a Happy New Year for Moon Cakes," Voice of America, February 21, 2007.

136. Zhu Jiefan, *Zhonghua Yanyu Zhi* (*A Compilation of Chinese Proverbs*) (Taipei: Shangwu, 1989), 6:3024.

137. Proctor, "Asian Pastries Take a Pounding."

138. Freeman, "Sung," 147.

139. Sidney Mintz, *Tasting Food, Tasting Freedom: Excursions into Eating, Culture, and the Past* (Boston: Beacon Press, 1996), 106.

140. Among those, who have tried to define the concept of cuisine, some see it as originating from a community's ongoing negotiating the surrounding natural environment. G. J. Armelagos writes, for example, that "a cultural system . . . defines the items in nature that are edible; how these items can be extracted, eaten, or processed into food; the flavors used to enhance the taste of the food; and the rules about consuming it" ("The Omnivore's Dilemma: The Evolution of the Brain and the Determinants of Food Choice," *Journal of Anthropological Research* 66 [2010]: 164).

8. THE CHINESE BRILLAT-SAVARIN

1. *Pengtiao Jishu Ziliao Huibian* (*Compilation of Information on Cooking Techniques*) (Guangzhou tielou ju bangongzshi [Guangzhou Railroad Bureau Office], 1973), 162, 231.

2. There are some interesting discussions of some Chinese-food cookbooks in J. A. G. Roberts, *China to Chinatown: Chinese Food in the West* (London: Reaktion, 2002), 187–197, though the assertion that Chinese food writing in the United States first appeared in the 1920s and 1930s is clearly incorrect. An insightful and interesting paper is Malinda Lo, "'Authentic' Chinese Food: Chinese American Cookbooks and the Regulation of Ethnic Identity" (paper presented at the annual conference of the Association for Asian American Studies, March 2001), http://www.malindalo.com /nonfiction/research/chinese-food/ (accessed December 7, 2012). A close reading of

Buwei Yang Chao, *How to Cook and Eat in Chinese* (New York: Day, 1945), can be found in Janet Theophano, "Home Cooking: Boston Baked Beans and Sizzling Rice Soup as Recipes for Pride and Prejudice," in *Kitchen Culture in America: Popular Representations of Food, Gender, and Race,* ed. Sherrie A. Inness (Philadelphia: University of Pennsylvania Press, 2001), 138–156.

3. In collecting the information about the number of Chinese-food cookbooks, I have consulted diverse sources, including my own cookbook collection and Jacqueline M. Newman's extensive bibliography *Chinese Cookbooks: An Annotated English Language Compendium/Bibliography* (New York: Garland, 1987). My tally does not include those published in English but outside the United States or reprinted versions. Professor Gordon Chang kindly shared the list of his Chinese-food cookbook collection with me several years ago.

4. Buwei Yang Chao, *How to Cook and Eat in Chinese,* 3rd ed. (New York: Vintage, 1972); Wallace Yee Hong, *The Chinese Cook Book* (New York: Crown, 1952); Clara Tom, *Old Fashioned Method of Cantonese Chinese Cooking,* 11th ed. (Honolulu: Hawaiian Service, 1983).

5. Jeffrey Pilcher, "Cultural Histories of Food," in *The Oxford Handbook of Food History* ed. Jeffrey Pilcher (New York: Oxford University Press, 2012), 47.

6. F. Volant and J. R. Warren, *The Economy of Cookery for the Middle Class, the Tradesman, and the Artisan* (London: Diprose & Bateman, 1860), iv.

7. Jane Cunningham Croly, *Jennie June's American Cookery Book, Containing Upwards of Twelve Hundred Choice and Carefully Tested Receipts . . .* (1866; New York: Excelsior, 1878), v.

8. U.S. Bureau of the Census, *Statistical Abstract of the United States: 2001,* sec. 26, "Arts, Entertainment, and Recreation," 752, https://www.census.gov/prod/2002pubs/01statab/arts.pdf (accessed November 9, 2012).

9. Edouard Cointreau, "A Loaf of Bread, a Jug of Wine, and Thou(sands of Books)," *LOGOS: Journal of the World Book Community* 12, no. 4 (2001): 210–214. See also Edouard Cointreau, "One Billion Cookbooks," *Gourmand,* http://www.former.cookbookfair.com/html/one_billion_cookbooks.html (accessed November 8, 2012).

10. Stacy Finz, "Cookbook Sales Flourish," *San Francisco Chronicle,* May 7, 2011, http://www.sfgate.com/business/article/Cookbook-sales-flourish-2373044.php (accessed November 8, 2012).

11. "Cookbook Trends," Favorite Recipes Press, http://www.frpbooks.com/publish/publish_trends.aspx (accessed May 30, 2014).

12. Gwen Schock Cowherd, "Cookbook Obsession," *Minnesota Women's Press,* July 2011, 15, http://library.ndsu.edu/grhc/foods/recipe/images/obsession.pdf (accessed February 10, 2014).

13. Traci Marie Kelly, "'If I Were a Voodoo Priestess': Women's Culinary Autobiographies," in Inness, *Kitchen Culture in America*, 255.

14. Janet Theophano, *Eat My Words: Reading Women's Lives Through the Cookbooks They Wrote* (New York: Palgrave, 2002), 122. Lynne Ireland has also noted the autobiographical nature of cookbooks in "The Compiled Cookbook as Foodways Autobiography," *Western Folklore* 40, no. 1 (1981): 107–114.

15. David Belman, "200 Years of Cooking by the Book: The American Cookbook Celebrates Its Bicentennial," *Restaurants USA*, November 1996, http://www.restaurant.org/tools/magazines/rusa/magArchive/year/article/?ArticleID=631 (accessed November 9, 2012).

16. Lu Yaodong, *Yi Fei Jiu Shi Wei* (*No Longer the Old Flavor*) (Taipei: Yuan shen chu ban she, 1992), 159; Ute Engelhardt, "Dietetics in Tang China and the First Extant Works of *Materia Dietetica*," in *Innovation in Chinese Medicine*, ed. Elisabeth Hsu (Cambridge: Cambridge University Press, 2001), 173, 175.

17. This is most clearly seen in Jia Sixie, *Qi Min Yao Shu* (*Critical Techniques for the Welfare of the People*, ca. 535 C.E.). One of ancient China's most important agroeconomic texts, Jia's work also includes extensive instructions on how to make food.

18. Lee Su Jan and May Lee, "Confucius, Taoism, and Nutrition," in *The Fine Art of Chinese Cooking* (New York: Gramercy, 1962), chap. 1.

19. *Yin Shan Zheng Yao* (*The Essentials of Food and Beverage*, 1320) was written by a Mongolian author and reflects Mongolian influence. For example, it includes numerous dishes that use different parts of the sheep, ranging from sheep skin to sheep head. For the text in Chinese, see http://www.zhongyiyao.net/book/show/%D2%FB%C9%C5%D5%FD%D2%AA.html (accessed February 10, 2014).

20. Jia Ming, *Yingshi Xu Zhi* (*All You Must Know About Food*), in *Yin Zhuan Pu Lu* (*A Collection of Writings on Drinks and Food*), ed. Yang Jialuo (Taipei: Shijie shuju, 1992); Gao Lian, *Yin Zhuan Fu Shi Jian* (*Discourse on Food and Drink*) (1591; repr., Beijing: Chinese Commerce Publishing, 1985), 1. This is the title of the food segment of Gao's *Zun Sheng Ba Jian* (*Eight Treatises on the Principles of Life*).

21. Gu Zhong, *Yang Xiao Lu* (*The Little Book on Nurturing Life*, 1698), in Yang, *Yin Zhuan Pu Lu*, 105.

22. Ibid., 108.

23. Zhu Yizun, *Shi Xian Hong Mi* (*The Grand Secrets of Diets*) (early Qing; repr., Beijing: Chinese Commerce Publishing, 1984), 1.

24. Li Huanan, *Xing Yuan Lu* (*Records of the Xing Garden*) (eighteenth century; repr., Beijing: Chinese Commerce Publishing, 1984), 1–3.

25. Yuan Mei, *Suiyuan Shidan* (*Food Menu of the Suiyuan Garden*, 1792), in *Yuan Mei Quan Ji* (*Complete Works of Yuan Mei*), ed. Wang Yingzhong (Nanjing: Jiangsu gu ji chu ban she, 1993), 5:1.

26. Yuan Mei, "Chu Zhe Wang Xiaoyu Zhuan" (Biography of Chef Wang Xiaoyu), in *Yuan Mei Sanwen Xuan Ji (Selected Essays of Yuan Mei)*, ed. Li Mengsheng (Tianjin: Bai hua wen yi chu ban she, 2009), 32.

27. Yuan, *Suiyuan Shidan*, 8.

28. Li offered a recipe for *xi yang* steamed cake in *Xing Yuan Lu*, 43.

29. Fannie Merritt Farmer, *The Boston Cooking-School Cook Book* (Boston: Little, Brown, 1896), 1.

30. Lizzie Black Kander, *The "Settlement" Cook Book: The Way to a Man's Heart* (Milwaukee, 1901), 4.

31. Farmer, preface to *Boston Cooking-School Cook Book*.

32. U.S. Department of Agriculture, *The Soy Bean as a Forage Crop* (Washington, D.C.: Government Printing Office, 1897); Walter Charles Blasdale, *A Description of Some Chinese Vegetable Food Materials and Their Nutritive and Economic Value* (Washington, D.C.: Government Printing Office, 1899).

33. *Good Housekeeping Everyday Cook Book*, facsimile ed. (1903; New York: Hearst Books, 2002), ix. Kander also included the same classification, as well as other nutrition information, in *"Settlement" Cook Book*, 5–6.

34. *The Good Housekeeping Cook Book*, 7th ed. (New York: Farrar & Rinehart, 1943), 3–24.

35. Harriet Beecher Stowe and Catharine Esther Beecher, *The American Woman's Home: or, Principles of Domestic Science; Being a Guide to the Formation and Maintenance of Economical, Healthful, Beautiful, and Christian Homes* (New York: Ford, 1869), 24.

36. Carol Fisher, *The American Cookbook: A History* (Jefferson, N.C.: McFarland, 2006), 12.

37. Amelia Simmons, preface to *American Cookery, or The Art of Dressing Viands, Fish, Poultry, and Vegetables . . .* (Hartford, Conn.: Hudson & Goodwin, 1796).

38. Nell Giles Ahern, ed., *The Boston Globe Cookbook for Brides* (1918; Boston: Globe Newspaper Company, 1963), 1.

39. For more detailed discussions of community cookbooks, see Anne Bower, ed., *Recipes for Reading: Community Cookbooks, Stories, Histories* (Amherst: University of Massachusetts Press, 1997).

40. Benedict Anderson, *Imagined Communities: Reflections on the Origins and Spread of Nationalism* (New York: Verso, 1983).

41. Arjun Appadurai, "How to Make a National Cuisine: Cookbooks in Contemporary India," *Comparative Studies in Society and History* 30, no. 1 (1988): 20.

42. Jeffrey M. Pilcher, *Que Vivan Los Tamales! Food and the Making of Mexican Identity* (Albuquerque: University of New Mexico Press, 1998), 48.

43. Department of Agriculture, *Soy Bean as a Forage Crop*; Blasdale, *Description of Some Chinese Vegetable Food Materials*.

44. Jessie Louise Nolton, *Chinese Cookery in the Home Kitchen: Being Recipes for the Preparation of the Most Popular Chinese Dishes at Home* (Detroit: Chino-American, 1911), 2.

45. Sara Bosse and Onoto Watanna, *Chinese-Japanese Cook Book* (Chicago: Rand McNally, 1914), 1.

46. Pearl Buck and Lyle Kenyon Engel, *Pearl Buck's Oriental Cookbook* (New York: Simon and Schuster, 1972). It covers the cuisines of ten different countries, and the section on China is the longest. See also Emily Hahn, with editors of Time-Life Books, *The Cooking of China* (New York: Time-Life Books, 1968).

47. James Beard, *The Essential James Beard Cookbook: 450 Recipes That Shaped the Tradition of American Cooking* (New York: Macmillan, 2012), xiv. See also Arnold Goldman, Barbara Spiegel, and Lyn Stallworth, eds., *The Great Cooks' Guide to Woks, Steamers, and Fire Pots: America's Leading Food Authorities Share Their Home-Tested Recipes and Expertise on Cooking Equipment and Techniques* (New York: Random House, 1977); and Craig Claiborne and Virginia Lee, *The Chinese Cookbook* (Philadelphia: Lippincott, 1972).

48. See, for example, La Choy Food Products, *The Art and Secrets of Chinese Cookery* (Detroit: La Choy, 1937); and Del Monte Corporation, *Foolproof Oriental Cooking with Chun King* (San Francisco: Del Monte, 1982).

49. Betty Crocker Editors, *Betty Crocker's Chinese Cookbook: Recipes by Leeann Chin* (New York: Random House, 1981). In 1945, *Fortune* ranked her as the second most popular woman after Eleanor Roosevelt, calling her "America's First Lady of Food." See Susan Marks, *Finding Betty Crocker: The Secret Life of America's First Lady of Food* (Waterville, Maine: Thorndike Press, 2005), 116. Betty Crocker's nature as a symbol of America's white identity stands out in comparison with images of African American women, such as Aunt Jemima, also created by Washburn-Crosby, as low-paid cooks and housekeepers.

50. In tallying the non-Chinese authors, I included non-Chinese organizations that published Chinese-food cookbooks.

51. In 1930, for example, immigrants accounted for more than half of the Chinese population in the United States, which numbered about eighty thousand.

52. Buwei Yang Chao, *How to Cook and Eat in Chinese*, 2nd ed., rev. (London: Faber and Faber, 1968), 142.

53. Hsiang-ju Lin and Tsuifeng Lin, *Chinese Gastronomy* (1969; repr., New York: Pyramid, 1972), 9–10.

54. Pacific Trading Company, *Mandarin Chop Suey Cook Book* (Chicago: Pacific Trading, 1928).

55. See, for example, Mei-Mei Ling, *Chop Suey: A Collection of Simple Chinese Recipes Adapted for the American Home* (Honolulu: South Sea Sales, 1953). In spite of its title, the book actually has only one recipe called chop suey, giving us a sense of the extent to which the notion had come to epitomize Chinese cooking.

56. Calvin Lee, *Calvin Lee's Chinese Cooking for American Kitchens* (New York: Putnam, 1958), 29.

57. Buwei Yang Chao, *How to Cook and Eat in Chinese*, 2nd ed. (London: Faber and Faber, 1956), 131, and *How to Cook and Eat in Chinese* (1968), 141–144.

58. Hahn, *Cooking of China*, 11, 14.

59. Susan B. Gall and Timothy L. Gall, eds., *Statistical Record of Asian Americans* (Detroit: Gale Research, 1993), 411, 572.

60. Andrew Coe, *Chop Suey: A Cultural History of Chinese Food in the United States* (New York: Oxford University Press, 2009), 238–239.

61. Wonona W. Chang, Irving B. Chang, Helene W. Kutscher, and Austin H. Kutscher, eds., *An Encyclopedia of Chinese Food and Cooking* (New York: Crown, 1970).

62. Florence Lin, *Florence Lin's Chinese Regional Cookbook: A Guide to the Origins, Ingredients, and Cooking Methods of over 200 Regional Specialties and National Favorites* (New York: Hawthorn Books, 1975); Calvin B. Lee and Audrey Evans Lee, *The Gourmet Chinese Regional Cookbook* (New York: Putnam, 1976); Lucille Liang, *Chinese Regional Cooking: Authentic Recipes from the Liang School* (New York: Sterling, 1979); Kenneth H. C. Lo, *The Encyclopedia of Regional Chinese Cooking* (New York: A and W, 1979).

63. Chao, *How to Cook and Eat in Chinese* (1968), 259 (this discussion was not in the 1945 edition of the cookbook). For dim sum cookbooks, see Rhoda Yee, *Dim Sum* (New York: Random House, 1977); and Lonnie Mock, *Dim Sum Cookbook* (Walnut Greek, Calif.: Alpha Gamma Arts, 1977), and *Favorite Dim Sum*, ed. Nancy Haggerty (Walnut Greek, Calif.: Alpha Gamma Arts, 1979).

64. Kenneth H. C. Lo, *Peking Cooking* (New York: Pantheon, 1971); Linda Lew, Agnes Lee, and Elizabeth Brotherton, *Peking Table Top Cooking* (North Hollywood, Calif.: Gala Books, 1972); Louise Stallard, *Cooking Hunan-Style* (New York: Drake, 1973), and *The Szechuan and Hunan Cookbook* (New York: Drake, 1976); Jung-Feng Chiang, with Ellen Schrecker, *Mrs. Chiang's Szechwan Cookbook: Szechwan Home Cooking* (New York: Harper & Row, 1976).

65. Gary Lee, *Chinese Vegetarian Cook Book* (Concord, Calif.: Nitty Gritty Cookbooks, 1972); Kenneth H. C. Lo, *Chinese Vegetarian Cooking* (New York: Pantheon, 1974); Florence Lin, *Florence Lin's Chinese Vegetarian Cookbook* (New York: Hawthorn Books, 1976); Catherine Y. C. Liu, *Nutrition and Diet with Chinese Cooking* (Ann Arbor, Mich.: Liu, 1977); James Leong, *Low Calorie Chinese Gourmet Cookbook* (Los Angeles: Corwin Books, 1978).

66. See for example, Maggie Jarvis Tove, *Simple Chinese Cookery for the American Cook* (New York: Peter Pauper Press, 1972); James C. Yao, *Chinese Cuisine Made Easy* (San Francisco, 1972); Kenneth H. C. Lo, *Quick and Easy Chinese Cooking* (Boston: Houghton Mifflin, 1972), and *Chinese Cooking on Next to Nothing* (New York: Pantheon, 1976); Flor-

ence Lin, *Chinese One-dish Meals* (New York: Hawthorn Books, 1978); To Chun Lee and Margaret Verner, *Chinese Cooking Made Easy: The Secret of a Great Cuisine Unveiled* (New York: Galahad Books, 1979); and Barbara Grunes, *Oriental Express: Chinese Menus for the Food Processor*, rev. ed. (Maplewood, N.J.: Good Food Books, 1979).

67. Cui Tongyue, ed., *Hua Ying Chu Shu Da Quan* (*Chinese-English Comprehensive Cookbook*) (San Francisco: Fa Ming Gong Si, 1910).

68. Nolton, *Chinese Cookery in the Home Kitchen.*

69. M. Sing Au, introduction to *The Chinese Cook Book* (Reading, Pa.: Culinary Arts Press, 1936).

70. Ling Yutang, foreword to Lin and Lin, *Chinese Gastronomy*, 7.

71. Pow Hay Se (Pao Xi Shi in pinyin) or Fu Xi Shi is the legendary man who taught people how to fish and how to domesticate animals for food. Many Chinese have also traced the origin of Chinese cooking to Yi Yin, who lived in the Shang dynasty (1600–1046 B.C.E.) and was an excellent chef before becoming a political figure. Yi Yin appears in several historical documents. In *Lu Shi Chun Qiu* (*Spring and Autumn Annals*), a book written in the third century B.C.E., Lu Buwei wrote about the life of Yi Yin, who developed the theory of five flavors. Yi Yin regarded water as the foundation of all flavors. He discussed boiling as a cooking method that would get rid undesirable odors of food. See "Ben Wei" (Fundamental Tastes), in Lu Buwei, *Lu Shi Chun Qiu* (Beijing: Chinese Commerce Publishing, 1983), 29. Contemporary food scholars in China have also mentioned Peng Zu, a legendary figure who lived in the Xia (2070–1600 B.C.E.) and Shang dynasties, in their discussions of the origins of Chinese cooking. See Wang Xuetai, *Zhongguo Yinshi Wenhua Shi* (*The History of Chinese Dietary Culture*) (Guilin, Guangxi: Guangxi Normal University Press, 2006), 13–14.

72. Shiu Wong Chan, *The Chinese Cook Book* (New York: Stokes, 1917), 2.

73. Hong, introduction to *Chinese Cook Book.*

74. Lee and Lee, *Fine Art of Chinese Cooking*, 15.

75. Isabelle C. Chang, *What's Cooking at Chang's: The Key to Cooking Chinese* (New York: Liveright, 1959), 13–23.

76. Sherrie A. Inness, *Secret Ingredients: Race, Gender, and Class at the Dinner Table* (New York: Palgrave Macmillan, 2006), 59.

77. Chan, *Chinese Cook Book*, 5.

78. Au, introduction to *Chinese Cook Book.*

79. Chao, *How to Cook and Eat in Chinese* (1945), 39–47.

80. Ibid., 3.

81. Samuel Wells Williams, *The Middle Kingdom: A Survey of the Geography, Government, Literature, Social Life, Arts, and History of the Chinese Empire and Its Inhabitants* (New York: Scribner, 1907) 1:772.

82. Doreen Yen Hung Feng, *The Joy of Chinese Cooking*, 3rd ed. (New York: Grosset & Dunlap, 1977), 13–14.

83. Johnny Kan, with Charles L. Leong, *Eight Immortal Flavors: Secrets of Cantonese Cookery from San Francisco's Chinatown* (Berkeley, Calif.: Howell-North Books, 1963), 16.

84. The English translation of the title is from Sucheta Mazumdar, *Sugar and Society in China: Peasants, Technology, and the World Market* (Cambridge, Mass.: Harvard University Press, 1998), 29. Lin Yutang's belief that Wu was from Jiangsu Province is apparently incorrect.

85. For the text of *Wu Shi Zhong Kui Lu* (*The Cookery of Manager's Records of Ms. Wu*) in Chinese, see Chinese Text Project, http://ctext.org/wiki.pl?if=en&chapter=150543 &remap=gb (accessed February 10, 2014).

86. Lin and Lin, *Chinese Gastronomy*, 42.

87. Ibid., 28, 46.

88. Hahn, *Cooking of China*; Gloria Bley Miller, *The Thousand Recipe Chinese Cookbook* (1966; repr., New York: Grosset & Dunlap, 1970).

89. George Kwon appears to be the first author to use the term "culinary art" in the title of a Chinese-food cookbook, *Oriental Culinary Art* (Los Angeles: Kwon, 1933).

90. Grace Zia Chu, *The Pleasures of Chinese Cooking* (New York: Simon and Schuster, 1962), 13.

91. Mai Leung, *The Classic Chinese Cook Book* (New York: Harper & Row, 1976), ix.

92. This figure does not include books without sufficient information about individual authors or their gender, including those issued by corporations. The ratio is about the same among both Chinese American cookbook writers and all Chinese-food cookbook authors.

93. Chao, *How to Cook and Eat in Chinese* (1968), xiii.

94. Mary Sia, *Mary Sia's Chinese Cookbook* (1956; repr., Honolulu: University of Hawai'i Press, 1967), ix.

CONCLUSION

1. Aviezer Tucker, "In Search of Home," *Journal of Applied Philosophy* 11, no. 2 (1994): 184.

2. Homer, *Odyssey*, ix, 84–85, in *The Odyssey of Homer*, trans. Richard Lattimore (New York: Harper Perennial, 1991), 139.

3. See, for example, Ah Quin, diary entry, November 30, 1877.

4. Thomas Wolfe, *You Can't Go Home Again* (1940; Mattituck, N.Y.: Amereon, 1981), 666.

5. John Hollander, "All It Depends," *Social Research* 58, no. 1 (1991): 44.

6. Huang Dingchong, "Ji Er Zhong De Zuguo" (The Motherland in Hunger), *Journal of the Yi Society of the Zhonghua School* (1943): 32; Wah-chung Leung, diary entry, April 3, 1939; Wah-chung Leung's papers. I am grateful to Sandy Yee Man Leung for permission to use her family documents.

7. Ted C. Fishman, *China, Inc.: How the Rise of the Next Superpower Challenges America and the World* (New York: Scribner, 2005), 1.

8. Allen L. Hammond, *Which World? Scenarios for the 21st Century* (Washington, D.C.: Island Press, 1998), 151.

9. This is based on the interpretation in the lexicon compiled by Xu Shen, *Shuo Wen Jie Zi* (*Explaining Texts and Analyzing Characters*, second century).

10. Yunxiang Yan, "McDonald's in Beijing: The Localization of Americana," in *Golden Arches East: McDonald's in East Asia*, ed. James Watson (Stanford, Calif.: Stanford University Press, 1997), 52.

11. For more discussions of the success of KFC in China, see Warren Liu, *KFC in China: Secret Recipe for Success* (New York: Wiley, 2008); and Diane Brady, "KFC's Big Game of Chicken," *Bloomberg Businessweek*, March 29, 2012, http://www.businessweek.com/articles/2012-03-29/kfcs-big-game-of-chicken (accessed October 23, 2012).

12. On April 23, 2006, during his visit to a dairy farm in Chongqing, Premier Wen Jiabao expressed publicly that it was his dream for every Chinese person, especially children, to have one *jin* of milk daily. See "Zongli Meng Xiang: Rang Mei Ge Zhongguo Ren Mei Tian He Yi Jin Nai" (The Premier's Dream: Let Every Chinese Drink One *Jin* of Milk Everyday), May 30, 2006, People.com, http://lady.people.com.cn/GB/4418527.html (accessed October 20, 2009). One *jin* in China equals 16.6 ounces, a bit more than one pint.

13. Shelley Mallett, "Understanding Home: A Critical Review of the Literature," *Sociological Review* 52, no. 1 (2004): 62.

14. Bertrand Russell, "Modern Homogeneity," in *In Praise of Idleness and Other Essays* (1935; repr., New York: Routledge, 2004), 132.

15. Lee Chew, "The Life Story of a Chinaman," *Independent*, February 19, 1903, 423.

16. For more information about the acquisition, see "Yum's Offer for Little Sheep Gets China Antitrust Clearance," *Bloomberg News*, November 8, 2011, http://www.bloomberg.com/news/2011-11-08/yum-s-offer-for-little-sheep-gets-clearance.html (accessed October 12, 2012). Yum! started to run Little Sheep in 2012. The official Web site of Little Sheep offers a brief history of the company. See http://www.littlesheep.com/company/Overview_Introduction.aspx (accessed October 12, 2012).

17. Xinhua News Agency, http://news.xinhuanet.com/food/2007-03/13/content_5838644.htm (accessed October 12, 2012).

18. Fuchsia Dunlop, "Hunan Resources," *New York Times*, February 4, 2007. See also Jennifer 8 Lee, *The Fortune Cookie Chronicles: Adventures in the World of Chinese Food* (New York: Twelve, 2008), 78–79.

19. Maurice Lim Miller, "Learning from Cambodian Donut Shops: The Family Independence Initiative," *Race, Poverty & the Environment* 9, no. 1 (2002): 50.

20. Katie Robbins, "Chinese and Doughnuts: A California Mystery," *Atlantic*, March 11, 2010, http://www.theatlantic.com/health/archive/2010/03/chinese-and -doughnuts-a-california-mystery/37319/ (accessed October 5, 2010).

21. Clarissa Wei, "50 Best Chinese Restaurants in the United States," CNN, March 6, 2012, http://travel.cnn.com/explorations/eat/usa/50-best-chinese-restaurants-usa -145368 (accessed October 12, 2012).

AFTERWORD

1. Representative publications include Mark Pendergrast, *Uncommon Grounds: The History of Coffee and How It Transformed Our World* (New York: Basic Books, 1999); Mark Kurlansky, *Salt: A World History* (New York: Walker, 2002); Lydia Gautier, *Tea: Aromas and Flavors Around the World* (San Francisco: Chronicle Books, 2006); and Dan Koeppel, *Banana: The Fate of the Fruit That Changed the World* (New York: Hudson Street Press, 2008).

2. Two good examples are Eric Schlosser, *Fast Food Nation: The Dark Side of the All-American Meal* (Boston: Houghton Mifflin, 2001); and Michael Pollan, *The Omnivore's Dilemma: A Natural History of Four Meals* (New York: Penguin Press, 2006).

3. See, for example, Pierre Laszlo, *Salt: Grain of Life* (New York: Columbia University Press, 2001); Gary Y. Okihiro, *Pineapple Culture: A History of the Tropical and Temperate Zones* (Berkeley: University of California Press, 2009); and Jeffrey Pilcher, *Planet Taco: A Global History of Mexican Food* (New York: Oxford University Press, 2012). Academic studies that have had a broad impact include Sidney Mintz, *Sweetness and Power: The Place of Sugar in Modern History* (New York: Viking, 1985); and George Ritzer, *The McDonaldization of Society: An Investigation into the Changing Character of Contemporary Social Life* (Thousand Oaks, Calif.: Pine Forge Press, 1996).

4. Emiko Ohnuki-Tierney, *Rice as Self: Japanese Identities Through Time* (Princeton, N.J.: Princeton University Press, 1993); Carole M. Counihan and Penny Van Esterik, eds., *Food and Culture: A Reader* (New York: Routledge, 1997); Jeffrey Pilcher, *Que Vivan Los Tamales! Food and the Making of Mexican Identity* (Albuquerque: University of New Mexico Press, 1998); Marion Nestle, *Food Politics: How the Food Industry Influences Nutrition and Health* (Berkeley: University of California Press, 2002); Solomon H. Katz, *Encyclopedia of Food and Culture* (New York: Scribner, 2003); James Watson and Melissa L.

Caldwell, eds., *The Cultural Politics of Food and Eating: A Reader* (Malden, Mass.: Blackwell, 2005); Fran Hawthorne, *Inside the FDA: The Business and Politics Behind the Drugs We Take and the Food We Eat* (Hoboken, N.J.: Wiley, 2005); Lorna Piatti-Farnell, *Food and Culture in Contemporary American Fiction* (New York: Routledge, 2011).

5. Waverley Root and Richard de Rochemont, *Eating in America: A History* (New York: Morrow, 1976), is one of the earliest comprehensive histories of American food and has interesting anecdotes. Food habits in early American history are covered in Trudy Eden, *The Early American Table: Food and Society in the New World* (DeKalb: Northern Illinois University Press, 2008); and James E. McWilliams, *A Revolution in Eating: How the Quest for Food Shaped America* (New York: Columbia University Press, 2005). As a nation known for its drinking habits, America's alcohol consumption has also received considerable scholarly attention. See, for example, Mark Lender and James Kirby Martin, *Drinking in America: A History* (New York: Free Press, 1982); Kathryn Grover, *Dining in America, 1850–1900* (Amherst: University of Massachusetts Press, 1987); W. J. Rorabaugh, *The Alcoholic Republic: An American Tradition* (New York: Oxford University Press, 1979); and Sharon V. Salinger, *Taverns and Drinking in Early America* (Baltimore: Johns Hopkins University Press, 2002). Andrew F. Smith focuses on critical events in *Eating History: 30 Turning Points in the Making of American Cuisine* (New York: Columbia University Press, 2009), and *Drinking History: Fifteen Turning Points in the Making of American Beverages* (New York: Columbia University Press, 2013).

6. Harvey A. Levenstein, *Revolution at the Table: The Transformation of the American Diet* (New York: Oxford University Press, 1988), and *Paradox of Plenty: A Social History of Eating in Modern America* (New York: Oxford University Press, 1993). Richard Pillsbury offers an interesting history of restaurants in America in *From Boarding House to Bistro: The American Restaurant Then and Now* (Boston: Unwin Hyman, 1990) and covers broader issues concerning America's diet—including technology, immigration, regional food, and cookbooks—in *No Foreign Food: The American Diet in Time and Place* (Boulder, Colo.: Westview Press, 1998).

7. The latest developments in studies of American foodways are explored in Jennifer J. Wallach, *How America Eats: A Social History of U.S. Food and Culture* (New York: Rowman & Littlefield, 2013).

8. Sherrie A. Inness, ed., *Kitchen Culture in America: Popular Representations of Food, Gender, and Race* (Philadelphia: University of Pennsylvania Press, 2001). An important topic explored in the book is advertising, as it is in Katherine J. Parker, *Food Is Love: Food Advertising and Gender Roles in America* (Philadelphia: University of Pennsylvania Press, 2006). The essays in another anthology, Arlene Voski Avakian and Barbara Haber, eds., *From Betty Crocker to Feminist Food Studies: Critical Perspectives on*

Women and Food (Amherst: University of Massachusetts Press, 2005), also apply gender as a tool for understanding the important issues in the development of food consumption in the United States and other contexts.

9. Sherrie A. Inness, *Dinner Roles: American Women and Culinary Culture* (Iowa City: University of Iowa Press, 2001), and *Secret Ingredients: Race, Gender, and Class at the Dinner Table* (New York: Palgrave Macmillan, 2006).

10. Wilbur Zelinsky, "The Roving Palate: North America's Ethnic Cuisines," *Geoforum* 16, no. 1 (1985): 51–72.

11. Linda K. Brown and Kay Mussell, eds., *Ethnic and Regional Foodways in the United States: The Performance of Group Identity* (Knoxville: University of Tennessee Press, 1984).

12. Donna Gabaccia, *We Are What We Eat: Ethnic Food and the Making of Americans* (Cambridge, Mass.: Harvard University Press, 1998).

13. Joel Denker, *The World on a Plate: A Tour Through the History of America's Ethnic Cuisines* (Boulder, Colo.: Westview Press, 2003).

14. Yong Chen, "Food, Race, and Ethnicity," in *The Oxford Handbook of Food History*, ed. Jeffrey Pilcher (New York: Oxford University Press, 2012), 428–443.

15. Frederick Douglass Opie, *Hog and Hominy: Soul Food from Africa to America* (New York: Columbia University Press, 2008). See also Tracy N. Poe, "The Origins of Soul Food in Black Urban Identity: Chicago, 1915–1947," *American Studies International* 37, no. 1 (1999): 4–33.

16. Psyche A. Williams-Forson, *Building Houses out of Chicken Legs: Black Women, Food, and Power* (Chapel Hill: University of North Carolina Press, 2006).

17. Gustavo Arellano, *Taco USA: How Mexican Food Conquered America* (New York: Scribner, 2012), 8. For discussions of the blending of Mexican food into regional foodways, see Amy Bentley, "From Culinary Other to Mainstream America: Meaning and Uses of Southwestern Cuisine," in *Culinary Tourism*, ed. Lucy M. Long (Lexington: University of Kentucky Press, 2004), 209–225. There are also several essays on the "chili queens." See Donna Gabaccia and Jeffrey Pilcher, "'Chili Queens' and Checkered Tablecloths: Public Dining Cultures of Italians in New York City and Mexicans in San Antonio, Texas, 1870s–1940s," *Radical History* 110 (2010): 109–126.

18. Gaye Tuchman and Harry Gene Levine, "New York Jews and Chinese Food: The Social Construction of an Ethnic Pattern," in *The Taste of American Place: A Reader on Regional and Ethnic Foods*, ed. Barbara Gimla Shortridge and James R Shortridge (Lanham, Md.: Rowman & Littlefield, 1998), 163–184. Hanna Miller continues to examine this connection in "Identity Takeout: How American Jews Made Chinese Food Their Ethnic Cuisine," *Journal of Popular Culture* 39, no. 3 (2006): 430–465.

19. Shun Lu and Gary Alan Fine, "The Presentation of Ethnic Authenticity: Chinese Food as a Social Accomplishment," *Sociological Quarterly* 36, no. 3 (1995): 536.

20. Sherrie A. Inness, "'Unnatural, Unclean, and Filthy': Chinese American Cooking Literature Confronting Racism in the 1950s," in *Secret Ingredients*, 39–60.

21. J. A. G. Roberts, *China to Chinatown: Chinese Food in the West* (London: Reaktion, 2002).

22. Haiming Liu and Lianlian Lin, "Food, Culinary Identity, and Transnational Culture: Chinese Restaurant Business in Southern California," *Journal of Asian American Studies* 12, no. 2 (2009): 135–162.

23. Jennifer 8 Lee, *The Fortune Cookie Chronicles: Adventures in the World of Chinese Food* (New York: Twelve, 2008); Andrew Coe, *Chop Suey: A Cultural History of Chinese Food in the United States* (New York: Oxford University Press, 2009); John Jung, *Sweet and Sour: Life in Chinese Family Restaurants* (Cypress, Calif.: Yin & Yang Press, 2009).

24. One of the first in-depth attempts to understand food and its importance in world history is Reay Tannahill, *Food in History* (New York: Stein & Day, 1973). Felipe Fernández-Armesto discusses eight great revolutions in food development in an effort to "treat food history as a theme of world history, inseparable from all the other interactions of human beings with one another and with the rest of the nature" (*Near a Thousand Tables: A History of Food* [New York: Free Press, 2002], xii). Jeffrey M. Pilcher thoughtfully illustrates the significance themes in human history through five themes, ranging from the diffusion of foods to the role of the state, in *Food in World History* (New York: Routledge, 2006). Tom Standage notes: "From the dawn of agriculture to the green revolution, food has been an essential ingredient in human history" (*An Edible History of Humanity* [New York: Walker, 2009], 242). An informative and ambitious account of important food systems in major regions and countries since prehistory is Linda Civitello, *Cuisine and Culture: A History of Food and People* (Hoboken, N.J.: Wiley, 2004), while Rachel Laudan takes a comprehensive look at the development of cuisines as styles of cooking in global history, in *Cuisine and Empire: Cooking in World History* (Berkeley, Calif.: University of California Press, 2013). Also worth noting are the numerous anthologies. See, for example, Kenneth F. Kiple and Kriemhild Coneè Ornelas, eds., *The Cambridge World History of Food* (New York: Cambridge University Press, 2000), an important reference book with a few noticeable omissions, such as classical Greece and Rome, and Jean-Louis Flandrin and Massimo Montanari, eds., *Food: A Culinary History from Antiquity to the Present* (New York: Columbia University Press, 1999), an accessible book that is useful for both food scholars and practitioners.

25. *Book of Rites* (*Liji-Lijun*). For a translation by James Legge, see Chinese Text Project, http://ctext.org/liji/li-yun (accessed February 10, 2014). Confucius used four Chinese characters for the words "eat," "drink," "man," and "woman" to designate "food" and "sex." Ang Lee used this notion as the title of his celebrated food film *Eat Drink Man Woman* (1994).

26. *Mencius-Gaozi*. In his translation of this phrase, Legge mistook the word *se*, which means "sex" or "lust" in this context, to mean "color." See Chinese Text Project, http://ctext.org/mengzi/gaozi-i (accessed February 10, 2014). Centuries later, Sun Yat-sen, founder of the Republic of China, also noted that "food is a most common matter but it is also the most important in life" (*Sun Wen Xueshuo* [*The Treatises of Sun Yat-sen*], facsimile of the 1918 manuscript [Taipei: Yanming, 1988]).

27. Jacques Pepin, *The Apprentice: My Life in the Kitchen* (New York: Houghton Mifflin, 2003), 212. I am grateful to my editor, Jennifer Crewe, for reminding me of this story.

28. M. F. K. Fisher, foreword to *The Gastronomical Me*, in Counihan and Van Esterik, *Food and Culture*, vii, which also appears in *American Food Writing: An Anthology with Classic Recipes*, ed. Molly O'Neill (New York: Literary Classics of the United States, 2007), 24.

29. Hasia Diner, *Hungering for America: Italian, Irish, and Jewish Foodways in the Age of Migration* (Cambridge, Mass.: Harvard University Press), xv.

30. Lin Yutang, *My Country and My People* (1936; London: Heinemann, 1939), 339.

31. Bernard Berenson, *Sunset and Twilight: From the Diaries of 1947–1958*, ed. Nicky Mariano, intro. Iris Origo (London: Hamish Hamilton, 1963), 350.

32. Ellen Henrietta Richards, *The Cost of Food: A Study of Dietaries*, 3rd ed. (New York: Wiley, 1917), 93.

33. Ibid., 94–95.

34. The supermarket numbers are from the Food Marketing Institute. For more details, see "Supermarket Facts," FMI: The Voice of Food Retail, http://www.fmi.org/facts_figs/?fuseaction=superfact (accessed November 21, 2011).

35. U.S. Department of Labor, Bureau of Labor Statistics, *100 Years of U.S. Consumer Spending: Data for the Nation, New York City, and Boston*, BLS Report 991 (Washington, D.C.: Department of Labor, Bureau of Labor Statistics, 2006), 6, 63.

Bibliography

ARTICLES

Anderson, E. N., Jr., and Chun-hua Wang. "Changing Foodways of Chinese Immigrants in Southern California." *Annals of the Chinese Historical Society of the Pacific Northwest* 3 (1965–1986): 63–69.

Appadurai, Arjun. "How to Make a National Cuisine: Cookbooks in Contemporary India." *Comparative Studies in Society and History* 30, no. 1 (1988): 3–24.

Austen, Ben. "End of the Road: After Detroit, the Wreck of an American Dream." *Harper's Magazine*, August 2009, 26–36.

Balleck, Barry J. "When the Ends Justify the Means: Thomas Jefferson and the Louisiana Purchase." *Presidential Studies Quarterly* 22, no. 4 (1992): 679–696.

Barinaga, Marcia. "Salmon Follow Watery Odors Home." *Science*, October 22, 1999, 705–706.

Bell, Emily, with Katherine Martinelli. "2009 StarChefs.com Salary Survey," June 2010. Starchefs.com, http://www.starchefs.com/features/editors_dish/salary_survey/2009/index.shtml.

Bentley, Amy. "From Culinary Other to Mainstream America: Meaning and Uses of Southwestern Cuisine." In *Culinary Tourism*, edited by Lucy M. Long, 209–225. Lexington: University of Kentucky Press, 2004.

"Bits of Chinatown." *New York Tribune*, May 2, 1880, 2.

Bogue, Allan G. "Farming in the Prairie Peninsula, 1830–1890." *Journal of Economic History* 23, no. 1 (1963): 3–29.

Bonner, John. "The Labor Question of the Pacific Coast." *Californian Illustrated Magazine*, April 1892, 410–419.

Breen, Timothy H. "Narrative of Commercial Life: Consumption, Ideology, and Community on the Eve of the American Revolution." *William and Mary Quarterly* 50, no. 3 (1993): 483–484.

Brooks, Noah. "Restaurant Life in San Francisco." *Overland Monthly*, November 1868, 465–473.

Cassel, Susie Lan. "To Inscribe the Self Daily: The Discovery of the Ah Quin Diary." In *The Chinese in America: A History from Gold Mountain to the New Millennium*, edited by Susie Lan Cassel, 54–74. Walnut Creek, Calif.: AltaMira Press, 2002.

Chan, Sucheng. "Chinese Livelihood in Rural California: The Impact of Economic Change, 1860–1880." *Pacific Historical Review* 53, no. 3 (1984): 273–307.

Chapman, Arthur. "Why All the Chinese Restaurants?" *New York Tribune*, December 25, 1921, 6.

Chen, Yong. "Food, Race, and Ethnicity." In *The Oxford Handbook of Food History*, edited by Jeffrey Pilcher, 428–443. New York: Oxford University Press, 2012.

"Chicago Chinamen." *Wisconsin State Register* (Portage), August 24, 1889, col. C.

"China as Affected by Protestant Missions." *Biblical Repertory and Princeton Review* 42, no. 4 (1870): 613–622.

"The Chinese as Servants: What Happened When Bridget and Maggie Retired, and Ching Took Charge of the House." *New York Times*, April 4, 1880, 5.

"A Chinese Banquet." *New York Times*, March 15, 1877, 2.

"Chinese Cooks." *Current Literature* 31, no. 3 (1901): 315–316.

"Chinese Directory." *Oriental* (San Francisco), February 8, 1856.

"Chinese Fond of Sauerkraut." *Sausalito (Calif.) News*, March 31, 1900.

"The Chinese in New York." *New York Times*, March 6, 1880, 8.

"The Chinese in New York." *New York Tribune*, October 8, 1870, 11.

"The Chinese in San Francisco: How Cook and Eat in Their Theatres." *Frank Leslie's Illustrated Newspaper*, June 14, 1879, 248.

"Chinese Restaurants." *Atchison (Kan.) Daily Champion*, December 23, 1890, 6.

"The Chinese Restaurants." *Boston Daily Advertiser*, August 12, 1899, 4.

"Chinese Restaurants." *New York Tribune*, February 3, 1901, B6.

"The Chinese to the President." *Record of the Year* 1, no. 6 (1876): 600–602.

"Chop Suey Best of All." *Guthrie (Okla.) Daily Leader*, July 8, 1907, 5.

Chu, Louis. "The Chinese Restaurants in New York." Master's thesis, New York University, 1939.

Collier, Ellen C. "Instances of Use of United States Forces Abroad, 1798–1993." 1993. Naval History and Heritage Command, http://www.history.navy.mil/wars/foabroad .htm.

"Consumption of Meat." *Southern Planter* 1, no. 6 (1841): 119.

Corson, Juliet. "Chinese Cookery." *Harper's Bazaar*, July 17, 1897, 593.

Coser, Lewis. "Servants: The Obsolescence of an Occupational Role." *Social Forces* 52, no. 1 (1973): 31–40.

Cox, Thomas W. "The Coming Man." *Frank Leslie's Illustrated Newspaper*, May 21, 1870, 154.

Craddock, Susan. "Embodying Place: Pathologizing Chinese and Chinatown in Nineteenth-Century San Francisco." *Antipode* 31, no. 4 (1999): 351–371.

Cross, M. H. "Seeing Chinatown." *New York Times*, April 28, 1905, 8.

Davis, Netta "To Serve the 'Other': Chinese-American Immigrants in the Restaurant Business." *Journal for the Study of Food and Society* 6, no.1 (2002): 70–81.

Deck, Alice A. "'Now Then—Who Said Biscuits'? The Black Woman Cook as Fetish in American Advertising, 1905–1953." In *Kitchen Culture in America: Popular Representations of Food, Gender, and Race*, edited by Sherrie A. Inness, 69–94. Philadelphia: University of Pennsylvania Press, 2001.

Dickens, Charles. "The Italian Peasant." *All the Year Round* 4, no. 97 (1870): 438–443.

Earle, E. Lyell. "Character Studies in New York's Foreign Quarters." *Catholic World* 68, no. 408 (1899): 782–793.

"Eating in China." *New York Times*, March 16, 1873, 2.

Engelhardt, Ute. "Dietetics in Tang China and the First Extant Works of *Material Dietetica*." In *Innovation in Chinese Medicine*, edited by Elisabeth Hsu, 173–191. Cambridge: Cambridge University Press, 2001.

Faison, Jane. "The Virtues of the Chinese Servant." *Good Housekeeping*, March 1906, 279–280.

Foner, Eric. "Why Is There No Socialism in the United States?" *History Workshop*, no. 17 (1984): 57–80.

Gabaccia, Donna, and Jeffrey Pilcher. "'Chili Queens' and Checkered Tablecloths: Public Dining Cultures of Italians in New York City and Mexicans in San Antonio, Texas, 1870s–1940s." *Radical History* 110 (2010): 109–126.

Gallagher, John, and Ronald E. Robinson. "The Imperialism of Free Trade." *Economic History Review*, 2nd ser., 6, no. 1 (1953): 1–15.

Gay, Malcolm. "St. Louie Chop Suey." *Riverfront Times*, November 15, 2006. http://www.riverfronttimes.com/2006-11-15/news/st-louie-chop-suey/.

Glickman, Lawrence B. "Introduction: Born to Shop? Consumer History and American History." In *Consumer Society in American History: A Reader,* edited by Lawrence B. Glickman, 1–14. Ithaca, N.Y.: Cornell University Press, 1999.

Gratton, Brian. "The Poverty of Impoverishment Theory: The Economic Well-Being of the Elderly, 1890–1950." *Journal of Economic History* 56, no. 1 (1996): 39–61.

Grimes, William. "American Culture Examined as a Force That Grips the World." *New York Times,* March 11, 1992, C17.

Hamilton, Clara E. "A Woman's View of Chinese Exclusion." *Independent* 54, no. 2781 (1902): 692–693.

Harrison, Alice A. "Chinese Food and Restaurant." *Overland,* June 1917, 527–532.

Hart, Jerome A. "The New Chinatown in San Francisco." *Bohemian Magazine,* May 1909, 593–605.

Hildebrand, George H. "Consumer Sovereignty in Modern Times." *American Economic Review* 41, no. 2 (1951): 19–33.

Hing, Bill Ong. "No Place for Angels: In Reaction to Kevin Johnson." *University of Illinois Law Review* 2 (2000): 559–601.

Ho Yow. "The Attitude of the United States Towards the Chinese." *Forum* 29 (1900): 385–396.

Hodgson, Maria. "The Setting Can Be as Important as the Food." *New York Times,* February 3, 1982, C6.

Hoganson, Kristin. "Food and Entertainment from Every Corner of the Globe: Bourgeois U.S. Households as Points of Encounter, 1870–1920." *Amerikastudien* 48, no. 1 (2003): 115–135.

Inveen, Emma. "Up the Yangtze River." *Baptist Missionary Magazine,* September 1894, 444–449.

Ireland, Lynne. "The Compiled Cookbook as Foodways Autobiography." *Western Folklore* 40, no. 1 (1981): 107–114.

Jefferson, Thomas. "The President to the Territorial Legislature," December 28, 1805. Indiana Historical Bureau, http://www.in.gov/history/2893.htm.

Jia Ming. *Yingshi Xu Zhi (All You Must Know About Food).* In *Yin Zhuan Pu Lu (A Collection of Writings on Drinks and Food),* edited by Yang Jialuo. Taipei: Shijie shuju, 1992.

Joffe, Natalie F. "Food Habits of Selected Subcultures in the United States." In *The Problem of Changing Food Habits: Report of the Committee on Food Habits, 1941–1943,* edited by Committee on Food Habits, 97–103. Washington, D.C.: National Research Council, 1943.

Johnson, Bryan R. "Let's Eat Chinese Tonight." *American Heritage,* December 1987, 98–107.

Johnston, Josée. "The Citizen–Consumer Hybrid: Ideological Tensions and the Case of Whole Foods Market." *Theory and Society* 37, no. 3 (2008): 229–270.

Kalcik, Susan. "Ethnic Foodways in America: Symbol and the Performance of Identity." In *Ethnic and Regional Foodways in the United States: The Performance of Group Identity*, edited by Linda K. Brown and Kay Mussell, 37–65. Knoxville: University of Tennessee Press, 1984.

Kelly, Traci Marie. "'If I Were a Voodoo Priestess': Women's Culinary Autobiographies." In *Kitchen Culture in America: Popular Representations of Food, Gender, and Race*, edited by Sherrie A. Inness, 251–269. Philadelphia: University of Pennsylvania Press, 2001.

"King Wah Lo." *Chicago Daily Tribune*, December 18, 1909, 24.

Krout, Mary H. "Cookery Among the Chinese." *New York Tribune*, October 30, 1904, 10.

Langenwalter, Paul E., II. "The Archaeology of 19th-Century Chinese Subsistence at the Lower China Store, Madera County, California." In *Archaeological Perspectives on Ethnicity in America: Afro-American and Asian American Culture History*, edited by Robert L. Schuyler, 102–112. Farmingdale, N.Y.: Baywood, 1980.

Lee, Rose Hum. "The Decline of Chinatowns in the United States." *American Journal of Sociology* 54, no. 5 (1949): 422–432.

Lee Chew. "The Life Story of a Chinaman." *Independent*, February 19, 1903, 417–423. In *The Life Stories of Undistinguished Americans as Told by Themselves*, edited by Hamilton Holt, 174–185. 1906. Reprint, New York: Routledge, 1990.

L'Enfant. "Odd and Ends from a Barrel of Shakings." *Spirit of the Times: A Chronicle of the Turf, Agriculture, Field Sport, Literature, and the Stage*, June 25, 1853, 217.

Libby, Gary W. "Historical Notes on Chinese Restaurants in Portland, Maine." *Chinese America: History and Perspectives* 20 (2006): 48–56.

Light, Ivan. "From Vice District to Tourist Attraction: The Moral Career of American Chinatowns, 1880–1940." *Pacific Historical Review* 43 (1974): 367–394.

Lin Shuanglin. "It Is Urgently Important to Have Well-Managed and Sufficiently Funded Retirement Accounts." *People's Daily*, November 23, 2011. http://finance.people.com.cn/GB/226375/16355736.html.

Liu, Haiming, and Lianlian Lin. "Food, Culinary Identity, and Transnational Culture: Chinese Restaurant Business in Southern California." *Journal of Asian American Studies* 12, no. 2 (2009): 135–162.

Loomis, A. W. "The Old East in the New West." *Overland Monthly*, October 1868, 360–367.

Lu, Shun, and Gary Alan Fine. "The Presentation of Ethnic Authenticity: Chinese Food as a Social Accomplishment." *Sociological Quarterly* 36, no. 3 (1995): 535–553.

Lutz, Mark A. "The Limitations of Karl Marx's Social Economics." *Review of Social Economy* 37, no. 3 (1979): 329–344.

MacPhail, Elizabeth C. "When the Red Lights Went Out in San Diego: The Little Known Story of San Diego's 'Restricted' District." *Journal of San Diego History* 22, no. 2 (1974): 1–28.

Madison, James. "Detached Memoranda" [Amendment 1, Document 64]. Ca. 1817. In *The Founders' Constitution*, edited by Philip B. Kurland and Ralph Lerner. Chicago: University of Chicago Press, 2012. http://press-pubs.uchicago.edu/founders/documents/amendI_religions64.html.

Mallett, Shelley. "Understanding Home: A Critical Review of the Literature." *Sociological Review* 52, no. 1 (2004): 62–89.

"Maxims of a Chinese Gourmand." *New York Times*, October 25, 1885, 4.

McClain, Charles J., and Laurene Wu McClain. "The Chinese Contribution to the Development of American Law." In *Entry Denied: Exclusion and the Chinese Community in America, 1882–1943*, edited by Sucheng Chan, 3–24. Philadelphia: Temple University Press, 1991.

Mead, Margaret. "Ethnicity and Anthropology in America." In *Ethnic Identity: Cultural Continuity and Change*, edited by George A. DeVos and Lola Romanucci-Ross, 298–320. Palo Alto, Calif.: AltaMira Press, 1995.

Means, Gardiner C. "The Consumer and the New Deal." *Annals of the American Academy of Political and Social Science* 173 (1934): 7–17.

Meloney, William Brown. "Slumming in New York's Chinatown." *Munsey's Magazine*, September 1909, 818–830.

Mieder, Wolfgang. "'No Tickee, No Washee': Subtleties of a Proverbial Slur." *Western Folklore* 55, no. 1 (1996): 1–40.

Miller, Hanna. "Identity Takeout: How American Jews Made Chinese Food Their Ethnic Cuisine." *Journal of Popular Culture* 39, no. 3 (2006): 430–465.

Morrison, Toni. "What the Black Woman Thinks About Women's Lib." *New York Times Magazine*, August 22, 1971, 14–15, 63, 64, 66.

"Mott-Street Chinamen Angry." *New York Times*, August 1, 1883, 8.

Mulford, Prentice. "California Culinary Experiences." *Overland Monthly*, June 1869, 556–562.

"Odd Chinese Dishes." *New York Tribune*, August 30, 1903, B2.

O'Meara, James. "The Chinese in Early Days." *Overland Monthly*, May 1884, 477–481.

——. "Pioneer Sketches–4: To California by Sea." *Overland Monthly*, April 1884, 375–381.

"Our Chinese Colony." *Harper's Weekly*, November 22, 1890, 910.

Palmer, Richard. "In Bad Odour: Smell and Its Significance in Medicine from Antiquity to the Seventeenth Century." In *Medicine and the Five Senses*, edited by W. F. Bynum and Roy Porter, 61–68. New York: Cambridge University Press, 1993.

Pang, Sunyowe. "The Chinese in America." *Forum* 32, no. 5 (1902): 598–607.

Paul, Rodman W. "The Origin of the Chinese Issue in California." *Mississippi Valley Historical Review* 25, no. 2 (1938): 181–196.

Press, Gerald A. "History and the Development of the Idea of History in Antiquity." *History and Theory* 16, no. 3 (1977): 280–296.

"Queer Chinese Traits." *New York Tribune*, May 22, 1887, 13.

Ray, Krishnendu. "Ethnic Succession and the New American Restaurant Cuisine." In *The Restaurants Book: Ethnographies of Where We Eat*, edited by David Beriss and David Sutton, 97–114. Oxford: Berg, 2007.

Roosevelt, Franklin D. "Address of Governor Franklin D. Roosevelt in Forbes Field, Pittsburgh, Pennsylvania, October 19, 1932." FDR Presidential Library, http://www.fdrlibrary.marist.edu/aboutfdr/pdfs/smCampaign_10-19-1932.pdf.

Rubinstein, Murray A. "American Board Missionaries and the Formation of American Opinion toward China, 1830–1860." In *America Views China: American Images of China Then and Now*, edited by Jonathan Goldstein, Jerry Israel, and Hilary Conroy, 67–79. Bethlehem, Penn.: Associated University Presses, 1991.

Schor, Juliet B. "In Defense of Consumer Critique: Revisiting the Consumption Debates of the Twentieth Century." *Annals of the American Academy of Political and Social Science* 611, no. 1 (2007): 16–30.

Schudson, Michael. "Delectable Materialism: Second Thoughts on Consumer Culture." In *Consumer Society in American History: A Reader*, edited by Lawrence B. Glickman, 341–358. Ithaca, N.Y.: Cornell University Press, 1999.

Seitz, Don. "A Celestial Farm on Long Island." *Frank Leslie's Popular Monthly* 35, no. 4 (1893): 489–496.

Selden, Catherine. "The Tyranny of the Kitchen." *North American Review* 157, no. 4 (1893): 431–440.

Sheraton, Mimi. "A Jewish Yen for Chinese." *New York Times Magazine*, September 23, 1990, 71–72.

Siegel, Reva B. "Home as Work: The First Woman's Rights Claims Concerning Wives' Household Labor, 1850–1880." *Yale Law Journal* 103, no. 5 (1994): 1073–1217.

"Six Chinese Students Sent to New Bedford." *Friend: A Religious and Literary Journal*, November 4, 1905, 130–131.

Smith, Mark M. "Producing Sense, Consuming Sense, Making Sense: Perils and Prospects for Sensory History." *Journal of Social History* 40, no. 4 (2007): 841–858.

Speer, William. "The First Stone in the Foundation of the Synod of China." *Chinese Recorder and Missionary Journal* 30 (1899): 472–479.

Spier, Robert F. G. "Food Habits of Nineteenth-Century California Chinese." *California Historical Society Quarterly* 37, no. 1 (1958): 79–84.

Spiller, Harley. "On Menus in Motown, Detroit's Chinatown." *Flavor and Fortune* 11, no 3 (2004): 17–18.

Spiro, Melford E. "Acculturation of American Ethnic Groups." *American Anthropologist* 57, no. 6 (1955): 1240–1252.

Steel, Ronald. "When Worlds Collide." *New York Times*, July 21, 1996, E15.

Tang Fuxiang. "The Crisis Facing Chinese Restaurants and the Solution." *Zhongguo Pengren* (*Chinese Cooking*) 8 (1988): 43.

Thurman, Wallace. "Negro Life in New York's Harlem: A Lively Picture of a Popular and Interesting Section." In *The Collected Writings of Wallace Thurman: A Harlem Renaissance Reader*, edited by Amritjit Singh and Daniel M. Scott III, 39–62. New Brunswick, N.J.: Rutgers University Press, 2003.

Tillotson, James E. "Our Ready-Prepared Ready-to-Eat Nation." *Nutrition Today* 37, no. 1 (2002): 36–38.

"To His Excellency Gov. Bigler." *Daily Alta California* (San Francisco), May 5, 1852.

Tuchman, Gaye, and Harry Gene Levine. "New York Jews and Chinese Food: The Social Construction of an Ethnic Pattern." In *The Taste of American Place: A Reader on Regional and Ethnic Foods*, edited by Barbara Gimla Shortridge and James R Shortridge, 163–184. Lanham, Md.: Rowman & Littlefield, 1998.

Tucker, Aviezer. "In Search of Home." *Journal of Applied Philosophy* 11, no. 2 (1994): 181–187.

"Uncle Sam's Thanksgiving Dinner." *Harper's Weekly*, November 20, 1869, 745.

United Nations Population Fund. "Linking Population, Poverty and Development." http://www.unfpa.org/pds/trends.htm.

Wallace, Alexander. "Seeing Chinatown." *New York Times*, April 28, 1905, 8.

Ward, Eunice. "Ah Gin." *Overland Monthly and Out West Magazine*, May 1907, 393–396.

Wayside, Gleason's Pictorial Drawing-Room Companion, January 21, 1854, 47.

"White Cooks Must Keep Sober or Go." *New York Times*, November 7, 1885, 3.

Wilson, Woodrow. "Address on International Trade, Before the Salesmanship Congress." In *President Wilson's Foreign Policy: Messages, Addresses, Papers*, edited by James Brown Scott, 218–224. New York: Oxford University Press, 1918.

Wing, Richard. "General George Marshall and I." *Gum Saan Journal* 30 (2007): 33–34.

Wong, Charles Choy. "The Continuity of Chinese Grocers in Southern California." *Journal of Ethnic Studies* 8 (1980): 63–82.

Wong Chin Foo [spelled Wing Chinfoo]. "Chinese Cooking." *Brooklyn Daily Eagle*, July 6, 1884, 4.

——. "The Chinese in New York." *Cosmopolitan*, June 1888, 297–311.

"Wong Chin Foo." *New York Times*, October 4, 1873, 4.

Wong Sam and Assistants. *An English-Chinese Phrase Book*. In *The Big Aiiieeeee! An Anthology of Chinese American and Japanese American Literature*, edited by Jeffery Paul Chan, Frank Chin, Lawson Fusao Inada, and Shawn Wong, 94–110. New York: Penguin, 1991.

Wright, Minna. "My Chinese Cook." *Ladies' Repository*, April 1870, 301–304.

Wu, Ching Chao. "Chinatowns: A Study of Symbiosis and Assimilation." Ph.D. diss., University of Chicago, 1928.

Wu Zhengge. "Gongbao Ji Ding Tan Yuan" (Exploring the Origins of Gongbao Chicken). *Zhongguo Shi Pin* (*China Food*) 6 (1986): 38–39.

Yang, Grace I-Ping, and Hazel M. Fox. "Food Habit Changes of Chinese Persons Living in Lincoln, Nebraska." *Journal of the American Dietary Association* 75, no. 10 (1979): 420–424.

Young, Alexander. "Chinese Food and Cookery." *Appleton's Journal of Literature, Science and Art*, September 14, 1872, 291–293.

Yu, Renqiu. "Chop Suey: From Chinese Food to Chinese American Food." *Chinese America: History and Perspectives* 1 (1987): 87–100.

Yuan Mei. "Chu Zhe Wang Xiaoyu Zhuan" (Biography of Chef Wang Xiaoyu). In *Yuan Mei Sanwen Xuan Ji* (*Selected Essays of Yuan Mei*), edited by Li Mengsheng, 27–32. Tianjin: Bai hua wen yi chu ban she, 2009.

Zelinsky, Wilbur. "The Roving Palate: North America's Ethnic Cuisines." *Geoforum* 16, no. 1 (1985): 51–72.

Zhang, Qingsong. "The Origins of the Chinese Americanization Movement: Wong Chin Foo and the Chinese Equal Rights League." In *Claiming America: Constructing Chinese American Identities During the Exclusion Era*, edited by K. Scott Wong and Sucheng Chan, 41–63. Philadelphia: Temple University Press, 1998.

BOOKS

Ahern, Nell Giles, ed. *The Boston Globe Cookbook for Brides*. 1918. Boston: Globe Newspaper Company, 1963.

American Federation of Labor. *Some Reasons for Chinese Exclusion: Meat vs. Rice. American Manhood Against Asiatic Coolieism. Which Shall Survive?* Washington, D.C.: American Federation of Labor, 1901.

Anderson, Eugene N. *The Food of China*. New Haven, Conn.: Yale University Press, 1988.

Andrew, Kenneth W. *Chop Suey*. Elms Court Ilfracombe, Eng.: Stockwell, 1975.

Applebaum, Herbert A. *The Concept of Work: Ancient, Medieval, and Modern*. Albany: State University of New York Press, 1992.

Appleton's Dictionary of New York and Vicinity. New York: Appleton, 1892.

Archer, Robin. *Why Is There No Labor Party in the United States?* Princeton, N.J.: Princeton University Press, 2010.

Arellano, Gustavo. *Taco USA: How Mexican Food Conquered America*. New York: Scribner, 2012.

Au, M. Sing. *The Chinese Cook Book*. Reading, Pa.: Culinary Arts Press, 1936.

Austin, Alvyn. *China's Millions: The China Inland Mission and Late Qing Society, 1832–1905*. Grand Rapids, Mich.: Eerdmans, 2007.

Avakian, Arlene Voski, and Barbara Haber, eds. *From Betty Crocker to Feminist Food Studies: Critical Perspectives on Women and Food*. Amherst: University of Massachusetts Press, 2005.

Bacevich, Andrew. *The Limits of Power: The End of American Exceptionalism*. New York: Metropolitan Books, 2008.

Bailey, Jeremy D. *Thomas Jefferson and Executive Power*. Cambridge: Cambridge University Press, 2007.

Bancroft-Whitney and Edward Thompson Co., comps. *American Annotated Cases*. San Francisco: Bancroft-Whitney, 1916.

Banner, Stuart. *How the Indians Lost Their Land: Law and Power on the Frontier*. Cambridge, Mass.: Belknap Press of Harvard University Press, 2005.

Barnard, Frederick A. P., ed. *Johnson's (Revised) Universal Cyclopaedia*. Vol. 8. New York: Johnson, 1886.

Barth, Gunther Paul. *Bitter Strength: A History of the Chinese in the United States, 1850–1970*. Cambridge, Mass.: Harvard University Press, 1974.

Bauman, Zygmunt. *Work, Consumerism, and the New Poor*. Milton Keynes, Eng.: Open University Press, 1998.

Beard, James. *The Essential James Beard Cookbook: 450 Recipes That Shaped the Tradition of American Cooking*. New York: Macmillan, 2012.

Beardsworth, Alan, and Teresa Keil. *Sociology on the Menu: An Invitation to the Study of Food and Society*. New York: Routledge, 1997.

Beck, Louis Joseph. *New York's Chinatown: An Historical Presentation of Its People and Places*. New York: Bohemia, 1898.

Beckert, Sven. *The American Bourgeoisie: Distinction and Identity in the Nineteenth Century*. New York: Palgrave Macmillan, 2010

Bellamy, Edward. *Looking Backward: 2000–1887*. 1887. Reprint, Bedford, Mass.: Applewood Books, 2000.

Berenson, Bernard. *Sunset and Twilight: From the Diaries of 1947-1958.* Edited by Nicky Mariano. Introduction by Iris Origo. London: Hamish Hamilton, 1963.

Betty Crocker Editors. *Betty Crocker's Chinese Cookbook: Recipes by Leeann Chin.* New York: Random House, 1981.

Bickers, Robert. *Britain in China: Community, Culture, and Colonialism, 1900-49.* New York: St. Martin's Press, 1999.

Blasdale, Charles. *A Description of Some Chinese Vegetable Food Materials and Their Nutritive and Economic Value.* Washington, D.C.: Government Printing Office, 1899.

Blumin, Stuart. *The Emergence of the Middle Class: Social Experience in the American City, 1760-1900.* Cambridge: Cambridge University Press, 1989.

Bonner, Arthur. *Alas! What Brought Thee Hither? The Chinese in New York, 1800-1950.* Madison, N.J.: Fairleigh Dickinson University Press, 1997.

Boorstin, Daniel J. *The Americans.* Vol. 3, *The Democratic Experience.* New York: Random House, 1973.

Borthwick, John David. *Three Years in California.* Edinburgh: Blackwood, 1857.

Bosse, Sara, and Onoto Watanna. *Chinese-Japanese Cook Book.* Chicago: Rand McNally, 1914.

Bourdieu, Pierre. *Distinction: A Social Critique of the Judgment of Taste.* Cambridge, Mass.: Harvard University Press, 1984.

Bower, Anne, ed. *Recipes for Reading: Community Cookbooks, Stories, Histories.* Amherst: University of Massachusetts Press, 1997.

Bowles, Samuel. *Our New West: Records of Travel Between the Mississippi River and the Pacific Ocean.* New York: Dennison, 1869.

Bowman, S. A., M. Lino, S. A. Gerrior, and P. P. Basiotis. *The Healthy Eating Index: 1994-96.* CNPP-5. Washington, D.C.: U.S. Department of Agriculture, Center for Nutrition Policy and Promotion, 1998.

Boyd's Copartnership and Residence. Business Directory of Philadelphia City. Philadelphia: Boyd's Directory Office, 1900.

Bracken, Peg. *I Hate to Cook Book.* Greenwich, Conn.: Fawcett Crest, 1960.

Braudel, Fernand. *Civilization and Capitalism, 15th-18th Century.* Vol. 1, *The Structures of Everyday Life.* Translated by Siân Reynolds. 1981. Reprint, Berkeley: University of California Press, 1992.

——. *Civilization and Capitalism, 15th-18th Century.* Vol. 2, *The Wheels of Commerce.* Translated by Siân Reynolds. New York: Harper & Row, 1982.

Breen, Timothy H. *The Marketplace of Revolution: How Consumer Politics Shaped American Independence.* New York: Oxford University Press, 2004.

Brewer, William H. *Up and Down California in 1860–1864: The Journal of William H. Brewer.* Edited by Francis P. Farquhar. 1933. Reprint, Berkeley: University of California Press, 1966.

Brillat-Savarin, Jean Anthelme. *The Physiology of Taste or Transcendental Gastronomy.* Translated by Fayette Robinson. Philadelphia: Lindsay & Blakiston, 1854.

Brooks, Benjamin S. *The Chinese in California: To the Committee on Foreign Relations of the United States Senate* (1876).

Brownson, Ross C., Graham A. Colditz, and Enola K. Proctor. *Dissemination and Implementation Research in Health: Translating Science to Practice.* New York: Oxford University Press, 2012.

Buchanan, Patrick. *A Republic, Not an Empire: Reclaiming America's Destiny.* Washington, D.C.: Regnery, 1999.

Buck, Pearl, and Lyle Kenyon Engel. *Pearl Buck's Oriental Cookbook.* New York: Simon and Schuster, 1972.

Buel, J. W. *Metropolitan Life Unveiled; Or the Mysteries and Miseries of America's Cities.* St. Louis: Linahan, 1882.

Burnett, John. *A History of the Cost of Living.* New York: Penguin, 1969.

Canada Royal Commission on Chinese Immigration. *Report of the Royal Commission on Chinese Immigration: Report and Evidence.* Ottawa: Printed by order of the Commission, 1885.

Carcopino, Jerome. *Daily Life in Ancient Rome: The People and the City at the Height.* New Haven, Conn.: Yale University Press, 1960.

Carey, Joseph. *By the Golden Gate: Or, San Francisco, the Queen City of the Pacific Coast; with Scenes and Incidents Characteristic of Its Life.* Albany, N.Y.: Albany Diocesan Press, 1902.

Chan, Paul, and Kenneth Baker. *How to Order a Real Chinese Meal.* New York: Guild Books, 1976.

Chan, Shiu Wong. *The Chinese Cook Book.* New York: Stokes, 1917.

Chan, Sucheng. *Asian Americans: An Interpretive History.* Boston: Twayne, 1991.

Chang, Isabelle C. *What's Cooking at Chang's: The Key to Cooking Chinese.* New York: Liveright, 1959.

Chang, Jung, and Jon Holiday. *Mao: The Unknown Story.* New York: Knopf, 2005.

Chang, Kwang-chih. *Food in Chinese Culture: Anthropological and Historical Perspectives.* New Haven, Conn.: Yale University Press, 1977.

Chang, Wonona W., Irving B. Chang, Helene W. Kutscher, and Austin H. Kutscher, eds. *An Encyclopedia of Chinese Food and Cooking.* New York: Crown, 1970.

Chao, Buwei Yang. *How to Cook and Eat in Chinese.* New York: Day, 1945. Reprint, New York: Vintage, 1972.

——. *How to Cook and Eat in Chinese.* 2nd ed. London: Faber and Faber, 1956.

——. *How to Cook and Eat in Chinese.* 2nd ed., rev. London: Faber and Faber, 1968.

——. *How to Cook and Eat in Chinese.* 3rd ed. New York: Vintage, 1972.

Chappell, George. *The Restaurants of New York.* New York: Greenberg, 1925.

Chen, Ben John. *Chen Benchang Wen Ji (Selected Works of Ben John Chen).* New York: Asian American Republican National Federation, 1998.

Chen Benchang. *Meiguo Huaqiao Canguan Gongye (The Chinese Restaurant Industry).* Taipei: Yuandong Books, 1971.

Chêng, Tê-chao. *Acculturation of the Chinese in the United States: A Philadelphia Study.* Foochow [Fuzhou]: Fukien Christian University Press, 1948. [Ph.D. diss., University of Pennsylvania, 1943]

Chevalier, Michel. *Society, Manners and Politics in the United States: Being a Series of Letters on North America.* Boston: Weeks, Jordan, 1839.

Chiang, Jung-Feng, with Ellen Schrecker. *Mrs. Chiang's Szechwan Cookbook: Szechwan Home Cooking.* New York: Harper & Row, 1976.

Chicago City Directory. Chicago: Chicago Directory Company, 1900.

China and the Chinese: A Compend of Missionary Information from Various Sources. Toronto: Methodist Society, 1892.

Chinatown Declared a Nuisance! San Francisco, 1880.

Chiu, Ping. *Chinese Labor in California, 1850–1880: An Economic Study.* Madison: State Historical Society of Wisconsin for the Department of History, University of Wisconsin, 1963.

Cho, Lily. *Eating Chinese: Culture on the Menu in Small Town Canada.* Toronto: University of Toronto Press, 2010.

Chou, Cynthia L. *My Life in the United States.* North Quincy, Mass.: Christopher, 1970.

Chow, Gregory C. *Knowing China.* River Edge, N.J.: World Scientific, 2004.

Chu, Grace Zia. *The Pleasures of Chinese Cooking.* New York: Simon and Schuster, 1962.

Civitello, Linda. *Cuisine and Culture: A History of Food and People.* Hoboken, N.J.: Wiley, 2004.

Claiborne, Craig, and Virginia Lee. *The Chinese Cookbook.* Philadelphia: Lippincott, 1972.

Cobbold, Robert Henry. *Pictures of the Chinese, Drawn by Themselves.* London: Murray, 1860.

Cockburn, Alexander. *Corruptions of Empire: Life Studies and the Reagan Era.* New York: Verso, 1988.

Cocks, Catherine. *Doing the Town: The Rise of Urban Tourism in the United States, 1850–1915.* Berkeley: University of California Press, 2001.

Coe, Andrew. *Chop Suey: A Cultural History of Chinese Food in the United States.* New York: Oxford University Press, 2009.

Cohen, Lizabeth. *A Consumers' Republic: The Politics of Mass Consumption in Postwar America*. New York: Vintage, 2003.

Cohen, Warren I. *Pacific Passage: The Study of American-East Asian Relations on the Eve of the Twenty-first Century*. New York: Columbia University Press, 1996.

Cohen, William A. *Filth: Dirt, Disgust, and Modern Life*. Minneapolis: University of Minnesota Press, 2004.

Condit, Ira. *The Chinaman as We See Him and Fifty Years of Work for Him*. Chicago: Revell, 1900.

Confucius, *Confucian Analects (Lunyu-Shuer)*.

The Constitution of Oregon. Portland: McCormick, 1857.

Conwell, Russell Herman. *Why and How: Why the Chinese Emigrate, and the Means They Adopt for the Purpose of Reaching America*. Boston: Lee & Shepard, 1871.

Coolidge, Mary. *Chinese Immigration*. New York: Holt, 1909.

Cott, Nancy. *The Bonds of Womanhood: "Woman's Sphere" in New England, 1780–1835*. New Haven, Conn.: Yale University Press, 1977.

Counihan, Carole M., and Penny Van Esterik, eds. *Food and Culture: A Reader*. New York: Routledge, 1997.

Croly, Jane Cunningham. *Jennie June's American Cookery Book, Containing Upwards of Twelve Hundred Choice and Carefully Tested Receipts; Embracing All the Popular Dishes, and the Best Results of Modern Science, Reduced to a Simple and Practical Form*. 1866. Reprint, New York: Excelsior, 1878.

Cross, Gary. *An All-Consuming Century: Why Commercialism Won in Modern America*. New York: Columbia University Press, 2000.

Cui Guoyin. *Chushi Meirimiguo Riji (Journal of Chinese Minister to the United States, Spain, and Peru)*. 2 vols. 1894. Reprint, Taipei: Wen Hai.

Cui Tongyue, ed. *Hua Ying Chu Shu Da Quan (Chinese-English Comprehensive Cookbook)*. San Francisco: Fa Ming Gong Si, 1910.

Culin, Stewart. *China in America: A Study in the Social Life of the Chinese in the Eastern Cities of the United States*. Philadelphia, 1887.

Dalby, Andrew. *Empire of Pleasures: Luxury and Indulgence in the Roman World*. New York: Routledge, 2000.

Daniels, Roger. *Asian America: Chinese and Japanese in the United States Since 1850*. Seattle: University of Washington Press, 1995.

Dauvergne, Peter. *The Shadows of Consumption: Consequences for the Global Environment*. Cambridge, Mass.: MIT Press, 2008.

Davis, David Brion. *Antebellum American Culture: An Interpretive Anthology*. University Park: Penn State University Press, 1979.

Dean, Betty. *The New Jewish Cook Book*. New York: Hebrew Publishing, 1947.

Debow, J. D. B. *The Seventh Census of the United States*. Washington, D.C.: Robert Armstrong, Public Printer, 1853.

———. *Statistical View of the United States*. Washington, D.C.: Beverley Tucker, Senate Printer, 1854.

DeConde, Alexander. *This Affair of Louisiana*. New York: Scribner, 1976.

Del Monte Corporation. *Foolproof Oriental Cooking with Chun King*. San Francisco: Del Monte, 1982.

Denker, Joel. *The World on a Plate: A Tour Through the History of America's Ethnic Cuisines*. Boulder, Colo.: Westview Press, 2003.

Densmore, G. B. *The Chinese in California: Descriptions of Chinese Life in San Francisco, Their Habits, Morals and Manners*. San Francisco: Pettit & Russ, 1880.

Dikötter, Frank. *Mao's Great Famine: The History of China's Most Devastating Catastrophe, 1958-1962*. New York: Walker, 2010.

Diner, Hasia. *Hungering for America: Italian, Irish, and Jewish Foodways in the Age of Migration*. Cambridge, Mass.: Harvard University Press, 2001.

Dobie, Charles. *San Francisco's Chinatown*. New York: Appleton-Century, 1936.

Dorfman, Rachelle A., ed. *Paradigms of Clinical Social Work*. 2 vols. New York: Brunner/Mazel, 1988.

Douglas, Mary. *Purity and Danger: An Analysis of Concepts of Pollution and Taboo*. New York: Praeger, 1966.

Douglas, Norman. *Good-bye to Western Culture: Some Footnotes on East and West*. New York: Harper, 1930.

Doxey, William. *Guide to San Francisco and the Pleasure Resorts of California*. San Francisco, 1897.

Du Bois, W. E. Burghardt. *The Philadelphia Negro: A Social Study, Together with A Special Report on Domestic Service by Isabel Eaton*. Philadelphia: University of Pennsylvania, 1899.

Durning, Alan Thein. *How Much Is Enough? The Consumer Society and the Future of the Earth*. New York: Norton, 1992.

Dyce, Charles M. *Personal Reminiscences of Thirty Years' Residence in the Model Settlement Shanghai, 1870-1900*. London: Chapman & Hall, 1906.

Eden, Trudy. *The Early American Table: Food and Society in the New World*. DeKalb: Northern Illinois University Press, 2008.

Engen, Trygg. *Odor Sensation and Memory*. New York: Praeger, 1991.

Ethington, Philip J. *The Public City: The Political Construction of Urban Life in San Francisco, 1850-1900*. Berkeley: University of California Press, 2001.

Farmer, Fannie Merritt. *The Boston Cooking-School Cook Book*. Boston: Little, Brown, 1896.

Farwell, Willard B., and San Francisco Board of Supervisors. *The Chinese at Home and Abroad: Together with the Report of the Special Committee of the Board of Supervisors of San Francisco, on the Condition of the Chinese Quarter of That City.* San Francisco: Bancroft, 1885.

Feng, Doreen Yen Hung. *The Joy of Chinese Cooking.* 3rd ed. New York: Grosset & Dunlap, 1977.

Ferguson, Niall. *Colossus: The Rise and Fall of the American Empire.* New York: Penguin, 2004.

Fernández-Armesto, Felipe. *Near a Thousand Tables: A History of Food.* New York: Free Press, 2002.

Fisher, Carol. *The American Cookbook: A History.* Jefferson, N.C.: McFarland, 2006.

Flandrin, Jean-Louis, and Massimo Montanari, eds. *Food: A Culinary History from Antiquity to the Present.* New York: Columbia University Press, 1999.

Fletcher, C. R. L., and Rudyard Kipling. *A School History of England.* Oxford: Clarendon Press, 1911.

Gabaccia, Donna. *We Are What We Eat: Ethnic Food and the Making of Americans.* Cambridge, Mass.: Harvard University Press, 1998.

Galbraith, John. *The Affluent Society.* Boston: Houghton Mifflin, 1958.

Gall, Susan B., and Timothy L. Gall, eds. *Statistical Record of Asian Americans.* Detroit: Gale Research, 1993.

Galster, Vernon. *Chinese Cook Book, in Plain English.* Morris, Ill.: Galster, 1917.

Gao Lian. *Yin Zhuan Fu Shi Jian (Discourse on Food and Drink).* 1591. Reprint, Beijing: Chinese Commerce Publishing, 1985.

Gautier, Lydia. *Tea: Aromas and Flavors Around the World.* San Francisco: Chronicle Books, 2006.

Gay, Ruth. *Unfinished People: Eastern European Jews Encounter America.* New York: Norton, 2001.

Gibson, Otis. *The Chinese in America.* Cincinnati: Hitchcock & Walden, 1877.

Glazer, Nathan, and Daniel Moynihan, *Beyond the Melting Pot: The Negroes, Puerto Ricans, Jews, Italians, and Irish of New York City.* Cambridge, Mass.: MIT Press, 1992.

Goldberg, Betty S. *Chinese Kosher Cooking.* Middle Village, N.Y.: Jonathan David, 1984.

Goldman, Arnold, Barbara Spiegel, and Lyn Stallworth, eds. *The Great Cooks' Guide to Woks, Steamers, and Fire Pots: America's Leading Food Authorities Share Their Home-Tested Recipes and Expertise on Cooking Equipment and Techniques.* New York: Random House, 1977.

The Good Housekeeping Cook Book. 7th ed. New York: Farrar & Rinehart, 1943.

Good Housekeeping Everyday Cook Book. Facsimile ed. 1903. New York: Hearst Books, 2002.

Green, Joey. *Contrary to Popular Belief: More Than 250 False Facts Revealed*. New York: Random House, 2005.

Greenberg, Brian, and Linda S. Watts. *Social History of the United States: The 1990s*. Santa Barbara, Calif.: ABC-CLIO, 2009.

Grover, Kathryn. *Dining in America, 1850–1900*. Amherst: University of Massachusetts Press, 1987.

Grunes, Barbara. *Oriental Express: Chinese Menus for the Food Processor*. Rev. ed. Maplewood, N.J.: Good Food Books, 1979.

Gu Zhong. *Yang Xiao Lu (The Little Book on Nurturing Life, 1698)*. In *Yin Zhuan Pu Lu (A Collection of Writings on Drinks and Food)*, edited by Jialuo Yang. Taipei: Shijie shuju, 1992.

Gutman, Richard J. S. *American Diner Then and Now*. Baltimore: Johns Hopkins University Press, 2000.

Haenni, Sabine. *The Immigrant Scene: Ethnic Amusements in New York, 1880–1920*. Minneapolis: University of Minnesota Press, 2008.

Hahn, Emily, with editors of Time-Life Books. *The Cooking of China*. New York: Time-Life Books, 1968.

Hale and Emory's Marysville City Directory. Marysville, Calif.: Printed at the Marysville Herald Office, 1853.

Haley, Andrew P. *Turning the Tables: Restaurants and the Rise of the American Middle Class, 1880–1920*. Chapel Hill: University of North Carolina Press, 2011.

Hamilton, Alexander, James Madison, and John Jay, *The Federalist Papers*. Edited by Clinton Rossiter. New York: New American Library, 1961.

Hammond, Allen L. *Which World? Scenarios for the 21st Century*. Washington, D.C.: Island Press, 1998.

Hardt, Michael. *Empire*. Cambridge, Mass.: Harvard University Press, 2000.

Hardy, Iza Duffus. *Between Two Oceans: Or, Sketches of American Travel*. London: Hurst & Blackett, 1884.

Hart, Virgil C. *Western China: A Journey to the Great Buddhist Centre of Mount Omei*. Boston: Ticknor, 1888.

Hawthorne, Fran. *Inside the FDA: The Business and Politics Behind the Drugs We Take and the Food We Eat*. Hoboken, N.J.: Wiley, 2005.

Higginson, Francis. *New-England's Plantation: With the Sea Journal and Other Writings*. 1630. Reprint, Salem, Mass.: Essex Book and Print Club, 1908.

Higman. B. W. *How Food Made History*. Malden, Mass.: Wiley-Blackwell, 2012.

Hochschild, Arlie, with Anne Machung. *The Second Shift: Working Families and the Revolution at Home*. New York: Penguin, 2012.

Homer. *The Odyssey of Homer*. Translated by Richard Lattimore. New York: Harper Perennial, 1991.

Hong, Wallace Yee. *The Chinese Cook Book*. New York: Crown, 1952.

Hoobler, Dorothy, and Thomas Hoobler. *The Chinese American Family Album*. New York: Oxford University Press, 1998.

Hummel, Thomas, and Antje Welge-Lüssen, eds. *Taste and Smell: An Update*. Basel: Karger, 2006.

Hunter, W. C. *The "Fan Kwae" at Canton Before Treaty Years, 1825-1844*. London: Paul, Trench, 1882.

Igler, David. *Industrial Cowboys: Miller & Lux and the Transformation of the Far West, 1850-1920*. Berkeley: University of California Press, 2001.

Ignatiev, Noel. *How the Irish Became White*. New York: Routledge, 1995.

Inness, Sherrie A., ed. *Kitchen Culture in America: Popular Representations of Food, Gender, and Race*. Philadelphia: University of Pennsylvania Press, 2001.

——. *Secret Ingredients: Race, Gender, and Class at the Dinner Table*. New York: Palgrave Macmillan, 2006.

Jung, John. *Sweet and Sour: Life in Chinese Family Restaurants*. Cypress, Calif.: Yin & Yang Press, 2010.

Kan, Johnny, with Charles L. Leong. *Eight Immortal Flavors: Secrets of Cantonese Cookery from San Francisco's Chinatown*. Berkeley, Calif.: Howell-North Book, 1963.

Kander, Lizzie Black. *The "Settlement" Cook Book: The Way to a Man's Heart*. Milwaukee, 1901.

Katzman, David M. *Seven Days a Week: Women and Domestic Service in Industrializing America*. 1978. Reprint, Urbana: University of Illinois Press, 1981.

Kimball, Charles P. *The San Francisco City Directory*. San Francisco: Journal of Commerce Press, 1850.

Kiple, Kenneth F., and Kriemhild Coneè Ornelas, eds. *The Cambridge World History of Food*. 2 vols. New York: Cambridge University Press, 2000.

Koeppel, Dan. *Banana: The Fate of the Fruit That Changed the World*. New York: Hudson Street Press, 2008.

Kraut, Alan. *The Huddled Masses: The Immigrant in American Society, 1880-1921*. Wheeling, Ill.: Harlan Davidson, 1982.

Kurlansky, Mark. *Salt: A World History*. New York: Walker, 2002.

Kwang Chang Ling [Alexander del Mar]. *Why Should the Chinese Go? A Pertinent Inquiry from a Mandarin High in Authority*. San Francisco: Bruce's, 1878.

Kwon, George. *Oriental Culinary Art*. Los Angeles: Kwon, 1933.

Kwong, Peter. *The New Chinatown*. Rev. ed. New York: Hill and Wang, 1996.

La Choy Food Products. *The Art and Secrets of Chinese Cookery*. Detroit: La Choy, 1937.

LaFeber, Walter. *The American Century: A History of the United States Since the 1890s*. 2nd ed. New York: Wiley, 1979.

Lai, H. Mark. *Becoming Chinese American: A History of Communities and Institutions*. Walnut Creek, Calif.: AltaMira Press, 2004.

Lampe, Peter. *Christians at Rome in the First Two Centuries: From Paul to Valentinus*. London: Continuum, 2006.

Lanctot, Benoni. *Chinese and English Phrase Book, with the Chinese Pronunciation Indicated in English, Specially Adapted for the Use of Merchants, Travelers and Families*. San Francisco: Roman, 1867.

Langley, Henry G., comp. *The San Francisco Directory*. San Francisco, 1878.

——. *The San Francisco Directory*. San Francisco, 1882.

Lasch, Christopher. *The Culture of Narcissism: American Life in an Age of Diminishing Expectations*. New York: Norton, 1978.

Laszlo, Pierre. *Salt: Grain of Life*. New York: Columbia University Press, 2001.

Laudan, Rachel. *Cuisine and Empire: Cooking in World History*. Berkeley: University of California Press, 2013.

Leach, William. *Land of Desire: Merchants, Power, and the Rise of a New American Culture*. New York: Vintage, 1992.

LeCount and Strong's San Francisco City Directory for the Year 1854. San Francisco: San Francisco Herald Office, 1954.

Lee, Gary. *Chinese Vegetarian Cook Book*. Concord, Calif.: Nitty Gritty Cookbooks, 1972.

Lee, Jennifer 8. *The Fortune Cookie Chronicles: Adventures in the World of Chinese Food*. New York: Twelve, 2008.

Lee, Rose Hum. *The Chinese in the United States of America*. Hong Kong: Hong Kong University Press, 1960.

Lee, To Chun, and Margaret Verner. *Chinese Cooking Made Easy: The Secret of a Great Cuisine Unveiled*. New York: Galahad Books, 1979.

Lee Su Jan and May Lee. *The Fine Art of Chinese Cooking*. New York: Gramercy, 1962.

Lender, Mark, and James Kirby Martin. *Drinking in America: A History*. New York: Free Press, 1982.

Leong, James. *Low Calorie Chinese Gourmet Cookbook*. Los Angeles: Corwin Books, 1978.

Leong-Salobir, Cecilia. *Food Culture in Colonial Asia: A Taste of Empire*. New York: Routledge, 2011.

Leung, Mai. *The Classic Chinese Cook Book*. New York: Harper & Row, 1976.

Levenstein, Harvey A. *Paradox of Plenty: A Social History of Eating in Modern America*. New York: Oxford University Press, 1993.

——. *Revolution at the Table: The Transformation of the American Diet*. New York: Oxford University Press, 1988.

Lew, Linda, Agnes Lee, and Elizabeth Brotherton. *Peking Table Top Cooking*. North Hollywood, Calif.: Gala Books, 1972.

Li Gui. *Huan You Diqiu Xin Lu* (*New Accounts of Travels Around the Globe*). In *Wang Tao: Man You Sui Lu* (*Accounts of Travels*), edited by Zhong Shuhe. Shangsha: Yue lu shushe, 1985.

Li Huanan. *Xing Yuan Lu* (*Records of the Xing Garden*). Eighteenth century. Reprint, Beijing: Chinese Commerce Publishing, 1984. [Originally published by his son]

Li Shu-fan. *Hong Kong Surgeon*. New York: Dutton, 1964.

Liang Qichao. *Xindalu Youji* (*My Journey to the New Continent*). 1904. In *Jindai Zhongguo Zhiliao Congkan* (*Historical Documents Concerning Modern China*), edited by Shen Yun-long. Vol. 10. Shanghai: Wen-hai, 1967.

Limerick, Patricia. *The Legacy of Conquest: The Unbroken Past of the American West*. New York: Norton, 1987.

Lin, Florence. *Florence Lin's Chinese One-dish Meals*. New York: Hawthorn Books, 1978.

——. *Florence Lin's Chinese Vegetarian Cookbook*. New York: Hawthorn Books, 1976.

Lin, Hsiang-ju, and Tsuifeng Lin. *Chinese Gastronomy*. 1969. Reprint, New York: Pyramid, 1972.

Lin Yutang. *The Importance of Living*. New York: Day, 1937.

——. *My Country and My People*. 1936. London: Heinemann, 1939.

Lind, Michael. *Land of Promise: An Economic History of the United States*. New York: HarperCollins, 2012.

Ling, Huping. *Chinese St. Louis: From Enclave to Cultural Community*. Philadelphia: Temple University Press, 2004.

Lippmann, Walter. *Men of Destiny*. 1927. Reprint, with a new introduction by Paul Roazen, Piscataway, N.J.: Transaction, 2003.

Liu, Catherine Y. C. *Nutrition and Diet with Chinese Cooking*. Ann Arbor, Mich.: Liu, 1977.

Liu Zongren. *Two Years in the Melting Pot*. 1984. Reprint, San Francisco: China Books, 1988.

Lloyd, Gordon. *The Two Faces of Liberalism: How the Hoover–Roosevelt Debate Shapes the 21st Century*. Salem, Mass.: Scrivener Press, 2006.

Lo, Kenneth H. C. *Chinese Cooking on Next to Nothing*. New York: Pantheon, 1976.

——. *Chinese Vegetarian Cooking*. New York: Pantheon, 1974.

——. *Peking Cooking*. New York: Pantheon, 1971.

——. *Quick and Easy Chinese Cooking*. Boston: Houghton Mifflin, 1972.

Lou Chenghao and Xue Shunsheng. *Xiao Shi De Shanghai Lao Jian Zhu* (*Disappearing Historical Buildings in Shanghai*). Shanghai: Tongji University Press, 2002.

Lui, Mary Ting Yi. *The Chinatown Trunk Mystery: Murder, Miscegenation, and Other Dangerous Encounters in Turn-of-the-Century New York City*. Princeton, N.J.: Princeton University Press, 2004.

MacCannell, Dean. *The Tourist: A New Theory of the Leisure Class*. New York: Schocken, 1976.

Madeley, John. *A People's World: Alternatives to Economic Globalization*. London: Zed Books, 2003.

Madison, James. *The Writings of James Madison*. Edited by Gaillard Hunt. Vol. 3. New York: Putnam, 1908.

——. *The Writings of James Madison*. Edited by Gaillard Hunt. Vol. 5. New York: Putnam, 1904.

Maier, Charles S. *Among Empires: American Ascendancy and Its Predecessors*. Cambridge, Mass.: Harvard University Press, 2006.

Marks, Robert. *The Origins of the Modern World: A Global and Ecological Narrative*. Lanham Md.: Rowman & Littlefield, 2002.

Marks, Susan. *Finding Betty Crocker: The Secret Life of America's First Lady of Food*. Waterville, Maine: Thorndike Press, 2005.

Marx, Karl. *Critique of the Gotha Program*. 1875. Reprint, Rockville, Md.: Wildside Press, 2008.

Marx, Karl, and Frederick Engels. *The German Ideology*. 3rd rev. ed. Moscow: Progress, 1976.

Matthews, Glenna. *"Just a Housewife": The Rise and Fall of Domesticity in America*. New York: Oxford University Press, 1987.

McWilliams, James E. *A Revolution in Eating: How the Quest for Food Shaped America*. New York: Columbia University Press, 2005.

Meng Yuanlao. *Dongjing Meng Hua Lu (A Reminiscence of the Glory of Bianjin)*. Reprint, with four other books, Beijing: Zhonghua, 1962.

Mieder, Wolfgang. *Politics of Proverbs: From Traditional Wisdom to Proverbial Stereotypes*. Madison: University of Wisconsin Press, 1997.

Miller, Gloria Bley. *The Thousand Recipe Chinese Cookbook*. 1966. Reprint, New York: Grosset & Dunlap, 1970.

Mintz, Sidney. *Sweetness and Power: The Place of Sugar in Modern History*. New York: Viking, 1985.

——. *Tasting Food, Tasting Freedom: Excursions into Eating, Culture, and the Past*. Boston: Beacon Press, 1996.

Mock, Lonnie. *Dim Sum Cookbook*. Walnut Greek, Calif.: Alpha Gamma Arts, 1977.

——. *Favorite Dim Sum*. Edited by Nancy Haggerty. Walnut Creek, Calif.: Alpha Gamma Arts, 1979.

Münkler, Herfried. *Empires: The Logic of World Domination from Ancient Rome to the United States*. Cambridge: Polity, 2007.

Nestle, Marion. *Food Politics: How the Food Industry Influences Nutrition and Health*. Berkeley: University of California Press, 2002.

New York Chamber of Commerce. *Fifty-sixth Annual Report of the Corporation of the Chamber of Commerce of the State of New York*. New York: Press of the Chamber of Commerce, 1914.

Newman, Jacqueline M. *Chinese Cookbooks: An Annotated English Language Compendium/ Bibliography*. New York: Garland, 1987.

Niebuhr, Reinhold. *The Irony of American History*. 1952. Reprint, with a new introduction by Andrew J. Bacevich, Chicago: University of Chicago Press, 2008.

Nolton, Jessie Louise. *Chinese Cookery in the Home Kitchen: Being Recipes for the Preparation of the Most Popular Chinese Dishes at Home*. Detroit: Chino-American, 1911.

Nordhoff, Charles. *California: For Health, Pleasure and Residence, a Book for Travellers and Settlers*. New York: Harper, 1873.

Norton, Mary Beth, Carol Sheriff, David W. Blight, Howard P. Chudacoff, Fredrik Logevall, and Beth Bailey. *A People and a Nation: A History of the United States*. 9th ed. Boston: Wadsworth, 2011.

Ohnuki-Tierney, Emiko. *Rice as Self: Japanese Identities Through Time*. Princeton, N.J.: Princeton University Press, 1993.

Okihiro, Gary Y. *Margins and Mainstreams: Asians in American History and Culture*. Seattle: University of Washington Press, 1994.

——. *Pineapple Culture: A History of the Tropical and Temperate Zones*. Berkeley: University of California Press, 2009.

O'Neill, Molly, ed. *American Food Writing: An Anthology with Classic Recipes*. New York: Literary Classics of the United States, 2007.

Opie, Frederick Douglass. *Hog and Hominy: Soul Food from Africa to America*. New York: Columbia University Press, 2008.

Ow, Yuk, H. Mark Lai, and P. Choy, eds. *Yumei Sanyi Zonghuiguan Jianshi (A Brief History of the Three-District Association)*. San Francisco: Three-District Association, 1975.

Pacific Trading Company. *Mandarin Chop Suey Cook Book*. Chicago: Pacific Trading, 1928.

Parker, Katherine J. *Food Is Love: Food Advertising and Gender Roles in America*. Philadelphia: University of Pennsylvania Press, 2006.

Pendergrast, Mark. *Uncommon Grounds: The History of Coffee and How It Transformed Our World*. New York: Basic Books, 1999.

Pepin, Jacques. *The Apprentice: My Life in the Kitchen*. New York: Houghton Mifflin, 2003.

Peters, Richard, ed. *The Public Statutes at Large of the United States of America*. Vol. 1. Boston: Little and Brown, 1845.

Pfaelzer, Jean. *Driven Out: The Forgotten War Against Chinese Americans*. New York: Random House, 2007.

Piatti-Farnell, Lorna. *Food and Culture in Contemporary American Fiction*. New York: Routledge, 2011.

Pilcher, Jeffrey M. *Food in World History*. New York: Routledge, 2006.

——. *Planet Taco: A Global History of Mexican Food*. New York: Oxford University Press, 2012.

——. *Que Vivan Los Tamales! Food and the Making of Mexican Identity*. Albuquerque: University of New Mexico Press, 1998.

Pillsbury, Richard. *From Boarding House to Bistro: The American Restaurant Then and Now*. Boston: Unwin Hyman, 1990.

——. *No Foreign Food: The American Diet in Time and Place*. Boulder, Colo.: Westview Press, 1998.

Pollan, Michael. *The Omnivore's Dilemma: A Natural History of Four Meals*. New York: Penguin Press, 2006.

Pollock, Alan J. *Barnstorming to Heaven: Syd Pollock and His Great Black Teams*. Tuscaloosa: University of Alabama Press, 2012.

Pops, Gerald M. *Ethical Leadership in Turbulent Times: Modeling the Public Career of George C. Marshall*. Lanham, Md.: Lexington Books, 2009.

Potter, David. *People of Plenty: Economic Abundance and the American Character*. Chicago: University of Chicago Press, 1954.

Preston, Diana. *The Boxer Rebellion: The Dramatic Story of China's War on Foreigners That Shook the World in the Summer of 1900*. New York: Walker, 2000.

Providence Directory. Providence: Sampson, Davenport, 1878.

Providence Directory and Rhode Island Business Directory. Providence: Sampson, Murdock, 1900.

R. L. Polk & Co., comp. *Michigan State Gazetteer and Business Directory*. Detroit: Tribune, 1875.

——. *Polk's Detroit City Directory, 1928–1929*. Detroit: Polk, 1929.

Randolph, Mary. *The Virginia Housewife: or, Methodical Cook*. Baltimore: Plaskitt, Fite, 1838.

Reeves, Terrance J., and Claudette E. Bennett. *We the People: Asians in the United States*. Census 2000 Special Reports (CENSR-17). Washington, D.C.: U.S. Economics and Statistics Administration and U.S. Bureau of the Census, December 2004.

Richards, Ellen Henrietta. *The Cost of Food: A Study in Dietaries*. New York: Wiley, 1902.

Rifkin, Jeremy. *Beyond Beef: The Rise and Fall of the Cattle Culture*. New York: Plume, 1992.

Riis, Jacob August. *How the Other Half Lives: Studies Among the Tenements of New York*. New York: Scribner, 1890.

Risse, Guenter B. *Plague, Fear, and Politics in San Francisco's Chinatown*. Baltimore: Johns Hopkins University Press, 2012.

Ritzer, George. *The McDonaldization of Society: An Investigation into the Changing Character of Contemporary Social Life*. Rev. ed. Thousand Oaks, Calif.: Pine Forge Press, 1996.

Roberts, J. A. G. *China to Chinatown: Chinese Food in the West*. London: Reaktion, 2002.

Roberts, Robin Michael. *Hanford: 1900–2000*. San Francisco: Arcadia, 2007.

Roediger, David R. *The Wages of Whiteness: Race and the Making of the American Working Class*. New York: Verso, 1991.

Rollins, Judith. *Between Women: Domestics and Their Employers*. Philadelphia: Temple University Press, 1985.

Root, Waverley, and Richard de Rochemont. *Eating in America: A History*. New York: Morrow, 1976.

Rorabaugh, W. J. *The Alcoholic Republic: An American Tradition*. New York: Oxford University Press, 1979.

Rosenwaike, Ira. *Population History of New York City*. Syracuse, N.Y.: Syracuse University Press, 1972.

Roth, Philip. *Portnoy's Complaint*. New York: Random House, 1969.

Russell, Bertrand. *In Praise of Idleness and Other Essays*. 1935. Reprint, New York: Routlege, 2004.

Russell, J. H. *Cattle on the Conejo*. Pasadena, Calif.: Ward Ritchie Press, 1959.

Ryan, Mary. *Cradle of the Middle Class: The Family in Oneida County, New York, 1790–1865*. Cambridge: Cambridge University Press, 1981.

Sahlins, Marshall. *Stone Age Economics*. Chicago: Aldine-Atherton, 1972.

Salinger, Sharon V. *Taverns and Drinking in Early America*. Baltimore: Johns Hopkins University Press, 2002.

Sampson, Davenport, & Co. *The Boston Directory, Embracing the City Record, a General Directory of the Citizens, and a Business Directory for the Year Commencing July 1, 1875*. Boston Streets: Mapping Director Data, http://bcd.lib.tufts.edu/view_text.jsp?urn=tufts:central:dca:UA069:UA069.005.DO.00020&chapter=d.1875.su.Wah.

Sandmeyer, Elmer Clarence. *The Anti-Chinese Movement in California*. Urbana: University of Illinois Press, 1991.

Schlosser, Eric. *Fast Food Nation: The Dark Side of the All-American Meal*. New York: Houghton Mifflin, 2001.

Seward, George Frederick. *Chinese Immigration in Its Social and Economical Aspects*. New York: Scribner, 1881.

Shah, Nayan. *Contagious Divides: Epidemics and Race in San Francisco's Chinatown.* Berkeley: University of California Press, 2001.

Sharpless, Rebecca. *Cooking in Other Women's Kitchens: Domestic Workers in the South, 1865-1960.* Chapel Hill: University of North Carolina Press, 2010.

Shaw, Steven A. *Turning the Tables: Restaurants from the Inside Out.* New York: Harper-Collins, 2005.

Shaw, William. *Golden Dreams and Waking Realities.* London: Smith, Elder, 1851.

Sherry, John E. H. *The Laws of Innkeepers: For Hotels, Motels, Restaurants, and Clubs.* Ithaca, N.Y.: Cornell University Press, 1993.

Shortridge, Barbara, and James R. Shortridge, eds. *The Taste of American Place: A Reader on Regional and Ethnic Foods.* New York: Rowman & Littlefield, 1998.

Sia, Mary. *Mary Sia's Chinese Cookbook.* 1956. Reprint, Honolulu: University of Hawai'i Press, 1967.

Simmons, Amelia. *American Cookery, or The Art of Dressing Viands, Fish, Poultry, and Vegetables, and the Best Modes of Making Pastes, Puffs, Pies, Tarts, Puddings, Custards and Preserves, and All Kinds of Cakes, from the Imperial Plumb to Plain Cake. Adapted to This Country, and All Grades of Life.* Hartford, Conn.: Hudson & Goodwin, 1796.

Simoons, Frederick J. *Food in China: A Cultural and Historical Inquiry.* Roca Raton, Fla.: CRC Press, 1991.

Siu, Paul C. P. *The Chinese Laundryman: A Study of Social Isolation.* Edited by John Kuo Wei Tchen. New York: New York University Press, 1988.

Smil, Vaclav. *Feeding the World: A Challenge for the Twenty-first Century.* Cambridge, Mass.: MIT Press, 2001.

Smith, Andrew F. *Drinking History: Fifteen Turning Points in the Making of American Beverages.* New York: Columbia University Press, 2013.

——. *Eating History: 30 Turning Points in the Making of American Cuisine.* New York: Columbia University Press, 2009.

Spang, Rebecca. *The Invention of the Restaurant: Paris and Modern Gastronomic Culture.* Cambridge, Mass.: Harvard University Press, 2000.

Speer, William. *China and California: Their Relations, Past and Present.* San Francisco: Marvin & Hitchcock, 1853.

——. *An Humble Plea, Addressed to the Legislature of California, in Behalf of the Immigrants from the Empire of China to This State.* San Francisco: Oriental, 1856.

——. *The Oldest and the Newest Empire: China and the United States.* Cincinnati: National, 1870.

Stallard, Louise. *Cooking Hunan-Style.* New York: Drake, 1973.

——. *The Szechuan and Hunan Cookbook*. New York: Drake, 1976.

Standage, Tom. *An Edible History of Humanity*. New York: Walker, 2009.

The Statutes at Large of the United States of America. Vol. 22. Washington, D.C.: Government Printing Office, 1883.

Stedman, Thomas Lathrop, and K. P. Lee, *A Chinese and English Phrase Book in the Canton Dialect: Or, Dialogues on Ordinary and Familiar Subjects for the Use of the Chinese Resident in America, and of Americans Desirous of Learning the Chinese Language; with the Pronunciation of Each Word Indicated in Chinese and Roman Characters*. New York: Jenkins, 1888.

Storti, Craig. *Incident at Bitter Creek: The Story of the Rock Springs Chinese Massacre*. Ames: Iowa State University Press, 1991.

Stout, Arthur B. *Chinese Immigration and the Physiological Causes of the Decay of the Nation*. San Francisco: Agnew & Deffebach, 1862.

Stowe, Harriet Beecher, and Catharine Esther Beecher. *The American Woman's Home: or, Principles of Domestic Science; Being a Guide to the Formation and Maintenance of Economical, Healthful, Beautiful, and Christian Homes*. New York: Ford, 1869.

Street, Richard. *Beasts of the Field: A Narrative History of California Farmworkers, 1769–1913*. Stanford, Calif.: Stanford University Press, 2004.

Sun Yat-sen. *Memoirs of a Chinese Revolutionary: A Program of National Reconstruction for China*. 1918. Reprint, Taipei: Sino-American, 1953.

——. *Sun Wen Xueshuo (The Treatises of Sun Yat-sen)*. Facsimile of the 1918 manuscript. Taipei: Yangming, 1988.

Sutton, David E. *Remembrance of Repasts: An Anthropology of Food and Memory*. New York: Berg, 2001.

Tannahill, Reay. *Food in History*. New York: Stein & Day, 1973.

Tate, E. Mowbray. *Transpacific Steam: The Story of Steam Navigation from the Pacific Coast of North America to the Far East and the Antipodes, 1867–1941*. Cranbury, N.J.: Cornwall Books, 1986.

Taylor, Bayard. *Eldorado: or, Adventures in the Path of Empire, Comprising a Voyage to California, via Panama; Life in San Francisco and Monterey; Pictures of the Gold Region; and Experiences of Mexican Travel*. New York: Putnam, 1894.

Tchen, John Kuo Wei. *New York Before Chinatown: Orientalism and the Shaping of American Culture, 1776–1882*. Baltimore: Johns Hopkins University Press, 1999.

Theophano, Janet. *Eat My Words: Reading Women's Lives Through the Cookbooks They Wrote*. New York: Palgrave, 2002.

Thurman, Wallace. *The Collected Writings of Wallace Thurman: A Harlem Renaissance Reader*. Edited by Amritjit Singh and Daniel M. Scott III. New Brunswick, N.J.: Rutgers University Press, 2003.

Thurston, G. H., and J. H. Diffenbacher, comps. *Directory of Pittsburgh and Allegheny Cities for 1875-1876.* Pittsburgh: Anderson, 1874.

Tiffany, Osmond. *The Canton Chinese: Or, The American's Sojourn in the Celestial Empire.* Boston: Munroe, 1849.

Tocqueville, Alexis de. *Democracy in America.* 1835, 1840. Reprint, New York: Walker, 1947.

Todd, Frank Morton. *Eradicating Plague from San Francisco: Report of the Citizens' Health Committee and the Account of Its Work.* San Francisco: Murdock, 1909.

Tom, Clara. *Old Fashioned Method of Cantonese Chinese Cooking.* Honolulu: Hawaiian Service, 1983.

Tove, Maggie Jarvis. *Simple Chinese Cookery for the American Cook.* New York: Peter Pauper Press, 1972.

Tow, J. S. *The Real Chinese in America.* New York: Academy Press, 1923.

Turner, Frederick Jackson. *The Frontier in American History.* New York: Holt, 1921.

U.S. Bureau of the Census. *Abstract of the Fourteenth Census of the United States, 1920.* Washington, D.C.: Government Printing Office, 1923.

——. *Fifteenth Census of the United States: 1930. Population.* Washington, D.C.: Government Printing Office, 1930.

——. *Fourteenth Census of the United States.* Vol. 4, *Population 1920: Occupations.* Washington, D.C.: Government Printing Office, 1923.

——. *Historical Statistics of the United States: Colonial Times to 1970.* Washington, D.C.: Government Printing Office, 1975.

——. *1980 Census of Population: Subject Reports. Asian and Pacific Islander Population in the United States, 1980.* Washington, D.C.: Bureau of the Census, 1988.

——. *Thirteenth Census of the United States.* Vol. 4, *Population 1910: Occupational Statistics.* Washington, D.C.: Government Printing Office, 1914.

——. *We, the American Asians.* Washington, D.C.: Government Printing Office, 1993.

U.S. Bureau of Economic Analysis and U.S. Bureau of the Census. *Long-Term Economic Growth.* Washington, D.C.: Government Printing Office, 1973.

U.S. Census Office, *Abstract of the Twelfth Census of the United States, 1900.* Washington, D.C.: Government Printing Office, 1902.

——. *Compendium of the Tenth Census.* Washington, D.C.: Government Printing Office, 1883.

——. *Ninth Census of the United State: Statistics of Population.* Washington, D.C.: Government Printing Office, 1872.

——. *Report on Population of the United States at the Eleventh Census: 1890.* Washington, D.C.: Government Printing Office, 1897.

U.S. Congress. *Report of the Joint Special Committee to Investigate Chinese Immigration.* Washington, D.C.: Government Printing Office, 1877.

U.S. Department of Agriculture. *The Soy Bean as a Forage Crop.* Washington, D.C.: Government Printing Office, 1897.

U.S. Department of Labor, Bureau of Labor Statistics. *100 Years of U.S. Consumer Spending: Data for the Nation, New York City, and Boston.* BLS Report 991. Washington, D.C.: Department of Labor, Bureau of Labor Statistics, 2006.

Veblen, Thorstein. *The Theory of the Leisure Class.* 1899. Reprint, New York: Kelley, 1965.

Volant, F., and J. R. Warren. *The Economy of Cookery for the Middle Class, the Tradesman, and the Artisan.* London: Diprose & Bateman, 1860.

Waley, Arthur. *Yuan Mei: Eighteenth Century Chinese Poet.* Stanford, Calif.: Stanford University Press, 1956.

Walker, Francis A. *Compendium of the Ninth Census.* Washington, D.C.: Government Printing Office, 1872.

Wallach, Jennifer J. *How America Eats: A Social History of U.S. Food and Culture.* New York: Rowman & Littlefield, 2013.

Walvin, James. *Fruits of Empire: Exotic Produce and British Taste, 1660–1800.* New York: New York University Press, 1997.

Wang Xuetai. *Zhongguo Yinshi Wenhua Shi (The History of Chinese Dietary Culture).* Guilin, Guangxi: Guangxi Normal University Press, 2006.

Watson, James, and Melissa L. Caldwell, eds. *The Cultural Politics of Food and Eating: A Reader.* Malden, Mass.: Blackwell, 2005.

Wells Fargo. *Directory of Principal Chinese Business Firms.* San Francisco, 1878.

——. *Directory of Principal Chinese Business Firms.* San Francisco, 1882.

Willcox, Walter Francis, et al. *Supplementary Analysis and Derivative Tables: Twelfth Census of the United States, 1900.* Washington, D.C.: Government Printing Office, 1906.

Williams, Mary Floyd. *History of the San Francisco Committee of Vigilance of 1851: A Study of Social Control on the California Frontier in the Days of the Gold Rush.* Berkeley: University of California Press, 1921.

Williams, Samuel Wells. *The Middle Kingdom: A Survey of the Geography, Government, Literature, Social Life, Arts, and History of the Chinese Empire and Its Inhabitants.* 2 vols. 1848. Reprint, New York: Paragon Book, 1966.

Williams, William Appleman. *Empire as a Way of Life: An Essay on the Causes and Character of America's Present Predicament, Along with a Few Thoughts About an Alternative.* Introduction by Andrew Bacevich. 1980. Reprint, New York: Ig, 2007.

——. *The Tragedy of American Diplomacy.* Rev. ed. New York: Dell, 1962.

Williams-Forson, Psyche A. *Building Houses out of Chicken Legs: Black Women, Food, and Power.* Chapel Hill: University of North Carolina Press, 2006.

Wilson, James Harrison. *China Travels and Investigations in the "Middle Kingdom": A Study of Its Civilization and Possibilities.* New York: Appleton, 1887.

Wolfe, Thomas. *You Can't Go Home Again.* 1940. Reprint, Mattituck, N.Y.: Amereon, 1981.

Wong, J. Y. *Yeh Ming-Ch'en: Viceroy of Liang Kuang, 1852–58.* Cambridge: Cambridge University Press, 1976.

Wong, K. Scott, and Sucheng Chan, eds. *Claiming America: Constructing Chinese American Identities During the Exclusion Era.* Philadelphia: Temple University Press, 1998.

Wong, Marie Rose. *Sweet Cakes, Long Journey: The Chinatowns of Portland, Oregon.* Seattle: University of Washington Press, 2004.

Worden, Helen. *The Real New York: A Guide for the Adventurous Shopper, the Exploratory Eater and the Know-it-all Sightseer Who Ain't Seen Nothin' Yet.* Indianapolis: Bobbs-Merrill, 1933.

Work, Monroe N., ed. *Negro Year Book.* Tuskegee, Ala.: Negro Year Book, 1919.

Wu, Blanche Ching-Yi. *East Meets West.* Baltimore: Huang, 1985.

Xiang Dingrong. *Guofu Qi Fang Mei Tan Kao Shu (The Founding Father's Seven Visits to the Continental United States and Hawaii).* Taipei: Shibao, 1982.

Xu Ke. *Qing Bai Lei Chao (Qing Unofficial History Categorized Extracts).* 48 vols. Shanghai: Shangwu, 1917.

Yao, James C. *Chinese Cuisine Made Easy.* San Francisco, 1972.

Yee, Alfred. *Shopping at Giant Foods: Chinese American Supermarkets in Northern California.* Seattle: University of Washington Press, 2003.

Yee, Rhoda. *Dim Sum.* New York: Random House, 1977.

Yuan Mei. *Suiyuan Shidan (Food Menu of the Suiyuan Garden, 1792).* In *Yuan Mei Quan Ji (Complete Works of Yuan Mei),* edited by Wang Yingzhong. Vol. 5. Nanjing: Jiangsu gu ji chu ban she, 1993.

Yue, Gang. *The Mouth That Begs: Hunger, Cannibalism, and the Politics of Eating in Modern China.* Durham, N.C.: Duke University Press, 1999.

Zhang Guangzhi (Kwang-chih Chang). *Zhongguo Qingtong Shidai (The Bronze Age of China).* Hong Kong: Chinese University of Hong Kong Press, 1982.

Zhang Yinhuan. *Sanzhou Riji (Journal of the Journey to Three Continents).* 8 vols. Beijing Yuedong xinguan, 1896.

Zhao Yang Fan Shu (Foreign Cookery in Chinese). 1866. Reprint, Shanghai: American Presbyterian Mission Press, 1909.

Zhu, Liping. *A Chinaman's Chance: The Chinese on the Rocky Mountain Mining Frontier.* Niwot: University Press of Colorado, 1997.

Zhu Jiefan. *Zhonghua Yanyu Zhi (A Compilation of Chinese Proverbs).* 11 vols. Taipei: Shangwu, 1989.

Zhu Yizun. *Shi Xian Hong Mi (The Grand Secrets of Diets)*. Early Qing. Reprint, Beijing: Chinese Commerce Publishing, 1984.

Zunz, Olivier. *The Changing Face of Inequality: Urbanization, Industrial Development, and Immigrants in Detroit, 1880-1920*. Chicago: University of Chicago Press, 2000.

Zuo Qiuming. *Zuo Zhuan (Chronicle of Zuo)*. Fourth century B.C.E.

Index

Italicized page numbers refer to recipes, and *plate* refers to an illustration in the photo gallery.

frontier thesis (Turner), 36

frying, *17, 98, 115. See also* stir-fry; wok

Fuji (food brand), 140

Gabaccia, Donna, 183

Gage, Henry, 50

Galbraith, John Kenneth, 28, 187

Gallagher, John, 25

Gao Lian, 134, 157

Gao Zi, 185

gender roles. *See* women and gender roles

General Tso's chicken, 6, 146, 179, 184

General Tso's dishes, 147

German immigrants, 56–57

Gibson, Otis, 83, 90, 123

Gilmore Girls (television show; 2000–2007), 114

Gleason's Pictorial Drawing-Room Companion (magazine), 16

Glickman, Lawrence B., 29

globalization and transnationalization, 14–15, 20, 184

Gold Rush, ix, 23, 73, 77

Goldberg, Betty S., 138, 145

Golden Bowl Chop Suey (restaurant; Detroit), 110, *plate*

Good Housekeeping (magazine), 40, 49, 160

Goodman, Matthew, 114

Great Depression (1930s), 37

Great Leap Forward, 29

Great Wall (restaurant; Detroit), 110

Green Max (Ma Yu Shan) Black Sesame Cereal, *180*

Greenberg, Brian, 15

Gu Zhong, 157–158

Guangdong Province, 130

Gumbo, *64*

Hahn, Emily, 163, 164, 170

Haley, Andrew P., 42, 103

hamburger, 136, 144–145, 175–176

Hamilton, Alexander (doctor), 39

Hamilton, Clara E., 47, 51

Han, cooking style of, 159

Hanford (Calif.), 61, 69, 80, 135

Hardy, Iza D., 84

Harrison, Alice A., 48

Hart, Jerome A., 131

Hart, Virgil C., 85

Have You Eaten Yet? (exhibition; Museum of Chinese in America, New York), *plate*

Hayes, Rutherford B., 96

health, 140, 149–150, 157–160, 165–166

Hell's Canyon Gorge massacre (Ore., 1887), 95

Henry Yee's Forbidden City (restaurant; Detroit), 109

Higginson, Francis, 31–32

Higman, B. W., 131

Hildebrand, George H., 30

Hing, Bill Ong, 228n.54

Ho Yow, 49

Hodgson, Moira, 147

Hollander, John, 174

home, concept of, 173–177, 181

"Home as Work" (Siegel), 200n.91

"Home Cooking" (Theophano), 233n.2

home delivery and takeout, 4, 119, *plate*

Hong, Wallace Yee, 110, 143, 154, 168

Hong Far Low (restaurant; Boston), 81

Hong Fer Low (restaurant; Portland, Ore.), 80–81

Hong Fer Low (restaurant; San Francisco), 81, 121, 123, 131

Hong Ping Lo (restaurant; New York), 134

Hoover, Herbert, 37